AF352747

JAPAN AND THE EMOTIONAL POLITICS OF NATIONAL IMAGE

JAPAN AND THE EMOTIONAL POLITICS OF NATIONAL IMAGE

PAUL A. KOWERT

GEORGETOWN UNIVERSITY PRESS / WASHINGTON, DC

The publisher is not responsible for third-party websites or their content. URL links were active at time of publication.

Library of Congress Cataloging-in-Publication Data

Names: Kowert, Paul, 1964–author
Title: Japan and the emotional politics of national image / Paul A. Kowert.
Description: Washington, DC : Georgetown University Press, [2026] |
    Includes bibliographical references and index.
Identifiers: LCCN 2025020681 (print) | LCCN 2025020682 (ebook) |
    ISBN 9781647126971 paperback | ISBN 9781647126964 hardcover |
    ISBN 9781647126988 ebook
Subjects: LCSH: Emotions—Political aspects | Japan—Public opinion | Japan—
    Relations—China | China—Relations—Japan | Japan—Relations—Korea
    (South) | Korea (South)—Relations—Japan
Classification: LCC DS806 .K774 2026 (print) | LCC DS806 (ebook) |
    DDC 327.5205—dc23/eng/20251118
LC record available at https://lccn.loc.gov/2025020681
LC ebook record available at https://lccn.loc.gov/2025020682

♾ This paper meets the requirements of ANSI/NISO Z39.48-1992 (Permanence of Paper).

EU GPSR Authorized Representative
LOGOS EUROPE, 9 rue Nicolas Poussin, 17000, LA ROCHELLE, France
Email: Contact@logoseurope.eu

27 26   9 8 7 6 5 4 3 2   First printing

Printed in the United States of America

Cover design by Nathan Putens
Interior design by Westchester Publishing Services

CONTENTS

FIGURES

TABLES

ACKNOWLEDGMENTS

A swift writer might finish up a book before accumulating too many debts. My own interest in how we form impressions of countries in general, and Japan in particular, began about thirty years ago. I've incurred many debts, personal and professional, since then. Evidently, I am not so swift.

Long-term projects like this one have multiple beginnings, but I can trace the origins of this book to a single event. Not long out of graduate school, I had developed an interest in the way national identity affects foreign policy. Constructivism gave me tools to think about this problem, and I began to work with Nicholas Onuf and Vendulka Kubálková on a book about constructivism in international relations. Joined by several students and colleagues who contributed chapters to the book, we made plans to present our first drafts at a joint meeting of the International Studies Association and the Japan Association of International Relations to be held at the newly built Makuhari Messe Convention Center in Chiba, Japan. The Makuhari district of Chiba City is built on reclaimed land across the bay from Tokyo, not so far from Tokyo Disneyland. A long flight from Miami deposited me there just days before a typhoon moved ashore, and the storm prompted me to stay in Chiba rather than venturing further afield. Makuhari had its own attractions, in any case. It was a landscape out of *Bladerunner* that Steven Poole describes in his book *Trigger Happy* as a "shrine to techno-optimism." Thus began my interest in Japan.

To make the point that our "construction" or image of countries matters to the conduct of foreign policy, Japan and the United States seemed like good cases precisely because both are said to have some sort of essential national character. I set out to explore the ways that, essential character notwithstanding, Japanese and Americans have changed their minds about each other repeatedly and dramatically. I was fortunate to receive support (Grant P-97272) from the Social Science Research Council and the Japan Society for the Promotion of Science to begin this research. Nick Onuf put me in contact with Tamamoto Masaru, the first of many Japanese colleagues who went far out of their way to answer my naïve questions and to provide all sorts of other assistance. They obtained for me an affiliation with the

Department of International Relations at Ritsumeikan University in Kyoto, where I arrived in January 1998 with a knowledge of Japanese language and culture that even those in a generous mood could only describe as rudimentary. The director of Ritsumeikan's Institute of Area Studies, Karasawa Kei, took me under his wing (and into his institute), graciously extending help of many kinds, as did his colleague, Kobayashi Makoto. There, I also benefited from conversations with Nakatsuji Keiji and Okubo Shiro. Additionally, I received help from many members of the department's office staff, and I particularly want to express my gratitude to Shinji Kazue and Tsujimoto Ritsuko.

Beyond the enormous debt I owe to Professors Tamamoto, Karasawa, and Kobayashi, I've accumulated many other debts during research trips to Japan and other parts of East Asia. For support in the earliest stages of my research, I am deeply grateful to Kansai University for a summer research grant and to Professor Kusunoki Sadayoshi for his gracious help during my time there. I am also grateful to Aichi University, Yonsei University, National Chengchi University, and the Taipei Economic and Cultural Office of Miami for support that permitted me to attend conferences from which I learned a great deal. Professor Suzuki Norio at Aichi University has patiently encouraged me and provided thoughtful guidance for many years. I thank the Fulbright Foundation and the Japan–United States Educational Commission (JUSEC) for a Fulbright Fellowship that permitted me to spend ten months at Tōhoku University beginning in September 2008. David Satterwhite, Iwata Mizuho, and the other JUSEC staff members in Tokyo provided a warm welcome, and Professor Satō Yoshimichi graciously welcomed me into his research group at Tōhoku University while also sorting out countless pragmatic details and making my time in Sendai a delight. Professor Ogihara Satoshi, whose office at Tōhokudai was next to mine, also provided assistance with mundane and intellectual matters alike, as did Professors Takenaka Koji and Yokota Masaaki.

As I learned more about the dynamics of Japan's relations with the United States, and as I continued to study the way Japanese and Americans formed impressions of each other, I also realized that Japanese concerns with national image were shifting. Leaders in Japan, China, and South Korea had all begun to marshal new forms of populist support through nationalist appeals, and this had a predictable effect on their diplomatic relations. It struck me as naïve and simplistic to attribute the problems in Japan's relations with its closest neighbors solely to historical memory and the immutable legacy of wartime animosity. Increasingly, therefore, I began to focus on the triangular relationship among Japan, China, and South Korea. My colleagues in the

Asian Studies Program at Florida International University (FIU) served as a sounding board for my poorly formed initial ideas. The director of this program, Steven Heine, has been a friend and especially valuable resource for many years. Equally, my colleagues in the Department of Politics and International Relations at FIU provided much support and thoughtful advice, and I particularly wish to thank Tom Breslin, Harry Gould, Félix Martín, Mohiaddin Mesbahi, Richard Olson, Lisa Prügl, and Julie Zeng.

Stephen Walker and I received support from the International Studies Association to hold a workshop on sociological role theory, and this greatly improved my ability to think about Japan's role within East Asia. Not only has Steve been a valuable sounding board and collaborator, but he has also been remarkably patient with me as I postponed other projects with him in order to focus on this one. I am also grateful for helpful conversations and advice from the other role theory workshop participants, especially Klaus Brummer, Cristian Cantir, Sebastian Harnisch, Hirata Keiko, Julie Kaarbo, Ulrich Krotz, Akan Malici, and David McCourt. Cameron Thies, another workshop participant, organized a follow-on conference on "Role Theory and International Relations" at Arizona State University, and I owe him a special debt. Not only did he provide a good deal of thoughtful feedback on this project, but his workshop gave me the opportunity to try out many of the ideas that helped this book take form.

When I moved to UMass Boston (UMB), Sammy Barkin took the lead in organizing a faculty research group that gave me another place to present first drafts and get valuable feedback. I am grateful to Sammy for his wise advice and also to Joseph Brown, Leila Farsakh, Andrés Henao Castro, Luis Jiménez, Shuai Jin, Michelle Jurkovich, Jeffrey Pugh, and Stacy VanDeveer for their thoughtful comments and suggestions. Another UMB colleague, Paul Watanabe, kindly included me in trips he organized both to Japan and to the Manzanar concentration camp in Southern California, and we were the beneficiaries of generous support from the Japan International Cooperation Center, the Kakehashi Project, and UMass Boston. More generally, I am enormously grateful for the institutional support I received over many years from Florida International University and the University of Massachusetts Boston, as well as the Harvard-Yenching Library for visiting access in 2021 and 2022.

Along the way, many other colleagues in addition to those already mentioned have graciously shared their time and thoughts about topics related to this book, helping me to avoid more than a few errors and dead ends. I am indebted to Marijke Breuning, Allen Carlson, Amy Catalinac, June Dreyer, Yoi Herrera, Jacques Hymans, Ted Hopf, Patrick Thaddeus Jackson,

Jay Jang, Michal Kolmaš, Simon Koschut, Deborah Larson, Richard Ned Lebow, Claire Lee, David Leheny, Daniel Levine, Jonathan Mercer, Jennifer Mitzen, Andrew Ross, Vaughn Shannon, David Sylvan, and David Wessels. I presented early drafts of chapters contained in this book at various conferences and workshops, including research seminars at Aichi University, Florida International University, Kansai University, Ochanomizu University, Reitaku University, Ritsumeikan University, the University of Tampa, Tōhoku University, UMass Boston, and Yonsei University. For their generosity in reading and discussing these drafts or other parts of the project with me, in addition to those already mentioned previously, I also wish to thank Abe Yuki, Edward Ashbee, Philippe Beauregard, Louis Bélanger, Cristian Cantir, Tereza Capelos, Roxanne Doty, Sebastian Harnisch, Hayashi Naoki, Valerie Hudson, Stuart Kaufman, Koga Kei, Greg Moore, Dani Nedal, Park Hwee-Rhak, Maria Rost Rublee, Bruce Stronach, and Saskia van Wees. Peter Gries, Suzuki Norio, and Tamamoto Masaru have been especially generous with their time over the years, reading the things I write and discussing with me many topics that directly informed this book. I am also deeply grateful to Manfred Elfstrom, Jeremy Wallace, and Jessica Chen Weiss for their kind willingness to make available to me their datasets, which permitted the statistical analysis in Chapter 5. And I thank my research assistant, Kristin Hynes, for her help compiling the sample of articles from *Chosun Ilbo* coded in Chapter 8.

It has been a real pleasure to work with Don Jacobs, my editor at Georgetown University Press, who has provided a lot of terrific advice and guided the project along expertly. I am also grateful for the thoughtful and extensive comments from anonymous reviewers that forced me to abandon a few cherished conceits and improved the manuscript in numerous other ways. Writing a book also competes, of course, with other demands on one's time. Sarah Carnes, Roisin and Jimmy Kinneen, and Marga Varea were wonderful sources of support when I needed them.

Several people have been trusted sources of guidance over many years. Peter Katzenstein was a superb mentor when I was a graduate student, and he has remained a source of inspiration and advice ever since. I'm always a bit surprised by his generosity in reading the things I send him, but never by how helpful and insightful his advice invariably turns out to be. John Clark has been a cherished friend and colleague for the entirety of my professional career. I count myself very lucky to have someone who, despite knowing my personal and intellectual shortcomings, still manages to be an unflinching supporter. Finally, I return to where this story began, with Nick Onuf. Nick started me down the path to studying Japan, deepened my understanding of many topics, and held me to his own high standards. Traveling around Japan from our home base in Kyoto with him and his wife, Sandy Keowen, was always a pleasure. To each of these individuals, I owe debts too great to repay.

Finally, most of all, I am grateful to my wife, Michelle Kneissl. Her limitless support and occasional impatience were indispensable, each in its own way. This book is dedicated to her.

CONVENTIONS

Consistency is not only the hobgoblin of little minds but an impossibility in rendering Asian names across different contexts. In the following pages, the family name will generally precede the given name, as is common practice with Chinese, Japanese, and Korean names even when writing in English. This practice is also observed for historical figures such as Mao Zedong, though academics publishing in English-language journals often place their family name last. In the latter cases, I try to preserve the order of authors' names as they are best known. I incline toward Hanyu Pinyin romanization except when historical figures are known in some other fashion, following common editorial practice. Mao's name exemplifies this transition, as Mao Tse-tung (the Wade-Giles romanization) is largely giving way to Mao Zedong (the Pinyin romanization). Similarly, Japanese historical figures (e.g., Tokugawa Ieyasu) are typically rendered with the family name first, but Japanese authors writing in English frequently adopt the Western name order (e.g., D. T. Suzuki). Again, I attempt to preserve the order of names by which authors are best known, while preferentially attempting to follow the current editorial practice of using the traditional name order with Japanese names. Finally, I include diacritical marks for Japanese words, except for names and other terms widely used in Western languages (thus, Tokyo rather than Tōkyō).

PART I

The Importance of Image

CHAPTER 1

Introduction

In 2023, for the first time since the creation of the Anholt-Ipsos Nation Brands Index (NBI) in 2005, an Asian country was ranked as the most popular country in the world. The NBI relies on annual surveys to assess the political, economic, and cultural appeal of sixty countries. Japan, which had steadily been climbing in the rankings, surpassed Germany to reach the top in 2023, where it remained in 2024.[1] Its perceived cultural popularity, combined with the relatively weak yen, has led to such explosive growth in Japan-bound tourism that it now ranks as the country's second-biggest export after automobiles.[2] Indeed, the Japan Tourism Agency has been compelled to explore ways of managing the problem of overtourism, and Kyoto even issued a ban on nonresidents in certain parts of its geisha district.[3]

To say that a country is popular is one thing, but the notion that a country is also a brand strikes some as repugnant. It injects a crass element of commercialism into international relations in a way that draws ire on both the left and the right. Yet countries do guard their images jealously, and the way they are perceived internationally confers certain diplomatic, economic, and strategic advantages. Whether out of a sense of national pride or in pursuit of the leverage afforded by soft power, therefore, national leaders take pains to burnish their country's image abroad. And they worry, when they detect an "image problem," that their country is being misunderstood. Indeed, its recent success in the NBI ranking notwithstanding, Japan has practically made a cottage industry out of bemoaning the various ways it is misunderstood abroad.

Worry about Japan's image abroad focuses above all on China and the Korean Peninsula.[4] It is in these two places, after all, that public attitudes depart so strikingly from the general approbation that Japan receives elsewhere. Surveys repeatedly show that Japan is deeply unpopular in China and South Korea.[5] In Spring 2014, to take just one example, a Pew Global Attitudes survey found that only 8 percent of Chinese citizens and 22 percent of South Koreans viewed Japan favorably.[6] These are, moreover, two crucially important countries for Japan. Japan cannot afford to overlook China's economic importance, and yet Japanese diplomats and businesses fight considerable headwinds in China. China's growing military capabilities also mean that the relationship with South Korea is important both in its own right and as part of the trilateral alliance with the United States. It is not surprising, therefore, that Chinese and South Korean attitudes take on special importance in Japan.

This book will focus on the puzzle of why attitudes toward Japan are so much more negative in China and South Korea than elsewhere. It often seems, in fact, that there is no better Rorschach test in the contemporary Asia–Pacific region than the story one tells about Japan. During and after the Second World War, American attitudes toward Japan were just as negative as in China and South Korea today. A National Opinion Research Center (NORC) poll conducted roughly a year before Japan's surrender found that 57 percent of Americans agreed with the statement that "the Japanese people will always want to go to war," and fully 13 percent of Americans advocated killing all Japanese.[7] Only six years later, however, Douglas MacArthur proclaimed that the Japanese people "have undergone the greatest reformation recorded in modern history" and having drawn "abreast of many free nations of the earth . . . [Japan] will not again fail the universal trust."[8] Today, Americans tend to see Japan as the kind of success story that eluded their grasp after interventions in Iraq and Afghanistan. US occupation forces managed in Japan, at least, to leave a democratic, prosperous, and stable society in their wake. Japan rapidly made the transition from fascist adversary to responsible international citizen. And if Japan had become a feared economic rival by the 1980s, it also became one of the world's largest foreign aid donors, a close ally in the global war on terror, and a reliable supporter of the rule of law internationally. The Spring 2014 Pew survey found that 70 percent of US citizens had favorable attitudes toward Japan.[9] It is certainly possible, therefore, for attitudes toward a former adversary to change dramatically.[10]

Against the temptation to say that the attitudes of Chinese and South Koreans are simply stuck in the past, perhaps because they suffered more or for a longer time, this book will also show that attitudes in these two countries are more variable than many realize. Indeed, both countries seem driven by emotions that take on a life of their own, at least partly independent from geopolitical conditions and domestic political incentives. This book explores each of these possibilities in some detail. Wartime experiences and contemporary strategic alliances may set the stage for Chinese and South Korean attitudes, but they do not explain the emotional dynamics very well. Domestic political maneuvering also clearly plays an important role, but it appears that both Chinese and South Korean politicians respond to public desires at least as much as they lead. If *realpolitik* and *innenpolitik* (domestic politics) do not suffice, then a third level of *psychopolitik* is also necessary to account for Japan's shifting image within these countries.

In China, official views of Japan have actually been something of a roller coaster, though heading downward more often than upward. Under Mao Zedong, Sino-Japanese relations had noticeably warmed by the 1970s, but this trend changed under Mao's successors, particularly after the Tiananmen uprising in 1989. By early 2014—as the Pew Global Attitudes polls were showing positive attitudes toward Japan almost everywhere—China's ambassador to the United Nations, Liu Jieyi, turned the clock all the way back to the Second World War: "whether the Japanese leaders choose to abide by the principles and purposes of the Charter of the United Nations by accepting the victory in the war against Fascism and the post-war international order or to support the war criminals is a fundamental question of principle. The Japanese leaders should recognize and reflect on the history of aggression and redress their mistakes through actions so as to regain the trust of the international community, including Japan's neighbouring States."[11] Liu's comments came in reaction to the decision of Japanese Prime Minister Abe Shinzō to pay an official visit to Yasukuni Shrine on December 26, 2013. Yasukuni memorializes Japan's war dead, including some who were classified as war criminals after World War II (hence Liu's reference to war criminals). Yasukuni is a place that crystallizes different interpretations of history, and Chinese opinions of Japan tumbled toward rock bottom in the wake of Abe's visit.

The same was true in South Korea, where fears of Japan were arguably more deep-seated, dating back to a long history of pirate raids and Japan's two sixteenth-century attempts to invade Korea. The trauma of Japanese colonization in the early twentieth century and the associated policies of cultural assimilation also provide context for Korean sensitivity to anything that might resemble historical whitewashing. Prime Minister Abe's appeals to Japanese nationalism undeniably touched a raw nerve, therefore, and they have become something of a staple among Liberal Democratic Party (LDP) politicians, particularly in more rural parts of Japan. In South Korea as well, however, attitudes toward Japan have changed over time, improving recently after the low point of the Abe years.

China and South Korea therefore present a two-fold puzzle to scholars and policymakers alike. First, Japan faces an unusually persistent image problem in these two countries. They are consequently interesting cases for an exploration of the difficulties of moving beyond historical traumas in international diplomacy. Second, attitudes toward Japan in China and South Korea are also interesting because they do in fact vary even if they remain negative on the whole. If one only consults opinion data in the past two decades or so, it is easy to conclude that anti-Japanese sentiment is reliably entrenched within these countries. Yet a more careful examination of public attitudes over time and across issue areas reveals a more complex and interesting picture. For both of these reasons, therefore, it makes sense for those interested in Japan's international image to pay special attention to the cases of China and South Korea.

OVERVIEW OF THE BOOK

Unlike many works of social science that begin with a scholarly puzzle, advance a theory to explain the puzzle, and then present evidence in support of that theory, this book presents a sequence of puzzles, each related to the problem of how Japan is seen in China and South Korea. Each of the following chapters stands on its own, blending theoretical and empirical discussions. In the fashion of Akira Kurosawa's classic film *Rashomon*, these chapters tell the story of Japan's image within Northeast Asia from multiple perspectives. In doing so, broadly speaking, the book progresses through three tasks and is thus divided into three parts.

In general, the first part makes the case that the way we see countries—and Japan in particular—is an important problem, worthy of attention. It is possible that a country's international image is only a reflection of other, more important concerns, but this book begins by making the case that image matters. The second part of the book then turns to the two most common accounts of Japan's image in the minds of its neighbors: perspectives that depend on either geopolitics or domestic politics. Each of these perspectives is important, and these chapters present a dialogue of theory and evidence about their relevance to Japan's image. This section makes the case, however, that neither of these perspectives suffices to explain the way Japan is seen in China and South Korea. Finally, the third part of the book develops a model of the way emotion shapes national imagery. This third part of the book is not intended to serve as an explanatory alternative to the explanations presented in Part II, but rather as a complementary account without which the other explanations are drastically incomplete. The argument advanced in Part III might well be applied to other countries, but doing so is beyond the scope of this book.

Chapter 2 presents a detailed overview of Japan's international image. It pays special attention to attitudes in China and South Korea, but it also devotes some attention to attitudes elsewhere to provide context. It demonstrates not only that China and South Korea stand out as special cases of countries in which Japan's image is unusually negative, but also that the picture is more complex in both of these countries when Japan's image is considered over time. Understanding Japan's image and the way it has evolved historically sheds light, in turn, on the role Japan is capable of playing in international politics and on the resources it must expend to do so. This chapter gives a clearer sense, therefore, of the challenge Japan faces.

Those seeking an explanation for Japan's image problems in China and South Korea might next turn directly to Chapter 4, skipping the intervening chapter. Some will wonder, however, about how national image or brand differs from several other concepts, including national character, national identity, national role, and even a nation's soft power. Chapter 3 clarifies the differences between *image* (perhaps the most generic of these terms) and other related terms as they are used by scholars of politics, international relations, and foreign policy. This chapter is also self-consciously historical, tracing the genealogy of these related concepts and the rise and fall of interest in them. Among students of international relations, in particular, interest in these phenomena seems more robust than ever, no doubt because of constructivist attention to problems of state identity. This chapter places recent interest in historical context. Taken together, Chapters 2 and 3 make the case that a country's image matters both to policymakers and scholars, and that Japan's image specifically is more complicated than one might assume at first blush.

The apparent puzzle of Chinese and South Korean attitudes will turn out not to be much of a puzzle if it is readily explained by geopolitics or domestic politics, the topics of the two chapters in Part II. As already noted, historical grudges have not remained an obstacle in most of Japan's other former adversaries. Still, realpolitik suggests other explanations for concern about Japan that go beyond simplistic inferences about historical enmity. Japan's strategic alignment with the United States, for example, may itself be cause for concern in China. Of course, this same alignment should promote positive attitudes in South Korea. Chapter 4 considers such explanations and establishes through careful historical process tracing that neither international alliances nor geopolitical vulnerabilities are especially good predictors of fluctuations in postwar Chinese and South Korean attitudes toward Japan.

Realpolitik cannot be dismissed out of hand, but if it is only weakly associated with Japan's image, then perhaps innenpolitik will serve as a better guide. In Shakespeare's *Henry IV*, the dying King Henry counsels his son to "busy giddy minds with foreign quarrels" in times of unrest.[12] The so-called "diversionary hypothesis" of foreign policy has long been a staple in political science.[13] And in the case of China, it is clear that patriotic education campaigns in the wake of the 1989 Tiananmen Square protests have found a suitable and useful target in Japan. It is equally plausible that South Korean politicians, particularly those on the left, find a convenient foil in nearby proximity, just across the Korea Strait. Chapter 5 considers the influence of domestic politics on Japan's image, reviewing the postwar history of domestic political shifts in China and South Korea. China is perhaps the more interesting of the two cases, since one might not expect public opinion to influence the Chinese Communist Party (CCP) very much. This chapter digs more deeply into the relationship between domestic political unrest and anti-Japanese attitudes with a new statistical analysis of data on citizen protest movements in China. The evidence suggests that, although innenpolitik undoubtedly contributes to swings in attitudes toward Japan, it does not completely account for these attitudes any more than does realpolitik. In both cases, a closer look reveals, public opinion more often leads than follows official state policies. If it is not simply the result of manipulation by Chinese and South Korean leaders, then the question remains: what else shapes attitudes toward Japan?

Part III develops a third explanation, arguing that emotion has its own dynamics in East Asia, a psychopolitik that provides a crucial piece of the puzzle to explain Japan's international image. Chapter 6 draws on the recent and rapidly growing scholarship on emotion and international politics to argue that differing international relationships give rise to different patterns of emotion in foreign policy. Two emotional patterns, in particular, are likely to dominate Japan's relations with China and South Korea. One, a politics of anger and fear, is more likely when Japan is seen to have the upper hand, or when attention shifts to the record of its wartime behavior and the adequacy of its penitence. The other, a politics of disdain, is more likely when Japan's interlocutors believe themselves to have the upper hand.

The remaining chapters apply this model of emotional psychopolitik to the cases of China and South Korea before concluding with a discussion of how these emotional politics play out in Japan. Chapter 7 reviews statements by Chinese officials and reports the results of a more formal text analysis of editorial content in the *People's Daily*. Chapter 8 undertakes a similar analysis of official statements and newspaper content in South Korea. Leaders in Beijing and Seoul often remark that their counterparts in Tokyo would be well advised to reflect carefully on their country's past and on the necessity of a properly remorseful attitude. Whether an acceptable politics of emotion can be devised by Japanese leaders remains to be seen. It is probably fair to say that few people are as attentive to their country's international image as are the citizens of Japan. This book's concluding chapter explores the implications of emotional psychopolitik for Japan's foreign policy, as well as some of the ways that Japan's freedom to do what others desire is limited by its own internal politics of emotion.

One further word about the organization of this book is in order. Works that address academic specialists often do a poor job of speaking to more general audiences, and vice versa. I nevertheless try in the following pages to write for both generalists and specialists with the hope that neither group will be too slighted. Most chapters blend some background material familiar to specialists with new arguments and new empirical findings. For example, Chapter 2 describes the observations of many scholars who have written about the perception of Japan in different parts of the world, but it also synthesizes this work in the hope of offering a new perspective on how Japan has been seen over time, particularly in China and South Korea. Scholars of East Asian diplomatic history will be well acquainted with the general pattern of Japan's relations with China and South Korea summarized in Chapter 4, to take another example. Even though these stories are familiar, however, it is important to establish that the patterns of Japan's diplomacy themselves do not always predict attitudes toward Japan. Likewise, the argument of Chapter 5—that patterns of domestic politics in China and South Korea influence but do not dictate attitudes toward Japan—is not novel. But the question of whether leader opinion drives public opinion or the reverse remains the subject of debate, and this chapter presents new evidence bearing on the formation of Chinese attitudes in particular.

IMPLICATIONS FOR POLICY

Although this book is not intended to develop and test a general theory of emotion and national image, it is nevertheless tempting to say that the account of Chinese and South Korean attitudes it develops will have important policy implications, particularly for Japanese leaders. Still, there are good reasons to be cautious about such claims. The better and more detailed our explanations for specific developments in Japanese diplomacy, the more likely that our accounts—tailored to those details—will be inadequate to explain future events. It is possible that generalizable arguments about emotion and foreign policy might be developed, and such arguments might well complement theories of structural constraint and rational choice. A degree of analytical humility is in order, however, since emotion operates at the level of individuals whose reactions may also change over time in response to events. Moreover, even if the following chapters succeed in showing, as they purport, that neither accounts rooted in geopolitics nor those focused on domestic pressures suffice in themselves, to account for Japan's image within neighboring countries, they certainly do not establish that realpolitik and innenpolitik are irrelevant to Japan's image. Thus, when we consider the myriad influences on Japan's image at each level—the international, the domestic, and the psychological milieu—we are likely to regard deterministic arguments with skepticism. For precisely this reason, a simple roadmap toward improved Japanese relations with China and South Korea is not likely to be forthcoming. There are too many competing pressures at work.

Simple prescriptions to improve Japan's image are thus likely to be met with frustration. The recent history of Japan's relations with China and South Korea tells us that much. We might slightly reframe this question, however, to ask whether efforts to improve these relationships are necessarily futile. Those who believe that national image among these three countries is locked in a pattern deeply engrained by historical memories might well think so. After all, controlling history is fundamental to the way countries play out certain roles on the international stage, and it is the linchpin of their efforts to take on new roles. By controlling stories about the past, they control what seems reasonable and proper for their future actions. Perhaps this is one reason that the politics of apology has taken on such importance in East Asia.[14] Apologies are crucial pieces of theater through which countries and their leaders seek to translate history into policy. When Japan's apologies are seen as tepid and insincere, rather than the product of genuine reflection and remorse, Japan's image and its diplomacy suffer. In consequence, the roles Japan can play are sharply constrained. And yet many of Japan's former adversaries have accepted its apologies and embraced new relationships with Japan.

One illustration of the policy stakes, and one reason that Japan's recent efforts have mostly met with little success in Beijing and Seoul, may be that neither the People's Republic of China (the PRC) nor Korea (North or

South) was a signatory to the San Francisco Peace Treaty. Signed on September 8, 1951, this treaty formally ended World War II, restored Japanese sovereignty, and settled issues of compensation for the forty-eight signatories. Because of the ongoing Chinese civil war, however, the PRC was not represented at the San Francisco Conference, and a formal peace treaty between Japan and the PRC was not signed until August 12, 1978. And because Korea was at the time of the San Francisco conference an occupied and partitioned territory, it also went unrepresented and still has not signed a formal peace treaty with Japan (although diplomatic relations between Japan and South Korea were established by treaty in 1965). Kept secret at the time, it was later revealed that the 1965 Treaty on Basic Relations between Japan and South Korea provided for $800 million in grants and soft loans from Japan, and that South Korea in turn would renounce any further reparations claims.[15]

The persistence of issues from World War II not adequately resolved by these agreements may be one reason why Tokyo's relations with Beijing and Seoul sometimes appear to be stuck in the past. The official position of the Japanese Foreign Ministry is that all issues of wartime reparations have been settled by Japan's acceptance of the San Francisco treaty and by its settlements with other combatants.[16] And yet Japanese leaders do sporadically acknowledge that more is needed. On the 50th anniversary of the end of World War II in 1995, the Japanese National Diet passed a formal resolution of apology:

> On the occasion of the 50th anniversary of the end of World War II, this House offers its sincere condolences to those who fell in action and victims of wars and similar actions all over the world. Solemnly reflecting upon many instances of colonial rule and acts of aggression in the modern history of the world, and recognizing that Japan carried out those acts in the past, inflicting pain and suffering upon the peoples of other countries, especially in Asia, the Members of this House express a sense of deep remorse.[17]

The same day, Japan's Prime Minister, Murayama Tomiichi, issued what has become known as the Murayama Statement. In a formal address to the Diet, he declared, "I would like to take this opportunity to express my most sincere condolences to all victims in Japan and abroad, and, based on our deep remorse for the past, to reaffirm my personal conviction that we must make every possible effort to build world peace."[18] Roughly two months later, Murayama again affirmed,

During a certain period in the not too distant past, Japan, following a mistaken national policy, advanced along the road to war, only
to ensnare the Japanese people in a fateful crisis, and, through its
colonial rule and aggression, caused tremendous damage and suffering to the people of many countries, particularly to those of Asian
nations. In the hope that no such mistake be made in the future,
I regard, in a spirit of humility, these irrefutable facts of history,
and express here once again my feelings of deep remorse and state
my heartfelt apology. Allow me also to express my feelings of profound mourning for all victims, both at home and abroad, of that
history.[19]

Emperor Akihito additionally made several statements of apology, beginning in 1990.[20] More recently, and after provoking strong emotions by
calling for a commission to investigate whether the Japanese Army had
really forced Korean women into sexual slavery, Prime Minister Abe
affirmed that Japan's formal apology stands.[21] These and similar statements
by other Japanese leaders notwithstanding, however, Chinese and South
Korean officials frequently implore Japan to apologize, or to apologize properly, or to apologize more sincerely. Polling by the Pew Research Center
in Spring 2013 found that an overwhelming 98 percent of South Koreans,
and 78 percent of Chinese, believe that Japan has *not* "sufficiently apolo-
gized for its military actions during the 1930s and 1940s."[22] Meanwhile, the
Japanese electorate has grown somewhat weary of the continued demands
for apologies.

On the face of it, therefore, one might make a plausible case that historical memories have congealed in a way that is very resistant to change, no
matter what Japan does now. If this is so, then as the Japanese themselves
often say, *shiyō ga nai* (nothing can be done). If the arguments developed in
the following chapters are correct, however, this at least is an argument we
should reject. The evidence suggests that Japan's image in China and South
Korea is more malleable than is widely appreciated. Moreover, it appears
to be driven not just by the imperatives of geopolitical strategizing and
domestic favor-seeking but also by the way emotion is structured in specific policy domains. Understanding why different sorts of problems tend
to provoke different reactions in Beijing and Seoul is the first step toward a
Japanese foreign policy that can finally move beyond the repeated cycles of
recrimination and apology that still poison Japan's relations with its closest
neighbors.

Notes

1. McGrath, Frankel, and Leidel, "Nation Brands Index 2023"; Place Brand Observer, "Anholt Nation Brands Index (NBI) 2024."
2. Kanaoka, "Tourism Surges."
3. Japan Tourism Agency, "Efforts to Prevent and Control Overtourism"; McCurry, "Kyoto Bans Tourists."
4. Japanese worries about the country's international image go beyond China and South Korea, to be sure. As Japan became less relevant on the global economic stage, it sometimes seemed to attract only negative attention as a country that was locked in the past. It refused to abandon its traditional whaling practices. Its decades of economic mismanagement and poor oversight gave it enormous national debt. And the failures of its regulatory bureaucracy to keep up with the times were on vivid display after the 2011 Tōhoku earthquake, tsunami, and radiological disaster. Reviewing Japan's diplomatic efforts in the first part of the twenty-first century, *Fortune* concluded, "Japan has a major international image problem!"; see Fitzpatrick, "Japan Has a Major International Image Problem."
5. The findings of these surveys are discussed extensively in Chapter 2. Attitudes toward Japan are also presumably negative in North Korea, although opinion research is more difficult there for obvious reasons.
6. Pew Research Center, "How Asians View Each Other."
7. Cole, "American Professors on Postwar Japan," 530.
8. MacArthur, "Farewell Address to Congress."
9. Pew Research Center, "How Asians View Each Other."
10. The Spring 2014 Pew survey also found, for example, that 81 percent of Thais and 80 percent of Filipinos held positive attitudes toward Japan; see Pew Research Center, "How Asians View Each Other."
11. Liu, "Comments."
12. Shakespeare, *2 Henry IV*, IV.v.184. For a related discussion of power and politics in Shakespeare's history plays, see Kizelbach, *Pragmatics of Early Modern Politics*.
13. For early statements, see Simmel, *Conflict*; and Coser, *Functions of Social Conflict*. Levy, "Diversionary Theory of War," provides a thoughtful overview and critique.
14. Lind's *Sorry States* offers an excellent, extensive treatment of this topic, contrasting Japanese and German diplomacy. See also Berger and Bong, "To Apologize and to Forgive"; Daase et al., *Apology and Reconciliation*; and Hanke et al., "When the Past Haunts the Present."
15. UPI, "S. Korea Discloses Sensitive Documents." Another former adversary that did not sign the San Francisco Treaty was the Soviet Union. Instead, it waited until 1956 to sign its own Joint Declaration with Japan, reestablishing diplomatic relations between the two countries.
16. The most obvious exception to this statement is North Korea, which has never normalized relations with Japan. Although Japan has at times appeared willing to negotiate with North Korea in exchange for assistance resolving the cases of Japanese citizens abducted by the North Korean government in the 1970s and 1980s, and although these negotiations did lead to the release of five abductees in 2002, North Korea's nuclear weapons program has mostly pushed the issue to the back burner since then. See

Manyin, "North Korea–Japan Relations"; Hagström and Söderberg, "Taking Japan–North Korea Relations Seriously."

17. Japan, National Diet, "Resolution to Renew the Determination for Peace."
18. Murayama, "Prime Minister's Address."
19. Murayama, "Statement."
20. Weisman, "Japanese Express Remorse to Korea."
21. Yamaguchi, "Review Confirms Basis."
22. Pew Research Center, "Japanese Public's Mood Rebounding."

CHAPTER 2

Images of Japan

For centuries the European world never doubted its superiority. In matters of technology and science, philosophy, literature, religion, politics, and culture, the West placed itself advantageously in a hierarchy over the East. This judgment rested in good measure on a racially inflected worldview that served as the bedrock of Western supremacy. "For nearly three hundred years," journalist and China specialist Harold Issacs says, the foundation of this outlook "was the assumption of Western superiority: a whole vast political-military-social-economic-racial-personal complex was built upon it. Almost every Western image of Asian and other non-Western peoples was based on it."[1] Edward Said baptized this phenomenon *Orientalism*, and it remains a powerful insight into the persistent force of us-versus-them distinctions in international relations.[2] Perhaps more than any other Asian country, however, Japan has resisted this simple binary in the Western imagination—and in its own.

Instead Japan carved out for itself a position somewhere between East and West. When Japanese Foreign Minister Mamoru Shigemitsu delivered Japan's first formal speech as a newly seated member of the United Nations at the eleventh session of the General Assembly in 1956, he proclaimed "the substance of Japan's political, economic and cultural life is the product of the fusion within the last century of the civilizations of the Orient and the Occident. In a way Japan may well be regarded as a bridge between the East and the West."[3] Historian and professor of international relations Akio Watanabe similarly construes Japan's "place in the history of civilization" as a "bridge between East and West."[4] Even Nitobe Inazō, the Meiji-era intellectual and diplomat best known for his popular study of Japan's samurai culture, also wrote that it was distinctively in Japan "where the thought and the influence of the East and of the West find their meeting ground."[5]

If Japan has succeeded in occupying a middle ground, then we might expect to find no great difference in attitudes toward Japan when comparing Eastern and Western countries. Or perhaps if we consider the influence of cultural and racial similarity, we might expect greater understanding and somewhat more positive attitudes toward Japan in the East than in the West. Instead, the pattern of attitudes toward Japan is more complex, and more difficult to explain. Although Japan benefits from a very positive image in the vast majority of countries, China and the two Koreas stand out as exceptions, where the public takes a much dimmer view of Japan. In many other Eastern countries—including Vietnam, Malaysia, and the Philippines—attitudes are quite positive. And even in China and South Korea, the available public opinion data suggests that there is more variability in attitudes toward Japan than is widely appreciated. It makes sense to begin by gaining a more nuanced sense of how Japan is seen in different parts of the world. This sets the stage for the discussion that follows, and it puts into context the challenges Japan faces in China and South Korea.

Rather than beginning this book with an elaborate conceptual framework parsing the differences in meaning of terms such as *national image, national role, national brand,* and *national identity*—clarifications that will in fact be helpful, and that will be undertaken in the following chapter—this book thus begins by "staying close to the ground" empirically. This chapter asks how Japan is actually seen on the world's stage, from different vantage points, and across time.

WARTIME MEMORIES

The inevitable starting point for a discussion of Japan's current image problem is the early twentieth century. To be sure, Japanese fascination with how outsiders see the country and its people goes back much further than this.[6] By the turn of the century, however, Japan had not only emerged from almost three centuries of isolation but quickly moved on to accomplish something that the great generals who unified the country in the latter half of the sixteenth century had been unable to do. Eager to replicate Western tactics of colonial expansion and sustained by ideologies such as Okakura Tenshin's notion that "Asia is one" with Japan as its natural leader, Japan used the pretext of Korean independence (from China) to effect Korean subordination.[7] After successively defeating Chinese forces on land and Russian forces at sea, Japan gained control of Taiwan, the Liaodong Peninsula, railroad concessions in Manchuria, part of Sakhalin Island, and Korea, which it formally annexed in 1910. Japan thus established itself as a major regional power.

At the same time, the terms of the Treaty of Portsmouth and the concessions exacted by Theodore Roosevelt, who had agreed to mediate between Japan and Russia, meant that Japan began to nurture grievances about how it was seen by Europeans and Americans. From this moment it was harder and harder to avoid sentiment in Japan that international relations were race relations pitting East against West.[8] Japan's Kwantung Army, formed to protect its interests on the Liaodong Peninsula and in Manchuria, became the sharp end of Japan's colonial wedge on the continent. Partly driven by Japan's own sense of racial superiority and stimulated by the rising prominence of pro-army factions in Japanese domestic politics, Kwantung Army officers grew ever bolder and more ruthless.[9] After fabricating a pretext in 1931 to seize Manchuria and establish a puppet state there, they moved on to Inner Mongolia before finally invading China itself in 1937, beginning the Second Sino-Japanese War. In December of that year, Japanese troops seized Nanjing from Chiang Kai-shek's nationalists and went on a rampage of rape, murder, and mayhem horrifying to even the most jaded observers.[10]

As the war progressed and merged into the broader cataclysm of the Second World War, accusations of wartime atrocities levied against Japan were neither limited geographically to the Chinese mainland nor in scope to the problem of soldiers running amok. Japan enslaved the civilian population of conquered territories and condemned them to forced labor and sexual servitude, tortured and murdered prisoners of war (POWs), carried out medical experiments on both civilians and POWs, and waged biological and chemical warfare. The Congressional Research Service estimates that roughly 40 percent of American POWs held by Japan died in captivity, compared with a little over 1 percent of POWs captured by Germany.[11] These acts were directed not only against Chinese, Koreans, and Americans but also against Australians, Indians, Pakistanis, Indochinese, Malaysians, Thai, Indonesians, Filipinos, and others.[12] Even as the war drew to a close and the US Army advanced into Manila in March 1945, Japanese troops unleashed a frenzy of violence that killed over 100,000 Filipino civilians in the Battle of Manila.[13] In fact an estimated one in every twenty Filipinos died during the Japanese occupation—an even higher ratio than in China or Korea.[14] Overall, plausible estimates suggest that civilian and POW casualties at Japanese hands numbered in the millions during the Pacific War.[15]

The deep wounds, both material and psychological, produced by these events are widely offered up to account for the resolutely negative attitudes toward Japan that are common in China and Korea. Writing about another traumatic event, the Holocaust, historian Dominick LaCapra says that "especially for victims, trauma brings about a lapse or rupture in memory that breaks continuity with the past, thereby placing identity in question to the point of shattering it."[16] We must either repress such memories or, if we cannot, find some way to harness the emotions such as shame and anger that they produce.[17] Building on LaCapra's point, Peter Gries argues that for China the "Century of Humiliation" represents a break with the narrative of Chinese superiority encapsulated in the notion of "5000 years of glorious civilization."[18] The shock or rupture produced by these contending histories is the deep well spring from which Chinese and, similarly, Korean emotions now flow. In the case of China specifically, Gries says, another form of anger is layered over this deep reservoir of hatred: "What sets anti-Japanese sentiment apart from other anti-foreign sentiments in China today is that while it includes a lower, visceral anger stemming from Japanese atrocities (like the Nanjing Massacre) in China during World War II, it also contains a higher, ethical anger stemming from the perceived injustice of "little brother" Japan's humiliating defeat of "big brother" China during the Sino-Japanese Jiawu War of 1894–95. It is such indignation, in my view, that sustains anti-Japanese anger in China today."[19]

The past, with all its indignities, is thus a potent feature of the present. Nicholas Kristof calls this "the problem of memory."[20] Kristof begins his well-known essay of that title by retelling the story of a dinnertime conversation with an underground Chinese democracy activist in the dark days after the Tiananmen Square uprising. There seemed to be few good prospects for advancing the cause of democracy in the wake of the government's crackdown, and Kristof leaned in to hear the activist's plans.

> "We're going to kill Japanese," he said brightly.
> "What?"
> "We're going to kill Japanese businessmen. That'll scare them so they won't invest here. And then the government will really be screwed!"
> "You're not serious?"
> "Of course we're serious. We can't demonstrate these days and we can't publish. The only thing we can do for democracy is kill Japanese businessmen."

> I protested that it seemed odd to promote human rights by mur-
> dering innocent businessmen. But he just smiled at my narrow-
> mindedness, with a "you-will-never-understand-Asia" grin.
> "They're Japanese," my friend said dismissively. "Japanese devils."[21]

Kristof surmises that his friend never actually murdered Japanese business-men. Yet he continues, "the vitriol in his voice underscored Asia's histor-ical tensions."[22] The problem with memory, in Asia, is that it often seems irrepressible.

On its face the perpetual resurgence of wartime memories offers a com-pelling explanation for attitudes toward Japan in many quarters. As a general account of how Japan is or must be seen, however, this explanation survives only passing scrutiny. The problem with this account is not that it is com-pletely wrong but rather that it is so drastically incomplete. The list of Japan's victims is fairly long—as it is for most states whose history is measured in centuries. And yet attitudes toward Japan differ markedly among the citizens of countries formerly subjected to Japan's rule.

In fact, the 2015 Pew Global Attitudes Survey finds that Japan is seen in a positive light within the Asia-Pacific region as a whole: "a median of 71% in the region have a favorable view of Japan, with positive views exceeding negative sentiment by more than five-to-one."[23] This survey, like the ones discussed in Chapter 1, reveals a common pattern in late-twentieth-century attitudes toward Japan: attitudes are strongly negative in China and South Korea and quite positive elsewhere. Even in countries that suffered greatly, such as Indonesia and the Philippines, over 70 percent of citizens now express favorable attitudes toward Japan, as shown in Figure 2.1.

The chief puzzle of historical memory and attitudes toward Japan is that there is such wide variation in attitudes, even among Japan's former adversaries. Explanations for these differences readily suggest themselves. Perhaps strategic vulnerabilities, international alliances, or trade and investment opportunities account for these attitudes in some states. Per-haps domestic politics can explain whether Japan is more usefully imagined as a threatening enemy, a diplomatic partner, or a source of economic lar-gesse. Explanations such as these will be considered in Chapters 4 and 5. The principal concern of this chapter is empirical, however, rather than explanatory. The remainder of this chapter delves more deeply into the available evidence about how Japan is seen by citizens of other countries in the Asia-Pacific region, exploring patterns of change across the region and across time.

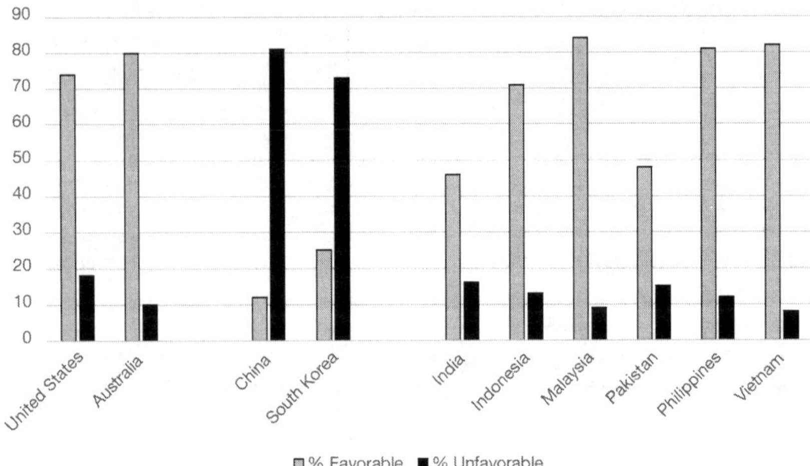

Figure 2.1. Attitudes toward Japan in the Asia-Pacific, 2015
(Data from Pew Global Attitudes Survey 2015; see Pew Research Center, "How Asia-Pacific Publics See Each Other.")

CULTURAL SIMILARITY AND DIFFERENCE

Two of the most prominent Western authors writing about Japan in the late nineteenth and early twentieth centuries were Lafcadio Hearn and Basil Hall Chamberlain. The former was a journalist and prolific translator who was born in Greece and spent his early adulthood in the United States before moving to Japan in 1890. The latter was a British professor of Japanese at Tokyo Imperial University, also widely known as a commentator on Japanese society and a translator of literature and poetry. In one of their many letters, Hearn relates a moment of reflection shared with W. B. Mason, another British author and translator. As the two looked over a scene of daily life in Japan, Mason lamented, "if those people could only feel for us the sympathy we feel toward them!"[24]

The dominant theme of international relations scholarship is that feelings such as these are completely beside the point. As threats and opportunities present themselves, our feelings about other countries will accommodate themselves to these "realities," and not the other way around. And yet iconoclasts have always taken the contrary point of view that our feelings about other countries matter independently. A simplistic version of this argument might hold that we have positive feelings toward countries we regard as similar to our own and negative feelings toward countries that are different. Cultural distance is a subjective matter, and it is our subjective assessment of similarity that looms larger in such arguments than any underlying material similarities. Such notions particularly reasserted their importance after the end of the Cold War.

A highly visible example of the claim that cultural distance and a general lack of sympathy predisposes countries toward conflict is Samuel Huntington's expectation that cultural differences lead to "clashes of civilization."[25] "World politics is entering a new phase," he says, in which "the great divisions among humankind and the dominating source of conflict will be cultural."[26] Addressing the case of Japan specifically, Huntington goes on to say that, "however strong the trade and investment links Japan may develop with other East Asian countries, its cultural differences with those countries inhibit and perhaps preclude its promoting regional economic integration like that in Europe and North America."[27] In this view difference is destiny, and so Japan is destined to be the target of suspicion if not outright hostility not because of what it did, but because it is recognizably different from other Asian countries.

More recent explorations of the relationship between culture and conflict have lamented Huntington's treatment of the topic not so much because they completely reject it, but rather because they conclude it represents a caricature that will only dissuade further exploration of cultural difference and international relations. Jacinta O'Hagan argues, for example, that encounters across cultural or civilizational divides are as often (perhaps *more* often) constructive rather than conflictual and that Huntington's facile linkage of difference and conflict is too simplistic.[28] Taking another tack, Erik Gartzke and Kristian Skrede Gleditsch use language, ethnicity, and religion as measures of difference.[29] They find that some forms of cultural similarity are actually associated with more conflict rather than less. Perhaps this is simply because conflict is more likely in general among neighboring states (which are more likely to be culturally similar compared with distant states), or perhaps it is because disputes are more intense when they are with the groups one knows best.[30]

Because Japanese authors have themselves taken such pains to emphasize Japanese distinctiveness—giving rise to a voluminous *nihonjinron* literature—it is worth exploring the way images of Japan may be influenced by cultural difference.[31] There is no better place to start this discussion than with China.

China

For most of Chinese history, Japan did not figure very prominently in the cosmology of the Middle Kingdom. Japan was part of a periphery that orbited around the Chinese center, acknowledged mostly to the extent it exhibited proper deference to China's rulers.[32] The crisis of Western imperialism shattered that worldview and upended the relationship between the two countries. As Chalmers Johnson observes, "China and Japan reacted to the influence of Western imperialism in the nineteenth century in almost diametrically opposite ways: within a few decades after the Western intrusion Japan had accommodated herself to and incorporated modern technology, whereas China disintegrated as a social system and required a century before she could begin her own modernization under conditions of national unity."[33] Although Japan briefly served as inspiration for Chinese modernizers, the Soviet Union quickly took over that role. Johnson continues: "just as in the case of the Sino-Soviet conflict, this earlier relationship has tended to color later antagonisms with feelings of ingratitude on the one hand and betrayal on the other."[34] Injecting its own colonial aspirations into the ongoing imperial scramble for Asia, Japan eliminated any possibility of further sympathy or admiration from China. After this, Johnson argues, the die was cast:

> Japan's progressive development from the Twenty-one Demands on China in 1915 to the seizure of Manchuria in 1931 ultimately filled all Chinese nationalists with enmity against Japan, a sentiment bolstered by fury against Japan's parvenu imperialism and betrayal of her fellow Asians. When, in the 1930s, the Japanese militarists tried to revive an anti-Western Asian nationalism led by Japan, they were too late. In Chinese eyes Japan was no longer Asian; it was imperialist, pure and simple.[35]

Johnson produced this assessment in 1972, and it would appear that little has changed on this score in the ensuing half-century.[36]

One reason for the intensity of these emotions, Gries has argued, is that China's Confucian cosmology suggested a family-based model for social order.[37] In this model Japan plays the role of a "younger brother" who does not know his proper place. The result, as noted earlier in this chapter, is what Gries calls righteous or ethical anger. Righteous anger is not merely episodic, stemming from Japan's wartime actions, but is predicated on the violation of status that is essential to China's self-image. Like Johnson, Gries finds that this sense of a natural order in which Japan is subservient to Chinese designs continues to exert a powerful influence on modern attitudes toward Japan. And yet Gries's approach also opens the door to a more nuanced understanding of Chinese attitudes, for it places Japan's image within a malleable social context. As the social context (and Japan's role within it) changes,

Japan's image shifts as well. Rather than looking in microscopic fashion at the details of Japan's wartime sins, this approach instead suggests the metaphor of a kaleidoscope through which Japan takes on different attributes as the viewer's own perspective shifts.

Focusing on the cultural embrace of Japanese food, music, fashion, and other elements of popular culture among China's younger generation, Wang Min argues that a "longing" for Japanese culture coexists alongside the far more negative emotions stirred up by wartime history and anti-Japanese education.[38] The result, according to Wang, is a "love-hate duality" that ebbs and flows, sometimes propelled by political controversy and sometimes lifted by the more encouraging waters of cultural exchange. Wang's argument calls to mind another duality proposed by Joshua Fogel, describing the Ming-era vision of Japan as a nation of pirates and monks.[39] In this image as well, Japan possesses the desirable traits of the "sagacious monk" as well as the less savory qualities of the "bloodthirsty warrior." Fogel goes on to argue that this understanding became even more complex later as Qing scholars variously emphasized Japan's economic, scholarly, artistic, and technological accomplishments. A recent two-volume study of the Chinese view of Japan produced by Japanese scholars also covers a range of topics—from international education to the Russo-Japanese War and Japan's annexation of Korea—and supports the conclusion that multiple views of Japan were evident in Qing China.[40]

Inquiry into the Chinese view of Japan is further complicated by the evident diversity of views within the Chinese-speaking world. In Taiwan, for example, both official and popular opinion is far more approving of Japan than in mainland China. Opinion polls conducted by the Japan–Taiwan Exchange Association between 2009 and 2018 show that when Taiwanese adults are asked to name their favorite country (other than their own), a far greater percentage choose Japan (an average of 50.2 percent across five polls) than either China or the United States (each of which averaged in single digits).[41] Deng Qingbo, a political commentator on Taiwan strait issues in China, argues that the attractiveness of Japanese culture in Taiwan goes a long way toward explaining these attitudes.[42] Others point out that close economic cooperation and a mutual sense of threat from China serve to draw them together.[43] And He Yinan finds at work a more subtle identity politics that seeks to balance Taiwan's relations between China and Japan in order to serve the interests of Taiwan's ruling elite.[44]

In Singapore, to take one more example, attitudes toward Japan more closely resemble those in Taiwan than in mainland China. An overwhelming majority of Singaporeans today regard their country's relationship with Japan as either "very friendly" (44 percent) or "somewhat friendly" (52 percent).[45] In 2002 the two negotiated a bilateral economic partnership treaty, and a combination of economic and cultural interests is commonly cited as an explanation for their good relationship.[46] In this case, because Singapore also has a close relationship with China, perceived military threat from the latter is evidently not part of the explanation.

If relations between Japan and the Chinese-speaking world are any guide, cultural distance by itself is an uncertain predictor of positive or negative diplomatic relationships. In Ian Nish's perceptive phrasing, "the relationship between China and Japan is a many-layered cake, impossible to eat all at once."[47] It entails many different relationships: economic, military-strategic, political, cultural, linguistic, religious, philosophical, and so on. Their complex variability is precisely what make Chinese relations with Japan an interesting puzzle.

South Korea

Even more than China, however, the country with the strongest claim of cultural proximity to Japan is undoubtedly Korea and, today, South Korea in particular. Japan was a more important other for Korea, all told, than for China. Historically, Korea's kingdoms were forced to reckon with their vulnerable position, sandwiched between China and Japan. For centuries, the primary Japanese threat to Korea was piracy, but this changed with Toyotomi Hideyoshi's invasion of Korea in the late sixteenth century. After the interregnum of the Tokugawa era, Japanese armies finally succeeded where Hideyoshi had failed, first eliminating Chinese influence and then seizing Korea outright. Their brutal murder of Korea's popular Queen Min was particularly traumatic.[48] And so, as with China, Japan's history of conflict with Korea—to say nothing of the horrors of the Pacific War—provides ample reasons for many Koreans to dislike Japan. Although "China has been the most persistent invader," as Brad Glosserman and Scott Snyder point out, "Japan was the most recent. Its conquest and bloody occupation from 1910 left an indelible mark on Korean memories."[49]

Despite this history and despite a simmering territorial dispute over the Liancourt Rocks, called Dokdo by South Korea and Takeshima by Japan, the relationship between the two countries has also had its ups as well as downs. As Cheol Hee Park perceptively explains, historical animosity in relations between South Korea and Japan is a variable rather than a constant: it "can either be escalated or de-escalated by political leaders and civic groups, and this produces different outcomes in cooperation and conflict between Korea and Japan."[50] Working in favor of de-escalation are the close economic and cultural ties between the two countries. Trade and tourism between the two countries have expanded steadily, and even when frictions over disputed issues flare, economic boycotts have never gained the same traction in South Korea that they have in China.[51] South Korea lifted its ban on cultural imports from Japan in 1998, ushering in a new era of cultural cross-fertilization between the two countries.[52] Not only did Japanese music, anime, and other elements of pop culture enjoy great success in South Korea, but a reciprocal Korean wave or *hallyu* (*hanryū* in Japanese) also took root in Japan.[53] Nissim Otmazgin argues that such cultural attractions are no mere epiphenomena but rather "a tail that wags the dog," exerting their own strong and independent influence on state and industrial policy.[54] Each government has recognized popular culture as an important source of soft power, but it is one that neither can completely or directly control.

Rather than trying to resolve the Japan–South Korea relationship into a simple equation between culture and conflict (or its absence), Glosserman and Snyder ultimately suggest a more nuanced view:

> Today members of each public are increasingly interacting directly with each other, through business relationships, tourism, education exchanges, sister-city relationships, and even marriage. . . . Exposure has heightened expectations of the other as the two societies recognize similarities between themselves. They now expect their partner to understand and appreciate their concerns. When that does not happen—when one country does something that hurts or offends the other—the feeling is more akin to betrayal and the pain seemingly more acute.[55]

From this perspective, culture similarities work more as intervening variables that intensify other rationales for either conflict or cooperation. Glosserman and Snyder believe that these other rationales often have roots in the "domestic political considerations [that are] a chronic flashpoint in Korea-Japan relations."[56] This is a plausible hypothesis, one that will be examined in greater detail in Chapter 5, but it will suffice for now to recognize that a simple equation of Korean and Japanese cultural proximity with either conflict or cooperation is problematic. And thus, at the very least, Korea calls into question the Huntingtonian expectation that cultural distance is the root of conflict.

United States

If Korea and Japan share many cultural traits, the United States serves as an obvious example of cultural distance. In contrast to those who see Japan as a bridge between East and West, many other scholars (including many Japanese scholars) argue that Japan typifies the contrast between West and East. In Edward Said's familiar conception of Orientalism, the West exemplifies a rational, mature, virile, and intrinsically superior contrast with Eastern cultures, nations, and peoples.[57] Ian Littlewood's study of Western images of Japan illustrates this genre nicely. The Western "idea of Japan," Littlewood argues, makes use of four distinct stereotypes either alone or in combination: exotic aliens, artistically refined aesthetes, feminine butterflies, and aggressive samurai.[58] Littlewood's treatment of each stereotype is extensive, but there is an unavoidable tension between his expressed desire to challenge these stereotypes and his sense that they are nonetheless deeply entrenched in the Western mindset.[59] Moreover, racial difference amplifies Rudyard Kipling's often-misappropriated maxim that "East is East, and West is West, and never the twain shall meet."[60] For Littlewood, racism helps to explain how samurai are transmuted into the "yellow peril," and how even the benign virtues of Japanese aesthetics take on a certain exotic absurdity.

Another telling illustration of the conviction that Eastern and Western countries are fated to view each other across a deep cultural chasm can be found in the writings of Endymion Wilkinson, the British sinologist and diplomat who established the European Commission's permanent delegation to Japan. Wilkinson wrote at the height of Japan's trade frictions with many Western countries in the 1970s and 1980s.[61] Although these frictions provided an occasion for his commentary, one of Wilkinson's main themes was the enduring contrast between Japan and the West:

> In many ways the images of Japan in the West have been the most extreme embodiment of the myths of the Orient. Japan is the furthest East, indeed, in the earliest European literature it was actually thought to be the Antipodes. Europeans and Americans never tired of writing that in Japan everything was antipodal, topsy-turvy and back to front; an absurd, Alice-in-Wonderland world, not worth taking seriously. Thus, the fundamental image of Japan in the West was of a country of extreme and paradoxical contrasts.[62]

To develop the point Wilkinson cites Sir Rutherford Alcock (the first British minister in Tokyo), who proclaimed: "Japan is essentially a country of paradoxes and anomalies, where all, even familiar things, put on new faces and are curiously reversed."[63] Alcock and Wilkinson are among the very many Western observers of Japan who stress what Basil Hall Chamberlain called its "topsy-turvydom."[64] In the span of several chapters Wilkinson reflects that this image of difference has several guises, portraying Japan as a country of exotic aliens in general, but also of refined artists, of seductive geisha, and finally of aggressive warriors (whether literally during Japan's colonial era or figuratively, in business, thereafter).[65] Thus, reaching back as far as these observations from the mid-nineteenth century, Wilkinson foreshadows the same categories employed by Littlewood. And like Littlewood, Wilkinson senses that these perceptions have become ossified in the Western imagination.

There are many other examples of Americans treading along this familiar path. In what was probably the most influential American treatise on Japan in the immediate postwar era, Ruth Benedict begins *The Chrysanthemum and the Sword* with the pronouncement that "the Japanese were the most alien enemy the United States had ever fought in an all-out struggle."[66] A few decades later, in a superb essay that begins with Benedict and surveys many of the studies that followed, Nathan Glazer concludes:

> The following points seem to characterize the present attitude of the best-educated Americans toward Japan: that they are *characterized by radical paradoxes*; that connected with this sense of radical paradox is a sense of *alienness*—and whether we see Japanese as alien because they are paradoxical, or paradoxical because they are alien, I am not sure; that one aspect of their alienness is their *insensitivity* to others, their peculiar relations to other people; that because of this paradoxicality they are basically *unpredictable*—they may change from one thing to another overnight; that because they are unpredictable one must approach their present prosperity, growth, and stability with a sense of extreme caution—in effect they are fundamentally *unstable*; that since they are unstable, we must in particular be distrustful of the *Japanese commitment to democracy*.[67]

As Glazer suggests, the stress so often placed on Japan's perceived exotic difference also translates into a sense that it is a land of extremes. The Japanese must be either superhuman or substandard.[68] They may even be both at the same time, as when Yoichi Funabashi described the country as an "'economic giant' and 'military dwarf.'"[69] They must be either ruthless warriors or gentle artists, aggressively masculine or seductively and submissively feminine.[70] This tendency toward extremes, in turn, reinforces the sense that Japan is not normal and that it can scarcely be understood by Americans. Glazer sums it up this way: "Underlying sophisticated American attitudes toward Japan, I argue, is the sense of alienness, paradoxicality, instability, and unpredictability, and these attitudes have remained as a basic component of the American image of Japan since World War II."[71]

The most significant update to this image is perhaps what David Roh calls *techno-orientalism*.[72] In place of the emotion-laden portrayals of aggressive samurai and beguiling geisha, this more futuristic orientalism envisions a society that is cold, unfeeling, and hypertechnical. Far from the creations of Kipling, it is a postmodern Asia of *Blade Runner* landscapes in which analog and digital realities meld seamlessly. The image remains recognizably Orientalist, however, in its moral critique of robotic collectivism at the expense of individual liberty. In this, it hearkens back to Benedict's distinction between shame cultures and guilt cultures and Takeo Doi's classic notions of social obligation and dependence (or *amae*).[73] What these several versions of Orientalism share is a two-fold conviction: first, that American perceptions (and mis-perceptions) of Japan are grounded in robust cultural convictions; and, second, that these convictions are highly resistant to change. The result is at best a "perception gap," if not "Japan-bashing" or something worse.[74] Arguments such as these certainly provide fodder for Huntingtonian expectations of East–West conflict. Equally striking, however, is that very few contemporary American observers seem to view such conflict as inevitable. As the dean of postwar Japanese studies in the United States, Edwin Reischauer argued during one of the many moments when tensions flared between the two countries, their "broken dialogue" could always be repaired by a willingness to listen to the other's perspective.[75]

Other Countries

This book will primarily focus on Chinese and South Korean perceptions of Japan along with some brief attention to contrasting American perceptions. In just these three cases, we see that perceptions run the gamut from attraction to repulsion, from familiarity to exoticism. We can also see very clearly that no single image will suffice to sum up the way citizens of any one of these countries see Japan. The realization that Japan's image is variable and complex is only deepened by extending our gaze to other parts of the world.

Other countries, particularly in Southeast Asia, suffered at Japan's hands during the war. In the war's immediate aftermath, their perceptions of Japan—like those of the three countries discussed previously—were negative. Some of these countries, such as the Philippines, had a history of interactions with Japan stretching back to the sixteenth century.[76] Some, like Australia, developed extensive contact with Japan only in the modern era or as a result of Japan's colonial expansion preceding the Pacific War.[77] Yet nearly all of Japan's former adversaries in Southeast Asia have developed positive attitudes toward Japan as memories of the war receded into the past. As previously noted and as shown in Figure 2.1, the Pew Research Center's 2015 Global Attitudes Survey found favorable attitudes toward Japan among 84 percent of Malaysians, 82 percent of Vietnamese, 81 percent of Filipinos, 80 percent of Australians, and 71 percent of Indonesians.[78] These views are generally corroborated in a series of "Country Ratings Polls" conducted by the BBC World Service. The BBC poll found that impressions of Japan's "influence in the world" are overwhelmingly positive in Indonesia (85 percent), in the Philippines (84 percent), and in Australia (60 percent).[79] Of these, the most culturally distant would seem to be Australia, yet cultural distance is once again a poor guide to these countries' changing impressions of Japan.[80] The contributors to one book surveying attitudes toward Japan in Southeast Asia suggest that contemporary impressions of Japan have less to do with culture and more to do with Japanese foreign aid and close bilateral business relationships.[81] In view of the security challenges posed by China, other observers also see the necessity of strategic cooperation with Japan and the United States as an impetus for positive trilateral relations, at least in the cases of Australia and the Philippines.[82]

Heading north rather than south, the situation is murkier. Russian attitudes toward Japan are mixed, perhaps reflecting the up-and-down character of Russian–Japanese relations over the past century and a half. As their competition for control over Manchuria and Korea intensified in the late nineteenth century and culminated in the Russo-Japanese war, their nascent relationship quickly deteriorated.[83] Just as quickly it rebounded, and the decade that followed has been called a "Golden Age" of Russian–Japanese relations as intensified contacts helped to demystify Japan in the minds of many Russians.[84] In the aftermath of World War II, Japan's alliance with the United States conditioned Soviet perceptions, and Soviet propaganda portrayed Japan as a potential threat to the Soviet Union's territorial integrity.[85] Contemporary Russia–Japan relations are also overshadowed by the countries' incompatible claims to the Southern Kuril Islands. And yet a 2018 opinion poll conducted by the Levada Center found that 61 percent of Russians have a positive opinion of Japan, versus 20 percent with a negative opinion.[86] Despite apparent cultural differences, some authors have suggested that perceptions of cultural similarities or, more recently, the attractions of Japanese popular culture help to explain such relatively approving attitudes.[87]

Much more has been written about the image of Japan in other parts of the world. For some, as argued at the beginning of this chapter, Japan serves as a bridge between East and West. For others it is the quintessence of the Orient: further to the East, more fantastically different, more pernicious in its vices, more sublime in its virtues, and thus more perfectly embodying the difference between East and West than any other place. For this very reason, perspectives of Japan in countries that do not cleave neatly to the East–West binary—in Africa or the Middle East, for example—are likely to be complicated by factors beyond perceived cultural distance.[88] It is therefore difficult to offer a neat summary of the relationship between cultural distance and attitudes toward Japan. If one can generalize at all, one might say that cultural difference is a useful trope for making a variety of arguments about national others. And a very wide variety of arguments have been made about Japan. Increasing cultural distance does not lead inevitably to negative or positive images in general, although it does lend itself to a certain exotic treatment of the other. At the same time, the French proverb *tout comprendre, c'est tout pardonner* is equally hard to defend, and some of Japan's closest neighbors have persistently been its harshest critics.

Exactly how persistent their criticism has been raises another issue, to which we now turn: variation in attitudes across time rather than across cultural distance. Many who comment on Japan's image—including most of those discussed in this section—tend to treat attitudes toward Japan as a static phenomenon, rooted in culture or race or history or something else understood to be immutable. Yet arguably culture, race, and history are all imminently susceptible to continuous reinterpretation. It makes sense to ask not only how Japan is seen, therefore, but also how perceptions of Japan have evolved.

CHANGES OVER TIME

The history of Western perceptions of Japan is mostly circumscribed by the fact of Tokugawa Japan's formal seclusion policy (*sakoku*), lasting until Commodore Perry's second trip to Japan in 1854. Before this, Japan was not well or widely known. After Perry's voyages, a period of great fascination with Japan began.[89] Lacking the wherewithal to place Japan in any meaningful context and working with very limited information, most Western writers insisted on its distinctiveness in the ways described in the previous section. Gilbert and Sullivan's 1885 comic opera, *The Mikado*, was emblematic and opened in this fashion:

> If you want to know who we are,
> We are gentlemen of Japan:
> On many a vase and jar—
> On many a screen and fan,
> We figure in lively paint:
> Our attitude's queer and quaint—
> You're wrong if you think it ain't, oh![90]

Thus begins one of the most popular English operettas in history. From this starting point, when so little was known about Japan in the West that its inhabitants seemed to be little more than two-dimensional images painted on screens and fans, it would be surprising if impressions did not change.

Of course, impressions did change. In the Western imagination, Japan was sometimes considered an exemplary "civilizing" influence in Asia, attractively and thoughtfully appreciative of European and American political and scientific models. At other times, particularly after demonstrations of growing Japanese independence and power in its turn-of-the-century wars against China and Russia, Japan also seemed reckless and dangerous.[91] After the Second World War Japan was soon in the good graces of the West once again, somewhat less so as its economic clout grew in the 1980s, and more so once again as China replaced Japan as the dominant Asian economy.[92] Summing up the evident volatility of American impressions of Japan over just a part of this history, Sheila Johnson says: "American attitudes toward Japan have changed enormously over the past half century. I believe this would not have been possible if such attitudes were, in fact, based on something as long-lasting and deeply rooted as national character."[93]

The previous section of this chapter strongly implies that our sense of national character is more in the eye of the beholder than in the target of our gaze. Thus estimations of what Japan is really like vary greatly from place to place, as discussed in the previous section, but also over time along with changes in the perspective of viewers. In the case of the United States, a growing body of polling data documents these changes. Japan did not often command the attention of mid-twentieth century American pollsters, but the polls that were conducted were unequivocal. Glazer reports that "in 1942, a poll showed that 56 percent of Americans thought Japanese cruel,

73 percent thought them treacherous, 63 percent sly. The parallel figures for Chinese were 3, 4, and 8."[94] As late as 1960, "55 percent of respondents thought Japan was 'not dependable,'" and only "31 percent thought it was."[95] From the late 1980s onward polling data are more plentiful thanks to the Gallup poll's Country Ratings surveys. The longitudinal extent of the data varies from country to country, but the Gallup poll has asked Americans how favorably they view Japan almost every year since 1989. Grouping "very favorable" and "mostly favorable" responses together as "favorable," and "very unfavorable" and "mostly unfavorable" responses together as "unfavorable," Figure 2.2 shows changes in American attitudes toward Japan over the past three decades. In the early 1990s, as the United States struggled with a recession and 77 percent of Americans saw Japan as an "economic threat," Japan's favorability and unfavorability ratings both fluctuated between 40 and 50 percent.[96] Since that time, Japan's favorability rating in the United States has steadily climbed, reaching a peak of 87 percent in 2018.[97]

On the face of it, data such as the favorability ratings presented in Figure 2.2 suggest that we are better served by asking how Americans see Japan under specific historical circumstances rather than in general. With this in mind, we might again turn to the central preoccupation of this book, the persistently negative

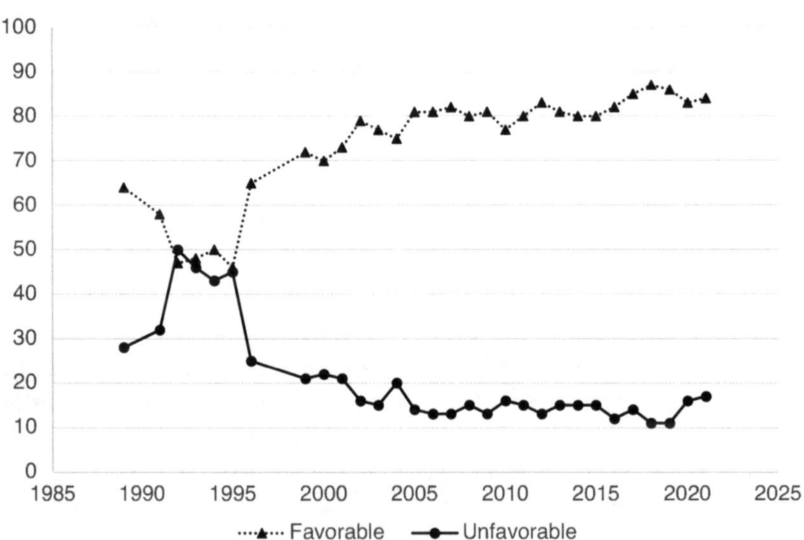

Figure 2.2. American Attitudes toward Japan, 1989–2021
(Data from Gallup Country Ratings Polls; see Gallup, "Country Ratings." In years with multiple polls—1989, 1991, and 1999—poll results are averaged.)

attitudes toward Japan held by Chinese and South Koreans. In fact, we might proceed by asking how just how persistent these attitudes have really been.

China

China's earliest impressions of Japan were conditioned mainly by its encounters with Japanese scholars, merchants, and pirates, but it is safe to say that the relationship between the two countries developed in radically new ways and took on new gravity as the late nineteenth century gave rise to the Sino-Japanese War. That China's humiliation fostered implacably hostile attitudes toward Japan and that these attitudes were only deepened by ensuing conflict in the first half of the twentieth century constitutes the received wisdom about this relationship. Most commentators emphasize how deeply ingrained Chinese hatred of Japan has become.[98] The strength of this conviction, unfortunately, has worked against treating this proposition as an empirical question. Are Chinese attitudes truly so unyielding?

Longitudinal public opinion data that might shed light on this proposition are a comparatively recent phenomenon in China. A part of the challenge, of course, is the control exerted by the Chinese Communist Party over research activities in China. Historically, it has been difficult to undertake objective, large-scale opinion surveys in China, and even the advent of the internet and new communication technologies has not completely changed this situation.[99] News organizations and enterprising scholars have nevertheless conducted numerous inquiries over the years, and a careful review of their findings allows us to draw some interesting, if tentative, conclusions.

Beginning with a recent series of polls from the Pew Research Center, we find a picture that is broadly in keeping with the assertion that animosity directed at Japan is entrenched and persistent in China. The Pew Global Attitudes Survey finds, in seven polls over a span of a decade, that Chinese attitudes toward Japan are consistently negative, hovering somewhere between 70 and 90 percent unfavorable (see Figure 2.3). These are probably the polls most familiar to American scholars interested in Chinese views of Japan. The Pew data begin in 2005, when the streets of large Chinese cities erupted into protests against a new Japanese textbook accused of whitewashing Japan's wartime atrocities. As historian Qiu Jin points out, "these were the first nation-wide anti-Japanese demonstrations since 1985 and probably the largest mass demonstrations in China since June 1989."[100] Relations between the two countries, Qiu goes on to say, "plunged to their lowest point since the two countries restored formal diplomatic relations in

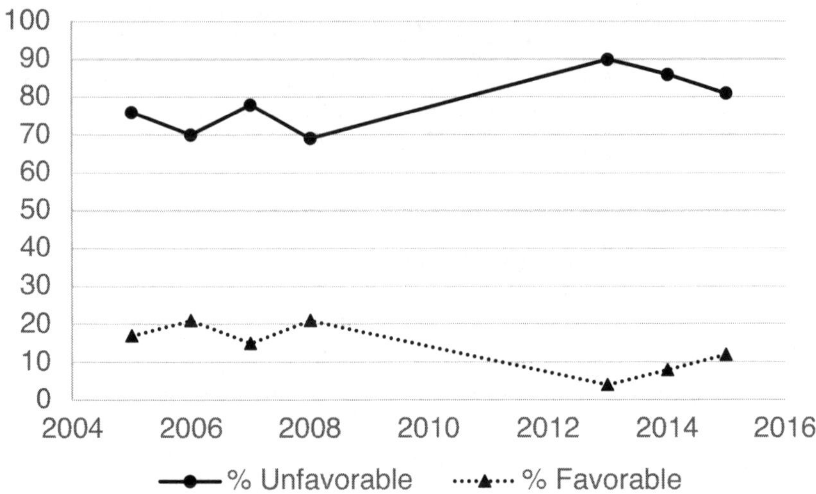

Figure 2.3. Chinese Attitudes toward Japan, 2005–2015, Pew Data
(Data from Pew Global Attitudes Survey 2015; see Pew Research Center, "How Asia-Pacific Publics See Each Other.")

1972."[101] The cumulative picture painted by the Pew polls, however, is that Chinese attitudes were not so much responses to particular events as they were the result of persistent and deeply entrenched animus.

A somewhat different picture emerges, however, when we consider polls conducted by Genron NPO, a Japanese think tank specializing in public opinion research and inter-Asian dialogue, over a slightly greater time span (2005–2021). The Genron NPO data, shown in Figure 2.4, indicate that Chinese attitudes toward Japan gradually improved following the 2005 protests. By 2007 the gap between unfavorable and favorable attitudes was only about 12 points (36.5 percent favorable, 24.4 percent unfavorable). After the two countries' dispute over the Senkaku/Diaoyu Islands was inflamed by Japan's nationalization of the islands in 2012, the percentage of Chinese with an unfavorable view of Japan increased dramatically (92.8 percent unfavorable). Yet views of Japan once again improved to the point that, by 2019, there was only a 7-point gap (52.7 percent unfavorable, 45.9 percent favorable).[102]

The picture painted by the Genron NPO data is one of at least some variability rather than consistent and entrenched anti-Japanese views. The Genron NPO data represent the longest series of opinion polls of Chinese attitudes toward Japan conducted by a single organization, but the results of additional polls have been compiled by Kobayashi Yoshiki, a researcher at Waseda University.[103] Kobayashi's data are derived from thirty opinion polls

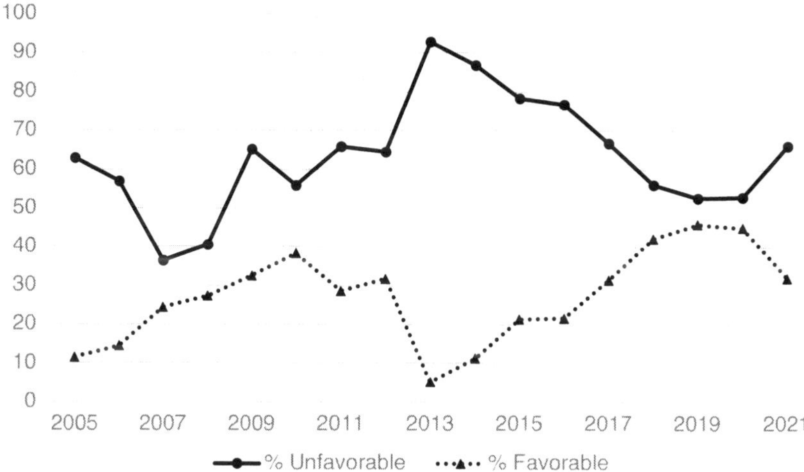

Figure 2.4. Chinese Attitudes toward Japan, 2005–2017, Genron NPO Data
(Data from Genron NPO Japan-China Public Opinion Surveys; see Genron NPO, "Japan-China Public Opinion Survey 2021.")

conducted by a wide range of news organizations, think tanks, and universities between 1988 and 2007.[104] For many years, Kobayashi has data from multiple polls (e.g., in 2007 he has polls conducted in April, August, and September by various organizations). And although Kobayashi groups responses into three categories—"positive," "negative," and "neutral" reactions to Japan—it is doubtful that all the polls on whose data he relies used the same wording.

Although the resulting data must therefore be treated cautiously, they are still useful to give a fuller picture of Chinese attitudes. To this end, I have computed annual averages of Kobayashi's poll results and added to these the post-2007 data discussed previously. Figure 2.5 shows the result of this combined dataset.[105] What is perhaps most striking is how different the picture becomes when we look at opinion data over a span of more than thirty years. If we were to look only at the Pew Global Attitudes data (Figure 2.3), it would be easy to conclude that Chinese attitudes toward Japan are negative and that this is the end of the story.

The longer time span shown in Figure 2.5 makes it clear that the story is actually much more interesting. Popular opinion about Japan fluctuates within China more than is commonly appreciated. Far from expressing implacably hostile attitudes, the Chinese public appears to react not only to perceived wrongdoing or threats from Japan but also to opportunities for rapprochement. To be sure, some events such as the imbroglio over the

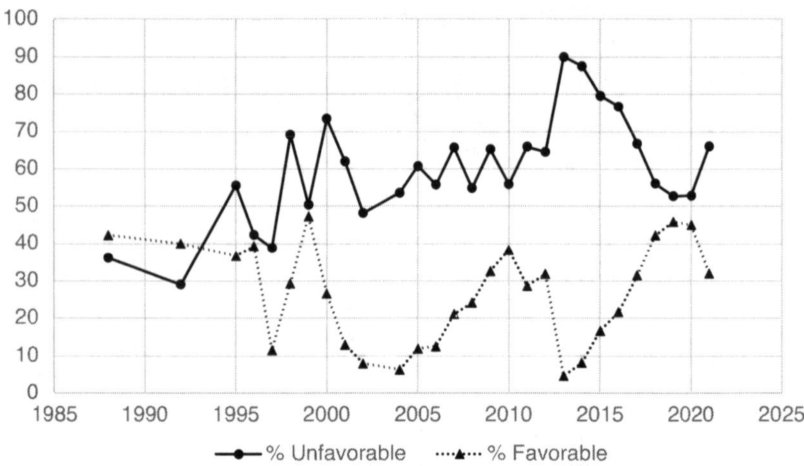

Figure 2.5. Chinese Attitudes toward Japan, 1988–2021, Combined Data
(Data from multiple sources. See Kobayashi, "Chūgoku ni okeru 'Tainichi Kanjō' ni Kan Suru Kōsatsu"; Genron NPO, "Japan-China Public Opinion Survey 2021"; Pew Research Center, "How Asia-Pacific Publics See Each Other.")

Senkaku/Diaoyu Islands in 2012 have a pronounced and clearly observable negative effect on popular attitudes in China. At other times—in the years preceding the Tiananmen Uprising, for example, but also as recently as 2019–2020—Japan's image has benefited both from a decline in negative attitudes and a rise in positive ones.

This chapter began with one question about Japan's international image: Why is Japan seen so negatively in China and South Korea when it has developed much better relations with—and is seen in a much better light by—many of its other former adversaries? A careful look at the available evidence of public opinion in China suggests, however, that this simple formulation is somewhat misleading or at least incomplete. We might also ask what governs shifts in attitudes toward Japan within China, where there is more variability than is sometimes acknowledged. It is also worth asking whether the same is true in South Korea.

South Korea

Reflecting on the state of relations between South Korea and Japan in 2013, David Kang and Jiun Bang lamented that they resembled the movie *Groundhog Day*, in which the character played by Bill Murray lives the same day over and over again.[106] Despite changes in leadership, South Korean and Japanese leaders seemed fated act out the same disputes following the same well-worn story lines. A few years later, Kang and Bang changed their metaphor but not their argument, arguing that "What Goes Up, Must Come Down" and that the momentary improvement in Seoul–Tokyo relations in late 2016 was destined to be brief because of domestic pressures on both sides.[107] The persistent tension between Japan and South Korea, despite their evident strategic interests in cooperating, makes the difficulty of "getting beyond history" in this relationship all the more notable.

As with China–Japan relations, however, a slightly more long-term perspective puts things in a new light. If long-term opinion data are limited for China, this is even more the case with South Korea. During the prewar period, when Japan's imperial expansion made it Korea's enemy, the relationship was reduced to its simplest and most antagonistic elements. Yet V. M. Tikhonov's excellent study of Korea's national "others" in the formative years of its early modern era (the 1880s to 1945) documents more complex attitudes than simple resentment or hatred directed against a colonizer. Tikhonov argues that Korean elites admired Japan's achievements and saw them as a model even as they despised Japan's policies toward Korea.[108]

Postwar attitudes have also had their ups and downs. As Karl Friedhoff and Kang Chungku observe, "the current negativity towards Japan did not always prevail. . . . As recently as 2010, Japan was viewed almost as favorably as China."[109] Systematic opinion poll data are, unfortunately, even more limited than in the case of China–Japan relations. Between 2007 and 2015, however, the Pew Research Center did include both South Korea and Japan in its Global Attitudes Survey, and since 2013 Genron NPO has also conducted an annual Japan–South Korea Public Opinion Poll. Figure 2.6 presents the results of these two polls, combined and averaged in the years when both polls were conducted.

The fifteen years of public opinion data on South Korean attitudes toward Japan presented in Figure 2.6 do not show unabated hostility but rather variability, as with Chinese attitudes. To be fair, at no point in this span of time did the majority of South Korean respondents have positive views of Japan. But even in this relatively brief period, Japan's unfavorability rating has swung from a high of 77 percent in 2013 to a low of around 50 percent (in 2008 and again in 2018–2019). Japan's favorability rating, meanwhile, peaked at a high of 47 percent in 2008 and fell to a low of 12 percent in the 2020 poll.[110] Friedhoff and Kang conclude that, compared with South Korean attitudes about China, North Korea, or even the United States, "the favorability of Japan is more volatile. Because the favorability of Japan declined sharply from 2010 through 2012, this also suggests that it could rebound quickly given the correct conditions."[111]

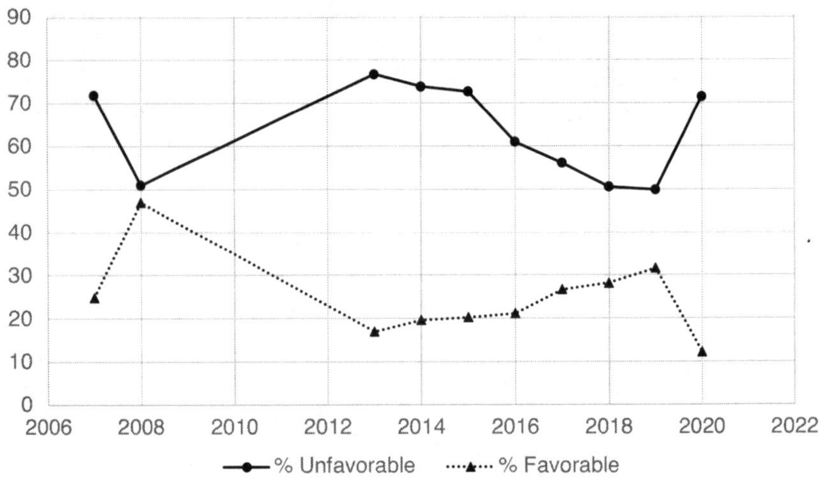

Figure 2.6. South Korean Attitudes toward Japan, 2007–20, Combined Data (Data from multiple sources. See Pew Research Center, "How Asia-Pacific Publics See Each Other"; Kudo, "South Korean Attitudes toward Japan Have Worsened Dramatically.")

MIRROR IMAGES

The first purpose of this chapter, announced at the outset, has been to review the variety of ways Japan has been and currently is seen by other countries. Perhaps the most succinct statement one could make on this topic is that Japan is seen, and has been seen, in many different ways. More than most countries, Japan has served as a mirror for people to understand their own country. Occupying a vaguely defined position somewhere between East and West, Japan is especially well suited to this role.

In a thoughtful interview with John Dower, Patrick Lawrence—a journalist and long-time Asia correspondent for the *International Herald Tribune* and *The New Yorker*—explores the notion of Japan as mirror in some detail. When Lawrence arrived to conduct the interview, he discovered not only John Dower but also Herbert Bix seated at the table, presenting him with the opportunity to interview not one but two of the leading Japan scholars of their generation. They got no further than Dower's PhD dissertation before the notion of Japan as a mirror surfaced.

> DOWER: At Harvard the expectation was that I would do a PhD
> on a writer named Mori Ogai, who was famous as a literary figure
> in the Meiji period [1868–1912]. Mori Ogai was fascinating

because, as you know, when you're immersed in a culture like Japan, partly you become immersed in the culture and partly you become immersed in rethinking your own culture. It's never that you go to Japan and just become a Japanophile; you also are reflecting on your own culture.

LAWRENCE: Japan as mirror. I came to that realization myself over time.

DOWER: Japan as a mirror. That was a period when "national character" and cultural difference were very strong. National character studies came up in World War II, with "Know Your Enemy" and the "national character" of the Japanese. You always, in national character studies, focus on what makes people different from you. You don't dwell on similarity, you dwell on differences. It's not just Americans or Westerners who are ethnocentric. Japanese love to do this: "What makes us different? . . ." It's called *nihonjinron* in Japanese. . . .

I had lived in Japan a number of years by this time. My wife was Japanese, I had a child who at the time was less than 2 and speaking only Japanese. Herb came back the same year. He, too, was married to a Japanese woman. I had spent a great deal of time with my wife's family—lots of siblings, mother and father—and I didn't spend my time thinking about how different these people are from me. I had no sense of us/me, self and other, of a big divide. And I also had no sense that they were all the same, that you could generalize about the Japanese, because I couldn't even generalize about my in-laws' family.[112]

It is not surprising that someone like Dower, who has spent a career studying Japan, should resist simple generalizations. Yet he goes on to say, "I always tried to see myself and others in a comparative way."[113] Like Dower, many other observers have found in Japan a highly polished surface reflecting their own society and culture in interesting ways.[114] And so, we might begin by observing that one's image of Japan is likely to be a measure of national self as much as an indication of Japan's own qualities.

Pushing a little further into the evidence but still hovering far above the details, we might offer a second generalization about Japan: although it is widely admired, this is not the case within China and South Korea. The conclusion that scholars often draw from this pattern is that the legacy of Japanese conquest and occupation of those two countries is reflected in popular attitudes toward Japan to this day. The second purpose of this chapter has been to establish, through a more careful examination of public opinion data, that attitudes toward Japan in both China and South Korea are not set in stone. What Japan means to citizens of both countries has changed over time and across issue areas (much as it has done in the United States). The puzzle is better framed in terms of the causes of shifts in public attitudes toward Japan rather than simply by asking why Chinese and South Koreans dislike Japan. Empirically, it would be more accurate to say that, at times, intensely negative sentiments toward Japan are prevalent in China and South Korea. Determining how and why this should be the case is the objective of the remainder of this book.

As this chapter has reviewed various images of Japan, it has also implicitly raised the question of what, exactly, one might mean by Japan's "image." The term suggests a predominantly cognitive approach, appearing to propose that Japan be understood by way of analogy. Japan is seen to be *like* something else, often anthropomorphized, and thus rendered as friend or enemy, barbarian or civilized, a leader or a follower, senior or junior, and so on. If Japan was once seen within China, to borrow Fogel's terms, as a land of pirates and monks, then Japan is either rapacious or refined.

These images either leave out or presuppose one of the central concerns of this book: why Japan is either liked or disliked. By conceiving of images only in cognitive terms, we leave out the emotional content of our views. This impoverishes our understanding of how and why such images matter. Before turning to the question of why Japan is seen in different ways, liked and disliked, some discussion of why image matters—and of how scholars in the fields of international relations and foreign policy analysis have approached the topic—is in order.

Notes

1. Isaacs, *Scratches on Our Minds*, 407.
2. Said, *Orientalism*. Said's concern with the East as a defining interlocutor for Western civilization led him to focus on the Ottoman Empire and the "Near East." "The Orient," he says, "is not only adjacent to Europe; it is also the place of Europe's greatest and richest and oldest colonies, the source of its civilizations and languages, its cultural contestant. In addition, the Orient has helped to define Europe (or the West) as its contrasting image, idea, personality, experience" (Said, *Orientalism*, 1–2; see also Neumann, *Uses of the Other*). As Europe's interests expanded to reach a global scale, the ambit of "Orientalism" kept pace to include the "Far East" as well.
3. Shigemitsu, "Address."
4. Watanabe, "Japan between East and West."

5. Nitobe, *Japanese Nation*, 12; on samurai culture, see Nitobe, *Bushidō*. Other thoughtful discussions of Japan's position between East and West include Naff, "Reflections"; Hutchinson, *Nagai Kafu's Occidentalism*; and, on the pre-Meiji era, Chang, *Prejudice to Tolerance*.

6. See, inter alia, Kawakami, *Japan and the Japanese*; and Tsuzuki, "Social Intercourse." Long before the imposed modernity of the Meiji era, in fact, Japanese authors took up the question of Japanese distinctiveness. The *kokugaku* ("national learning") movement beginning in the late seventeenth century stressed the unique qualities of Japanese scholarship, initially contrasted primarily with Confucian and Buddhist perspectives (see Nosco, *Remembering Paradise*).

7. Okakura, *Ideals of the East*. Also see Tankha, *Okakura Tenshin*.

8. On the broader importance of race in the events leading up to the Pacific War, see Dower, *War without Mercy*; and on the rationale for pan-Asian racial sentiment, see Hotta, *Pan-Asianism* and Saaler and Koschmann, *Pan-Asianism in Modern Japanese History*.

9. Orbach, *Curse on This Country*.

10. For a good documentary history of the "rape of Nanking," see Brook, *Documents*.

11. Reynolds, "U.S. Prisoners of War."

12. Tanaka and Dower, *Hidden Horrors*.

13. Connaughton, Pimlott, and Anderson, *Battle for Manila*.

14. For estimates of deaths caused by the Japanese military, see Gruhl, *Imperial Japan's World War Two*, 97 and 143–44. On the percentage of Filipino deaths, see Day, *Philippines*, 106. Gruhl's numbers would put Filipino losses at about 3.5 percent of the Philippines' population—comparable to losses in China and South Korea. Deaths in the Dutch East Indies (Indonesia) also amounted to about 5 percent of the total population; see Dower, *War without Mercy*, 295–96.

15. Rummel, *Statistics of Democide*.

16. LaCapra, *History and Memory*, 9.

17. The literature on individual trauma and emotion is sizable. On emotion and national trauma, specifically, see Demertzis, *Political Sociology of Emotions*.

18. Gries, "Nationalism, Indignation."

19. Gries, "Nationalism, Indignation," 113.

20. Kristof, "Problem of Memory."

21. Kristof, "Problem of Memory," 37.

22. Kristof, "Problem of Memory," 38.

23. Pew Research Center, "How Asia-Pacific Publics See Each Other."

24. Hearn, *Japanese Letters*, 359.

25. Huntington, "Clash of Civilizations?" Huntington leans heavily on religion as a marker of cultural difference. And in principle, at least, his argument is about civilization as difference rather than civilization as hierarchy (although one might harbor suspicions to the contrary after he turns, in this piece, to a discussion of the "West against the rest"). For a more thorough discussion of the antinomy between civilization and barbarism, see Salter, *Barbarians and Civilization*. Salter argues that notions of civilization as high culture are woven throughout postcolonial power structures and inevitably continue to sustain international hierarchies in the modern world.

26. Huntington, "Clash of Civilizations?," 22.

27. Huntington, "Clash of Civilizations?," 28.

28. O'Hagan, "Civilisational Conflict?"

29. Gartzke and Gleditsch, "Identity and Conflict."
30. Gartzke and Gleditsch control for distance and still find that their "identity" variables (language, ethnicity, religion) have meaningful effects on conflict. Yet one suspects that multicollinearity might be a problem, making it hard to disentangle physical and cultural distance.
31. Important overviews of the nihonjinron (theories of Japanese distinctiveness) literature include Dale, *Myth of Japanese Uniqueness*; Befu, *Hegemony of Homogeneity*; Befu and Kazufumi, "Empirical Status of Nihonjinron"; Minami, *Nihonjinron*; and Yoshino, *Cultural Nationalism*. An interesting comparative discussion of exceptionalist discourses in China, Japan, and Korea is to be found in Kim, "West and East Asian National Identities."
32. Thoughtful discussions of Chinese attitudes toward Japan in the Ming and Qing eras (from the late fourteenth century through the early twentieth century) can be found in Fogel, *Sagacious Monks and Bloodthirsty Warriors*.
33. Johnson, "How China and Japan See Each Other," 711.
34. Johnson, "How China and Japan See Each Other," 711.
35. Johnson, "How China and Japan See Each Other," 715.
36. See, e.g., Whiting, *China Eyes Japan*; Gries, *China's New Nationalism*; Suzuki, "Importance of 'Othering.'"
37. Gries, "Nationalism, Indignation."
38. Wang, *Nihon ni Akogareru Chūgoku-jin*.
39. Fogel, *Sagacious Monks and Bloodthirsty Warriors*.
40. Chinese View of Japan Editorial Committee, *Chūgokujin no Nihon Kan*. For another statement of prewar Chinese views on Japan, see Shinano, *Shinajin no Mita Nihonjin*.
41. Japan–Taiwan Exchange Association, "Public Opinion Poll of Taiwan."
42. Deng, "Pro-Japan but Anti-China."
43. See, e.g., Fouse, "Japan–Taiwan Relations"; Dreyer, "Japan–Taiwan Relationship"; and Fukuda, "Recent Developments."
44. He, "Identity Politics and Foreign Policy."
45. Michishita, "Japan, Singapore." A 2008 opinion poll commissioned by Japan's Ministry of Foreign Affairs obtained similar results (TNS Singapore, "Opinion Poll on Japan").
46. Michishita, "Japan, Singapore." Also see Koh, "Japan, Singapore"; Lim, *Merlion and Mt. Fuji*.
47. Nish, "Overview of Relations," 601.
48. For a discussion of the role this assassination continues to play in Korean popular culture, see Lee, "Female Body."
49. Glosserman and Snyder, *Japan–South Korea Identity Clash*, 7.
50. Park, "Cooperation Coupled with Conflicts," 16.
51. Vekasi and Nam, "Boycotting Japan."
52. See, inter alia, Han, "Consuming the Modern"; Shin, "Reconsidering Transnational Cultural Flows"; Otmazgin, "Tail that Wags the Dog?"
53. Creighton, "Japanese Surfing the Korean Wave"; Jung, "Transnational Korea." Indeed, Korean musicians were responsible for more than a third of the highest-selling albums in Japan in 2021, including the top-selling album by Korean band BTS (Soompi, "K-Pop Artists").
54. Otmazgin, "Tail that Wags the Dog?"
55. Glosserman and Snyder, *Japan–South Korea Identity Clash*, 7.

56. Glosserman and Snyder, *Japan–South Korea Identity Clash*, 4.

57. Said, *Orientalism*.

58. Littlewood, *Idea of Japan*.

59. For an elaboration of this point, see Dickinson, "Idea of Japan."

60. Kipling, *Departmental Ditties*, 3 (pagination restarts in the second half of this edition). Kipling's "Ballad of East and West" was originally entitled "Kamal," published in 1889, and collected in various anthologies (under its better-known title) thereafter. Although this line is widely used to signify racialized and Orientalist attitudes, the first stanza of the poem, taken as a whole, subverts this purpose (italics in original):

    Oh, East is East and West is West, and never the twain shall meet,
    Till Earth and Sky stand presently at God's great Judgment Seat;
    But there is neither East nor West, Border, nor Breed, nor Birth,
    When two strong men stand face to face, tho' they come from the ends of the earth!

    In any case, race has certainly figured in British accounts of Japan as in the American accounts on which Littlewood focuses. For a discussion of how this has affected Britain–Japan diplomatic relations, see, e.g., Búzás, "Color of Threat."

61. Wilkinson, *Japan versus the West*. One of Wilkinson's first major works focused on trade frictions between Japan and Europe and was entitled *Gokai*, or "Misunderstanding" (Wilkinson, *Gokai*).

62. Wilkinson, *Japan versus the West*, 100.

63. Alcock, *Capital of the Tycoon*, 357; quoted in Wilkinson, *Japan versus the West*, 101.

64. Chamberlain, *Things Japanese*, 480.

65. Wilkinson, *Japan versus the West*, 97–152.

66. Benedict, *Chrysanthemum and the Sword*, 1.

67. Glazer, "Ruth Benedict to Herman Kahn," 157 (emphasis in original). Glazer's essay is included in Akira Iriye's *Mutual Images*, itself a major contribution to the literature on Japanese and American views of one another.

68. Thorsten, *Superhuman Japan*.

69. Funabashi, "Japan and the New World Order," 65.

70. The militarist/pacifist or aggressive/submissive binary is at the heart of Benedict's analysis in *The Chrysanthemum and the Sword*; see also Berger, "Sword to Chrysanthemum"; Berger, *Cultures of Antimilitarism*; and Katzenstein and Okawara, *Japan's National Security*. For more recent echoes of the same antinomy, see Lind, "Pacifism or Passing the Buck"; Gustafsson, Hagström, and Hanssen, "Japan's Pacifism Is Dead"; and Gustafsson, Hagström, and Hanssen, "Long Live Pacifism!" For thoughtful and extensive treatments of the gender binary in US–Japan relations, see Johnson, *Japanese through American Eyes*, 73–92; Morris-Suzuki, *Re-Inventing Japan*, 110–39; and Shibusawa, *America's Geisha Ally*.

71. Glazer, "Ruth Benedict to Herman Kahn," 163. That Japan is dangerously unpredictable is also the central theme of Zbigniew Brzezinski's 1972 treatise, *The Fragile Blossom*.

72. Roh, *Techno-Orientalism*.

73. Benedict, *Chrysanthemum and the Sword*; Doi, *Amae no Kōzō*. In a similar vein, see Caudill and Scarr, "Japanese Value Orientations"; Lebra, *Japanese Patterns of Behavior*. For thoughtful critiques of the collectivist/individualist binary in its various guises as applied to Japan, see Befu, *Hegemony of Homogeneity*; Dale, *Myth of Japanese*

Uniqueness; Mouer and Sugimoto, *Images of Japanese Society*; Sugimoto and Mouer, "Reappraising Images"; and Yoshino, *Cultural Nationalism*. Wagenaar argues that techno-orientalism is giving way to an even newer conception of Japan as other that is simply bizarre and incomprehensible, in contrast to the normality of the West; see Wagenaar, "Wacky Japan." Yet this seems like new wine in old-bottle notions of Japan as alien and exotic.

74. Keizo Nagatani and David Edgington have highlighted the problem of a "perception gap" between the United States and Japan; see Nagatani and Edgington, *Japan and the West*. Also see Hammond, *Cultural Difference*. And, on Japan-bashing, see Abney, "Japan Bashing"; Morris, *Japan-Bashing*.

75. Reischauer, "Broken Dialogue."

76. On the history of Japan's trade relationship with the Philippines and the intermediary role of Portuguese Jesuits in the late sixteenth century, see Moran, *Japanese and the Jesuits*. Not long thereafter, Spain began to supplant the Portuguese in the Philippines, and Franciscans replaced the Portuguese Jesuits; see Thanh, "Role of the Franciscans." Many Japanese fleeing from Toyotomi Hideyoshi and Tokugawa Ieyasu's anti-Christian edicts escaped to the Philippines in the early seventeenth century, while in Japan both the Portuguese and the Spanish were replaced by a Dutch mission that showed less interest in proselytizing; see Boxer, *Christian Century*; Kataoka, "Takayama Ukon."

77. Piesse, "Japan and Australia."

78. Pew Research Center, "How Asia-Pacific Publics See Each Other." These numbers do not diverge greatly from those found in Pew's 2014 Global Attitudes Survey; see Pew Research Center, "How Asians View Each Other."

79. BBC, "2011 BBC Country Rating Poll." Interestingly, South Koreans also reported generally positive impressions of Japan's influence in this poll (68 percent versus 20 percent who saw Japan's influence as negative), but this finding was not repeated in the 2012 and 2013 BBC polls, which saw a return to more negative numbers for Japan in South Korea (67 percent versus only 21 percent with a positive impression); see BBC, "2012 BBC Country Rating Poll"; BBC, "2013 BBC Country Rating Poll." In the BBC's 2012 poll, Japan was the most highly regarded country in the world by respondents in the BBC's sample of 22 countries.

80. One recent study finds, in any case, that Japanese cultural exports have generally proven to be popular in postwar Australia; see Chapman and Hayes, *Japan in Australia*.

81. Constantino, *Southeast Asian Perceptions of Japan*.

82. Villacorta, "Japan's Asian Identity"; Yee and Storey, *China Threat*; Bisley, "Japan-Australia Security Declaration."

83. For a good discussion of the importance of both China and Japan in the Russian imagination, beginning in the late seventeenth century, see Lim, *China and Japan*. And, for a discussion of similarities in the challenges faced by Russia and Japan as they responded to Western imperialism, see Anno, *National Identity and Great-Power Status*.

84. Berton, "Enemies to Allies"; Saveliev and Pestushko, "Dangerous Rapprochement"; Baryshev, *Nichiro Dōmei no Jidai*; Mikhailova, "Representations of Japan."

85. Mikhailova, "Japan's Place." For an impressive two-volume overview of Russo-Japanese relations during the Cold War, see Kimura, *Japanese–Russian Relations under Brezhnev and Andropov*; Kimura, *Japanese–Russian Relations under Gorbachev and Yeltsin*.

86. Levada Center, "Rossiysko-Yaponskiye Otnosheniya." The 2011 BBC World Service poll of country attitudes found that 65 percent of Russians viewed Japan's influence

favorably and only 7 percent considered it to be negative; see BBC, "2011 BBC Country Rating Poll."

87. Mikhailova, "Representations of Japan"; Mikhailova and Torchinov, "Images at an Impasse." More generally, see Mikhailova and Steele, *Japan and Russia*.

88. See, inter alia, Goldstein-Gidoni, "Producers of 'Japan' in Israel"; Morikawa, "Japan and Africa"; Jain, "Japan–India Relations"; Worringer, *Ottomans Imagining Japan*.

89. See, e.g., Yokoyama, *Japan in the Victorian Mind*.

90. Gilbert and Sullivan, *Mikado*, Act. 1, No. 1.

91. For thoughtful discussions of this shift from early approbation to fear and disillusionment, see Lehmann, *Image of Japan*; Holmes and Ion, "Bushidō and the Samurai"; Saitō, *Omoiyari Jidai no Shūen*; Pham, "Edge of the Orient"; Towle, *Ally to Enemy*; Davidann, *Cultural Diplomacy*; Kowner, *Impact of the Russo-Japanese War*; Jacob and Linhart, *War and Stereotypes*; Best, *British Engagement with Japan*. For a discussion of the role race played in these growing fears, see Heere, *Empire Ascendant*; Henning, *Outposts of Civilization*; Yoshihara, *Embracing the East*; Morris-Suzuki, *Re-inventing Japan*.

92. On Japan's shift from "enemy" back to "ally" in the United States and Britain, see Ball, *Japan*; Chiba, "Enemy to Ally"; Mettler, *How to Reach Japan*. On the deterioration of Japan's image in the United States as its economic power rose, see Trezise, "Japan, the Enemy?" Finally, for an interesting comparison of late nineteenth and late twentieth century "Japonisme," see Lehmann, "Old and New Japonisme."

93. Johnson, *Japanese through American Eyes*, ix.

94. Glazer, "Ruth Benedict to Herman Kahn," 144.

95. Glazer, "Ruth Benedict to Herman Kahn," 141.

96. A 1991 Gallup poll found that 77 percent of Americans saw Japan as an "economic threat"; see Reinhart, "Eve of Summit."

97. Gallup, "Country Ratings." The Gallup data are partially corroborated by data from the Pew Global Attitudes Survey between 2006 and 2015. The Pew survey finds that unfavorable attitudes toward Japan in the United States hover between 10 and 20 percent in this period and that favorable attitudes gradually climb from around 65 percent to around 75 percent (slightly lower than in the Gallup poll, but still very high); see Pew Research Center, "How Asia-Pacific Publics See Each Other."

98. See, e.g., Christensen, "Chinese Realpolitik"; Deng, "Chinese Relations with Japan"; Gries, *China's New Nationalism*; Kristof, "Problem of Memory."

99. Rosen, "Public Opinion and Reform"; Mei and Brown, "Conducting Online Surveys in China."

100. Qiu, "Politics of History," 25–26.

101. Qiu, "Politics of History," 26.

102. Genron NPO, "Japan–China Public Opinion Survey 2021."

103. See Kobayashi, "'Chūgoku ni okeru Tainichi Kanjō' no Jittai to Akka Yōin ni Kan Suru Kenkyū."

104. Kobayashi's data includes some Pew Global Attitudes and Genron NPO data, as well as polls conducted by major Japanese newspapers (Asahi, Yomiuri), Chinese organizations (the Chinese Academy of Social Sciences, the Chinese National Studies Association), and universities (Jilin University, Fudan University), among others. See Kobayashi, "Chūgoku ni okeru 'Tainichi Kanjō' ni Kan Suru Kōsatsu," 89.

105. The inclusion of a third "neutral" category in many of the polls reported by Kobayashi may increase the apparently volatility of the "positive" and "negative" responses. In

some years (and some polls), a large number of respondents availed themselves of this neutral category, whereas it does not figure prominently in other polls. This is perhaps one reason why, prior to about 2009, the "favorable" and "unfavorable" lines shown in Figure 2.5 do not move together inversely as they do thereafter.

106. Kang and Bang, "Groundhog Day in Foreign Policy."
107. Kang and Bang, "What Goes Up, Must Come Down."
108. Tikhonov, *Modern Korea and Its Others*.
109. Friedhoff and Kang, "Rethinking Public Opinion," 2.
110. This sharp drop in Japan's approval rating within South Korea actually began in 2019; see Kim and Kang, "South Korean Attitudes."
111. Friedhoff and Kang, "Rethinking Public Opinion." Friedhoff and Kang rely on data from opinion polls produced by the Asan Institute for Policy Studies, a think tank based in Seoul that has also conducted the Asan Annual Survey of Korean opinion on a variety of topics (including relations with Japan and Japanese leaders) for more than a decade. The Asan survey uses a Likert scale to calculate a favorability rating. Although this rating cannot be integrated with the favorable/unfavorable percentages reported in Figure 2.6, the Likert scale approach has the advantage of greater sensitivity to variability in responses than binary response categories. This may be one reason why Friedhoff and Kang perceive greater variability in South Korean attitudes toward Japan than many other observers.
112. Dower and Lawrence, "Japan and the United States."
113. Dower and Lawrence, "Japan and the United States."
114. Yuge Toshihiro describes Japan as an *awase-kagami*—a lacquered double mirror used by geisha—reflecting visions of modern China and Taiwan; see Yuge, *Chūgoku Taiwan ni Okeru Nihonzō*. Similarly, Park Sang-Hyun (*Kankokujin wa Nihonjin o Dō Omotte Iru no ka*) discusses Japan as a mirror for Koreans, and Robert Rosenstone (*Mirror in the Shrine*) explores the way Meiji-era Japan served as a mirror for Americans.

CHAPTER 3

Image Matters

That we must study perceptions of things is either obvious or dangerous, or both. In an age of simulation and fake news, perception is itself an important reality. Especially in the social sciences, constructivists of many stripes investigate the social construction of perceived realities, while some other scholars recoil from this state of affairs as a dangerous affront to science. In our efforts to study subjective appraisals of the world, we may appear to suggest that one perceived reality is as good as another. Quite apart from the challenge this poses to scientific progress, it also creates moral problems. To criticize a behavior as unethical is to vouch for our ability to identify it when we see it. Ethics and science both depend on our having some acquaintance with reality. Of course, the same dilemma infects civic life as partisans challenge not just the political programs but also the facts asserted by their opponents. From antiquity to the present, the relationship of perceived truths to some other, greater reality has been a crucial problem. Broadly speaking it divides philosophers of science into two camps: those who offer some form of epistemology, or theory of knowledge, and skeptics who deny the possibility of knowledge about the real world external to ourselves.[1]

A book about the way we perceive a single country, Japan, can and should leave most of these broader philosophical concerns to others. It should be clear at the outset, however, that this book is not concerned with the question of how Japan *really* is. One could answer such a question only by defining one's terms so carefully that the answer is defined along with them. Otherwise we must acknowledge that Japan really is many different things, seen from different perspectives.

It is precisely the diversity of perspectives on Japan that makes the study of Japan's image so interesting. Japan is seen in a very positive light in many of the countries it once fought. And even in the two most obviously divergent cases—China and Korea, where it is seen much more negatively—it is also clear that perceptions of Japan fluctuate. These observations suggest interesting puzzles. Why is Japan disliked in these places? What causes perceptions of Japan to change? Even if these are interesting questions, of course, one might argue that they are of mostly academic interest. Those who believe that foreign policy is made on the basis of something more fundamental than the vagaries of perception—whether (or how) Japan chooses to rearm, whether it grants other countries more or less access to its markets, whether it offers or withholds diplomatic support, and so on—would expect material factors to matter more than Japan's international image. Indeed they would probably argue that image is effect rather than cause, that Japan's image can safely be treated as a dependent variable rather than an independent variable explaining diplomatic outcomes.

Constructivists in international relations, as in other fields, argue that our perceptions and understandings of the world *do* matter. Well before constructivism emerged as an important school of thought, however, several different groups of specialists in political science, international relations, and foreign policy analysis had already made similar arguments. One might even make the case that, far from being ignored, political perception has been studied in so many different ways, in various well-compartmentalized intellectual silos, that the result is a confusing jumble of partly related terms and poorly integrated theories.

One more discussion of the problem is unlikely to sort everything out. The more modest purpose of this chapter, however, is two-fold. First, it seeks to give some clarity to the wide variety of ways country perceptions have been studied. To this point, I have mostly used the term "image" to suggest a perception of the way a country is. There is considerable ambiguity in this definition. It might refer to various properties of a country, or its people, or its government. It might refer to the way countries behave in general or specifically to their interactions with other countries. That is to say, it may be a property of countries themselves, or it might be a phenomenon of international society. It is also likely that, however defined, countries have multiple identities: the way they see themselves, for example, presumably differs from the way they are seen by other countries. With distinctions such as these in mind, scholars variously speak of *national images, national identities, national roles, national brand,* and related terms such as *soft power* denoting qualities (like image or identity) that make a country attractive or influential.

After sorting through some of the terminological confusion that afflicts our study of the way countries are perceived, the second purpose of this chapter is to offer a brief defense of the claim that a country's image matters. This problem will be taken up once again at the end of this book. Indeed, one of the purposes of this book is to explain more fully how perceptions of countries are formed—specifically how perceptions of Japan are formed in China and South Korea—and how such perceptions matter in their interactions.

Those who do not require persuasion can, if they wish, turn ahead to the next chapter, which considers the first widely discussed explanation for Japan's image—that its own diplomacy is the principal determinant of how the country is seen. For those who are less familiar with the variety of ways country perceptions have been discussed among social scientists, on the other hand, this chapter serves the purpose of organizing that conversation. It will focus on the study of national imagery in the fields of international relations and foreign policy analysis, although the topic has received some attention in fields ranging from economics and sociology to history and cultural studies. It is fair to say that national image and national identity have become topics of considerable interest to international relations scholars in the past two decades.

THE PERCEPTION OF COUNTRIES

As a scholarly enterprise the field of international relations has many beginnings. It is arbitrary to single out one scholar as a starting point. Even if we set aside such early precursors as Thucydides and Machiavelli, we might for example look to Alfred E. Zimmern, a liberal internationalist who held the first endowed professorship of international politics, the Woodrow Wilson Chair at the University College of Wales, Aberystwyth, from 1919 to 1921.[2] Alternatively, E. H. Carr was the progenitor of realist thought who gave the nascent field its early definition.[3] And Hans Morgenthau was the first prominent, self-conscious advocate for the creation of international relations as a field of study. To the extent Morgenthau was an instrumental midwife to the birth of international relations as a distinctive field of inquiry, then it is also fair to say (borrowing Dean Acheson's pithy phrase) that the problem of national character was "present at the creation."[4] In *Politics among Nations,* Morgenthau not only articulates principles of realism that later served to homogenize accounts of the state but also, and in contrast to the way later realists employed these principles, draws sharp distinctions among kinds of states.[5] In particular he draws a distinction, evidently motivated by Cold War politics, between "status quo" and "revisionist" states. This is not terribly different from Stephen Walt's characterization of some states as more "threatening" than others.[6] For Walt the difference is to be found not only in capabilities but also in intentions, associating his argument with state motives in at least a minimal fashion.

Such arguments stand out against the grain. As economistic models became more prominent in the study of international relations, sustaining a neo-utilitarian synthesis and emphasizing the rational interaction of like units within the international system, states were generally treated as interchangeable in the same way that firms or consumers are interchangeable in microeconomic theory.[7] This was less true in the study of foreign policy, where differences among states attracted more attention, but it was overwhelmingly true of international relations theory in general until the emergence of constructivism. To the extent that other subdisciplines within international relations embraced rational microeconomic models, the same rule applied. In strategic studies, peace science, and international political economy, efforts to build formal models tended to obscure rather than to highlight differences among states. In this fashion the new scholarly discipline of international relations diverged from the way states had typically been discussed and described for more than a century.

National Character

In the nineteenth century, as emerging nation-states embraced a mostly fictive isomorphism of state and nation, discussions of national character flourished. European colonialism was expansive by this time, which worked to extend the logic of racial hierarchy to international relations. Thus nationality and race were often conflated, bound up together as part of the justifying ideology for new alignments of nation and state.[8] As Peter Jackson and Jan Penrose have argued, "notions about the social hierarchy of human 'races' served the interests of mercantile and industrial capitalism as it moved into its expansionist phase through the development of overseas empires."[9] While providing a justifying ideology for European control, they also purported to offer a new science of human classification that introduced the term "race" into the discourse of nationality.

This ideology provided the foundation for Leopold von Ranke, the pre-eminent historian of the state in the mid-nineteenth century, to declare that "every nation has been endowed by god with its own special character, and the course of history was marked by 'each nation's independent development of its own specific character in the manner ordained by god.'"[10] Even before Ranke wrote these words, Alexis de Tocqueville had traveled to the United States, returned to France, and published his monumental work *Democracy in America*, attributing the particular form and success of American democracy to the distinctive soil in which it was planted. In Rogers Smith's apt summary of Tocqueville's thesis, the "combination of comparatively equal and open economic and social conditions and an ideological legacy conducive to republicanism and personal liberties made America the perfect laboratory to study the tendencies of a society that from the start was decisively free, egalitarian, and democratic in theory and practice."[11] Ignoring for a moment that only a certain, small segment of American society enjoyed these conditions, Tocqueville's perception was that they created a distinctive national character. Later commentators such as Louis Hartz were more critical of American liberalism, but they also found inspiration in Tocqueville to advance the thesis of American distinctiveness.[12]

National character was far from a uniquely American preoccupation. The advent of European Romanticism in the late eighteenth century amplified existing tendencies toward national hagiography. National folklore found a wide audience with the examples of the Brothers Grimm and Hans Christian Anderson.[13] Heroic poems such as *Beowulf*, the *Song of Roland*, and the *Nibelungenlied* were refashioned and widely disseminated as national epics in this era.[14] As the Revolutions of 1848—the so-called Springtime of Nations—swept across Europe, reformers on all sides presented nationalist justifications for their actions, whether they pursued democracy (with varying degrees of success in Denmark, Austria, Prussia, and Hungary among others), monarchism (as in France under the Second Empire), or simply respite from the turmoil (as in mid-Victorian England). Karl Marx famously wrote of the upheaval in France that the tragedy of Napoleon I was repeated later as farce with his nephew, Louis Napoleon.[15] We might extend Marx's aphorism to observe that the tragic romanticization of national character was to give rise to new generations of nationalists who, having fought Napoleon on the continent, later marched confidently into the Great War.

Their most absurd expression came next. In his 1926 study of the *Racial Origins of English Character*, Robert Bradley provides a good example of the farcical extreme, proclaiming the English to be "a virile race. They are men first and foremost and have the dominance, the masculinity and the strength of the male. With the Mediterranean the female is apt to dominate and the tone of the race is feminine, whereas the essential maleness of the Asiatic is enhanced by the accident of Nordic supremacy."[16] The crudeness of Bradley's racial and sexual essentialism is not far removed—either in time or in sentiment—from the romantic nationalism that took root among German and Italian fascists.[17] It was only a short step to a program of national racial purity. Ranging somewhere between the zenith of Tocqueville and the nadir of Joseph Goebbels's propaganda were a vast collection of nineteenth- and early twentieth-century musings on the essential qualities of national groups.[18]

Whereas nineteenth-century abstractions wedded a science of racial hierarchy to romanticized (and, when necessary, invented) traditions of national culture, the twentieth century ushered in the preoccupations of a new collection of social sciences. Psychology and anthropology found common cause, giving rise to a Culture and Personality School of anthropology. Early on, Margaret Mead's *Coming of Age in Samoa* was notable for its "sustained consideration of the relation between personality and culture."[19] But it was Ruth Benedict's *Patterns of Culture,* published in 1934, that provided the greatest impetus for a new anthropological field of "national character studies." Mead herself wrote the preface to Benedict's book and described Benedict's "view of human culture as 'personality writ large.'"[20] In this approach, national character was formalized as the "modal personality structure" of people organized into national groups, within which personality is presumably shaped by common experiences.[21] Mead applied the approach to the United States in *And Keep Your Powder Dry!,* while Benedict turned her attention to Japan in *The Chrysanthemum and the Sword.*[22] Geoffrey Gorer's studies of American and Russian national character were other notable examples, and David Riesman's *The Lonely Crowd* built a bridge from national character studies to sociology.[23]

The epilogue (and perhaps the epitaph) for the Culture and Personality School was delivered in a study authored by Antonio Terracciano and no fewer than eighty-six coauthors, published in *Science.* Terracciano and his colleagues designed a National Character Survey to measure perceptions of national character and, employing the NEO-PI-R instrument as a standard measure of personality, sought to determine whether there is any general correspondence between the way countries are perceived and modal personality traits. Their conclusions are effectively summed up in the title of their paper: "National character does not reflect mean personality trait levels in 49 cultures."[24] At present national character studies are of interest more for what they say about their authors, perhaps, than for insights into their subject.

Although it is probably fair to say that most contemporary scholars regard the nation as an "imagined community," in Benedict Anderson's pithy phrasing, what is especially striking about national character studies is their rejection of this premise.[25] By aligning nation first with race and later with modal personality, national character studies sought a scientific and material foundation for generalizations about national difference. To this end the focus of national character studies has always been on the way genetics, experience, geography, or some other shared circumstance affects the individuals who comprise a nation. When the equally materialist discipline of international relations took form and insisted on treating states as like units, distinctions of national character were pushed aside. They later reemerged, but as a matter of perception—an imagined character to go with the imagined community of the nation, all in contrast to the ostensibly material characteristics of the state with its defined territory, its governmental hierarchy, and its ability to wield military power. The national character approach is fundamentally different, therefore, from those that followed and that are discussed in the following sections. Its object was always to understand the individual as part of a collective rather than the country as a whole or the qualities of the state.

Even as national character studies emphasized the distinctive qualities of persons, the conception of a national people also benefited from analogies to the state as an embodied entity. This may seem a curious development since people, not states, have bodies. Yet Thomas Hobbes had long since developed the metaphor of the body politic in *The Leviathan*, and Samuel Pufendorf had extended the logic to treat states themselves as "compound moral persons."[26] That the state could be considered to have the qualities of a person, with associated moral duties within international society, no doubt facilitated the conception of a national people with common qualities. We rightly draw a distinction between the two for analytical purposes, but we cannot be overly purist about the extent to which people will observe this distinction in practice. Asked what they think of Japan, as in the surveys discussed in the previous chapter, people may well think of Japanese people as they form their impression of the state—or vice versa. This book is concerned with Japan's image as a corporate entity—as a state person in Pufendorf's terms—but this image undoubtedly owes something to assumptions about national character that continue to percolate in the space between nation and state.

National Image

Like specialists in the new discipline of international relations, economists generally tended to focus on the material, measurable characteristics of markets (rather than states). Whereas scholars of international relations abstracted from the material world to develop theories of unitary states interacting in an anarchical system of self-help, economists likewise theorized firms and the consumers in an abstracted market. Although equilibrium in markets (like the balance of power among states) is an abstract notion, its referents ultimately are material things: people, as either consumers or producers. Economic materialism notwithstanding, however, it was an economist who proposed a new science of *images*. Taking issue with the notion that the material properties of the world dictate the behavior of either markets or nations, Kenneth Boulding proposed that "we act according to the way the world appears to us, not necessarily according to the way it 'is.'"[27] In his book on the topic, entitled *The Image*, Boulding explored the implications of this simple proposition for a variety of scholarly disciplines, including organizational behavior, biology, psychology, sociology, economics, politics, and history.[28] His objective was to show that the study of images of the world deserves a science of its own, which he proposed to label "eiconics."

In an article focusing on national images specifically, Boulding begins with childhood socialization and patriotic instruction. Such images consist of the stories that people tell about their nation: "essentially a mass image, or what might be called a 'folk image,' transmitted through the family and the intimate face-to-face group, both in the case of the powerful and in the case of ordinary persons."[29] We learn that members of our own national group have certain (presumably admirable) qualities that set them apart from others. Boulding argues that this sort of image "is basically a lie, or at least a perspective distortion of the truth."[30] Boulding then turns to the problem of relations among states and thereby comes to his central argument: that we distinguish among states by making judgments along several "dimensions." The first of these is "the territorial aspect of the nation state" or the "image of the map-shape of [the nation]."[31] This is important, Boulding contends, because sovereignty requires territorial exclusivity. Although he does not say so, this is more a permissive condition for state images than a quality that distinguishes some states from others. The other two dimensions of state image are (1) hostility or friendliness, and (2) strength or weakness. In his subsequent analysis, these are the two dimensions on which Boulding focuses in order to distinguish states from one another. The former includes not only the extent of enmity or cooperation between two states but also the stability of that relationship. And the latter includes comparisons across a variety of measures of national capability—not only resources but also organizational effectiveness, willingness to sacrifice, loyalty, and so on.[32] Both of these dimensions are treated as relational constructs, intelligible through comparisons between or among states.

It is clear by this point that, in laying out these dimensions of national image, Boulding has shifted focus. Without quite saying so, his discussion has progressed from the stories people tell about themselves and the image of the *nation* to stories people tell about the *state* as an agent that can be compared with other states. Although his argument is muddled by the initial discussion of national folk histories, the gist of this essay is that different images are ascribed to states according to judgments about their intentions and capabilities. Methodologically, Boulding's approach is purely observational, and the way people arrive at their judgments remains obscure. Boulding's concluding comments are telling:

> The national image . . . is the last great stronghold of unsophistication. Not even the professional international relations experts have come very far toward seeing the system as a whole, and the ordinary citizen and the powerful statesman alike have naive, self-centered, and unsophisticated images of the world in which their nation moves. Nations are divided into "good" and "bad"—the enemy is all bad, one's own nation is of spotless virtue.[33]

This applies as much to Boulding as to anyone else. His scheme does just what he describes, assigning states to either hostile or friendly camps, and then endowing them with only one further quality—the capability (or lack thereof) to carry out their intentions. This is not a bad starting point, inductively and intuitively. But at this early stage of development, the study of state images could hardly be described as sophisticated either empirically or theoretically. Swimming so much against the tide of his own discipline, in any case, Boulding's work on eiconics passed into obscurity without producing the hoped-for interdisciplinary convergence of research on "images."[34] Almost two decades passed before another scholar, Richard Cottam, took up the same problem and began to study the way we ascribe different images to countries based on our assessment of their motives.

Cottam's first career was as a CIA operative. He served in the US embassy in Teheran at the pivotal moment when the Eisenhower administration authorized Operation Ajax to overthrow Iranian Prime Minister

Mohammad Mosaddegh. Whereas the Truman administration saw Mosaddegh as a nationalist, Eisenhower's Secretary of State John Foster Dulles feared that he would gravitate toward the Soviet orbit.[35] US policy thus hinged on Dulles's assessment of Mosaddegh's motives and intent, and this object lesson inspired Cottam, who left the CIA several years later, to devote much of his subsequent academic career to studying the way leaders form impressions or images of other countries and infer their motives.

Motives are notoriously difficult to infer. Indeed it was Eisenhower himself who, according to his leading biographer, "made it a rule to never question another man's motives."[36] As a maxim of interpersonal relations, this may be a good rule, but we nevertheless often wish to understand others' motives. And it is impossible to craft foreign policy without either knowing or, at least, making assumptions about the motivations of countries. In his best-known book, *Foreign Policy Motivation*, Cottam acknowledges the problem of measurement frankly:

> John Herz and Hans Morgenthau both warn of the perils of attempting to analyze motivation. Other writers, by ignoring the matter, seem to agree. Yet Herz, Morgenthau, and the others as well operate from implicit and usually simplistic motivational assumptions. The naïve optimism of idealist writers has been ridiculed and generally rejected today. Yet the idealists recognized motivational complexity and a vast diversity of individual and collective interests. Simplicity entered with the belief that with minor effort these competing interests could be brought into harmony. The idealist simplism has been replaced by two competing simplisms: the realist and the revisionist. The former, in the logical reductionist theory of William Riker, becomes a mechanical power determinism. The latter tends to be closer to C. Wright Mills's *Power Elite* than to Marx and thus is less an inexorable process dictated by the mode of economic production than a conspiracy of self-interested establishmentarians.[37]

Simplicity is desirable in a theory, other things being equal, but Cottam's proposition is that other things are not equal. Against the perspectives he describes as simplistic, Cottam maintains that states have a more complex variety of motivations.

Motivation, as Cottam understands it, is "a compound of factors that predispose a government and people to move in a decisional direction in foreign affairs."[38] Implicitly, therefore, it answers important questions about foreign policy: Why did a state choose to do A and not B? To this question,

Cottam adds another layer of interpretation. Whatever a state's actual motivations, if these can even be known, we might also choose to study the way motivations are imputed to states. These imputed motives constitute an *image* of the state, thus reprising Boulding's terminology with approximately the same meaning. Far more than Boulding, however, Cottam formalizes his argument by proposing a general theory of state images. For Cottam state images depend on judgments about several things, including motivation, capabilities, decisional style, decisional locus, and "domestic forces interaction." *Motivation* is perhaps the most basic judgment (and a confusing choice of terminology, since it is just one element of Cottam's general effort to explain state motivation). As one component of this theory, however, motivation refers to the positive or negative orientation of another state vis-à-vis one's own state. That is, does another state pose a threat of loss, or does it present opportunities for gain? *Capability* refers to that state's ability to bring about these conditions (of either loss or gain). Taken together, these two judgments account for much of the variation in state images and, one cannot help but notice, are essentially the same as Boulding's two dimensions of hostility–friendliness and strength–weakness.

The remaining three judgments describe aspects of the internal culture of the target state. *Decisional style* ranges from a formal and rational process to a less organized, "*ad hoc* incremental style."[39] *Decisional locus* distinguishes states with a "monolithic, hierarchical decisional structure" from those with a "highly differentiated, diverse decisional structure."[40] Finally, *domestic forces interaction* distinguishes states that are intolerant of dissent from those that are more accepting or ideologically pluralist. Each of these judgments represents a dimension on which another state could be judged as culturally similar to or different from one's own state. In more recent scholarship based on Cottam's scheme, these are collapsed into a single dimension conventionally labelled *cultural difference*.[41]

Cottam and those who have followed in this tradition of foreign policy image theory derive from these core judgments several ideal-type national images, including the *enemy* (a threat that is similar in capabilities and culture to one's own state), the *ally* (an opportunity with similar capabilities and culture), the *imperial* power (a threat, particularly an economic threat, from a state with advanced capabilities and culture), and the *colony* (an opportunity with inferior capabilities and culture).[42] Richard Herrmann and Michael Fischerkeller point out that many combinations of threat orientation, capabilities, and culture are possible, but that not every combination of ideal types makes sense.[43] A country with weak capabilities and a similar culture, for example, is unlikely to be seen as threatening. It is in this sense that Cottam's approach takes Fritz Heider's balance theory as inspiration, arguing for a certain logical coherence within state images.[44] Indeed, strategic and "cultural" capabilities usually seem to go hand-in-hand, effectively collapsing Cottam's three-dimensional typology to two dimensions for most purposes.[45]

Scholars working in this tradition thus anticipate the existence of a limited number of state images in practice. Of these, undoubtedly the best studied is the enemy image.[46] More recently, the *rogue* state received considerable attention.[47] As this research tradition has moved to apply Cottam's insights, however, it has increasingly drifted away from any serious attempt to identify the full range of conceivable (or policy-relevant) images.[48] Instead, foreign policy image theory has gradually become a nomothetic enterprise, devoted to underscoring the relevance of certain specific state images and their impact on foreign policies.[49] This is an important goal, and perhaps it reflects the increasingly widespread acceptance of a basic proposition about state images: that they are shaped principally by threat orientation and capabilities (and arguably, though perhaps to a lesser extent, by an additional dimension of cultural difference). We should not forget, moreover, that the purpose of identifying such images was to infer the motives that drive foreign policies. Although images appear as cognitive categories in much of the literature, they are wedded to implicit expectations about emotions or "drive states" that animate policy choices.

National Role

Even before Cottam made his effort to study state images more systematically, another foreign policy specialist had taken inspiration from sociology and set out to catalog types of states according to the international roles they play. This approach distinguished states not according to our image of what they are like—for instance big or small, powerful or weak—but rather according to what they do. Borrowing a page from George Herbert Mead's studies of social life as dialogue and his insistence that the self is a social phenomenon, Kal Holsti saw states as having different kinds of "selves" according to their roles in the international system.[50] States play out these roles, Holsti argued, in ways that are defined both by their own conception of "national self" and also by other states' conceptions of how they should behave.[51] Both *ego* and *alter*, to adopt Mead's terminology, thus participate subjectively and interactively in role definition. In foreign policy, for example, Holsti understands *bloc leader* as a role defined jointly by the behavior of the state adopting this role (e.g., issuing directives, endeavoring to oppose the authority of another bloc, etc.) and of other states, either *bloc members* (who acknowledge this leadership) or *bloc opponents* (who resist it).

Beginning with a survey of the foreign policy literature, Holsti set out to map the variety of "national role conceptions" as completely as possible. Initially, he identified nine national roles—revolutionary leader-imperialist, bloc leader, balancer, bloc member (ally), mediator, nonaligned, buffer, isolate, and protectee—listed here in order from most to least "active."[52] The activity of states can have either a threatening, a neutral, or a supportive purpose, and it might be sustained by either greater or lesser capabilities. In this way, therefore, Boulding's two dimensions of hostility–friendliness and strength–weakness are also present in Holsti's typology. Although Holsti doesn't invoke Boulding specifically, he does refer to other works that have made similar distinctions among national roles. Frederick Schuman distinguished, for example, between "satiated" and "unsatiated" states, William T. R. Fox between states seeking "security" and those seeking "domination," and Hans Morgenthau between "status-quo" and "revolutionary" states.[53] A. F. K. Organski adds the dimension of capabilities, yielding a fourfold typology of states that are satisfied and strong, dissatisfied and strong, satisfied but weak, and dissatisfied and weak.[54]

To move beyond roles such as "bloc leader," "balancer," or "neutral" that were already well established in the Cold War foreign policy literature, Holsti next sought to expand his account of possible state roles by assembling a database of general foreign policy statements made by the leaders of different countries.[55] Holsti reviewed each statement and identified seventeen distinct national role conceptions, which, as he points out, "is almost double that derived from past and contemporary treatises on international politics."[56] These roles are listed in Table 3.1, along with states that Holsti felt exemplified each role. A key finding, however, is that national leaders may articulate a commitment to more than one national role in their foreign policy rhetoric. In fact, in Holsti's sample, there were an average of 4.6 role conceptions per nation.[57] Chinese leaders saw the People's Republic of China as a "bastion of the revolution," for example, but also as a "liberator/supporter" of oppressed peoples. He even finds that states may sometimes embrace incompatible roles, as for example in French or Japanese professions to be both an "active independent" and a "faithful ally."[58] It is possible that such situations reflect an internal conflict over the appropriate national role, or that there are advantages to external dissembling. It is also possible that they reflect conceptual or methodological difficulties in measuring national roles.

Table 3.1: Holsti's National Role Conceptions[1]

National Roles	Examples (circa late 1960s)
Bastion of the revolution	Cuba
Regional leader	Egypt
Regional protector	United States, Soviet Union
Active independent	France, India
Liberator/supporter	China
Anti-imperialist agent	Syria
Defender of the faith	North Vietnam
Mediator/integrator	Sweden
Regional collaborator	Japan
Developer	Canada
Bridge	Pakistan
Faithful ally	Great Britain
Independent	Nepal
Example	Philippines
Internal development	Brazil
Isolate	Cambodia
Protectee	Czechoslovakia

[1]Holsti, Kal J. "National Role Conceptions in the Study of Foreign Policy." *International Studies Quarterly* 14 (1970): 233–309.

By relying on the statements of prominent national leaders, Holsti has limited expressions of national role to those of a very specific (powerful, well-educated, typically male, etc.) subset of the general population. He also relies on data from a limited span of time. And he spells out no way of distinguishing among beliefs about existing national roles, aspirations, and fears. Given that states in his sample typically adopt several national roles, it seems likely that *role* as an operational matter in his study is not quite equivalent to *role* as he originally defined it in behavioral terms. Instead, leaders would appear to engage simultaneously in declarations about ongoing and aspirational roles that change, moreover, depending on context. Such short-comings notwithstanding, Holsti's study was pathbreaking. He provided the first major empirical and inductive approximation of the sorts of roles states adopt and thus began to introduce Mead's sociology of roles to the field of foreign policy analysis.

A second wave of role theory scholarship took root about a decade after Holsti's initial study, formalizing the idea of national roles and applying the concept to numerous cases.[59] Then about a decade after that, a third wave of interest in the concept began with a trickle that has turned into a flood of new research.[60] Whereas Holsti's initial study was essentially descriptive, second- and third-wave scholars have done a great deal to formalize theories of role taking.[61] They have studied the conditions for national role adoption and role change.[62] They have explored the interaction of domestic politics and international roles.[63] And they have developed much more sophisticated methods for inferring national role conceptions from the statements of national leaders and for studying their effects.[64]

Surprisingly, one thing practitioners of role theory generally have *not* done is integrate their insights into national roles with scholarship on national image and foreign policy motivation.[65] Perhaps one reason for this separation of the two camps of scholars is that image theory grew out of efforts to infer state motives, whereas role theory typifies behavior as arising from social "scripts" appropriate to the performance of a given role. Role theorists also tend to stress the interactive, Meadian foundations of role definition, while social interaction is not central to Cottam's argument. Still, saying that another state seeks to play a dominant or hegemonic international role is not too different from ascribing to it Cottam's imperial image. And foreign policy image theorists have developed an interest in the ways images are defined through interactive processes, such as the spiral deterioration of relations that leads to the formation of enemy images.[66] So, although it is true that *image* tends to emphasize qualities ascribed to another state while *role* tends to emphasize a social interaction that requires role conceptions to be "accepted" rather than "ascribed," in practice there is overlap between the two concepts. Much the same is true of another related concept that has attracted considerable attention: national identity.

National Identity

The argument that some combination of foreign policy image theory and role theory, taken together, have established compelling typologies of state imagery would be more plausible were it not for the dramatic emergence of constructivist scholarship focusing on the *identity* of states after the end of the Cold War. As with the terms "national image" and "national role," "national identity" is frequently employed as a term of art within the field of international relations referring to qualities of the state rather than national peoples, or to a conception of the country as a whole that draws somewhat ambiguously on qualities of both the state and its people. Rodney Bruce Hall refers to "national collective identity," for example, as the prevailing identity "template" within the international system.[67] Ironically, a Westphalian past in which the needs of the state could be distinguished readily from those of national peoples legitimated an international order that increasingly effaces this distinction. Hall explains:

> As the state is privileged at the level of the "system," communities of shared identity construct states to serve their needs as "nations" in the course of systemic interaction. This was so in the past because the Westphalian system, organized under the legitimating principle of *raison d'état*, privileged the sovereign with rights and legitimacy. This is so in the newer era of national sovereignty, organized under the legitimating principle of national self-determination, because the state is still the privileged institutional form, with the provision that it must at least claim to serve as an institutional form of the collective action of a "national" collective identity.[68]

Alexander Wendt discusses "collective identity formation" and the "corporate identity" of the state in a similar fashion.[69] For the sake of clarity, the following discussion will employ the term "state identity" rather than "national identity" to refer to the qualities of the state as an agent within the international system, since the latter term may also refer to the degree of a state's internal cohesion and the extent of binding sentiments among people that allows them to constitute themselves as a nation.[70] In practice, however, many constructivists writing about international relations use the term "national identity" to refer to images of the state, and some use the two terms interchangeably.

Perhaps a theory of state identity is somehow different from a theory of images or roles. The body of constructivist identity scholarship is sufficiently large and diverse, however, that one would be hard pressed to defend any systematic distinction among the terms. Holsti's view that role entails behavioral prescriptions, for example, calls to mind Ron Jepperson, Alexander Wendt, and Peter Katzenstein's characterization of the relationship between *norms* and *identity*: "norms either define ('constitute') identities in the first place (generating expectations about the proper portfolio of identities for a given context) or prescribe or proscribe ('regulate') behaviors for already constituted identities (generating expectations about how those identities will shape behavior in varying circumstances)."[71] Some constructivists distinguish, therefore, between constitutive and regulative accounts of identity, though it might be better to say that identity serves both constitutive and regulative purposes.[72] Wendt's widely discussed *Social Theory of International Politics*, his most extensive treatment of state identity, says more about the constitution of identities than their regulative effects. Yet Wendt also specifically draws on role theory and Mead's "rich framework for thinking about how identities and interests are learned in social interaction," further emphasizing the social character of identity.[73]

Elsewhere Wendt has defined social identities as "sets of meanings that an actor attributes to itself while taking the perspective of others, that is, as a social object."[74] This is what foreign policy image theorists would call an *image*, although Wendt's focus here is on *self*, whereas Cottam was more concerned with accounts of *other*.[75] Constructivists have also tended to emphasize the malleability of identity, unlike image theorists who developed formal typologies of states organized by judgments about orientation, capabilities, and cultural difference. Wendt is something of an exception in this regard, having popularized the distinction among states as enemies, rivals, or partners depending on the culture of anarchy at play in their relations with other states.[76] Yet Wendt himself sees this typology more as an illustration of the possibilities than as a systematic effort, even a preliminary one, to build a constructivist theory of identity.[77] And while constructivists have been attentive to cultural difference as a source of state identity, they do not generally have in mind a formulaic set of cultural judgments about decision making and institutional structure such as those on which Cottam relies.[78] Nor, with the notable exception of Ned Lebow's effort to situate anxieties about identity within the broader context of modernity, have constructivists said much about the cultural milieu in which state identity matters.[79]

Rather than building typologies, constructivists have mostly been intent on exploring nuanced accounts of specific state identities and on showing how identity matters.[80] Ted Hopf digs deep into popular literature and other Russian-language texts, for example, to build a rich account of Soviet identity and of its transformation into a new Russian identity.[81] These Soviet and, later, Russian identities draw heavily on comparisons with other countries (notably the United States) in the fashion that image theorists would expect, and they certainly have something to do with Soviet or Russian (self-)conceptions about national capabilities. But they were also built out of competing visions of modernity and pride.[82] Hopf shows, for example, that Russian identity is crucial for understanding the persistent importance of nuclear armament for the Russian state. Pride also plays a role in Erik Ringmar's illuminating account of Swedish identity as it was transformed during and by the Thirty Years' War.[83] Perhaps even more than territory, Ringmar finds, Sweden sought recognition and major power status through the war. By focusing on what Sweden sought to become rather than on how it was seen by other European states of the era, Ringmar captures a dynamic aspect of identity that is generally ignored by typological theories. Finally, to take just one more example from among many, Iver Neumann adds a multilevel aspect to his account of state identity by showing how European identity is made possible through juxtaposition with the East at the pan-European, regional, and national levels.[84] It is through encounters with a multifaceted Eastern other, he argues, that Europeans come to know themselves and to define a hierarchy that places the West advantageously.

Hopf, Ringmar, and Neumann's studies of identity in international relations are bold in their exposition, rich in nuance, and powerful as defenses of the claim that state identity matters to the conduct of foreign policy. Yet none of these authors attempt a general theory (or even typology) of state identity, and it is quite possible that none of them would see the effort as likely to bear much fruit. Indeed, Hopf makes this sentiment fairly explicit, criticizing "those accounts of identity that assume too much about the social world, making too many a priori foundational claims that both hinder the social context from speaking for itself and often put words in its mouth," and arguing instead for work that is "thickly inductive."[85] Each of these scholars seeks to understand identity in a provisional, local, and historical context. One comes away from their work feeling that one understands better the way Russians, Swedes, or Europeans in general have seen themselves at certain points.

Constructivist scholarship on state identity is a vast and still-growing enterprise.[86] Indeed, Ned Lebow has characterized identity as a "master variable" for constructivists.[87] He regards this conception as problematic, moreover, precisely because identity is so malleable, so likely to bend to the will of various political projects, and so subjective that it is shifting sand on which to build a "theoretical house" of any weight. Talk of identity as a variable notwithstanding, the examples of constructivist identity scholarship discussed previously typify a tendency toward historical particularism that, while not entirely atheoretical, is far more intent on historicizing and contextualizing theoretical claims than on generalizing across cases of identity politics in international relations.[88] The result has been an accretion of studies demonstrating that identity matters in foreign policy but offering scant general guidance as to when or why. For the most part, moreover, constructivist scholars have probably been less attentive to the social aspects of identity definition than have role theorists. Ironically, given their nominally social (rather than individualist) ontology, constructivists have tended to treat identity as a claim about the properties of specific states. They may see states as "modern," "democratic," "hegemonic," "Islamic," "Western," or many other things, and they often pay careful attention to the way these claims are politically contested. Yet with the notable exception of a burgeoning literature on ontological security that does take emotions like anxiety and shame seriously, constructivists mostly tend to treat identity as cognitive content rather than emotion or motivation (as image theorists might) and as a property that is asserted rather than negotiated (as role theorists might).[89]

National Brand

This discussion of foreign policy images began with the philosophically minded work of an economist, Kenneth Boulding, musing about the importance of perception. Perhaps because Boulding was an economist, his work on images is less often appreciated by international relations specialists than is Richard Cottam's foreign policy image theory. This disciplinary myopia is also evident in scholarship on national brand. In much the same way that firms must concern themselves with the value of their brand, economists might argue that positive perceptions of a country also have market value. This value may be monetized and measured as the contribution (positive or negative) to GDP of a country's international image or brand, and it may also have other, even harder-to-measure but nevertheless important components such as diplomatic leverage.

The burgeoning literature on national brand falls mostly within the purview of business, communications, and economics journals, only rarely intruding into the awareness of political scientists.[90] When it does come to the attention of political scientists and international relations specialists, moreover, it often invites skeptical reactions. In fact Wally Olins suggests a much stronger adjective, marveling at the "violent reactions that the concept of branding the nation provokes. There is clearly something about it that sets some people's teeth on edge."[91] Indeed, he continues, "commentators from every part of the political and social spectrum have at different times in very different publications expressed their loathing and contempt for the idea as repellent and superficial."[92] Olins cites French political scientist Michel Girard as an example: "In France the idea of re-branding the country would

be widely unacceptable because the popular feeling is that France is something that has a nature and a substance. . . . A country carries specific dignity
unlike a marketed product. . . . In France it is unimaginable for Chirac to
attempt to re-brand France."[93]

Presumably constructivists are less likely to go along with Girard's sense
that countries have an unalterable nature. In any case the empirical evidence
favors Olins. Countries have long engaged in marketing campaigns. After
the famed 1851 Crystal Palace Exhibition in Hyde Park, London, countries
began to attach great importance to international expositions and world's
fairs as a means of promoting images of national power, prowess, and desir-
ability.[94] Global sporting events, and the Olympic Games above all, serve
this purpose as well.[95] The 2008 Beijing Summer Olympics stands out as
an especially impressive spectacle of national branding.[96] Three years later,
in the run-up to the London Games, the UK launched a massive advertising campaign with the intention of "putting the GREAT back into Britain."[97]
One study credited the campaign with adding £500 million to the British
economy.[98] Negative or failing brands are also possible, and Simon Anholt
goes so far as to argue that the entire continent of Africa suffers from an
image of "poverty, corruption, war, famine and disease" that constitutes a
negative "continent brand effect."[99]

That countries sometimes engage in national branding exercises is hard
to gainsay. One of the foremost scholars of national branding, Anholt argues
that "the rapid advance of globalization means that every country, every city
and every region must compete with every other for its share of the world's
consumers, tourists, investors, students, entrepreneurs, international sporting and cultural events, and for the attention and respect of the international
media, of other governments, and the people of other countries."[100] Yet one
might remain skeptical about whether the term "brand" adds anything to
our understanding of this necessity that is not conveyed by "image," "role,"
"identity," or more anodyne notions such as reputation or standing. In fact,
Anholt himself has gravitated toward the term "competitive identity" and
also discusses national image at length.[101] He observes that branding, ironically, has a "bad brand" because "there's a lot of mistrust about brands and
branding these days."[102] Like Olins, he is aware that the notion of "selling"
a country provokes strong reactions. Describing national image as a brand
implies commodification and an extension of the market into domains that
some might wish to protect from economic imperatives. The rejoinder, of
course, is that there is always a market when people are prepared to act as
though there is one.

Much of the research on national brand, like that on national image, begins with the question of whether a country is seen positively or negatively. Yet there is also one respect in which *brand* is more like *role*: both are clearly interactive notions. To put this somewhat differently, self-image or personal identity are perfectly intelligible notions, but self-branding is not. Countries can send messages about their brand, of course, but these messages do not function as branding unless they are received. Unsurprisingly, there is a considerable literature applying the sociological insights of symbolic interactionism to brand marketing.[103] National brand is a notion that only works in the context of international society wherein states can perceive another state's branding efforts.

The notion of brand is not only social, moreover, but also emotional. Unlike most conceptions of national identity, for example, brand implies attitudes that either attract or repel. In a thoughtful study of branding in political communication, Michael Serazio cites Tony Schwarz, the creator of Lyndon Johnson's famous "Daisy" advertisement:

> The best political commercials are similar to Rorschach patterns. They do not tell the viewer anything. They surface his feelings and provide a context for him to express those feelings. Commercials that attempt to tell the listener something are inherently not as effective as those that attach to something that is already in him.[104]

Serazio conducted in-depth interviews with thirty-eight professional campaign consultants to explore the role of emotion in political branding. As one of these consultants explained, "emotion leads to action and thinking leads to more thought. . . . If you can find an emotional wrapper to put around your issue, then you're just going to get further."[105] The emotional purpose of national branding undoubtedly diverges in some ways from that of candidate branding. One important difference, for example, is that nations have internal as well as external constituencies. Christopher Browning thus argues that national self-esteem is a crucial element of nation branding. The state must not only situate itself among others as a "competition state" but also respond to its own citizens' "desire for ontological security and self-esteem."[106] Nation branding campaigns are not only a response to these internal needs but are themselves made possible by the emotional support generated within. As Browning puts it, "the success of nation-branding campaigns may ultimately depend on whether citizens endorse them."[107] Brand thus stands out as a distinctively emotional as well as cognitive and intersubjective phenomenon.

HOW IMAGE MATTERS

The four overlapping notions of image, role, identity, and brand form a constellation of state-perception variables. They have enough in common that one might wish for a general term to subsume them all, yet none of them clearly has the upper hand. And although the differences among them are important, these differences are not crucial to the argument developed in the following chapters. Indeed, with some minor rhetorical adjustments, one might investigate the way Japan is seen by others as a matter of its state identity, its international role, its national brand, or its global image. The nuances of these terms are different, as described in the preceding sections, but they all refer to country perceptions.

For several reasons, I will mostly use the term "image" in this book to discuss the way countries are perceived. First, "image" is probably the most generic of the four terms. "Identity" can invite confusion about whether one has in mind the problem of a country's internal cohesion or its qualities as an agent, as seen from the outside. "Role" carries with it the specific baggage of sociological role theory and a focus on a country's behavior that narrows the concept beyond the general question of how a country is perceived. And "brand," likewise, more narrowly connotes market valuation. At the same time, in the study of foreign policy, "image" has its own association with theories of affect and motivation. Because I intend to inquire into the emotional foundations of how countries perceive Japan, this also makes the term "image" particularly suitable.

Figure 3.1 depicts some of the differences of nuance in the way identity, role, brand, and image are discussed, particularly among political scientists and other experts in international relations and foreign policy. Role and brand typically refer more to the social functions of country perceptions, whereas identity and image are often used to refer to the properties of countries as agents (even though these properties may well be defined through some social process). And although identity and role both seem to convey primarily cognitive content (i.e., the way a country is), image and brand more often tend to evoke feeling as well (i.e., the way we feel about a country). Of course, feelings about a country involve cognitive content, and for that matter society is comprised of individuals. The four quadrants of Figure 3.1 are not so much clear categorical distinctions, therefore, as overlapping general tendencies.[108]

That scholars have paid so much attention to these country perception variables suggests that they are widely seen as important determinants of state behavior. Decades of research by political psychologists in the field of

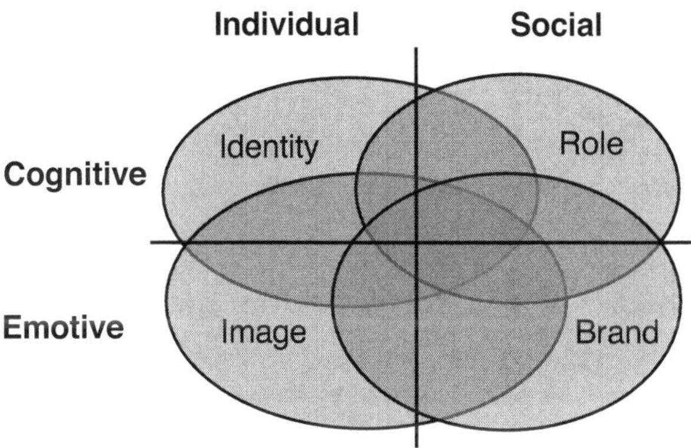

Figure 3.1. Research on the Perception of States

foreign policy analysis have served to establish the importance of perceptual variables, including country perceptions. In the field of international relations, the emergence of constructivist scholarship has accomplished much the same thing. Perhaps the most prominent discussion of the way a country's image affects its ability to get things done has been Joseph Nye's argument that countries rely on "soft" as well as "hard" power.

Soft Power

Prompted by growing concern among Americans about their country's loss of international influence in the 1980s, Nye set out to explain "the changing nature of American power" in his 1990 book, *Bound to Lead*.[109] He wrote at a time when theories of imperial overreach abounded, when "half the American public believed that the nation was in decline," and when "only one in five Americans believed that the United States was the top economic power, even though it remained by far the world's largest economy."[110] Nye argued that such declinism overstated the problem because, as the world was changing, the nature of power was changing along with it. Whereas Spain's power had once depended on its command of precious metal reserves and Britain's had depended on its navy, Nye saw power in the late twentieth century as having evolved to depend less on such material considerations. Instead, he argued, "the ability to establish preferences tends to be associated with intangible power resources such as culture, ideology, and institutions. This dimension can be thought of as *soft power*, in contrast to the *hard* command power usually associated with tangible resources like military and economic strength."[111]

Simply put, soft power is the ability to achieve objectives—Nye says, "to establish preferences"—derived from the ability to attract rather than the ability to coerce. It is not a synonym for "influence" since influence can be derived from coercion as well as attraction. Nor is it simply influence that depends on the carrot rather than the stick. Benefits, once offered, can also be withdrawn. So, offering something of benefit as a tool of persuasion also carries with it an implicit threat and is therefore more akin to hard power. Instead, soft power refers to a state's ability to attract cooperation and support not because of what it might do or refrain from doing, but instead because it is seen as an attractive model. Nye puts it this way:

> One way to think about the difference between hard and soft power is to consider the variety of ways you can obtain the outcomes you want. You can command me to change my preferences and do what you want by threatening me with force or economic sanctions. You can induce me to do what you want by using your economic power to pay me. You can restrict my preferences by setting the agenda in such a way that my more extravagant wishes seem too unrealistic to pursue. Or you can appeal to my sense of attraction, love, or duty in our relationship and appeal to our shared values about the justness of contributing to those shared values and purposes. If I am persuaded to go along with your purposes without any explicit threat or exchange taking place—in short, if my behavior is determined by an observable but intangible attraction—soft power is at work.[112]

A country's soft power, then, rests on its attractiveness. Attributes of a country—its culture, its institutional character, its ability to produce inspirational figures—that are judged as desirable lead others to emulate those qualities. A country's image, in other words, is the key to its soft power. A positive image can confer important soft power resources, and it is also worth keeping in mind that a negative image deprives a country of these same resources.

Nye's argument found an eager audience not only in the United States but also, at the dawn of the twentieth century, in China. China was attentive to the positive and negative aspects of soft power. It sought, on one hand, to maximize its growing influence at a time when the United States was still dominant by trading on the appeal of its influential cultural legacy and its economic dynamism. At the same time it hoped to minimize or deflect fears in the West about its growing economic and military power by projecting a narrative of "peaceful rise." In December 2003, commemorating the

110th anniversary of Mao Zedong's birthday, Chinese General Secretary Hu Jintao proclaimed that China would "insist on following the development path of a peaceful rise," a concept that was forcefully advocated by Chinese intellectuals such as Zheng Bijian.[113] More recently, as Xi Jinping has put his own stamp on China's foreign policy and moved more aggressively in some areas, such as the South China Sea, scholars have begun to ask whether the rhetoric of "peaceful rise" remains apt.[114]

The danger, for China, goes beyond losing the potential advantages of attractive soft power. A negative image not only deprives a country of soft power, after all, but can even produce an opposite effect: a generalized antipathy that leads others instinctively to work against a country's desires. After the triumphal moment of the end of the Cold War, American leaders have grown all too familiar with this problem. Anti-Americanism now attracts the attention of scholars and observers on both the left and right.[115] For the former it is often interpreted as a response to acts of American foreign policy that may also be condemned by domestic critics within the United States. From this perspective one might expect anti-Americanism to have increased as a result of protracted US interventions abroad and human rights abuses such as those infamously associated with the Abu Ghraib prison during the US occupation of Iraq. For the latter, on the other hand, anti-Americanism is more typically associated with a rejection of the American "way of life."[116] In either case, to the extent that anti-American attitudes harden, they may cause individuals or states to work actively against US interests out of a sense of revulsion that might be thought of as "negative soft power" or perhaps "soft weakness."

Interestingly, one of the few specific discussions of negative soft power in the scholarly literature focuses specifically on China's demonization of Japan. In a fanciful episode of name-calling in 2014, China's ambassador to Britain, Liu Xiaoming, compared Japan with the villain in J. K. Rowling's Harry Potter novels, Lord Voldemort, making an effort to improve Sino-British ties at Japan's expense.[117] William Callahan interprets this act as part of a "negative soft power" strategy, seeking to paint another state in an unflattering light while simultaneously attempting to enhance the soft power of one's own state.[118] Japan's own ambassador to Britain was forced into the comical position of declaring China to be Asia's true Voldemort.[119]

It should come as no surprise that Japan was quick to respond since Japan has also made soft power a centerpiece of its diplomacy in the past two decades. In a 2002 essay, Douglas McGray proclaimed that Japan's "Gross National Cool" was on the rise, even as its economic power waned. "Instead of collapsing beneath its political and economic misfortunes," McGray says,

"Japan's global cultural influence has only grown. In fact, from pop music to consumer electronics, architecture to fashion, and food to art, Japan has far greater cultural influence now than it did in the 1980s, when it was an economic superpower."[120] Although McGray interprets this as a largely uncoordinated outgrowth of trends in Japanese popular culture, Japan's government officials have clearly taken notice. In 2004, *Gaiko Forum* (the Japanese equivalent of *Foreign Affairs*, sponsored by the Ministry of Foreign Affairs) published a special issue on soft power featuring an essay by Joseph Nye introducing the topic.[121] Japan's minister of foreign affairs at the time, Asō Tarō, proclaimed that diplomacy in the modern world required "having a competitive brand image" and that it would be "necessary for us to draw on assistance from a broad spectrum of people who are involved in Japanese culture."[122] In 2005, NHK also began to air a weekly television program entitled "Cool Japan" that featured foreign (non-Japanese) guests reacting to various aspects of Japanese culture, technology, and everyday life.[123] And in 2010, the Ministry of Economy, Trade and Industry (METI) adopted "Cool Japan" (*kūru japan*) as a theme of its industrial strategy, and its Manufacturing Industries Bureau (*seizō sangyō kyoku*) created a Cool Japan Office.[124] "Cool Japan" is now well established as a self-conscious national branding strategy resembling the Blair administration's "Cool Britannia" campaign.[125]

Unsurprisingly, a number of scholars, both inside and outside Japan, have taken up the theme of soft power and its importance for Japanese diplomacy.[126] Many are fairly sanguine about Japan's ability to extend its influence through instruments of soft power.[127] Watanabe Yasushi and David McConnell proclaim Japan, along with the United States, to be a "soft power superpower."[128] Soeya Yoshihide speculates that cultural diplomacy may even enable Japan to erase its "militaristic" image in some quarters.[129] And Utpal Vyas provides some support for this claim by tracing the way both state and non-state actors have sought to translate cultural capital into Japanese influence in China.[130] On the other hand, Konno Shigemitsu worries that Japan has embraced the "soft" without actually gaining much power as a result.[131] In an excellent overview of Japan's soft power strategizing, David Leheny offers one explanation for this outcome. Leheny points out that Japan's efforts to deploy popular culture as an instrument of soft power may be limited insofar as its targets within other Asian countries see in Japan's success an illustration of their own future trajectories rather than as a distinctively Japanese model to be emulated.[132] Meanwhile, outside Asia, it is possible that proclaiming Japan's cultural uniqueness as a diplomatic tool will reinforce Orientalist conceptions of Japan's exoticism.[133] And Mihara

Ryūtarō even worries that Japan's cultural success is provoking a backlash that ultimately worsens its image abroad.[134]

Despite these notes of caution, a majority of observers seem to regard Japan's attractiveness as a trendsetter in entertainment, fashion, and other areas as a diplomatically beneficial phenomenon. Exactly how beneficial is hard to measure. As McGray has observed, "it is impossible to measure national cool," and "soft power doesn't quantify neatly."[135] And yet, although soft power may appear to be an intrinsically vague and difficult-to-measure form of national strength, Portland (a strategic communications consultancy) and the USC Center on Public Diplomacy published a formal ranking of countries' soft power for several years. To do so, they combined a range of measures in six categories—(1) digital infrastructure, (2) cultural output, (3) enterprise and capacity for business innovation, (4) education and human capital, (5) diplomatic engagement, and (6) government, including commitment to democracy and quality of institutions—along with polling data in order to develop a soft power scale. Their "Soft Power 30" reports the thirty highest-scoring countries out of 61 countries for which they gathered data for five consecutive years beginning in 2015. During this time span, Japan's highest rank was fifth, and it averaged a ranking of 6.8, typically exceeded only by the United States, the UK, France, Germany, and Canada.[136] It was the highest-ranking country for soft power in Asia by a sizable margin.[137] An earlier study by Christopher Whitney and David Shambaugh relying on public opinion data also gave Japan relatively high marks in several dimensions of soft power, often second only to the United States among the countries they surveyed.[138] Studies such as these seem to corroborate the argument that soft power is an important objective. And this is perhaps especially true in Asia, where Ian Hall and Frank Smith argue an arms race "for the weapons of 'soft power'" is now underway.[139] "Using traditional and new media, as well as cultural events and academic exchange programs," they go on to say, "Asian states now aim to project a better image than their neighbors to garner sympathy and support for their foreign policy objectives."[140] Japan's 2023 and 2024 ranking in the Anholt-Ipsos Nation Brands Index as the most popular country in the world thus appears to place it in a diplomatically advantageous position.[141]

Hard Power

Soft power presumes that a country's image is important. On the face of it, hard power does not. Hard power is seen by realists as the "power of last resort," the form of power that must be employed when efforts to win hearts and minds have failed, when persuasion hasn't worked, and when there is no other choice. Against the argument that hard and soft power are alternatives and that one comes into play only when the other has failed, however, is the notion that the two are often complementary.

Joseph Nye argues in favor of "an integrated strategy that combines hard and soft power."[142] He begins an essay on the topic, in fact, by quoting a statement made by Hillary Clinton at her confirmation hearing for the position of secretary of state: "America cannot solve the most pressing problems on our own, and the world cannot solve them without America. . . . We must use what has been called 'smart power,' the full range of tools at our disposal."[143] Effecting change may require both soft and hard power, and Nye admonishes us to remember that soft power is sometimes the more efficacious. "When the Berlin Wall finally collapsed," he recalls, "it was destroyed not by an artillery barrage but by hammers and bulldozers wielded by those who had lost faith in communism."[144]

Smart power requires both hard and soft power, and because a country's image is central to its soft power, a positive image is necessary for "smart" diplomacy. Yet the relevance of image goes beyond this. When coercion does become necessary, we might assume that states will focus on the material determinants of their advantage: economic and military might. Even in the case of military power, however, image matters. This is because the material determinants of power do not "speak" for themselves. For the United States, Britain's possession of nuclear weapons means something very different than Iran's. Nuclear weapons themselves are not a brute fact. They are threatening or not according to our image of the state that possesses them. In a very interesting study of the way military planners think of nuclear weapons, Lynn Eden has shown that even something as material as the damage from nuclear weaponry is subject to a great deal of social construction.[145] The military, as an organization, applied the conceptual framework of conventional bombing campaigns to nuclear weapons and focused almost exclusively on blast damage in its calculations. In the post–Cold War era, Eden shows, this tendency persists although the predictable thermal damage from modern high-yield nuclear weapons would be much larger than the blast effects. By her estimation, "under most circumstances, damage from mass fire would extend two to five times farther than blast damage."[146]

Japan offers a particularly good illustration of the way national image shapes the meaning of military hardware. The Japanese government interprets Article 9 of the Japanese constitution to allow for defensive military forces, but not to allow offensive "war potential."[147] For this reason, the

Japanese Self-Defense Forces (JSDF) deploys hardware that is primarily defensive rather than offensive. The Japanese Maritime Self-Defense Forces (JMSDF) surface fleet includes destroyers and helicopter carriers for the defense of Japan's coastal waters, for example, but not aircraft carriers for power projection. And the JMSDF submarine fleet includes diesel submarines but not nuclear submarines that would facilitate extended missions outside Japanese waters. Still, whether a vessel should be considered offensive or defensive is often in the eye of the beholder. Japan's newest generation of *Izumo* class helicopter destroyers might also be classified as light aircraft carriers, and the ships in this class are being refitted to permit deployment of F-35B V/STOL fighter aircraft.[148] Leaving aside the question of whether such light aircraft carriers are consistent with Article 9, it is clear that they will be seen in some quarters as a threat.[149] China has expressed "strong dissatisfaction and opposition" to the move, proclaiming that it is "not conducive to the development and improvement of Sino-Japanese relations."[150]

Hard power thus takes on different meanings depending on a country's image. In the long run, perhaps material capabilities will matter more than image, but a great deal can happen before the long run gets around to having an effect. It is hard to deny the importance of a country's image—or brand, or role, or identity. The way we see countries affects not only their ability to employ the tools of soft power but even the extent to which they are subject to the constraints of hard power. How Japan is seen is not only the subject of long-standing academic interest, as Chapter 2 revealed, but also a question of great practical importance. Chinese and South Korean animosity toward Japan matters. The remainder of this book takes up the question of how such animosity can be explained, beginning in the next chapter with the straightforward proposition that Japan's image depends on its own international behavior.

Notes

1. We might count Michel de Montaigne and David Hume among the skeptics; see Montaigne, *Essais*; and Hume, *Treatise*. In Bertrand Russell's wry observation, "Skepticism, while logically impeccable, is psychologically impossible, and there is an element of frivolous insincerity in any philosophy which pretends to accept it" (Russell, *Human Knowledge*, 9). Perhaps for this reason as much as any other, the grounds offered to reject skepticism are myriad. Thoughtful discussions of this problem include Huemer, *Skepticism*; Nagel, *View from Nowhere*; Pollock and Cruz, *Contemporary Theories*; Popkin, *History of Scepticism*; and Stroud, *Significance of Philosophical Skepticism*.
2. For an interesting study of the influences on Zimmern's thought, see Baji, *International Thought of Alfred Zimmern*.

3. Carr, *Twenty Years' Crisis*; for discussions of Carr's influence, see, inter alia, Cox, *E. H. Carr*; Howe, "Utopian Realism"; and Jones, *E. H. Carr and International Relations*.

4. Acheson, *Present at the Creation*.

5. Morgenthau, *Politics among Nations*.

6. Walt, "Alliance Formation"; Walt, *Origins of Alliances*.

7. Barnett, "Historical Sociology and Constructivism"; Evans, *Embedded Autonomy*.

8. See, inter alia, Anthias and Yuval-Davis, *Racialized Boundaries*; Balibar and Wallerstein, *Race, Nation, Classe*; Jackson and Penrose, *Constructions of Race, Place, and Nation*; Marx, "Race-making and the Nation-state"; and Mosse, "Racism and Nationalism."

9. Jackson and Penrose, *Constructions of Race, Place, and Nation*, 4.

10. Schulze, *States, Nations and Nationalism*, 164; Schulze cites Ranke, "Geschichte Deutschlands und Frankreichs," 78.

11. Smith, "Beyond Tocqueville," 551. To be clear, Smith's intent was to "challenge that thesis by showing that its adherents fail to give due weight to inegalitarian ideologies and conditions that have shaped the participants and the substance of American politics just as deeply"—not least the inequalities that attach to distinctions of race and gender in American society (Smith, "Beyond Tocqueville," 549).

12. Hartz, *Liberal Tradition*. Another prominent example of this tendency is Frederick Jackson Turner's claim—echoing Tocqueville's own commentary on the importance of open land for settler expansion, and originally presented to the American Historical Association in 1893—that the open Western frontier in the United States played a crucial role in shaping the national character (Turner, *Frontier*). For further discussion of Turner's argument about American character, see also Potter, *People of Plenty*; Hartshorne, *Distorted Image*.

13. On the role of folklore and folk tales in the emergence of nationalist sentiment, see Baycroft and Hopkin, *Folklore and Nationalism*. This was not a uniquely European phenomenon. In late Tokugawa Japan, for example, the *kokugaku* (national learning or nativist studies) movement refocused scholarly attention on Japanese traditional folklore and stories. It was one of the leading kokugaku scholars, Motoori Norinaga, who helped elevate the *Genji Monogatari* as a work expressing the "native Japanese voice" (see Marra, *Poetics of Motoori Norinaga*). The kokugaku movement was later extended, in turn, by the early twentieth century Kyoto School (*Kyōto-gakuha*) and its renewed focus on Japanese uniqueness. For a discussion of the Kyoto School and Japanese nationalism, see Heisig and Maraldo, *Rude Awakenings*.

14. For a contemporary compilation of these national epics, see Rabb, *National Epics*. Using the *Nibelungenlied* as the basis of his libretto, Wagner began to write the Ring cycle in 1848, further cementing its place as the German national epic.

15. Marx, *Eighteenth Brumaire*.

16. Bradley, *Racial Origins*, 139.

17. Stalin's conception of national character also drew heavily on romantic nationalist prejudices, dividing the world into hero and merchant countries and embracing the same anti-Jewish stereotypes that were circulated by Nazi ideologues such as Alfred Rosenberg; see Van Ree, "Heroes and Merchants."

18. Even in the eighteenth century, a literature on national stereotypes already flourished; see Hayman, "Notions on National Characters"; Neumann, "Cultural and Historical Imagology." The pace quickened dramatically, however, in the nineteenth century; see Baycroft and Hopkin, *Folklore and Nationalism*; Hobsbawm, *Nations and*

Nationalism; Mandler, *English National Character*; Patriarca and Riall, *Risorgimento Revisited*; Thaden, "Romantic Nationalism in Russia." It was, as Robert Nisbet puts it, "an age rich in reification. Typologies, entelechies, ideal types, and abstractions of all kinds flourished" (Nisbet, "Tocqueville's Ideal Types," 171).

19. Winthrop, *Concepts in Cultural Anthropology*, 214. Mead's work was also notable for the controversy it later produced over the challenge of cultural awareness in modernizing societies; see Mead, *Coming of Age in Samoa*; Côté, *Adolescent Storm and Stress*.

20. Mead, "Preface"; see Benedict, *Patterns of Culture*.

21. Du Bois, *People of Alor*.

22. Mead, *Keep Your Powder Dry!*; Benedict, *Chrysanthemum and the Sword*.

23. Gorer, *American People*; Gorer, *People of Great Russia*; Riesman, *Lonely Crowd*. For an application of the approach to the Soviet Union, see Inkeles and Bauer, *Soviet Citizen*. See also Riesman, "Psychological Types," for interesting reflections on psychological types and national character.

24. Terracciano, "National Character." Long before Terracciano's work, criticism of simplistic claims such as Gorer's attribution of Russian character to infant swaddling had effectively undermined national character studies and the Culture and Personality School; see Mead, "Swaddling Hypothesis"; LeVine, "Culture and Personality Studies."

25. Anderson, *Imagined Communities*.

26. Hobbes, *Leviathan*; Pufendorf, *Law of Nature and Nations*, 7. I am indebted to Nick Onuf for drawing my attention to the importance of this foundation for later, embodied conceptions of the nation (see Onuf, "World-Making, State-Building"). Nicholas and Peter Onuf argue that Pufendorf was the first to develop the notion of the state as a moral person (Onuf and Onuf, *Nations, Markets and War*, 69–74).

27. Boulding, "National Images and International Systems," 120.

28. Boulding, *Image*.

29. Boulding, "National Images and International Systems," 122.

30. Boulding, "National Images and International Systems," 122.

31. Boulding, "National Images and International Systems," 124.

32. Boulding, "National Images and International Systems," 124–25.

33. Boulding, "National Images and International Systems," 131.

34. In several fields—not only international relations, but also psychology and law, for example—constructivism has taken the place of Boulding's science of eiconics. A similar orientation toward problems of phenomenology can also be detected in postmodernist work on the provisionality of representations, and what Baudrillard (1993, 1994) calls "simulacra." In a sense, therefore, Boulding's vision of a science of images spanning the social sciences has at least partially come to fruition.

35. Gasiorowski, "1953 Coup d'Etat in Iran," 276. Cottam evidently shared the Truman administration's assessment and later said he was "horrified" by the decision to overthrow Mosaddegh (Akhavi, "Memoriam," 204).

36. Ambrose, "Comparing and Contrasting Ike and Dick," 19.

37. Cottam, *Foreign Policy Motivation*, 31.

38. Cottam, *Foreign Policy Motivation*, 31.

39. Cottam, *Foreign Policy Motivation*, 64.

40. Cottam, *Foreign Policy Motivation*, 64.

41. See Herrmann, *Perceptions and Behavior*; Herrmann, "Soviet Decision to Withdraw"; Herrmann and Fischerkeller, "Beyond the Enemy Image."

42. Following the lead of later scholars who adopted Cottam's scheme, I have reversed his labeling of the imperial and colonial images. Originally, Cottam treated the imperial image as one in which another state is held (by the imperial power) to represent an opportunity with inferior capabilities or culture; see Cottam, *Foreign Policy Motivation*. The other, in this case, is seen as a colony or pseudo-colony, and more recent work thus applies the *colony* label to a weaker state and the *imperial* label to a stronger one; see Herrmann and Fischerkeller, "Beyond the Enemy Image"; Alexander, Levin, and Henry, "Image Theory." This is more consistent with Cottam's use of other terms such as "enemy" or "ally."

43. Herrmann and Fischerkeller, "Beyond the Enemy Image."

44. Heider, *Psychology of Interpersonal Relations*.

45. See, e.g., Kowert, "National Identity," 24–26.

46. Herrmann and Fischerkeller, "Beyond the Enemy Image"; Shimko, *Images and Arms Control*.

47. Hoyt, "'Rogue State' Image"; O'Reilly, "Perceiving Rogue States."

48. For an overview of the development of this research tradition by one of its leading practitioners, see Herrmann, "Perceptions and Image Theory."

49. One recent example of this trend is Castano, Bonacossa, and Gries's very interesting investigation of subliminal priming of the *ally*, *enemy*, and *dependent* images; see Castano, Bonacossa, and Gries, "National Images as Integrated Schemas."

50. Mead, *Mind, Self, and Society*; Holsti, "National Role Conceptions."

51. See Holsti, "National Role Conceptions," 239. This insight also calls to mind the dramaturgical approach to social roles pioneered by Erving Goffman. Goffman held that people "play" out their own identity as though following a script in the drama of their own lives; see Goffman, *Presentation of Self*. Like Holsti's states, we can only play the roles that make sense both to ourselves and to others.

52. Holsti, "National Role Conceptions," 255.

53. Schuman, *International Politics*; Fox, *Super-Powers*; Morgenthau, *Politics among Nations*.

54. Organski, *World Politics*, chap 12.

55. To this end, Holsti collected 972 general foreign policy statements made by the national leaders of seventy-one countries; see Holsti, "National Role Conceptions," 256–60.

56. Holsti, "National Role Conceptions," 273.

57. Holsti, "National Role Conceptions," 277.

58. Holsti, "National Role Conceptions," 302.

59. Walker, "National Role Conceptions"; Walker, *Role Theory and Foreign Policy Analysis*; Wish, "Foreign Policy Makers"; Shih, "National Role Conception"; Cottam and Shih, *Contending Dramas*; Le Prestre, *Role Quests*. In an underappreciated contribution to this second wave of role theory scholarship, Bert Edström examined Japan's efforts to take on new international roles between 1969 and 1982; see Edström, *Japan's Quest*.

60. The third wave of role-theory scholarship is extensive. For good overviews of this evolving research tradition, see Breuning, "Role Theory"; Thies, "Role Theory." Some of the most important theoretical and empirical works include Brummer and Thies, "Contested Selection"; Elgström and Smith, *European Union's Roles*; Harnisch, "Conceptualizing in the Minefield"; Harnisch, Frank, and Maull, *Role Theory*; McCourt, "Roles States Play"; McCourt, *Britain and World Power*; Schafer and Walker, *Operational Code*

Analysis; Thies, "Social Psychological Approach"; Thies, *United States, Israel*; Thies and Nieman, *Rising Powers*; Walker, *Cognitive Architecture of British Appeasement Decisions*; Walker, Malici, and Schafer, *Rethinking Foreign Policy Analysis*; Wehner and Thies, "Role Theory, Narratives, and Interpretation."

61. See especially Schafer and Walker, *Operational Code Analysis*; Thies, *United States, Israel*; Walker, *Role Theory and Foreign Policy Analysis*.

62. Grossman, "Role Theory"; Karim, "Role Conflict"; Oppermann, Beasley, and Kaarbo, "British Foreign Policy"; Yoshimatsu, "Japan's Role Conception."

63. Cantir and Kaarbo, "Contested Roles"; Cantir and Kaarbo, *Domestic Role Contestation*; Friedrichs, *US Global Leadership Role*.

64. Important methodological contributions include Schafer and Walker, *Operational Code Analysis*; Wehner, "Narration of Roles." For an empirical study of the effects of national role conceptions, see Kowert and Thies, "(Babylonian) Lions."

65. One of the few exceptions to this rule is Shih, "National Role Conception."

66. See Herrmann and Fischerkeller, "Beyond the Enemy Image."

67. Hall, *National Collective Identity*.

68. Hall, *National Collective Identity*, 28.

69. Wendt, "Collective Identity Formation." Both Wendt and Hall are attentive to the way the international system socializes states as agents. Wendt refers to the outcome of this process as *state identity*, whereas Hall employs the phrase *national collective identity*; see Wendt, *Social Theory of International Politics*.

70. See Kowert, "National Identity"; Wendt, "State as Person."

71. Holsti, "National Role Conceptions," 239; Jepperson, Wendt, and Katzenstein, "Norms, Identity, and Culture," 54.

72. See Jepperson, Wendt, and Katzenstein, "Norms, Identity, and Culture"; Abdelal, Herrera, Johnston, and McDermott, "Identity as a Variable."

73. Wendt, *Social Theory of International Politics*, 327. James Fearon points out that identity, as constructivists typically understand it, also "refers at the same time to social categories and to the sources of an individual's self-respect or dignity"; see Fearon, "What Is Identity," 4.

74. Wendt, "Collective Identity Formation," 385.

75. Cottam, *Foreign Policy Motivation*.

76. Wendt, "Anarchy Is What States Make of It"; Wendt, *Social Theory of International Politics*. For constructivist applications of this typology, see Thies, "Construction of a Latin American Interstate Culture"; Kowert and Thies, "(Babylonian) Lions." And for a critique of Wendt's typologizing (and, presumably, other works in this vein) from the perspective of a critical constructivist, see Zehfuss, "Constructivism and Identity."

77. Wendt, *Social Theory of International Politics*.

78. Constructivist discussions of culture and state identity include Katzenstein, *Culture of National Security*; Hopf, "Promise of Constructivism"; Hopf, *Social Construction of International Politics*; Lebow, *Cultural Theory*; Lebow, *National Identities and International Relations*.

79. Lebow, *Politics and Ethics of Identity*. See also Varadarajan, "Constructivism, Identity and Neoliberal (In)security," which considers state identity in the context of the capitalist global economy.

80. Indeed, "Identity Matters . . . and How" was the theme of a multidisciplinary workshop at Ohio State University organized in 2003 by Ted Hopf that brought together

constructivists, social psychologists, and other scholars interested in the nexus of social identity, politics, and international relations. A more recent study by Hopf and Allan, *Making Identity Count*, is devoted especially to methodological concerns but again with the intention of documenting the importance of national (state) identity. And, to take but one more example, Freyburg and Richter's "National Identity Matters" studies EU efforts to promote democracy in the Balkans.

81. Hopf, *Social Construction of International Politics.*

82. See also Zevelev, "Russian National Identity."

83. Ringmar, *Identity, Interest and Action.* More generally, see Lebow's illuminating account of the role of pride—along with honor, prestige, glory, and other forms of what he calls "spirit," drawing on the ancient Greeks—in the history of international relations; see Lebow, *Cultural Theory.*

84. Neumann, *Uses of the Other.*

85. Hopf, *Social Construction of International Politics*, 2–3. Cf. Zehfuss, "Constructivism and Identity."

86. One of the earliest works in this tradition was Katzenstein, *Culture of National Security.* Among the many other examples that followed, see: Ashizawa, "When Identity Matters"; Bozdağlıoğlu, *Turkish Foreign Policy*; Browning, *Constructivism, Narrative and Foreign Policy Analysis*; Brysk, Parsons, and Sandholtz, "After Empire"; Bukh, *Japan's National Identity*; Cahan, "National Identity and the Limits of Constructivism"; Catalinac, "Identity Theory and Foreign Policy"; Cerutti and Lucarelli, *Search for a European Identity*; Flamm, *South Korean Identity*; Hagström, "'Abnormal' State"; Hopf and Allan, *Making Identity Count*; Leichtova, *Misunderstanding Russia*; Rieker, *Europeanization*; Schonberg, *Constructing 21st Century US Foreign Policy*; Shannon and Kowert, *Psychology and Constructivism.* For overviews of research on state identity, see Alexandrov, "Concept of State Identity"; Berenskoetter, "Identity in International Relations"; Bucher and Jasper, "Revisiting 'Identity'"; Kowert, "Foreign Policy and the Social Construction of State Identity"; Hopf, "Making Identity Count"; and Lebow, *National Identities and International Relations.* For an application to Japan that builds a bridge from scholarship on identity to role theory, see Klien, *Rethinking Japan's Identity.*

87. Lebow, *National Identities and International Relations.*

88. Hobden and Hobson, *Historical Sociology.* This same tendency exists, though perhaps to a lesser extent, in constructivist studies of national identity as a phenomenon of internal cohesion and "nationalism"; see Alemán and Woods, "Inductive Constructivism."

89. Key statements in the rapidly expanding literature on ontological security are Kinnvall, "Globalization and Religious Nationalism"; Mitzen, "Ontological Security"; and Steele, *Ontological Security.* Steele, to take one example, pays careful attention to the way honor and shame shape a state's need for certain identities. For good overviews of this literature, paying special attention to the role of anxiety, see Gustafsson and Krickel-Choi, "Returning to the Roots"; and Kinnvall and Mitzen, "Anxiety, Fear, and Ontological Security." There are numerous other exceptions to the general tendency of constructivist studies of state identity to ignore scholarship on emotion and role theory in foreign policy. For example, Patrick Flamm explores the links between identity and role at some length in order to gauge the implications of South Korea's evolving status as a middle power for its foreign policy; see Flamm, *South Korean*

Identity. And Jonathan Mercer, in "Feeling Like a State," makes the case that emotion is an important component of state identities. Still, these works stand out against the grain.

90. For a good overview of the nation branding literature, see Kaneva, "Nation Branding"; and, for a somewhat more circumspect review of the literature, Wang, "Power and Limits of Branding."

91. Olins, *Branding the Nation*, 17.

92. Olins, *Branding the Nation*, 17.

93. Michel Girard, quoted in Olins, *Branding the Nation*, 18.

94. See, e.g., Leerssen and Storm, *World Fairs*; Raizman and Robey, *Expanding Nationalisms*.

95. Tomlinson and Young, *National Identity and Global Sports Events*; Chen, "Branding National Images." Other contests, such as the Eurovision singing competition, also constitute sites of national brand comparison; see Jordan, *Modern Fairy Tale*.

96. Li and Kaplanidou, "Impact of the 2008 Beijing Olympic Games." Brady argues, in contrast, that the Beijing Olympic extravaganza was targeted especially at domestic audiences; see Brady, "Beijing Olympics."

97. Pamment, "Putting the GREAT Back into Britain."

98. See Pamment, "Putting the GREAT Back into Britain," 275.

99. Anholt, "Brand Africa," 72; see also Browning, "Nation Branding and Development."

100. Anholt, *Competitive Identity*, 1.

101. Anholt, *Competitive Identity*.

102. Anholt, *Competitive Identity*, 3.

103. See, e.g., Leigh and, "Symbolic Interactionism"; Solomon, "Role of Products as Social Stimuli." The economic literature on branding has also been applied by sociologists to symbolic interactionism; see Whitmer, "You Are Your Brand."

104. Tony Schwarz, quoted in Serazio, "Branding Politics," 225.

105. Serazio, "Branding Politics," 234.

106. Browning, "Nation Branding, National Self-Esteem," 196, 197. On the "competition state," Browning cites Weidner, "Nation Branding"; cf. Fougner, "State, International Competitiveness and Neoliberal Globalisation."

107. Browning, "Nation Branding, National Self-Esteem," 212.

108. It is also worth noting that one could differentiate accounts of country perception along dimensions other than those identified in Figure 3.1. For example, countries are primarily concerned with their own brands, although their leaders certainly perceive other countries' branding as well. Conversely, foreign policy image theorists, along with most constructivist accounts of state identity, are more concerned with how other countries are seen. And because it identifies relationships, role is necessarily concerned with both self and other.

109. Nye, *Bound to Lead*.

110. Nye, *Bound to Lead*, 2. Kennedy's *The Rise and Fall of the Great Powers* was especially influential. See also Calleo, *Beyond American Hegemony*; Snyder, *Myths of Empire*.

111. Nye, *Bound to Lead*, 32; emphasis added.

112. Nye, *Soft Power*, 6–7.

113. Cheng, "China's Peaceful Rise," 132. See also Zheng, "China's Peaceful Rise"; Li and Worm, "Building China's Soft Power." "Top level endorsement in China affected me directly," Nye writes. "Hardly a week went by in the year after Hu Jintao's use of the

concept without an e-mail asking me to write an article or participate in some soft power seminar or conference" (Nye, "Soft Power: The Origins"). For a thoughtful study of China's pursuit of soft power, see Lee, *Soft Power Made in China.*

114. Moore, "Bismarck or Wilhelm?"; Diamond, "No More Mr. Nice China"; Yue, "Limits to China's Peaceful Rise." Other scholars continue to find reason for cautious optimism about China's peaceful rise; see Gries, "China's Rise"; Johnston, "How New and Assertive"; Herrick, Gai, and Subramaniam, *China's Peaceful Rise.*

115. See, e.g., Ross and Ross, *Anti-Americanism;* Katzenstein and Keohane, *Anti-Americanisms in World Politics;* Chiozza, *Anti-Americanism.* There are numerous studies of anti-Americanism in various regions: in Asia (Kim, "Anti-Americanism in Korea"); Europe (Roger, *American Enemy*), Latin America (McPherson and Zelikow, *Yankee No!*), the Middle East (Baxter and Akbarzadeh, *US Foreign Policy*), and the Muslim world more generally (Gentzkow and Shapiro, "Media, Education and Anti-Americanism").

116. See Katzenstein and Keohane, *Anti-Americanisms in World Politics.*

117. Liu, "China and Britain."

118. Callahan, "Identity and Security in China."

119. Hayashi, "China Risks Becoming Asia's Voldemort."

120. McGray, "Japan's Gross National Cool," 47.

121. Nye, "Soft Power of Japan."

122. Asō, "New Look."

123. See Kokami, *Kūru Japan!?*

124. Mikami, "Nihon Oranda Denmāku," 55.

125. See Ishii, "Gaikokujin no Mita Nihon"; Shi, "Ekkyō Suru Bunka kara Miru 'Kūru Japan.'" On the Cool Britannia campaign, see Werther, "Rebranding Britain."

126. See, e.g., Leheny, "Narrow Place"; Ōishi and Yamamoto, *Imēji no Naka no Nihon;* Otmazgin, "Contesting Soft Power"; Heng, "Mirror, Mirror on the Wall"; Vyas, *Soft Power in Japan–China Relations;* Hayden, *Rhetoric of Soft Power,* chap. 3; Sun, *Japan and China as Charm Rivals.*

127. Akaha, "'Soft Power' in Japan's Security Policy"; Otmazgin and Otmazgin, "Japan Imagined"; Christensen, "Cool Japan, Soft Power"; Vyas, *Soft Power in Japan–China Relations.*

128. Watanabe and McConnell, *Soft Power Superpowers.*

129. Soeya, "Evolution of Japan's Public Diplomacy."

130. Vyas, *Soft Power in Japan–China Relations.*

131. Konno, "Sofuto Pawā." On the skepticism of some Japanese observers, see also Hayden, *Rhetoric of Soft Power,* 99. Thomas Berger also argues that Japanese soft power is overstated; see Berger, "Triumph of Hope."

132. Leheny, "Narrow Place."

133. Shi Jinkai hints at this problem by placing the Cool Japan campaign in the context of a long tradition of exporting Japanese exoticism going back to the role of Japonism in Europe; see Shi, "Ekkyō Suru Bunka kara Miru 'Kūru Japan.'" For another effort to put Cool Japan in a broader historical context, see Ishii, "Gaikokujin no Mita Nihon."

134. Mihara, "Kūru Japan." Hernandez and Hirai find that younger audiences in Taiwan, South Korea, and China respond positively to Japanese animation, but that older audiences respond negatively; see Hernandez and Hirai, "Reception of Japanese Animation." See also Hall and Smith, "Struggle for Soft Power," for additional discussion of the way efforts to enhance soft power can produce a backlash.

135. McGray, "Japan's Gross National Cool," 53.
136. This information is reported on the Soft Power 30 website: https://softpower30.com. For a description of the development of the Soft Power 30 index, see McClory and Harvey, "Soft Power 30"; and for a critical discussion of its construct validity, see Yun, "Overdue Critical Look."
137. See McClory, "Soft Power 30."
138. Whitney and Shambaugh, *Soft Power in Asia.*
139. Hall and Smith, "Struggle for Soft Power," 1.
140. Hall and Smith, "Struggle for Soft Power," 1.
141. Place Brand Observer, "Anholt Nation Brands Index (NBI) 2024."
142. Nye, "Get Smart," 162.
143. Hillary Clinton, quoted in Nye, "Get Smart," 160.
144. Nye, "Get Smart," 162.
145. Eden, *Whole World on Fire.*
146. Eden, *Whole World on Fire,* 2.
147. For a good overview of Article 9 and its evolving interpretation, see Auer, "Article Nine."
148. On the political and strategic implications of this decision, see Cannon and Rossiter, "Unraveling Japan's Aircraft Carrier Puzzle."
149. The *Izumo*-class helicopter destroyers are 27,000-ton vessels with flat flight decks. Although they are effectively light aircraft carriers, Cannon and Rossiter argue that they can only be seen as offensive if they are deployed with training and doctrine suited to offensive operations, and that the JMSDF shows no inclination toward either for the foreseeable future; see Cannon and Rossiter, "Offensive or Defensive."
150. Hiyama, "Japan to Get First Post-WWII Aircraft Carriers."

PART II

Explaining Country Images

CHAPTER 4

The Geopolitics of Japan's Image

There is a standard explanation among political scientists for why countries see themselves, and other countries, in a certain way. It has been elaborated at length in several distinct bodies of literature within the field of foreign policy analysis, and it is consonant with a long tradition of realist scholarship. It boils down to a very simple premise: the image of countries is determined, overwhelmingly, by their aggregate power within the international system and the use they make of it. Weak countries are seen as different from strong countries, and hegemons are different still from other great powers.

Realists would hasten to add that the way countries are seen doesn't really matter. What does matter are their objective capabilities, and not perceptions. Even the most committed structural realists are usually more doctrinaire in principle than in practice. As Stephen Walt has pointed out, it is hard to explain alliance relationships purely on the basis of capabilities without acknowledging that some states pose a greater threat than others for reasons apart from their structural position alone. Western European countries thus aligned themselves with the most powerful country in the international system after the Second World War because they saw the Soviet Union as a greater threat than the United States.[1] Insights such as this have motivated a new wave of neoclassical realism that explores the way a range of domestic and ideological variables inform various understandings of threat.[2] Yet even the most classical of the classical realists, Hans Morgenthau, drew a distinction between *status quo* and *revisionist* powers paralleling Walt's observation that some states pose a greater threat than others.[3]

For realists, our perceptions of states can never stray very far from capabilities, though, and this remains largely true for the image theorists, role theorists, identity theorists, and brand theorists discussed in Chapter 3 as well. We can afford to think differently of weak states than of strong states, but we cannot afford to ignore the possibility that the weak may someday become stronger, or that strong allies might over time become strong enemies. For this reason, Cameron Thies argues that relative power within the international system socializes states to adopt certain roles while discouraging them from playing others.[4] Role theorists, in particular, typically begin with the premise that a state's position in the international system matters because it weighs heavily on its interactions with other states.[5] These interactions, in turn, gradually define a state's role within the system.

If there is any simple lesson from almost a century of efforts to understand why countries sometimes see one another as enemies and other times as allies, it is that the power to inflict meaningful damage on another state is a crucial determinant of a state's image and ascribed role. In short, what a state *can* do plays a large role in shaping what we fear it *might* do. To this we might also add that what a country *has done* in the past also provides certain relevant information. These two premises are a good place to start.

REALPOLITIK AND JAPAN'S IMAGE

If a history of conflict leads us to expect negative attitudes toward a former aggressor, then Chinese and South Korean attitudes toward Japan are no surprise. Japan's wartime conduct made animosity in Beijing and Seoul inevitable, or so the argument goes. This logic should also yield the same expectation elsewhere in East Asia, however, and Chapter 2 shows that this expectation is not supported by the evidence. Although Filipinos, Indonesians, Vietnamese, and many others also suffered in various ways, these countries have generally positive attitudes toward Japan today. Indeed, there were more casualties in each of the latter countries than in South Korea. The total number of casualties was the highest in China, but deaths in Indonesia amounted to around 5 percent of the population, a proportionally higher figure than in China or South Korea.[6] Still, Indonesians mostly admire Japan today.

It is clear, therefore, that attitudes toward a former adversary can and do change. Of course, such attitudes might be more resistant to change when conflict lasts over a longer span of time. If we were to date South Korean conflict with Japan to Hideyoshi's sixteenth-century invasion attempts, then this is indeed a conflict with a long history. The most persistent invader of South Korea was China, however, and generalized animosity toward Japan within South Korea is more of a twentieth-century phenomenon, beginning with Japan's 1910 occupation. Taiwan had a similar history of Japanese occupation, to take another example, but Taiwanese attitudes are once again more positive. For that matter, longstanding conflicts in other parts of the world, such as those between France and Germany or France and Britain mostly gave way to positive diplomatic relationships (and public attitudes) by the twentieth century's end.

It is too simplistic, then, to argue that a conflictual past necessarily implies future hostility. To complement this argument, we might turn instead to the strategic needs of the present. It seems likely that rapprochement among Western European countries depended in good measure on their shared perception of threat from the Soviet Union. This is the case that led Walt to prioritize threat perception over capabilities as a determining factor in international alliances.[7] Similarly, it would be easy to attribute China's persistent distrust of Japan to the same postwar alliance framework that divided Europe into West and East. Although Tokyo's alliance with Washington might explain attitudes in Beijing, however, it does not explain those in Seoul. The same circumstances that divide China and Japan should push South Korea and Japan toward a positive relationship, as among erstwhile enemies in Western Europe. Indeed, this probably has been the effect of their trilateral alliance with the United States at least to a degree, but it remains difficult to reconcile these strategic circumstances with South Korea's mostly negative estimations of Japan.[8]

Broad generalizations from either past conflict or present strategic necessity seem inadequate, therefore, to explain Chinese or South Korean attitudes toward Japan. Chapter 2 argues that broad generalizations should be replaced, in any case, with a more nuanced appreciation of the fluctuations in Japan's relations with its closest neighbors. To determine whether changes in Japan's image correspond to changes in Japan's capabilities or other geopolitical circumstances, we must turn to a more detailed exploration of the way Japan's relations with each of these two countries has evolved over time.

JAPAN AND CHINA

From the Chinese perspective, the many geopolitical disasters that inform its contemporary relationship with Japan took place within the context of a grand cosmology that had always placed China at the cultural and political center of civilization. Japan, meanwhile, was a parvenu that had only begun by the seventh and eighth century CE to import elements of Sui and Tang Dynasty culture including Buddhist teachings, agricultural and city planning systems, and Chinese medicinal, artistic, and writing techniques.[9] These early contacts provide an important foundation for contemporary views of self and other in both China and Japan, a foundation that far predates the modern state system.[10]

For a millennium thereafter, this relationship evolved mostly in isolation from the West given the inherent limits of the Silk Road. Beginning in the late fifteenth century, however, European explorers and colonizers extended their reach across the globe, and by the nineteenth century, first China and then Japan were inexorably drawn into a new global state system. Whereas Japan succeeded in refashioning itself as a modern state, however, China remained mired in a feudal past until the dawn of the twentieth century. Then, just as a transformative civil war erupted in China, it was subsumed within a struggle for survival against Japan. After the Pacific War, it took several more years before the Chinese Communist Party was able to drive the Kuomintang off the mainland and establish control of the new People's Republic of China (PRC) in 1949. Relations between the PRC and Japan were not formally established until after Nixon visited China in September 1972, permitting Japanese Prime Minister Tanaka Kakuei to follow suit, flying to Beijing and signing a joint communiqué with Zhou Enlai that normalized relations between the two countries. Only by 1972, therefore, we can begin to speak of state-to-state relations between modern China and Japan in every meaningful sense.[11]

The broad contours of a realist account of Sino-Japanese relations in the latter twentieth century go something like this: after its defeat in the Pacific War, Japan was humbled and constrained by the United States, and these constraints persisted even after full Japanese sovereignty was restored. As US constraints loosened over time, however, Japan again appeared to pose a greater threat to China. Meanwhile, China's new rise to global prominence in the late twentieth century has posed a similar threat when viewed from Tokyo. In consequence, both countries adopted increasingly negative attitudes toward the other, and both increasingly doubted that the other could play a constructive role in Asian affairs. In contrast to the static notion that Japan's aggressive past makes negative attitudes inevitable, structural shifts in relative capabilities might thus appear to provide a better account of attitudes toward Japan.[12] Closer examination shows, however, that patterns in the Japan–China relationship are not well explained even by a more dynamic structural-realist perspective.

Somewhat surprisingly in the immediate aftermath of their war, Chinese attitudes toward Japan—at the level of officialdom, anyway—were remarkably benign even before diplomatic relations were restored in 1972. Mao Zedong issued a policy instruction within the CCP, shortly before normalization, that cooperation with Japan would "contribute to the struggle against American and Soviet hegemonism, especially Soviet revisionism" and was therefore useful.[13] Meanwhile Japan had already supplanted the Soviet Union as China's leading trade partner by 1965, and Chalmers Johnson goes so far as to describe this decade as "the high tide of Japanese intellectual flattery of China."[14] The Japanese left "projected onto China the feelings of war guilt that bothered many Japanese" or found in China "a vehicle for their anti-American attitudes during the Vietnam War" or "a utopian contrast to their own increasingly bureaucratized society."[15] After 1972 Sino-Japanese trade increased nearly another order of magnitude.[16] Japan also moved far more quickly than the United States to recognize the PRC's right to occupy China's seat in the United Nations.[17]

Chinese attitudes toward Japan improved under Mao Zedong not merely because Japanese power was suppressed but because Mao had other uses for Japan.[18] Zhou Enlai made a similar calculation at this juncture, embracing the useful fiction that a small military clique had seized control of Japan without broader popular support. In Yinan He's thoughtful analysis:

> By endorsing the Japanese "myth of military clique," the Chinese government avoided political disputes with Japan over historical memory and made way for their immediate strategic collaboration. In addition, to distinguish the many good Japanese from only a few bad Japanese also fit the communist ideology, the primary legitimacy foundation of the Chinese Communist Party (CCP) regime in Beijing. From the founding of the PRC until the end of the 1970s, communist propagandists premised national identity on the "defining fundamental fissure" between the Chinese Communists and the Capitalists, especially the Kuomingtang (KMT) government in Taiwan. As for foreign perpetrators, the class-based Marxist historiography claimed that the majority of people in a country were righteous proletarians and struggled with the evil capitalists, the militarist minority in the case of Japan.[19]

For the Chinese leadership, reconciliation with Japan fit within a broader narrative of communist triumphalism. Mao even permitted himself to remark, on the occasion of his meeting with Tanaka in 1972, that Japan need not apologize since it had actually helped the emergence of a modern China by hastening the communist revolution and the dissolution of the old feudal order.[20] This ideologically inflected understanding of history had a greater influence on the ebb and flow of Chinese attitudes toward Japan in this era than did any shifts in national capabilities.

The decade and a half after normalization constituted what some have called the "golden age" of China–Japan relations.[21] And yet these were precisely the years during which the Japanese economy blossomed, restoring Japan's status as a major power within Asia.[22] It is also worth noting that one of the first major controversies over Japan's depiction of its wartime conduct in textbooks occurred during this era (in 1982), as did the first official visit by a Japanese prime minister to Yasukuni Shrine (Prime Minister Yasuhiro Nakasone in 1985). Yet Japan's rise did not precipitate a reevaluation, on either side, of Sino-Japanese relations. And the textbook and Yasukuni Shrine controversies were interpreted largely as the misguided actions of a "handful of rightists."[23] Following student protests of Nakasone's Yasukuni Shrine visit, the CCP editorialized in the *People's Daily* that Chinese citizens should "treasure the hard-won China-Japan friendly relations."[24] What *did* transform the relationship, on the other hand, were changes set in motion by the Tiananmen Square protests in China as well as the electoral reforms put in place in Japan after 1994.

The Tiananmen Square protests of 1989, known as the June Fourth Incident in China, turned out to be the harbinger of a dramatic Chinese reassessment of Japan. With the collapse of communism in the Soviet Union and its replacement in China by an authoritarian system that was communist in name but nationalist in practice, the Chinese vision of Japan's international role suddenly became much darker. For Deng Xiaoping, who emerged as China's de facto leader after Mao's death in 1976, the fundamental task was to reconcile China's ongoing economic modernization with the continued dominance of the CCP. Meanwhile, shortly after events in Tiananmen Square sent political shockwaves throughout China, an equally fundamental shock struck Japan with the collapse of its bubble economy in the early 1990s. The Nikkei 225 lost over a third of its value in 1990.[25] The following year, the Nikkei continued its downward march, and urban land values began to plummet. The collapse of asset prices marked the end of Japan's economic miracle. One might imagine that both China and Japan would turn inward. In some ways they did, in fact, but the character of their relations also took on a new urgency, particularly in China.

For the CCP leadership, a new emphasis on patriotic education was intended as the glue that would hold the country together. To this end the

CCP undertook its own textbook revision campaign beginning in 1991. "In the new textbooks," Zheng Wang observes, "a patriotic narrative replaced the old class-struggle narrative. The official Maoist 'victor narrative' (China won national independence) was also superseded by a new 'victimization narrative,' which blames the 'West' for China's suffering."[26] The patriotic education strategy involved the creation of museums, landmarks, and other patriotic education bases. Forty of these one hundred sites were memorials of wars with foreign powers, and fully half of those were devoted to the "anti-Japanese war."[27] Thus, the KMT was increasingly supplanted by the West and, above all, by Japan as the villain in the story of China's suffering.[28] A technological transformation reinforced this strategic shift as well. Whereas ordinary Chinese citizens had previously been shut off from most sources of international news apart from those officially sanctioned in China, after the mid-1990s, internet bulletin boards flourished. These helped to mobilize popular sentiment and—combined with further Japanese missteps on a range of issues including the textbooks, the controversy over the Senkaku/Diaoyu Islands, and the Yasukuni Shrine visits—helped create a self-sustaining anti-Japanese nationalism in China partially independent of the CCP's efforts or control.[29]

The state of China–Japan relations continued to deteriorate in the early part of the new century under Jiang Zemin and Koizumi Junichirō, and it reached new lows under Xi Jinping and Abe Shinzō. Just before Xi took the reins of power from Hu Jintao—a pragmatist who somewhat improved China's relationship with both Taiwan and Japan—a particularly important crisis erupted when the Japanese government nationalized the Senkaku/Diaoyu Islands after a group led by Tokyo Governor Ishihara Shintarō threatened to buy them. China condemned Japan's actions, major anti-Japanese protests again broke out in China, and the following year Beijing declared that it would impose a new Air Defense Identification Zone (ADIZ) over parts of the East China Sea that included the disputed islands. Since then Chinese and Japanese Coast Guard ships have repeatedly confronted one another in the area. Needless to say, Abe's decision to pay an official visit to Yasukuni Shrine in December 2013 did nothing to help matters.[30]

Witnessing the degradation of China–Japan relations, more than a few experts have seen broader strategic designs in the actions of both Beijing and Tokyo. Jessica Chen Weiss argues that the ebb and flow of nationalist protests in China is not easily explained simply as a reaction to Japanese actions.[31] Even though anti-Japanese sentiment is genuine, she says, it finds expression in ways that are still controlled to a great degree by the Chinese government. When the government wishes to increase pressure on Japan—for example, to oppose Japan's 2005 bid for a permanent seat on the UN Security Council—it gives freer rein to the protests. Thus, the CCP permitted a grassroots campaign in China that gathered tens of millions of signatures in opposition to Japan's proposal.[32] When the government wishes to signal a more cooperative attitude, on the other hand, message boards on Baidu and other such social media websites are censored and protest is curtailed. Although it is clear that the CCP must take into account the feelings of the Chinese people, Weiss nevertheless argues that government also plays a big role in shaping protests as part of its broader diplomatic strategy.[33]

Mike Mochizuki argues that the Japanese government is similarly motivated by strategic calculations.[34] It must remain engaged with China for economic reasons, but it does so while hedging against the rise of Chinese power as much as possible. The result is a characteristic blend of cold politics and warm economics (*seirei keinetsu*).[35] Meanwhile the 1994 electoral reforms in Japan gradually injected more issue voting into national elections, increasing incentives for many politicians to play to a nationalist base.[36] Furthermore the 2015 revision of the US–Japan Defense Guidelines expanded cooperation between the US military and Japan's Self Defense Forces and lifted restrictions on the Japanese armaments industry. In June Dreyer's estimation, "the gradual movement of Japan toward becoming a 'normal' country with a standard military force seems irreversible."[37] As US–China relations have grown more antagonistic, moreover, it would seem logical for Chinese officials to view Japan as a greater threat too, given its close links with the United States. Japan's willingness to play politics with foreign policy and its deepening military cooperation with the United States no doubt bear directly on the issue of how Japan is seen in China.

Despite the gradual quasi-military normalization of the SDF and Japan's ongoing cooperation with the United States, however, it is impossible to ignore the fact that the balance of power in the new century had begun to shift decisively toward China. Earlier, during the so-called golden age of Sino-Japanese relations when Japan capabilities were growing rapidly, Mao displayed little concern. In the twenty-first century, on the other hand, attitudes toward Japan deteriorated even as China gained the upper hand. Nor is it the case that Japan has somehow been turned loose by the United States to embrace reckless new adventures. On the contrary Japan remains tightly integrated within what Peter Katzenstein calls the "American imperium."[38] The consistency of this alliance relationship makes it a poor explanation for the shift in Chinese attitudes.

It is tempting to argue, therefore, that geopolitics are much less important than the internal politics of the CCP's deliberately nationalist strategies.

Deng's patriotic education campaigns clearly plowed the field in which anti-Japanese sentiments grew. For this reason the next chapter will explore the domestic political determinants of attitudes toward Japan in greater detail. Even where such attitudes are controlled and deployed strategically by the Communist Party, however, it is hard to escape the sense that they have taken on a life of their own and that this may still have something to do with the geopolitical fears and aspirations of the Chinese public. Yinan He sums up the present situation as follows.

> Society has gone far beyond the official line in demonizing Japan. Regardless of its origins in official mythmaking, the extreme anti-Japanese nationalism in China today represents a public opinion that is distinct from state propaganda. . . . Beijing certainly has the coercive power to silence dissenting voices, as recently demonstrated in its crackdown of the Falun Gong and many scattered labor and rural riots. But to use that power against popular nationalism can be politically risky because it would contradict the government's own claims to be the foremost defender of national interest and pride. No Chinese government in modern history, the late Qing, Republican, or Nationalist, succeeded in putting down "patriotism"; each time they tried, it incurred massive anti-government revolts. Today's Communist government also fears the force of public opinion being used by anti-authority elites to defy its rule, and chooses to co-opt rather than suppress the popular sentiment.[39]

We are thus left with a geopolitical puzzle. Chinese attitudes toward Japan do not correspond particularly well to changes in the two countries' strategic positions. And yet it remains possible that geopolitical considerations—both historical enmities and more recent insults such as the Senkaku/Diaoyu standoff—are filtered through other lenses into forms of contemporary relevance.

JAPAN AND SOUTH KOREA

Perhaps even more than China, South Korea serves as an obvious test case for the way changing structural constraints and power politics might affect attitudes toward Japan. Nestled amid more powerful states throughout the past century, as it often was in earlier periods as well, South Korea's foreign policies have consistently been buffeted by the winds blowing from regional powers. It is not hard to imagine the depth of popular frustration with these shifting circumstances. In the late nineteenth century, Koreans could only look on helplessly as their kingdom was forced to concede territory and, ultimately, its own sovereignty, trapped in a contest between Japan and Russia. Then, emerging from the Second World War under occupation, Korea never enjoyed independence before it was again plunged into war and then partition. Heavily dependent on their superpower patrons, it is little wonder that both the North and the South have faced a struggle ever since between the necessity of alliance cooperation and the desire for independence and unification. In the North, this tension is manifest most prominently in the ideology of *juche,* or self-reliance.[40] In the South periodic waves of anti-Americanism give voice to a similar desire for greater independence. Both of the Koreas seem bound, therefore, by unusually tight geopolitical constraints.

If anti-Americanism rises and falls in South Korea, swings in sentiment against Japan have been more circumscribed. And the general tendency toward anti-Japanese sentiment is a puzzle that simply cannot be explained by South Korea's structural position. Almost from the beginning of South Korea's postwar emergence as a state, anti-Japanese feelings have run high. Sung-Hwa Cheong has shown in some detail, however, that these feelings were not simply the inevitable consequence of a half-century of Japanese rule.[41] Instead Cheong argues that the president of South Korea, Syngman Rhee, traded on and reinforced anti-Japanese feelings as the only available currency to bolster his own weak position. "Because politicians in South Korea were engaged in fierce struggles for power during this period," Cheong says, "'Japan-bashing' provided a powerful lever to manipulate public opinion and undercut their opponents."[42] Even though Rhee's own hatred of Japan was genuine, he favored rapid normalization of relations between the two countries. As in contemporary China–Japan relations, moreover, anti-Japanese sentiment could be used but not entirely controlled, and this prevented normalization until 1965.

Cheong also argues that the United States was much more concerned with extricating itself from South Korea than it was with brokering contacts between South Korean and Japanese officials that would help to improve the relationship between the two key American allies in East Asia. It is striking how little the United States did to institutionalize this trilateral relationship. After all, as Kohno Masaru pointedly asks, "if NATO was so successful in Europe, why was it not copied in East Asia in the aftermath of World War II?"[43] Cheong's answer to this question is consistent with another argument put forward by Christopher Hemmer and Peter Katzenstein—that

Washington sought to foster only bilateral relationships with its allies in Asia, unlike the multilateral institutions it helped to build in Europe, because it simply didn't trust its Asian partners.[44] "Throughout the Cold War," Hemmer and Katzenstein point out, "U.S. officials distinguished their NATO partners from other alliance members. Europe was seen as a 'center of world power' populated by a 'vigorous' people who had been powerful in the past and would be again in the future."[45] These views also had, they argue, "an undeniable racial component."[46]

Although Japan and South Korea were both bound separately to the "American imperium" in matters of foreign and security policy, the United States was never able to exert much control, in any case, over either country's internal politics. The result in Japan was a generation of political stability presided over by the Liberal Democratic Party (LDP) resting upon a bureaucratic bedrock that the United States scarcely penetrated even during the occupation.[47] In South Korea the United States was no more effective, but the resulting patterns of domestic politics were very different, and political upheavals were much more common.

Following on the heels of a brief experiment in parliamentary democracy (the Second Republic, 1960–61) and then two years of military rule (1961–63), Major General Park Chung-hee inaugurated the Third Republic by winning the presidency in 1963. Two years later, Park signed the Korea–Japan Treaty, normalizing relations with Japan, although the treaty and the lack of a formal apology from Japan sparked protests across South Korea.[48] In 1971 Park declared martial law to head off a challenge from opposition leader Kim Dae-jung. After forcing a new constitution through parliament in 1972 (the beginning of the Fourth Republic), strengthening his power and removing term limits on the presidency, Park continued to rule for seven more years despite growing protests. Finally, in 1979, he was assassinated by the director of the Korean Central Intelligence Agency.

The ensuing Fifth Republic (1979–87) brought another period of intense political turmoil. Major General Chun Doo-hwan's reimposition of martial law was met with nationwide protests. Chun eventually managed to consolidate his position, while the country's economy continued to grow. In 1983 Chun invited Japanese Prime Minister Nakasone Yasuhiro to Seoul, and the following year Nakasone issued a formal apology for the "great sufferings" Japan had inflicted on Korea during a reciprocal visit by Chun to Tokyo.[49] Protests favoring a direct presidential election meanwhile continued, and in 1987 Roh Tae-woo, the government's designated successor, gave in to the pressure. Roh's "June 29 Declaration" called for direct presidential elections and ushered in the Sixth Republic that has continued to the present.

A democratic political system thus finally took hold in South Korea not long before China veered decisively away from further democratization in the aftermath of the Tiananmen incident and the final days of the Cold War. In 1993 South Korea's first civilian president, Kim Young-sam, took office, and in 1998 he was succeeded by the country's first opposition president, left-wing party leader Kim Dae-jung. After Kim, Roh Moo-hyun and Lee Myung-bak each served five-year terms before Park Geun-hye's time in office was cut short in a corruption scandal. Moon Jae-in was the next elected president to serve a full term, but his successor, Yoon Suk Yeol, was impeached after briefly declaring martial law. The suspension of the Yoon presidency thus marks the third impeachment case in relatively recent memory, after those of Roh and Park. It is something of an understatement, therefore, to say that Korean democracy remains a tumultuous affair, and this may have some bearing on Japan's geopolitical "uses."

Although anti-Japanese attitudes have been more consistent in South Korea than in China, the democratic era of the Sixth Republic has nevertheless brought both highs and lows in the Japan–South Korea relationship. In 2002 the two countries jointly hosted the FIFA World Cup, and a "Korean Wave" of cultural exports including pop music stars and a hit television show, *Winter Sonata*, further warmed relations.[50] As with China, however, Japan's relationship with South Korea suffered after Koizumi's official visits to Yasukuni Shrine, eventually prompting Roh Moo-hyun to suspend further contact with Koizumi. In 2012 Roh's successor Lee Myung-bak paid an official visit to the disputed Liancourt Rocks (Dokdo in Korean, Takeshima in Japanese) and elevated the issue of Japanese wartime sexual enslavement of Korean women.[51] Following this, relations seemed to deteriorate further, with both President Park and Japanese Prime Minister Abe appearing to rely more heavily on nationalist appeals as a political strategy. In December 2015 Park and Abe somehow managed to conclude a deal to resolve the "comfort women" issue that included a formal apology from Abe on Japan's behalf as well as a payment of 1 billion yen to survivors.[52] After Park's impeachment, however, Moon Jae-in repudiated even this deal as inadequate. And whereas relations began to improve again under the more conservative administration of Yoon Suk Yeol, his impeachment introduced new uncertainties.[53]

As this discussion has begun to suggest, and as in post-Tiananmen China, it is hard to escape the sense that relations between South Korean and Japan have more to do with domestic politics than geopolitics. Still, Park Cheol Hee argues that the pattern of relations between South Korea and Japan has fundamentally changed since the end of the Cold War. Whereas Korean politicians in the earlier period may have been "pro-active" in mobilizing anti-Japanese sentiment to advance their own interests, Park argues that they have been "reactive" in the Sixth Republic. According to Park, "the logic of raising historical memory issues changed drastically from the mid-1990s. First of all, South Korea rarely initiated anti-Japanese claims on its own initiative. South Korea responded to the Japanese claims only when the Japanese side took a renewed position on the traditional history agenda. More often than not, Japanese actions came out of domestic political conflicts."[54]

At the level of foreign policy, in any case, it is hard to sustain the claim that South Korea–Japan relations have been defined to any great extent by realist strictures. As already discussed, South Korea and Japan's alliance relationship with the United States and their mutual economic interdependence should create strong pressures for cooperation. The rise of China introduces a dynamic element into these circumstances, causing strategic analysts in both South Korea and Japan to conclude that a closer relationship is necessary. And yet it has remained surprisingly elusive.[55] In fact, in 2014, the Pew Global Attitudes Survey data showed that the percentage of South Koreans who viewed Japan as their country's single greatest threat was almost as high (33 percent) as the percentage who saw North Korea in this light (36 percent).[56]

It is also increasingly difficult to attribute negative attitudes toward Japan within South Korea purely to political manipulation within the Sixth Republic. Although there are clear left–right differences in diplomacy toward Japan, politicians on both sides have attempted to broker deals with Tokyo, only to be frustrated by popular discontent. That Japan is still seen by many Koreans as a greater threat than China also exasperates American policymakers and strategic planners.[57] As in China, it appears that these attitudes sometimes take on a life of their own, driven by emotions that politicians do not reliably control.

CONSTRAINTS, NOT DECREES

The broad shifts in relative capabilities among Japan and its closest neighbors probably do have some effect on the attitudes citizens in these countries have toward one another. For this chapter to claim otherwise would be extraordinary. As a general and very crude rule of thumb, it is safe to say that rising Japanese economic and cultural power in the 1970s and 1980s concerned many South Koreans and Chinese. It did not seem far-fetched to imagine that this power would ultimately be put in the service of Japanese interests, particularly when Ishihara Shintarō and Akio Morita heralded the advent in 1989 of "the Japan that can say no."[58] In the same fashion, rising Chinese power is now a source of anxiety in Japan as well, and China has gained its own "naysayers."[59] South Korea's rise in stature has also awakened in that country the desire for a more independent foreign policy line.[60]

Still, Japan's image in China and South Korea does not track particularly well with changes in aggregate capabilities. The same is also true when we look beyond Japan's immediate neighborhood. Japan's most crucial relationship for much of the past two centuries has undoubtedly been with the United States. Yet even as the United States and Japan both began to expand their interests and nascent empires in the Asia-Pacific during the late nineteenth century, they took pains to avoid antagonizing each other. The United States held lucrative railroad and gold mine concessions on the Korean Peninsula, for example, but it looked the other way when Japan moved to check Russian and Chinese influence in the region. Japan returned the favor when the United States moved to annex Hawaii in 1898, despite the presence there of many more Japanese than Americans. And as the United States moved on after its war against Spain to annex the Philippines, Japan even supported American vessels in an encounter with German warships in Manila Bay. Although the Philippines were not that far from Japanese-controlled Formosa (Taiwan), and although Philippine rebels sought Japanese assistance to fight American rule, Tokyo refused to oppose the United States.

Throughout this era influential Japanese steadfastly saw the United States as an ally and partner. In Walter LaFeber's summation, "foreign threats, in Japanese eyes, did not include the United States."[61] Americans, aware of their superior military and economic capabilities, were more inclined to view Japan as a client than as a partner, and they did not hesitate to bring pressure to bear on Japan to achieve their own interests, as when McKinley rushed American warships to Hawaii to "encourage" Japanese moderation. Yet US attitudes, if condescending, were nevertheless positive. Lafcadio Hearn dispatched a series of laudatory reports to American magazines such as *Atlantic Monthly*, and one popular writer christened Japanese the "Yankees of the East."[62] Japan neatly fit into the simplistic American portrait of liberal, seafaring trading states struggling against land-locked colonialism.

It is true that Japan's destruction of Russia's Baltic Fleet in the Battle of Tsushima began to arouse concerns in Washington. Theodore Roosevelt detested Russia and admired Japan, but he joined other American leaders in worrying about Japan's rapidly growing strength.[63] Still, Roosevelt's concern over rising Japanese power did not stop him from directing his secretary of war, William Howard Taft, to conclude a secret agreement with Japanese Prime Minister Katsura Tarō in 1905 that specifically recognized Japanese control of Korea in return for Japanese acceptance of American control of the Philippines. It took another two decades before American attitudes toward Japan truly began to change. When they did so, the shift was conditioned more by the growing institutional divergence between American democracy and rise of military rule in Japan as Taishō-era democratic experiments came to an end.[64] And perhaps even more than this, the growing tendency in both countries to see international relations as a form of race relations began to produce hysteria in Japan and the United States alike.[65] What was new was not any great change in capabilities but rather a change in attitudes on both sides that depended heavily on the application of cultural lenses through which race and democracy were viewed. By the time Japan renewed its imperialist march in the 1930s, American attitudes had already shifted. As in the cases of China and South Korea, popular opinion had taken on a life of its own that was only loosely connected to underlying geopolitical conditions.

In general, therefore, shifts in capabilities and strategic position do not stand up to scrutiny as explanations for shifts in Japan's international image. The moments when Japan has been seen with the greatest alarm by China and South Korea, and even by the United States, are better explained by factors other than strategic position alone. When Japanese power grew rapidly during the Meiji era, and as Japan and the United States each expanded their Pacific empires, relations between the two nevertheless remained good. They soured only when institutional differences between the two countries, further influenced by racial attitudes, became more salient. And the two countries' relationship also remained strong in the late twentieth century, even as Japanese power again grew.[66] Like American attitudes toward Japan, China's attitudes also improved quickly after World War II, largely because this suited Mao's institutional purposes. Under Deng and after the post–Cold War hopes of democratization were dashed in China, the relationship grew far worse. Even though Chinese power was on the rise while Japan's was (relatively speaking) on the decline, moreover, this change in attitudes happened earlier and more rapidly in China, whereas the dips in China's favorability rating in Japan appear more reactive. Finally, in South Korea, postwar internal politics encouraged negative attitudes toward Japan rather than suppressing them as was the case in China. And even though the alliance with the United States and the rise of Chinese power should later have encouraged a far more constructive relationship, attitudes toward Japan within South Korea have mostly remained negative.

A purely structural account of Japan's international image and role taking within East Asia thus gets most of the particulars wrong. Cameron Thies's insight that new states are gradually socialized to play certain roles by the international system may be sound *ceteris paribus*.[67] A weak state cannot afford to act the part of a superpower, after all, and international roles do not "float freely" any more than other ideas that matter in international politics.[68] Yet powerful states do not always choose to take up the mantle of leadership even when it is possible to do so. If they do, they do not always lead in the same direction. And for "middle" or "regional" powers such as Japan, there has been even more leeway over the past century to act—and to be seen—in a variety of ways.

There might have been even more leeway, particularly in the postwar era, were it not for domestic political constraints. This chapter has repeatedly hinted at the important role played by domestic politics in South Korea and even in China, despite the dominance of the Communist Party. The crucial question, however, is whether domestic politics explains attitudes toward Japan or whether politicians are merely reacting to attitudes that must be explained in some other way. The next chapter takes up this question.

Notes

1. Walt, *Origins of Alliances*.
2. Lobell, Ripsman, and Taliaferro, *Neoclassical Realism*; Ripsman, Taliaferro, and Lobell, *Neoclassical Realist Theory*; Rose, "Neoclassical Realism."
3. Morgenthau, *Politics among Nations*.
4. Thies, *Search for International Order*.
5. Two other works that specifically link the microfoundations of threat assessment with broader, systemic constraints are Walker, Malici, and Schafer, *Rethinking Foreign Policy Analysis*; and Malici and Walker, *Role Theory and Role Conflict*.
6. For estimates of deaths caused by the Japanese military, see Gruhl, *Imperial Japan's World War Two*, 97, 143–44. Gruhl's numbers put Filipino losses at about 3.5 percent of the Philippines' population—comparable to losses in China and South Korea. On deaths in the Dutch East Indies (Indonesia), see Dower, *War without Mercy*, 295–96.
7. Walt, *Origins of Alliances*.
8. Michael Green argues that China has also exploited the divide between South Korea and Japan for strategic reasons; see Green, *By More than Providence*. Green does not claim that China is itself the primary cause of poor relations between South Korea and Japan, however, and it would seem a stretch to do so.
9. China's *Book of Han*, composed by a court official of the Western Han Dynasty, indicates Chinese awareness of a Kingdom of Wa on the Japanese islands in the first century CE; see Hoffman, "Cultures Combined." On Sui and Tang Dynasty contacts, see also Fogel, *Articulating the Sinosphere*.
10. See Wang, *Ambassadors from the Islands of Immortals*. For another thoughtful study of the way historical relations inform contemporary China–Japan relations, see Dreyer, *Middle Kingdom*.

11. See Johnson, "Patterns of Japanese Relations with China," 411. Johnson makes a strong case that, despite what he calls Japan's "studied passivity" toward China prior to 1972, Japanese politicians were in fact active under Tanaka's predecessor, Satō Eisaku, in establishing the groundwork for normalization and in advancing Japanese interests in China in other ways. In most meaningful respects, therefore, state-to-state relations existed between China and Japan well before 1972.

12. See, e.g., Bush, "China–Japan Tensions," for an example of an analysis that interprets China–Japan relations largely in these terms, suggesting that a security dilemma is to blame for the recurrent diplomatic challenges they face in their bilateral relations. Cheng's comprehensive historical analysis is also broadly consonant with the structural argument, though perhaps laying most of the blame on Japan; see Cheng, *China's Japan Policy*.

13. Mao Zedong, quoted in He, "Remembering and Forgetting," 50.

14. See Johnson, "Patterns of Japanese Relations with China," 406, 409.

15. Johnson, "Patterns of Japanese Relations with China," 409. Johnson cites Nakajima, "Mao and His Career."

16. He, "History, Chinese Nationalism," 4.

17. See Ogata, "Business Community," 196ff.

18. Realists might argue that Japan's image was positive because Japanese power was suppressed *or*, as He suggests, because rising Japanese power helped offset Soviet and American power; see He, "Remembering and Forgetting." Both arguments are plausible. Yet the claim that Japanese capabilities predict positive Chinese attitudes, no matter whether these capabilities are suppressed or growing, reveals just how ambiguous such arguments are.

19. He, "History, Chinese Nationalism," 5. He cites Mitter, "Behind the Scenes."

20. Buruma, "Dangerous Rift."

21. Vogel, Yuan, and Tanaka, *Golden Age*; also see Dreyer, *Middle Kingdom*, 156–87.

22. One might argue that despite the growth of Japanese power, the country's strong integration into the American orbit meant that Japan still could not pose a serious threat. Yet given the strongly anticommunist position of the United States and the US presence in Vietnam, both supported in crucial ways by Japan, it would have been equally reasonable for Beijing to conclude that Japanese power directly supported interests inimical to the Chinese state. This calculation did not come, however, until the 1990s.

23. Johnson, "Patterns of Japanese Relations with China," 421. As Johnson notes, no textbooks were actually changed in 1982, although an internal controversy was clearly brewing between the Japan Teachers' Union (*Nihon Kyōshokuin Kumiai*, or *Nikkyōso* for short) and more conservative bureaucrats in the Ministry of Education.

24. Zhang, "China's Relations with Japan," 198; and cf. Soeya, "Japan's Relations with China."

25. Over the course of 1990, the Nikkei 225 dropped 38 percent from 38,712.88 at the beginning of the year to 23,848.71 at the year's close. See the Nikkei's historical data website, http://indexes.nikkei.co.jp/en/nkave/archives/data.

26. Wang, "National Humiliation, History Education," 784.

27. Wang, "National Humiliation, History Education," 794–96.

28. For other accounts of Japan's postwar role as a key Chinese "other," see Suzuki, "Importance of 'Othering'"; Atanassova-Cornelis, "Chinese Nation Building"; Lindgren and Lindgren, "Identity Politics and the East China Sea."

29. See He, "Remembering and Forgetting," 62–63. On the burgeoning nationalism of this era, see also Gries, *China's New Nationalism*. The textbook revision controversies escalated considerably when a group of conservative historians published a *New History Textbook* (*Atarashii Rekishi Kyōkasho*) in 2000. Prime Minister Koizumi's repeated visits to Yasukuni Shrine beginning in 2001 also contributed greatly to the growing furor.

30. These events, and their effects on attitudes toward Japan, are discussed in detail in Chapter 7.

31. Weiss, *Powerful Patriots*.

32. Kahn, "If 22 Million Chinese Prevail."

33. Weiss, *Powerful Patriots*. Also see Wallace and Weiss, "Political Geography of Nationalist Protest"; Zhou and Wang, "Participation in Anti-Japanese Demonstrations."

34. Mochizuki, "Japan's Shifting Strategy."

35. See Maslow, "China and Japan," 189–206.

36. The 1994 reforms introduced a mixed system for elections to the National Diet that included both single-member districts and proportional voting for party lists. Amy Catalinac shows that this new system has caused a significant rise in issue voting at the national level; see Catalinac, *Electoral Reform*.

37. Dreyer, *Middle Kingdom*, 318.

38. Katzenstein, *World of Regions*.

39. He, "History, Chinese Nationalism," 18–19.

40. See Park, *North Korea*.

41. Cheong, *Politics of Anti-Japanese Sentiment*.

42. Cheong, *Politics of Anti-Japanese Sentiment*, xiii.

43. Kohno, "Limits of Neoliberal Institutionalism," 7.

44. Hemmer and Katzenstein, "Why Is There No NATO in Asia?" See also Hatch, *Ghosts in the Neighborhood*.

45. Hemmer and Katzenstein, "Why Is There No NATO in Asia?," 593–94.

46. Hemmer and Katzenstein, "Why Is There No NATO in Asia?," 593.

47. Johnson, "Japan: Who Governs?"; Pempel, "Bureaucratization of Policymaking"; Muramatsu and Krauss, "Bureaucrats and Politicians."

48. On June 3, 1964, as many as 50,000 demonstrators marched in Seoul against the normalization treaty, and the government was compelled to impose martial law. See Lee, "1960s in South Korea," 193. Victor Cha argues persuasively that the treaty itself was the result of American pressure, but this pressure evidently did little to change South Korean attitudes; see Cha, "Bridging the Gap."

49. Ross, "Nakasone Apologizes."

50. Lee, "Remembering 'Winter Sonata.'" Based in large measure on the success of *Winter Sonata*, Japanese tourism to South Korea surged in 2004 and 2005. See Kim et al., "Effects of Korean Television Dramas."

51. BBC, "South Korea's Lee Myung-bak Visits."

52. Kennedy and Nagakawa, "Public Divided."

53. Minegishi, "Yoon Era Stokes Hope."

54. Park, "Historical Memory," 195–96.

55. See Glosserman and Snyder, *Japan–South Korea Identity Clash*.

56. Pew Research Center, "How Asians View Each Other."

57. Increasing concern about China, particularly among younger voters, is gradually changing this. See Choe, "South Koreans Now Dislike China."

58. Morita and Ishihara, *"NO" to Ieru Nihon*. Ishihara's contributions were later published in English translation as well. See Ishihara, *Japan That Can Say No*.
59. Song et al., *Zhongguo keyi shuo bu*.
60. Ko, "South Korea's Search."
61. LaFeber, *Clash*, 47.
62. Curtis, *Yankees of the East*.
63. Kajima, *Emergence of Japan*, 180–201.
64. Takayoshi, "Development of Democracy in Japan." On the relationship of Taishō democracy to diplomacy and peaceful relations with other states, also see Thompson, "Democracy and Peace"; Samuels, *Rich Nation, Strong Army*, 95–99.
65. See Ngai for a detailed history of anti-immigration policies and the emergence of the "illegal alien" as a concept in early twentieth century American politics; Ngai, *Impossible Subjects*. Wilson's refusal to include a racial equality clause in the League of Nations Charter also stung many Japanese deeply; see Storry, *Japan and the Decline*, 87–99. For an account of how Yamagata Aritomo, a venerated general and "elder statesman" (*genrō*), gradually reached the conclusion that turn-of-the-century wars had racial origins, see Hackett, *Yamagata Aritomo*, 275.
66. Wick shows that perceptions of growing economic competition do not necessarily cause Americans to have more negative attitudes toward other countries; see Wick, "Capabilities, Cooperation, and Culture."
67. Thies, *United States, Israel*.
68. Risse-Kappen, "Ideas Do Not Float Freely."

CHAPTER 5

The Domestic Politics of Japan's Image

In the summer of 2017, Facebook hit a milestone with the addition of its 2 billionth active monthly user, continuing its reign as the largest social media platform in the world. In contrast, Twitter was much smaller, with only about 328 million active users.[1] Yet in its heyday it was Twitter, rather than Facebook, to which US President Donald Trump frequently resorted in dramatic and provocative fashion. The reason is aptly summarized by social media commentator Andrew Hutchinson: "Twitter's strength is real-time. No other social platform comes close on this front. While Facebook is trying to compete and Snapchat offers a unique perspective on the theme, Twitter remains our best indicator of the wider pulse of the world and what's happening within it."[2]

In China the equivalent service is provided by Sina Weibo (abbreviated as Weibo, meaning "microblog"), whose active users surpass those of Twitter, numbering about 340 million by 2017 and just short of 600 million in 2023.[3] Weibo is consequently one of the most influential social media platforms in the world. One notable difference between Weibo and services such as Facebook, Twitter, or Snapchat, however, is that Weibo is subject to direct control and censorship by the Chinese government (the popular Western services are banned in China). Weibo posts are automatically scanned by government software and, if any sensitive language is detected, passed directly to a government censor for approval or rejection.[4]

Surveillance and censorship of social media is not limited to China. It is evident that the United States also maintains an extensive program of government-run electronic surveillance of its own citizens and noncitizens alike.[5] States in general perceive an interest in monitoring and controlling various segments of society, and they have a wide range of mechanisms for doing so—arguably a greater range in the information age than ever before.[6] Nevertheless the so-called Great Firewall of China—the Golden Shield Project, or *jīndùn gōngchéng,* as it is more formally known—signals a particularly intrusive approach to surveillance and control in what remains an extremely strong state despite the gradual decline of its communist ideological trappings.[7] Freedom House ranks China as the world's "worst abuser of internet freedom" and notes that "a criminal law amendment added seven-year prison terms for spreading rumors on social media (a charge often used against those who criticize the authorities), while some users belonging to minority religious groups were imprisoned simply for watching religious videos on their mobile phones."[8] As Human Rights Watch sums up the situation in its annual country report, "China remains an authoritarian state, one that systematically curtails a wide range of fundamental human rights, including freedom of expression, association, assembly, and religion."[9]

So when protests occur in China against Japan, and to the extent that there is in China a robust nationalism targeting Japan as an unrepentant and still-threatening enemy, we might plausibly imagine that such nationalist expressions are fundamentally projects of the Chinese Communist Party (CCP) and the Chinese state. If they were not, they would not be permitted. Lokman Tsui argues that the modern Chinese state has at its disposal all of the tools—legal, economic, social, and technical—necessary to render contemporary Chinese society in the form of Bentham's Panopticon prison.[10] Zhao Yuezhi takes the somewhat more cautiously stated position that imperatives of economic growth and political control sometimes find themselves in tension in the online world of China, just as they have in other domains of Chinese society.[11] Nevertheless, she too argues that the Chinese media (traditional and social media alike) are fundamentally subservient to the political designs of the Chinese state.

The objective of the Chinese state, many observers have suggested, is stable control. With the collapse of communist ideology in the 1990s, a new rallying ideology was needed in China. "Patriotic passions help fill the spiritual void left by the loss of faith in communism," as Susan Shirk puts it, "and offer an idealistic alternative to the commercialism of Chinese society today."[12] China's current leader Xi Jinping himself has proclaimed: "The tasks our Party faces in reform, development, and stability are more onerous than ever—and the conflicts, dangers, and challenges are more numerous than ever."[13] Nationalist protest against Japan might be interpreted, then, as a response primarily to domestic needs. This claim is plausible, but the story of how Japan's image is affected by domestic politics in China (and in South Korea, for that matter) is not quite as simple as this story makes it appear.

THE SECOND IMAGE OF IMAGES

Standing against the argument that domestic politics stop at the border, and that a country's foreign policy is too important to be made subject to domestic political pressures, is the claim that such a sharp distinction has always been dangerously naïve. Kenneth Waltz called the latter perspective the "second image" of foreign policy.[14] Although he is widely known for the opposite claim—that international pressures constrain all states to behave in similar ways—even Waltz recognized that democracies differ from nondemocracies, and among themselves for that matter, in some elements of their foreign policies.[15] This argument runs against a realist orthodoxy that focuses entirely on the national interest and the pursuit of power or security within a complex international system. Yet ur-realist Hans Morgenthau, writing well before Waltz, similarly distinguished between what he called "revisionist" and "status quo" states, the former motivated by ideology or some other quirk of their domestic political arrangements to challenge the status quo internationally and the latter inclined by their own domestically institutionalized commitments to protect it.[16] Second image accounts of international relations gradually proliferated, notably including a large literature on the democratic peace and Peter Katzenstein's pathbreaking explorations of the way strong states differ from weak states in the formulation of their foreign policies.[17] Today it is probably more accurate to say that what distinguishes contemporary realists from other scholars is not the claim that domestic politics are unimportant but rather the claim that international considerations still take precedence over domestic ones.[18]

Broadly speaking, we might therefore contrast a logic of innenpolitik with realpolitik, of domestic with international primacy. The former holds that the most compelling constraints on the formulation and enactment of a state's foreign policy are not those of the international distribution of power or alliance requirements but rather concerns that are (literally) closer to home. As former speaker of the US House of Representatives Thomas "Tip" O'Neill was fond of observing, "all politics is local."[19] In the calculations of those in power, whether elected or not, patronage and negotiation are at the heart of policy. Although both can and frequently do cross national borders, as myriad examples of efforts by groups in one country to affect electoral outcomes in another attest, the densest networks of money politics and other favors are always at home. It should come as no surprise for domestic politics to shape foreign policy, therefore, bromides about politics stopping at the water's edge notwithstanding.

Yet the question at hand is not whether domestic politics have some sort of effect on foreign policy but the more specific problem of how this innenpolitik might shape attitudes toward another country. Even more specifically, how do domestic political arrangements in China and South Korea shape the attitudes of those countries' citizens toward Japan? This chapter will focus in greater detail on China, and much more briefly on South Korea. China is the more interesting case for this argument. On one hand, an authoritarian state can presumably afford to ignore domestic pressures more easily than a democracy. On the other, its leaders also presumably have less to gain than do leaders who might manipulate foreign policy for electoral purposes. A closer examination reveals that Chinese leaders are more constrained than their authoritarian image suggests, however, and that they also have more to gain. Their ability to reap such rewards is ultimately conditioned more by the effectiveness of their response to popular pressures than it is by their ability to create or direct public attitudes.

THE VIRTUE OF DEMONS

Having enemies pays certain dividends. The political "virtues" of demonizing outsiders were clear long before Donald Trump made this a centerpiece of contemporary American politics. Arguably, no people better understand the long-term advantages of building a wall than do the Chinese. The Great Wall insulated China for many centuries from the predations of aggressive kingdoms and nomadic raiders to its north and east.[20] Yet this point applies equally well to less literal contexts. The great firewall also protects the country from outside influences, and the notion that China's borders demarcate a barrier between civilized and uncivilized realms, between secure familial arrangements of China's inner political space and the insecurity of the outside world, is fundamental to Chinese cosmology.[21] China has long relied on metaphorical as well as physical walls between inside and outside to protect a sacred internal space from the profane world outside it.[22] "The task of leaders is to save China by expelling barbarians," as William Callahan puts it, and so "the civilization/barbarian distinction continues to be the structure of feeling that frames Chinese understandings of identity and security."[23]

It is not only the wall that has advantages, but also the enemy. In a metaphorical context, the wall is just a symptom of the distinction between inner and outer worlds, of the demarcation between self and a threatening or dangerous other. The literature on the political uses of the other is vast, and it is unnecessary to recapitulate here every conceivable way that external threats can be used for political advantage. In a survey of the literature on nationalism, to take just one example, Erica Downs and Phillip Saunders provide an excellent account of three prominent ways nationalist self/other distinctions are strategically deployed for political purpose: (1) to bolster weak or illegitimate regimes by blaming problems on "foreigners"; (2) to support the expansionist or militarist goals of specific groups within the state, or affiliated with the state; and (3) to gain an advantage in domestic electoral or other political competitions.[24] We might surmise that the first two nationalist strategies figure prominently in Chinese attitudes toward the United States and, even more, toward Japan. In a more democratic South Korea, on the other hand, the second and third strategies are presumably more relevant.

In either case, the virtue of finding external demons is that they provide justifications for policies—or politicians or political regimes—that would otherwise be unpopular. On the face of it, the Sino-Japanese relationship looks like a fairly easy case for this argument. After the Tiananmen uprising in particular, and the declining relevance of communist ideology in general, the CCP has needed a way of mobilizing popular support. By most accounts it has fostered new forms of nationalism specifically for this purpose.

The Tiananmen uprising concentrated the attention of China's leaders on their vulnerability, if any further reminder were needed, at a moment of extraordinary volatility and transformation for communist political regimes. This uprising might be thought of as the opening, and perhaps the most potent, salvo in a series of challenges to China's leadership brought on by its own efforts at reform and modernization. Roughly a decade later, the Falun Gong sect appeared to represent another challenge to the party's authority. As the first decade of the twentieth century wore on and ethnic separatism appeared to flourish in Tibet and Xinjiang, China's leaders identified still other threats to their power and position.

It is telling that, although all of these upswings in resistance to CCP authority came from internal actors, they were consistently represented by the party itself as external threats. In a very interesting study of the way party officials talk about such threats, Alistair Iain Johnston shows that statements decrying "hostile forces"—understood, in keeping with the inside/outside cosmology described previously, as outside forces—in the *People's Daily* and the *Liberation Army Daily* peak after moments of perceived threat.[25] These two newspapers are the definitive outlets of policy orthodoxy for the CCP and the Chinese military.

The most straightforward interpretation of this evidence is that upticks in CCP complaints about hostile forces represent, in each case, a response to moments of internal vulnerability. The first big peak in editorials decrying hostile forces occurs immediately after the Tiananmen uprising. The second, beginning around 1999, corresponds to the Communist Party's crackdown on Falun Gong. And the third, in 2009, follows the 2008 uprisings in Tibet and the Ürümqi riots in Xinjiang. This pattern corresponds to the first form of nationalist innenpolitik identified by Downs and Saunders.[26] In general Johnston's data appear to provide strong prima facie evidence that the CCP manages internal threats with a strategy of distraction that emphasizes external threats to the body politic instead.

Although this pattern of distraction is evident in editorials drawn from both the *People's Daily* and the *Liberation Army Daily*, an interesting divergence in these two key party organs also seems to emerge in recent years. After 2010 references to hostile forces began to climb again in the *Liberation Army Daily* but not in the *People's Daily*. Johnston's explanation for this is that beginning under Hu Jintao, and then increasingly under Xi Jinping, fostering greater support for the CCP leadership within the ranks of the military has been a greater preoccupation than popular support. Johnston believes that this explanation is "consistent with Xi's own analysis of the collapse of the Soviet Communist Party—namely, that a key reason for the collapse was the Soviet military's abandonment of the Party."[27] In consequence, Johnston concludes, Xi "is more worried about 'foreign' ideological subversion in the military than in society writ large."[28]

This explanation is certainly plausible, but it is also conceivable that a new era of military professionalization has created incentives for the military itself to emphasize external threats. David Shambaugh, undoubtedly one of the most careful Western observers of the Chinese military, has pointed out that the professionalization of the People's Liberation Army (PLA) has had far-reaching consequences in the past. "The PLA had, during the 1980s, been led (and trained) to believe that they should disengage from the political arena and prepare themselves to fight external enemies. When called upon by Deng and the Central Military Commission to enforce martial law, clear Tiananmen Square and reclaim Beijing, the PLA's new professional ethic was fundamentally challenged."[29] In some cases the PLA hesitated to act directly against the people, and so "in the wake of Tiananmen numerous reports of rank insubordination circulated inside and outside China."[30] It is precisely this threat of insubordination to which Johnston points. But the up-and-down pattern of emphasizing "hostile forces" since Tiananmen points to something more complex, and the divergence of emphasis on threats in the *Liberation Army Daily* from the *People's Daily* is a more recent phenomenon.

Downs and Saunders's second rationale for nationalist innenpolitik is to advance the interests of military or other leadership groups in a domestic competition for legitimacy and influence, and this argument suggests an alternative explanation for the post-2010 pattern seen in Figure 5.1. The existence of hostile forces is, of course, excellent justification for policies favoring the military and its growth in an era when sustaining China's overall economic growth is likely to become increasingly challenging. And formally, at least, the *Liberation Army Daily* is a publication of the PLA, not the CCP. Still, there is undeniably close political coordination of major PLA statements. As Shambaugh notes, "organizationally, the Communist Party penetrates the military structure from top to bottom."[31] And yet the reverse cannot always be said. PLA membership on the Politburo peaked in 1977, when fully 59 percent of Politburo members were members of the PLA. By 1987 that figure had fallen to just 12 percent.[32] In the Politburo announced

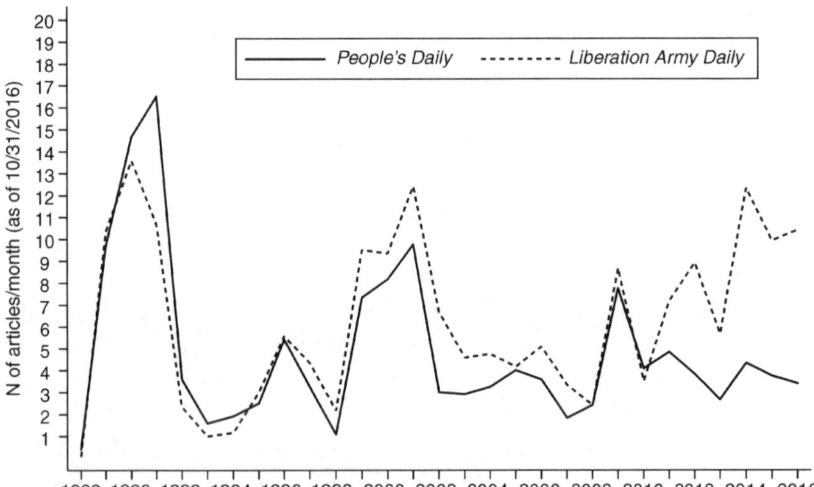

Figure 5.1. Average Monthly Number of Articles in the *People's Daily* and the *Liberation Army Daily* That Use the Term "Hostile Forces." *From Alastair Iain Johnston, "Is Chinese Nationalism Rising? Evidence from Beijing."* International Security, 41, no. 3 (Winter 2016/17): 7–43.

at the Nineteenth Party Congress by Xi Jinping in 2017, only two of twenty-five Politburo members (8 percent) were PLA members.[33]

To the extent that Johnston is correct and that PLA loyalty is a prime concern for Xi, this apparent distancing of the PLA from the Politburo is puzzling. It is possible, of course, that Xi simply believes his most loyal allies are elsewhere. But elevating his supporters in the military would make a great deal of sense if he were worried about PLA loyalty. It may well be, instead, that it is the PLA that must now worry about its position and privilege. To the extent this is true, the specter of external threats from Japan or the United States will improve the military's bargaining position.

The political status of the military will, no doubt, continue to be an interesting question for China-watchers. Whether Johnston's explanation or the one I have indirectly attributed to Shambaugh proves correct—whether Xi is worried about the military, or whether the military is worried about Xi, or perhaps both—the very divergence of *People's Daily* and *Liberation Army Daily* editorials provides some evidence for Downs and Saunders's second hypothesis. That different messages are sent to different parts of Chinese society implies a degree of jockeying for political position.

We should not lose sight of Johnston's overall argument that nationalism is *not* on the rise in China, notwithstanding the widespread claims that it is.[34] Johnston's point is that China is not, in general, experiencing greater nationalism than other countries. Nor, he argues, is the level of nationalism in China today greater than it has been in the past. Allen Carlson takes a similar position and argues that excessive preoccupation with Chinese nationalism obscures the more important problem of how Chinese national identity is formed and how it influences the country's behavior and policies.[35] In any case, the concern of this chapter is not with overall levels of nationalism in China but rather with the uses to which such nationalism can be put.

The term "hostile forces" on which Johnston focuses is ambiguous, but there is considerable other evidence that Japan in particular serves as the most prominent foil—even more than the United States—for nationalist sentiments within China. The post-Tiananmen national patriotic education campaign targeted Japan in particular. When the CCP created dozens of new museums and monuments to serve as "patriotic education bases," more of them memorialized conflict with Japan than any other foreign adversary.[36] Zhao Suisheng sees the "Communist state as the architect of nationalism in China" and argues that the post-Tiananmen patriotic education campaign was a key mechanism of this project.[37] William Callahan and Wang Zheng have also explored the political uses of "national humiliation" (*guóchǐ*) in great detail.[38] In textbooks, on maps, and through films, China's citizens are taught never to forget their one hundred years of national humiliation (*băinián guóchĭ*) at the hands of Britain, to be sure, but above all Japan.[39] What particularly stings about this humiliation, Peter Gries argues, was Japan's hubris in ignoring its proper place and filial duty to China.[40] Or, as Callahan puts it, "many Chinese people see Japan as a barbaric 'country of ingratitude' because it has turned on its teacher while still refusing to face up to its horrible crimes from the twentieth century."[41]

The CCP therefore has at its disposal powerful and resonant imagery for the purpose of securing its own position or to be deployed in internal power struggles. Yet the evidence that such considerations of innenpolitik are the prime drivers of anti-Japanese sentiment is mostly circumstantial. Japan is certainly a target of nationalist campaigns in China, and the timing of such campaigns suggests an effort by CCP officials to improve their position, either with respect to society in general or in struggles among elites. It is also plausible, however, that party officials are responding to public pressures as much as they are fomenting anti-Japanese attitudes. Even if contemporary anti-Japanese attitudes owe a good deal to the CCP's patriotic education campaigns, they also take on a life of their own, a phenomenon that Steven Van Evera termed "blowback."[42] Increasingly, these attitudes may constrain party officials rather than empowering them.

The notion that public patriotism constrains national elites is Downs and Saunders's third form of nationalist innenpolitik. One might expect this form to be more prevalent in a democracy than in a more authoritarian political system. And so, before considering the plausibility of this phenomenon in China, a brief consideration of the "easier" South Korean case is in order.

THE DEMON OF VIRTUE

South Korean officials, like those in China, have long resorted to anti-Japanese declarations as a way of establishing their bona fides with the more nationalist segments of the electorate. Particularly during the early postwar era, according to Cheong Sung-Hwa, anti-Japanese sentiment was virtually the only currency available to Korean politicians to bolster their legitimacy within a fundamentally undemocratic system.[43] With the advent of democracy under the Sixth Republic, on the other hand, Park Cheol-Hee argues that South Korean politicians have tended to be more reactive to perceived Japanese slights such as visits to Yasukuni Shrine rather than proactively seeking to demonize Japan.[44] Yet even so, Korean politicians must placate an electorate convinced of its own virtue in the context of Korea-Japanese relations. This unrequited sense of virtue remains far from satisfied by agreements such as the one reached by Park Geun-hye and Abe Shinzō in 2015 to resolve the issue of compensation for Korean comfort women.[45] The Korean sense of patriotic virtue has, in other words, itself become a "demon" that bedevils an important alliance relationship for both countries.

In a recent, brief essay, Robert Kelly identified three hypotheses to explain negative South Korean attitudes toward Japan. They parallel Downs and Saunders's hypotheses almost exactly: (1) Koreans have always been anti-Japanese, but their attitudes were manipulated by the government until the era of democracy; (2) the emergence of a newer generation of South Korean elites has brought more negative attitudes; and (3) with democratization, the South Korean government has been compelled to seek electoral legitimation to a greater extent than before.[46] In other words, South Korean politicians either manipulated patriotic attitudes, or specific groups of elites did, or elites were conversely forced by the electoral process to curry favor with public opinion.

Although the evidence in South Korea is somewhat ambiguous, it increasingly favors the third, electoral mechanism.[47] Efforts to recognize the fortieth anniversary of normalized relations by celebrating a year of South Korea–Japan friendship in 2005, for example, collapsed in acrimony in March of that year when the Shimane Prefectural Assembly in Japan proclaimed an annual Takeshima Day shortly after Japan's ambassador to South Korea, Takano Toshiyuki, had reiterated Japan's claim to the island.[48] These actions set off widespread protests in South Korea, prompting President Roh Moo-hyun to issue a strident condemnation of Japan. Rather than having orchestrated these tensions, however, Roh's behavior appears largely to be a reaction to popular sentiment that compelled him to speak out. Similarly, in her 2012 campaign for the presidency, Park Geun-hye laid out a vision of *trustpolitik* with North Korea and promised a "bonanza" associated with eventual Korean unification while decrying Japan's failure to arrive at a "correct view of history."[49] Park herself was disposed to cooperate with Japan, but she was also vulnerable on this score because her father (former President Park Chung-hee) was seen as overly sympathetic to Japan, and so electoral incentives weighed heavily on her rhetoric.

After Park's impeachment and removal from office in 2017, the frontrunner in the ensuing election was *not* compelled to demonize Japan. Rather, Park's impeachment gave Moon Jae-in's liberal Minjoo Party an alternative electoral strategy of campaigning against the corruption of Park's conservatives. Moon was associated with Roh and was widely expected in Japan to signal another potential turn toward ill will in this crucial relationship. After all, South Korea's progressives have generally tended to be more critical of Japan whereas conservatives have focused more often on the threat posed by China and North Korea.[50] And yet, during the election, Moon generally did not avail himself of the anti-Japanese strategy. Given the choice between appealing to anti-Japan nationalism and an anticorruption strategy that presents fewer diplomatic risks, Moon opted for the safer, less nationalistic course. On the other hand, once in office, the challenge of governing meant that Moon eventually found himself taking a page from Park's playbook, calling for rapprochement with North Korea while maintaining a studied distance from Japan.[51]

In sum, it is hard to dispute the claim that anti-Japanese nationalism plays some sort of role in South Korean party politics and electoral strategy. Yet for the most part South Korean politicians seem to react to public disapproval of Japan rather than to inflame it strategically. Recent history is more consistent with Downs and Saunders's third form of nationalist innenpolitik, that is, than with the first two. Turning back to the case of China, one might wonder whether a similar historical transition is underway. Although China cannot be said to have democratized—and observers as intellectually diverse as David Shambaugh and Daniel Bell argue it is moving *away* from democratization—it is nevertheless possible that Communist Party leaders increasingly react to public sentiment, rather than direct it, when it comes to anti-Japanese attitudes.[52]

The accounts of nationalist innenpolitik in China discussed so far have tended to emphasize the strategic objectives of the CCP, or of particular groups of Chinese elites, in fostering anti-Japanese sentiment. Yet party officials are well aware that nationalism can get out of hand. As Zheng Yongnian points out, "nationalism . . . is a double-edged sword. When a nationalistic movement becomes uncontrollable, socio-political stability will be endangered. This is what happened to Mao's China."[53] One consequence of this strategy is that, under Mao, CCP leadership itself was closely associated with the PLA. Deng began a process of reducing the military's sphere of influence to such an extent that Jiang Zemin was compelled to make new efforts to improve relations with the military even as he moved to cement party control after the Tiananmen uprising. In Zheng's view, even as Jiang's government responded to Tiananmen with new patriotic education campaigns, it was keenly aware that "popular nationalism needed to be constrained to some degree, and China's foreign policy-making could not be affected by such domestic nationalistic pressure."[54] Zheng goes on to explain,

The issue was how the "anti-China" theories could be responded to nationalistically so that popular nationalistic sentiments could be appeased and domestic stability not affected. The campaign against the "anti-China" theories could be well controlled if the military took charge of it. Thus, instead of a nationwide political movement, the government initiated a rhetoric campaign against such theories. Jiang Zemin and other senior leaders, especially those from the military, used different occasions to speak out, nevertheless in a moderate form. While social groups expressed their strong sentiments, the leadership remained pragmatic.[55]

In general Zheng perceives a civilian–military coalition at work seeking to manage popular nationalist uprisings so that the patriotic education campaigns do not lead to uncontrollable sentiments.[56] This is a more complex view that incorporates all three of Downs and Saunders's pathways (even in an undemocratic system).

Like Zheng, Zhao Suisheng argues that "although the Chinese government is hardly above exploiting nationalist sentiment when doing so suits its purposes, Beijing has practiced a pragmatic nationalism tempered by diplomatic prudence."[57] Nationalism may well be, Zhao acknowledges, "an instrument that the Chinese Communist Party (CCP) uses to bolster the population's faith in a troubled political system and to hold the country together during its period of rapid and turbulent transformation into a post-Communist society."[58] Yet it is also something that could easily get out of hand. And so the reality, Zhao argues, "is that Beijing is seeking to rein in rising Chinese nationalism, particularly its liberal strand, while preventing the even more threatening nativist and antitraditionalist strands from emerging."[59]

Of course, it is not only nationalist sentiment but also other forms of protest that might spiral out of control. David Shambaugh observes, for example, that "Tibet and Xinjiang simply seethe with hostility and frustration."[60] Susan Shirk characterizes China as a "fragile superpower," acutely aware of the potential for nationalist movements to spill over into other parts of Chinese society in ways that could threaten CCP control.[61] Joseph Fewsmith likewise argues that China's leaders are and must remain preoccupied with a growing internal legitimacy crisis.[62] And Manfred Elfstrom has documented with great care the growing incidence of labor protests in major Chinese cities.[63] Broadly speaking, Chinese labor protests have been on the rise since about 2007.[64] They are concentrated primarily in the large and economically dynamic urban areas that are the home of China's export manufacturing industries. Elfstrom's analysis suggests that such protests are linked in large measure to heightened public expectations associated with the growth of China's overall economy.[65] As with so many other challenges, rising expectations are a potent concern for CCP officials.

Clearly, the Chinese government has many forms of internal dissent—actual and potential—to manage, and there is a very real prospect that one form of protest (e.g., against Japan) could suddenly spill over into another (against Han control in Xinjiang, or for improved working conditions). Shirk's characterization of China as "fragile" and its leadership as vulnerable seems apt. This does not entirely negate the perspective with which this chapter began—that the state wields considerable authority and manages popular sentiment in ways that preserve its own position—but it makes clear that Chinese nationalism is not entirely a top-down morality play orchestrated by the CCP's propaganda departments.

One of the most prominent recent episodes of surging nationalist sentiment helps to illustrate this point. In August 2012, protests erupted in numerous Chinese cities after the Japanese government announced its decision to nationalize the disputed Senkaku/Diaoyu Islands. Jeremy Wallace and Jessica Chen Weiss have carefully documented the incidence and geography of these protests, which swept through 208 of China's 287 prefectural cities (including all of the largest urban agglomerations in the country).[66] At their peak, on September 18, there were protests in 128 different prefectural cities.[67] Of course there were also cities where protests did not occur. In general, protests were more common in the large, politically important cities of China's east with large populations of migrants and college students. These are also the cities in which patriotic education bases are more likely to be located. They were less likely in the cities of China's west with larger minority (non-Han) populations. Wallace and Weiss argue that "variation in nationalist mobilization reflects both grassroots propensity to protest and state willingness to tolerate popular mobilization. Citizens are galvanized by genuine anger at provocative foreign actions. Government statements and media coverage raise the salience of foreign insults and signal that nationalist outrage is politically acceptable."[68] In another study of the 2012 protests, Gries, Steiger, and Wang found it was popular sentiment that put pressure on the government, and not the other way around.[69] Yet they, too, acknowledge the role of signaling and the ability of the state to clamp down on protests when necessary.

To push the analysis of the 2012 protests somewhat further, it would be interesting to know whether the geography and the frequency of anti-Japanese protests correspond in any way to the occurrence of other forms of protests, such as labor protests. Elfstrom kindly supplied his labor protest data, and Wallace and Weiss the replication dataset from their study, in order to test this relationship. I combined the two in a composite dataset documenting both nationalist and labor protests from June 1 through September 30, 2012.[70] Both types of protests are recorded in the dataset, yielding labor and nationalist protest frequency counts for each of 286 prefectural cities in Wallace and Weiss's original dataset.[71] The data also includes measures of demographic considerations such as population (total and logarithmically transformed), the percentage of college students within the population, and an indexed measure of city-level GDP.

If the state-centric approach best captures the dynamics of nationalist innenpolitik in China, then we might expect to find a positive relationship between Elfstrom's data on one hand and Wallace and Weiss's on the other. To the extent that the state manages and directs popular dissent, then nationalist protests should serve as a mechanism for deflecting or distracting from labor protests. In areas where, or at times when, labor protests flourish, the state should be more inclined to redirect this dissent away from targets that might implicate CCP officials and, instead, toward external enemies of the state. In these circumstances, the state should encourage nationalist protests or, where they arise, it should allow them to flourish rather than tamping them down.

We might begin with a test resembling the analysis conducted by Wallace and Weiss in their study of where nationalist protests occur.[72] Table 5.1 shows a logistic regression test for two different models of the relationship between nationalist protests and several other variables, including labor protests. The two models are distinguished by the time lag between labor protests and the nationalist protests that erupted in mid-August 2012 after the Japanese government announced its decision to nationalize the Senkaku/Diaoyu Islands. Model 1 considers labor protests from June to August 14, 2012—prior to the beginning of widespread nationalist protests. Model 2 considers protests from the time that nationwide anti-Japan protests began on August 15, running through September 2012. By considering these two models independently, we are able to distinguish the effects of prior labor protests from those of concurrent labor protests.

Although the two models are divided temporally, the analysis is spatial: it asks *where* protests occurred. In both periods, the larger the city and the larger the percentage of college students within it, the more likely it was to experience nationalist protests. This is consistent with Wallace and Weiss's original findings. The occurrence of labor protests prior to August 15 also approaches significance as a predictor of nationalist protests (Model 1), whereas labor protests in the latter period (Model 2) are not a significant

Table 5.1: Logit Analysis of Nationalist Protests by Prefectural City

Variable	Model 1: June-Aug. 14			Model 2: Aug. 15-Sept.		
	B	S.E.	Sig.	*B*	S.E.	Sig.
Labor Protests	1.298	0.685	.058	0.306	0.398	.442
Log Total Population	1.086	0.246	.000	1.104	0.243	.000
College Student %	0.616	0.188	.001	0.620	0.186	.001
Constant	-6.062	1.442	.000	-6.098	1.423	.000

n=272
Model 1: Corrected Cox-Snell (Nagelkerke) $R^2 = 0.279$.
Model 2: Corrected Cox-Snell (Nagelkerke) $R^2 = 0.254$.

predictor of nationalist protests. This is to say, anti-Japanese nationalist protests in late August and September 2012 appear more likely to occur in cities that had experienced labor protests in the preceding two and a half months than in cities that had not. But they were *not* significantly more likely in cities that were experiencing ongoing labor unrest at the same time (or afterward). It is at least plausible, therefore, to imagine that authorities were more likely to allow nationalist protests in places where it could use them to turn public attention from labor disputes to Japanese malfeasance. Of course, it is also plausible that these are simply larger cities with larger groups of people (such as college students) who are easy to mobilize and better organized cadres of protesters in general. If the latter explanation is correct, then these are simply the spaces where *any* kind of protest is likely to happen. On the other hand, if this explanation were satisfactory, there should also have been an observed correlation between labor and nationalist protests in late August and September (if both tended to occur, that is, in the same kinds of spaces).

Potentially an even better way to test the willingness of authorities to allow nationalist protests is to consider not simply the spatial distribution but also the duration of anti-Japanese protests. Even where protests against Japan welled up spontaneously, it is consistent with the state-centric hypothesis to expect that such protests would be allowed to go on longer (and thus occur with greater frequency) in areas that had experienced other forms of unrest, such as more frequent labor protests. Table 5.2 shows the results of a regression analysis of protest frequency (the number of protests that occurred in each prefectural city from August 15 through September 30. Again, the analysis incorporates two models: the first includes labor protest data from June to mid-August, and the second includes labor protests from August 15 through September 30, the period of peak anti-Japanese protests.

Once again, and in both models, cities with larger populations in general and larger populations of college students were significantly more likely to experience anti-Japanese protests of greater frequency and duration. Wealthier cities, on the other hand, were less likely to experience anti-Japanese protests, suggesting as Wallace and Weiss found that "nationalist protests should be easiest to mobilize where socio-economic grievances are higher, perhaps owing to sluggish economic growth."[73] And as with the spatial analysis presented in Table 5.1, Table 5.2 shows that anti-Japanese protests occurred more frequently in areas that had experienced labor protest in the preceding months. In this case, however, Model 2 in Table 5.2 shows that nationalist protests were also more frequent in areas that experienced ongoing labor protests (in late August through September).

In other words, the protest frequency data suggest that anti-Japanese protests were more numerous both in the cities that had experienced labor unrest *and* in those that continued to experience ongoing labor unrest. It is plausible to think that Chinese authorities allowed the protests to go on, given their statistical association with labor protests. Yet if the protests against Japan were part of a conscious state-led strategy of distraction, they were not particularly effective, since the areas where they were allowed to go on seem to have continued to experience strikes and other forms of labor protests as well. In any case, the lack of statistical association between

Table 5.2: Regression Analysis of Nationalist Protest Frequency

Variables	B	S.E.	Standardized Beta	t	Sig.
			Model 1: June-Aug. 14		
Constant	0.834	0.716		-1.164	.245
College Student %	0.148	0.029	0.280	5.130	.000
Log Total Population	0.507	0.091	0.296	5.589	.000
GDP Index	-0.079	0.028	-0.153	-2.826	.005
Labor Protests (to 8/14)	0.177	0.084	0.116	2.096	.037
			Model 2: Aug. 15-Sept.		
Constant	-0.876	0.707		-1.239	.216
College Student %	0.123	0.030	0.233	4.076	.000
Log Total Population	0.503	0.090	0.294	5.615	.000
GDP Index	-0.075	0.028	-0.144	-2.705	.007
Labor Protests (8/15 on)	0.334	0.102	0.190	3.285	.001

n=271

Model 1: R^2=0.290; Adj. R^2=0.279.

Model 2: R^2=0.306; Adj. R^2=0.296.

ongoing labor protests and the location of anti-Japanese protests (as shown in Table 5.1, Model 2) suggests that the sudden, nationwide outbreak of anti-Japanese protests was more likely spontaneous than orchestrated by the CCP even if party officials may have allowed them to continue in places where they served a strategic purpose (Table 5.2).

The most plausible explanation for these protest frequency data, therefore, is probably the one offered by Wallace and Weiss, who advance a hybrid model of feedback loops between popular sentiment and CCP efforts to manage and direct public opinion. The general pattern of evidence—in their analysis as well as mine, and based on the conclusions of other observers including Johnston, Hyun and Kim, Reilly, and Gries, Steiger, and Wang—is that Chinese officials must increasingly worry about how best to respond to public pressures and sentiments regarding Japan irrespective of their own occasional efforts to manipulate these sentiments.[74] They do appear to make such efforts, but the truly large protests (protests that might risk getting out of hand) are unlikely to be their work. In another related analysis, Christopher Cairns and Allen Carlson studied microblog posts on Weibo during the 2012 anti-Japanese protests and found strong evidence for a genuine and powerful popular response in China to Japan's actions, including much invective aimed at the Chinese government itself for an ineffectual response.[75] Yet they also found evidence that censorship of this topic on Weibo dropped on August 18, near the peak of the first wave of protests, suggesting a coordinated government strategy of permissiveness. And an earlier investigation of Chinese protests over Japan's textbook revisions in 2005 also finds evidence that the protests began, at least, as a spontaneous popular movement.[76] Overall it seems likely that causation moves in both directions. Even though the government exercises a degree of control, it must also take popular sentiment into account, both for its own sake and because it is a meaningful currency in intra-elite competitions.

MANAGING HURT FEELINGS

Bruce Dickson, a specialist on the political consequences of economic reform in China, summarizes what he calls the "dictator's dilemma" as follows: "in the popular imagination, China's political system is a brutal authoritarian regime that represses its critics, is riddled with corrupt and venal officials, and is in danger of collapse if it does not sustain rapid economic growth."[77] There is truth in this account, he goes on to say, but it also ignores the comparatively high levels of popular support that the Chinese government enjoys. This chapter has explored the extent to which negative characterizations of Japan have played a role, alongside economic growth, in sustaining that support. And to the extent demonizing Japan does play such a role, it asks whether this because the CCP has orchestrated a certain image of Japan for its own purposes, or whether it is because the party is merely taking advantage of popular sentiments that are at least partly independent of its own efforts at image manipulation and control.

Broadly speaking, Dickson does not actually think that nationalist appeals (anti-Japanese or otherwise) are the most important elements of the CCP's strategy for survival and adaptation. Rather he focuses on the management of internal dissent, the provision of necessary public goods (including not only general economic growth but specific improvements in education, health care, and so on), and improvements in governance (including the reduction of public corruption). He sums up these three strategies as repression, cooptation, and legitimation. In general, Dickson is in broad agreement with Johnston and Carlson that the Western preoccupation with Chinese nationalism is overblown.[78]

Seen from the perspective of Tokyo, however, Chinese nationalism nevertheless remains a major concern. It has profound consequences for the two countries' relationship, as does Japanese nationalism for that matter. This chapter has said nothing about the latter, but it is worth noting that China has increasingly come to play the role of "demon" in Japan over the past two decades, just as Japan has done in China. Cheung Mong makes the case, for example, that the visits to Yasukuni Shrine by Koizumi Junichirō and Abe Shinzō were driven fundamentally by political calculations.[79] Even though the shrine visits consistently roil Japan's relations with China and South Korea, they are, according to Cheung, a means of shoring up support from an important segment of the Liberal Democratic Party's conservative base. Ku Yangmo and Stephen Nagy make similar arguments, although other observers point out that there is no general upswelling of support within Japan for changing the constitutional status of the Self-Defense Forces.[80]

In general, all three forms of nationalist innenpolitik identified by Downs and Saunders appear to offer insights into Chinese and South Korean attitudes toward Japan.[81] There are good reasons to believe that these countries' leaders perceive certain political advantages in demonizing Japan. Yet it is equally clear that a good part of this advantage, in both countries, depends on a genuine and direct public response to Japan's perceived affronts. We cannot reduce the question of how Japan is perceived in China and South Korea *purely* to considerations of domestic political manipulation in these countries. How Chinese and South Korean citizens perceive Japan is also a matter of their emotional response to its behavior, or that of its leaders, past and present.

It is easy to dismiss as hyperbolic Chinese claims that Japan has "hurt the feelings of the Chinese people" (*shānghài zhōngguó rénmín de gǎnqíng*), particularly because this has become such a common trope in recent years.[82] "Poor China," the editors of *The Economist* opine, "so vast and so sensitive."[83] It is also easy to dismiss such emotions because we have no general theories of how hurt feelings might be relevant in international relations, and barely even a lexicon with which to describe and discuss "national feelings." Feelings are hard things to see, and so we tend not to take them seriously. And yet if domestic politics is relevant to the way Japan is seen in other Asian capitals, then so are feelings. Psychopolitik is an important part of innenpolitik.

Notes

1. Ingram, "Facebook Hits 2 Billion." At the end of 2024, Facebook had over 3 billion monthly active users; see Geuens, "Top Social Media Platforms."
2. Hutchinson, "Here's Why Twitter Is So Important." Since its rebranding as X, Twitter's growth has stagnated, and current estimates of its monthly active users are similar to those in 2017; see Geuens, "How Many Users."
3. BBC, "Twitter User Numbers." At its peak in 2023, Sina Weibo surpassed 600 million monthly active users, and it retains about that many in 2025; see Geuens, "Top Social Media Platforms." As in the United States with Facebook, an even larger social media platform in China, WeChat (Wēixìn), offers a variety of commercial and communication services (resembling those of WhatsApp and Skype, combined with gaming and ecommerce apps) and has surpassed 1 billion active monthly users; see Deng, "Tencent's WeChat." The closest analog to pre-X Twitter, however, is Sina Weibo.
4. Wang, "Business of Censorship."
5. Gellman and Poitras, "US, British Intelligence Mining Data"; Greenwald and MacAskill, "NSA Prism Program."
6. Krueger, "Government Surveillance"; Slobogin, *Privacy at Risk.*
7. Denyer, "China's Scary Lesson."
8. Freedom House, "Silencing the Messenger."
9. Human Rights Watch, "China."
10. Tsui, "Panopticon."
11. Zhao, *Media, Market, and Democracy;* Zhao, *Communication in China.*
12. Shirk, *China,* 64.
13. Xi, "Shuoming"; cited in Shambaugh, "Contemplating China's Future," 121.
14. Waltz, *Man, the State, and War.*
15. Waltz, *Foreign Policy and Democratic Politics.*
16. Morgenthau, *Politics among Nations.*

17. Katzenstein, *Between Power and Plenty*; Katzenstein, *Small States*. An important early statement of the democratic peace hypothesis can be found in Doyle, "Kant, Liberal Legacies."

18. Rose, "Neoclassical Realism."

19. Matthews, *Hardball*.

20. Waldron, *Great Wall of China*.

21. Wang, *Empire and Local Worlds*.

22. For a more theoretical treatment of the inside/outside political binary, see Walker, *Inside/Outside*. A related, classic account of sacred and profane spaces is offered by Eliade, *Sacred and the Profane*. Edward Said and Iver Neumann offer invaluable discussions of the way this binary is typically applied to an East/West context; see Said, *Orientalism*; Neumann, *Uses of the Other*.

23. Callahan, *China*, 23.

24. Downs and Saunders, "Legitimacy," 114.

25. Johnston, "Is Chinese Nationalism Rising?," 37. It is also conceivable, of course, that CCP officials are more likely to direct the public's attention to outside threats when they actually face such threats. Jessica Chen Weiss makes the related argument that the CCP allows domestic protests as part of an international bargaining strategy; see Weiss, *Powerful Patriots*. By constraining leaders, domestic protests actually improve their hand in international negotiations (Chinese leaders can plausibly claim that their hands are tied as a result of domestic opinion). The problem with this argument, however, is that the broader pattern of worsening or improving relations between China and Japan doesn't correspond particularly well to moments of strategic necessity, as argued in the preceding chapter.

26. Downs and Saunders, "Legitimacy."

27. Johnston, "Is Chinese Nationalism Rising?," 38.

28. Johnston, "Is Chinese Nationalism Rising?," 38.

29. Shambaugh, "Soldier and the State," 552.

30. Shambaugh, "Soldier and the State," 552.

31. Shambaugh, "Soldier and the State," 550.

32. Shambaugh, "Soldier and the State," 534.

33. Li, "China's New Politburo."

34. Johnston, "Is Chinese Nationalism Rising?"

35. Carlson, "Flawed Perspective"; Carlson, "It Should Not Only Be about Nationalism."

36. Wang, "National Humiliation, History Education."

37. Zhao, "State-Led Nationalism," 288.

38. Callahan, "History, Identity, and Security"; Callahan, *China*; Wang, "National Humiliation, History Education"; Wang, *Never Forget National Humiliation*.

39. Wang, *Never Forget National Humiliation*.

40. Gries, *China's New Nationalism*.

41. Callahan, *China*, 162.

42. Van Evera, "Causes of War." Snyder adopts the same term to explain how German leaders before World War II came to believe what was largely propaganda before World War I; see Snyder, *Myths of Empire*.

43. Cheong, *Politics of Anti-Japanese Sentiment*.

44. Park, "Historical Memory."

45. Panda, "Final and Irreversible."

46. Kelly, "Three Hypotheses."

47. See, inter alia, Kim, "Escaping the Vicious Cycle"; Ku, "Role of Identity"; Seo, "Diagnosing Korea–Japan Relations."

48. Onishi, "Dispute over Islets Frays Ties." *Takeshima* is the Japanese name for a disputed island administered by South Korea, where it is called *Dokdo*.

49. Snyder, "South Korean Identity," 105–6.

50. See, e.g., Jo, "Memory, Institutions"; Koo and Choi, "Who Takes the Japanese Threat Seriously?" Cf. Chae and Kim, "Conservatives and Progressives."

51. Phillips, Lee, and Yi, "Future of South Korea–Japan Relations." Sakaki also argues that a deepening left/right political divide in South Korea left Moon with few options other than the time-honored one of appealing to anti-Japanese sentiment to bolster his support; see Sakaki, "Japan–South Korea Relations."

52. Shambaugh, *China's Future*; Bell, *China Model*. For a parallel discussion of the CCP's responsiveness to public pressure on economic matters, see Jin, *Politics of Economic Inequality*.

53. Zheng, *Discovering Chinese Nationalism*, 103.

54. Zheng, *Discovering Chinese Nationalism*, 104.

55. Zheng, *Discovering Chinese Nationalism*, 104.

56. Zheng, *Discovering Chinese Nationalism*, 102 ff.

57. Zhao, "China's Pragmatic Nationalism," 132.

58. Zhao, "China's Pragmatic Nationalism," 132.

59. Zhao, "China's Pragmatic Nationalism," 143. For a similar argument, see Liao, "Presentist or Cultural Memory."

60. Shambaugh, "Contemplating China's Future," 129.

61. Shirk, *China*.

62. Fewsmith, "Challenges of Stability."

63. Elfstrom, *Workers and Change*; Elfstrom and Kuruvilla, "Changing Nature of Labor Unrest."

64. See Elfstrom, *Workers and Change*.

65. Elfstrom, *Workers and Change*. Also see Jin, *Politics of Economic Inequality*.

66. Wallace and Weiss, "Political Geography of Nationalist Protest," 404.

67. Wallace and Weiss, "Political Geography of Nationalist Protest," 406.

68. Wallace and Weiss, "Political Geography of Nationalist Protest," 404.

69. Gries, Steiger, and Wang, "Popular Nationalism."

70. Elfstrom's data were truncated to fit this date range and recoded using Wallace and Weiss's classification of prefectural cities. In all but 4 out of 150 cases in this date range, the city coded by Elfstrom as the site of a labor protest corresponded to one of the prefectural cities in Wallace and Weiss's coding. One other case appeared to be a duplicate (two cases that appeared to refer to a single protest against NVC Lighting in Chongqing on July 17, 2012). This left a final list of 145 labor protest incidents in the relevant date range.

71. Wallace and Weiss exclude the 287th prefectural city—Lhasa, Tibet—from their analysis; see Wallace and Weiss, "Political Geography of Nationalist Protest."

72. Wallace and Weiss, "Political Geography of Nationalist Protest."

73. Wallace and Weiss, "Political Geography of Nationalist Protest," 420.

74. Johnston, "Is Chinese Nationalism Rising?"; Hyun and Kim, "Role of New Media"; Reilly, *Strong Society, Smart State*; Gries, Steiger and Wang, "Popular Nationalism." Johnston argues, for example, that while Chinese political elites seek to shape popular

opinion, they must also take "positions close to those of more nationalistic or hard-line publics" lest they give their elite competitors an advantage; see Johnston, "Is Chinese Nationalism Rising?," 41, fn. 73.

75. Cairns and Carlson, "Real-World Islands."
76. Tam, "Who Engineered the Anti-Japanese Protests in 2005?"
77. Dickson, *Dictator's Dilemma*, 1–2.
78. Dickson, *Dictator's Dilemma*; Johnston, "Is Chinese Nationalism Rising?"; Carlson, "It Should Not Only Be about Nationalism."
79. Cheung, "Political Survival."
80. Ku, "Irreparable Animosity?"; Nagy, "Nationalism, Domestic Politics." Among those who find no link between the shrine visits and popular support are Mochizuki and Porter, "Japan under Abe"; Penney and Wakefield, "Right Angles."
81. Downs and Saunders, "Legitimacy."
82. King, "Hurting the Feelings of the Chinese People."
83. Economist, "World of Hurt."

PART III

Emotion and Image in East Asia

CHAPTER 6

The Emotional Politics of Japan's Image

The worst thing one can say about someone is not the same in every society or in every epoch. In most societies, most of the time, the things that evoke the strongest emotional responses are linked to very basic human activities. Thus, our biological functions are linked to what we construe, in English, as four-letter words. The lexicographer and former American editor of the *Oxford English Dictionary*, Jesse Sheidlower, points out that our choice of profanity says a lot about us. Sexually explicit vocabulary has lost much of its shock value, he observes, and now "racial or ethnic epithets are the scourge."[1]

In Asia as elsewhere, racial or ethnic epithets abound as intense emotions born of wartime memories, strategic and economic competition, and domestic factionalism are linked to external scapegoating on a national level. Less surprising than the strength of these emotions or their ability to derail diplomatic initiatives is the comparative lack of attention they have received from specialists in international relations. Relations among countries evoke strong feelings. Yet our understanding of the field is indebted, overwhelmingly, to economic models that restrict emotion to the expression of positive or negative *utility*, whether we like or dislike a certain state of affairs. The rational model is a powerful aid to our ability to make and understand choices. Its two branches—utility theory and game theory—have had an enormous impact on the study of international relations. Rational models ignore the way emotions constrain our choices by design. To the extent that emotions distort our choice-making procedures, the resulting decisions are not rational, whether or not the outcomes they yield are desirable. The assumption that we are rational thus contains the assumption that emotional distortions are ephemeral, that they will cancel one another out, and that their effects are not profound.

A resurgent body of scholarship on emotion and politics argues, conversely, that emotion has persistent effects on politics, that these effects often add up in ways that systematically privilege certain choices over others, and that the results can be expensive and dangerous. It has long been clear that cooler heads do not always prevail, but that is not much of a theory. The challenge is to replace such trite observations with systematic accounts of the role emotion plays in politics. And to understand the structure of attitudes about other countries in particular, it is helpful to know more about the structure of political emotion in general.

EMOTION AND POLITICS

Emotions are conceptually and theoretically prior to most scholarship in international relations. They dwell in the unexamined background assumptions of international relations theory. Our efforts to explain foreign policy choices often hinge on what, exactly, people or states are assumed to want. Stephen Walt proposed "threat minimization" as a general alternative to Kenneth Waltz's assumption that "security maximization" is the fundamental goal of states.[2] And *security* maximization is not quite the same as *power* maximization. Once we know what states want, or assume that we do, our task is simply to trace the link from desire through constraint to foreign policy outcomes. Accomplishing this requires a theory of decision rather than a theory of desire. And so, although emotional responses to the world are fundamental to microeconomic models of politics, the development of rational modeling in international relations has mostly exiled the study of emotion from the field, except as an assumption or a by-product of decisions taken for "more serious" reasons.[3] Emotional reasons are not serious reasons. To put this another way, our goals always involve emotion (because we want them), but our decisions must not be emotional if they are to be rational.

This tendency to treat emotional decisions as fundamentally distinct from rational decisions characterized a generation of debates among international relations scholars over whether foreign policy decision making was appropriately seen as a rational phenomenon, and over whether the prescriptions of some rational choice theorists, such as rational deterrence theorists, were sound or pernicious.[4] Like most such efforts to draw sharp binary distinctions, this one has gradually succumbed to objections that neither people nor states really behave as proponents of either extreme would have it.

Instead decision theory has gravitated toward a new position that is neither monochromatic nor simply a mushy blend of rationalism and affective psychology. Emotion and reason are both increasingly regarded as integral features of decision making.[5] We might start, for example, by noting that people have feelings not only about outcomes but also about the decision-making process itself. As Irving Janis and Leon Mann noted in their introduction to their classic work on *Decision Making*, choosing is a stressful occupation.[6] Thus we often seek to avoid decisions themselves, as well as bad outcomes. Janis and Mann hypothesized that decision avoidance is one of the principal mechanisms of coping with the problem of decision making under stress, particularly when there is no realistic prospect of a good outcome.[7] They also recognize that we have feelings about risk and uncertainty as well—some people are much more tolerant of it than others. The study of decision making under conditions of risk and uncertainty has given rise to a branch of decision theory known as *prospect theory*.[8] If we were indifferent to risk, a 10 percent chance of winning a million dollars would be equivalent to having $100,000 in our pockets. But few of us are indifferent to such choices. We enjoy some risks. We might bet $10 on a coin toss just to see what happens. When the stakes are large, however, we typically become more risk averse.[9] Prospect theory thus finds that we have feelings not only about different outcomes—having $100,000 versus having nothing—but also about risk itself.

We might infer from these examples that our feelings influence the decision-making process. Most contemporary specialists in decision theory, however, would go further than this. Keith Stanovich and Richard West argue that two independent but complementary systems govern decision making. The first is "automatic, largely unconscious, and relatively undemanding of computational capacity."[10] This system—they label it *System 1*—relies heavily on emotional guides as heuristics to facilitate information processing. Our hunches and feelings of instinct constantly give us clues about how to behave whenever we encounter a problem. This happens almost instantly, well before we have a chance to think about the problem carefully. *System 2*, in contrast, is the careful process of slow, laborious, analytical thought that we typically associate with rationality. Daniel Kahneman, who has also written extensively about these two modes of thought, points out that the former is often a surprisingly accurate guide to answers that the latter eventually works out in more careful fashion.[11] And it is fair to say that we rely on System 1 far more heavily than System 2 most of the time. From this perspective, it makes less sense to see emotion and reason as two mutually opposed accounts of the decision process and instead to see them as parts of a dual reasoning process whereby we understand and devise responses to the world. Our feelings or instincts about a problem can be surprisingly good guides to the answer, particularly for simple problems. Even when they turn out to be poor guides, moreover, they are nevertheless excellent guides to our behavior.

Citing developments in neuropsychology over the past twenty years, Jonathan Haidt argues that our reasoning selves are usually no match for our emotional selves, even when we pause for careful reflection.[12] Like Stanovich, West, and Kahneman, Haidt sees emotion as an integral part of the decision process itself. Indeed it is the part that is often in charge. Haidt offers the metaphor of an elephant and a rider, in which the elephant represents our automatic and emotionally guided selves (System 1), and the rider our more deliberative selves (System 2). In *The Happiness Hypothesis*, he puts it this way: "I'm holding the reins in my hands, and by pulling one way or the other I can tell the elephant to turn, to stop, or to go. I can direct things, but only when the elephant doesn't have desires of his own. When the elephant really wants to do something, I'm no match for him."[13] Where the elephant really wants to go, the rider follows.

We flatter ourselves as the rider in this metaphor, struggling to master our emotional instincts. Yet in truth we are the elephant as much as, or really more than, the rider. By 2012 Haidt had somewhat reworked the metaphor:

> I called these two kinds of cognition the rider (controlled processes, including "reasoning-why") and the elephant (automatic processes, including emotion, intuition, and all forms of "seeing-that"). I chose an elephant rather than a horse because elephants are so much bigger—and smarter—than horses. Automatic processes run the human mind, just as they have been running animal minds for 500 million years, so they're very good at what they do, like software that has been improved through thousands of product cycles. When human beings evolved the capacity for language and reasoning at some point in the last million years, the brain did not rewire itself to hand over the reins to a new and inexperienced charioteer. Rather, the rider (language-based reasoning) evolved because it did something useful for the elephant.
>
> The rider can do several useful things. It can see further into the future (because we can examine alternative scenarios in our heads) and therefore it can help the elephant make better decisions in the

present. It can learn new skills and master new technologies, which can be deployed to help the elephant reach its goals and sidestep disasters. And, most important, the rider acts as the spokesman for the elephant, even though it doesn't necessarily know what the elephant is really thinking. The rider is skilled at fabricating post hoc explanations for whatever the elephant has just done, and it is good at finding reasons to justify whatever the elephant wants to do next. Once human beings developed language and began to use it to gossip about each other, it became extremely valuable for elephants to carry around on their backs a full-time public relations firm."[14]

The disparity in size between elephant and rider is intentional. Our emotional decision processes do most of the work, and most decisions are thus made on an emotional level before we ever really have time to think about them. We *do* think about them. We offer justifications for our actions. Yet by the time we marshal these reasons, the choice itself has usually been made.

Haidt's notion of System 2 as a PR firm is well suited to an analysis of national image and branding. It invites us to look not only at the justifications we offer for our own country's behavior and the criticisms we level at others but also at the emotional elephant employing this skillful PR firm. Again, however, it is worth stressing that justifying our impressions of the world is not the only thing System 2 does. If it were, then the field of economics would have little success in explaining the behavior of markets. The elephant needs to adapt to its environment. While System 1 often accomplishes this task quickly and efficiently, System 2 contributes capacities for learning and adaption that System 1 cannot.

In the field of international relations, scholars have also focused their attention on adaptation and learning. As the field grew out of the experience of two world wars, it seemed self-evident that states must adapt to the constraints of a dangerous international environment. Because this environment is inadequately governed by legal frameworks, it is anarchical by definition and dangerous as a result. Perhaps for this reason, a scholarship of rational adaptation drawn from economics has provided the guiding intellectual light more often than a scholarship of emotion drawn from psychology.

The methodological tendencies of these two fields have arguably had substantial theoretical consequences as well. No one will be surprised by the claim that our methods of studying the world influence the things we see. Arguably, one reason that economists focus so resolutely on System 2, whereas psychologists attend more often to System 1, is that their methods reinforce this difference. Psychologists rely on experimental methods that highlight either commonality or individual variance in response to environmental stimuli. Presented with a certain stimulus, experimental subjects may react similarly (they may seek, for example, to minimize cognitive dissonance). Or, perhaps they will react differently, highlighting the effects of personality variables. Either way, however, the constraints of society that provide a given stimulus are not themselves theorized. They are a matter for other social scientists. As a result, rational adaptation to those constraints is rarely a topic of psychological research. Economists, on the other hand, embrace formal models of how people react to the very important constraint of scarcity. Markets are necessary precisely because not all desires are met with abundance, and the field of economics enshrines exactly one reaction to this constraint. It assumes that we react to scarcity by seeking to maximize utility wherever we can find it. Economists are then free to devote their attention to equilibria in the pursuit of utility under particular conditions of constraint. And so formal microeconomic modeling is well suited to uncover stability or instability in our adaptation to market constraints, whereas psychological experiments are attuned to behavioral patterns in response to a wide variety of stimuli, but without any particular expectation on the part of the field in general about those stimuli. Thus it is easy for economists to see constraint, but only one sort of behavior. The methods of psychologists uncover many sorts of behavior (and attitudes, emotions, etc.) but with little concern for particular kinds of constraint.

Returning to Haidt's metaphor, economists focus on the way elephants negotiate obstacles (scarcity), and so the efforts of the rider are magnified. Psychologists place the elephant in a laboratory, where the rider is easily overwhelmed and usually irrelevant. The field of international relations has resembled economics far more than psychology. Unlike economics, it is power that is in short supply in international relations rather than wealth, but the effect on theory development has been similar. Theories of international relations privilege the rational responses of the rider (i.e., national leader) who must adapt to the constraints of the anarchical international system. Until recently efforts to incorporate emotion formally into accounts of foreign policy have been sparse. For specialists in international security during the Cold War, these efforts mostly took the form of observations that mutual fears reinforced conflict spirals and arms races.[15] One powerful image of other countries, the "enemy image," was driven by one powerful corresponding emotion: fear.[16] With the end of the Cold War, new fears have replaced the old, with terrorism taking the role formerly played by communism in the West, without doing much damage to existing models of emotional politics. Meanwhile, for specialists in international political economy, the assumptions of economists themselves already made sense, with the addendum that power as well as economic scarcity was an important source of constraints.

Richard Ned Lebow makes a strong case that this dual emotional orientation in the study of international relations gives rise to a crabbed and cramped understanding of people's political desires.[17] Dividing itself into realist and liberal camps, the field of international relations sees states as driven either by fear in an environment dominated by pervasive insecurity or by acquisitiveness in an environment of pervasive economic scarcity. Nowhere in this scheme is there a place for pride, honor, prestige, or other emotions that Lebow groups under the category of "spirit" and that, he argues, get short shrift despite their evident importance in both the ancient and contemporary worlds. It is impossible to understand Medieval Europe, he argues, without understanding the way a complex system of honor informed relations among proto-states. And it is equally impossible, having seen the world through this lens that he traces back to the ancient Greeks, to fail to recognize dynamics of national pride and honor at work in the world today. These are usually dismissed as subterfuge by international relations scholars. We are trained to reject as naïve the claim that countries build weapons or provoke conflicts simply to defend their honor. Rather, we ask what interests were at stake, or how the dynamics of the security dilemma may have provoked their fears.[18]

Lebow's work is part of the new wave of scholarship on emotional politics.[19] In the field of international relations, scholarship has finally begun to move beyond the outdated conception of emotion as an alternative to rationality, giving it independent analytical standing. Simon Koschut calls this the "emotional turn" in international relations and considers it "one of the most promising developments in the field."[20] In a compelling study of terrorism, ethnic conflict, and transitional justice, for example, Andrew Ross shows that emotions far beyond fear and hatred have profound effects in international relations.[21] Pride, revenge, empathy, enthusiasm, and frustration—as well as fear and hatred, to be sure—are all amply displayed at both the interpersonal and international level in the war on terror, the implosion of Yugoslavia, and the Rwandan genocide. Ross is sensitive to what one might call the "emotional exchanges" between political elites and mass audiences. As "social settings become linked as never before," he argues, "affective circulations create feedbacks and synergies among actors with differing degrees of formal authority."[22] Emotion percolates up and down the hierarchies of society as leaders and followers react to one another. Perhaps the top-down pathway is the more familiar. As Daniel Goleman, Richard E. Boyatzis, and Annie McKee argue in their book on emotion and leadership, "leaders have always played a primordial emotional role. . . . The leader acts as the group's emotional guide."[23] Yet leaders, to be successful, must also respond to the emotional tenor of the times and to the passions that inflame their constituents—passions that are, at best, only partially under their control.

Several other recent works have focused primarily on the way emotion shapes the behavior of leaders engaged in the conduct of foreign policy. In a study of emotional diplomacy, Todd Hall starts from the premise that emotional expressions are a form of communication among states just as they are among individuals.[24] Although the emotional performances of states may well be strategic, he argues, they are not merely rhetorical tactics deployed by national leaders. Instead, they perform many other functions: they reveal commitments, they solidify bonds of cooperation, they signal intent to repair damaged relationships, and they alert others to the potentially dangerous consequences of their own behavior. In particular Hall focuses on what he regards as three essential forms of emotional performance by states: diplomacies of anger, sympathy, and guilt. The outrage conveyed by the diplomacy of anger indicates that a line has been crossed. By construing "particular issues as sensitive and volatile, and thus outside the realm of standard cost-benefit calculations," it also warns other states that normal strategic equilibria may be unattainable.[25] It warns them to tread carefully. In contrast, diplomacies of sympathy and guilt work at the opposite end of the spectrum: rather than signifying implacable hostility, they seek either to deepen a positive relationship (sympathy) or to repair a damaged one (guilt). In all of these cases, emotional performances are crucial to demonstrating sincerity—the lynchpin of successful deterrent and compellent strategies.[26]

Such strategies are, in fact, the focus of another recent work on emotion and foreign policy: Robin Markwica's study of coercive diplomacy.[27] Markwica views emotion as an essential communicative device for states that seek to coerce without incurring the additional costs of armed hostilities. He points out that history contains many examples of the "curious failure of military might to afford success in coercive diplomacy. As early as in the fifth century BCE, Thucydides recounted how the inhabitants of the small island of Melos in the Aegean Sea rebuffed imperial Athens' call to give up their neutrality in the Peloponnesian War, only to be subdued and enslaved."[28] In their efforts to explain why coercive diplomacy fails, sometimes with disastrous consequences, Markwica argues that existing "rationalist, cognitivist, and constructivist accounts of coercive diplomacy either neglect or do not examine systematically . . . the role that emotions play in encounters between coercers and targets."[29] Stepping into this gap, Markwica proposes a model connecting the "logic of affect" to compliance decisions in the face of coercive diplomacy. Focusing on "five key emotions"—fear, anger, hope, pride, and humiliation—he suggests that fear and humiliation under certain circumstances will lead to compliance. In the well-known fight-or-flight response, flight (and thus compliance) is one possibility, but fighting is another. And the tendency to resist coercive demands is also amplified by anger, hope, pride, and humiliation (when the humiliation is seen as unjust).[30]

Summing up recent research on emotion and foreign policy, Thomas Dolan observes that it has primarily focused on three topics: (1) the way emotion influences decision processes; (2) the way emotion influences the process of diplomatic negotiation; and (3) the way emotion influences public attitudes that, in turn, define the context in which leaders must operate.[31] Emotion mediates the extent to which national leaders are willing to take risks in response to stressful international events such as the terrorist attacks examined by Ross or the coercive confrontations examined by Markwica.[32] It conditions diplomatic bargaining by fostering trust in some situations while undermining it in others, as Hall has shown.[33] In these and many other ways, emotion shapes the way leaders understand the international environment and their own possible behaviors within it. Given the importance of System 1 decision processes, it would be surprising to argue otherwise.

The arguments explored in Chapter 4—that geopolitical considerations such as the distribution of capabilities in the international system might suffice to explain whether countries are seen as enemies or allies—should therefore be recast in this light. Emotion plays an important part in the way we appraise capabilities. If Walt was right that countries balance against threat more than against power, for example, then emotion plays a crucial role in applying principles of *realpolitik*.[34] Theories of emotion do not replace geopolitical theories, but rather complement them.

Emotion is also constantly at work in the interplay between leaders and followers as each react to perceived emotional cues from the other. This is the third area of research identified by Dolan, and it is generally consistent with the argument developed in Chapter 5 about the way domestic politics shapes country perceptions. In China and South Korea, as elsewhere, leaders both respond to and attempt to manipulate public emotions. Ross's conception of the "circulation of affect" is a particularly nice way of capturing this flow of emotions within social hierarchies, shaped by the agendas of state leaders but also constraining them as popular attitudes and mass emotions take on a life of their own. For those interested in the way emotion sustains attitudes about countries, this notion of affect circulating within or among social groups is a good place to begin developing a model of the way emotion regulates national images.

EMOTIONAL PATTERNS IN INTERNATIONAL RELATIONS

As an account of how emotion works, the bodily metaphor of circulation is apt, for circulation within the body transports things—nutrients, oxygen, lymph, and so on—from one place to another. In the same way, the circulation of emotion transports attitudes about one thing so that they can be brought to bear on something else. By building on this metaphor of transport, Ross treats emotions as "fluid" devices of enormous utility, and motility, in politics. They lubricate certain understandings of other peoples and countries while pushing back with considerable hydrostatic pressure against others. Ross's purpose is to stress the variety and versatility of our emotional lives, even at the level of international politics. He does not argue for any particular constraints on the emotional politics of international relations, and one senses that he might look with skepticism on the claim that emotions must ordinarily run through specific, well-worn channels. Yet circulation within the body mostly does just that: the body regulates its fluids carefully, sending each to its proper place. And whereas Ross sees emotions as continuously moving through various channels, they may also become stuck, like platelets forming a blood clot or cholesterol obstructing arteries. They stick together in certain ways, and in certain combinations, under specific circumstances of constraint.

The preceding paragraph follows Ross by employing circulation as a bodily metaphor for something that happens in society, rather than in the body, treating emotion as a fluid that flows through social channels. Before proceeding with this metaphor, however, it may be helpful to step away from such figurative language for a moment to ask instead how specialists in psychology and neurobiology understand emotion. Although there has been a great deal of progress in recent decades studying the biophysical aspects of emotion, there is no consensus about the best way to explain exactly what emotions are. Beverley Fehr and James Russell infamously wrote of this state of affairs: "Everyone knows what an emotion is, until asked to give a definition. Then, it seems, no one knows."[35] Fehr and Russell's brief overview of the many different ways of thinking about emotion is apt:

> Attempts to define emotion can be traced back at least as far as Plato and Aristotle. The nature of emotion (or passion, as it was then called) was debated by philosophers, including Thomas Aquinas, Descartes, Hobbes, Hume, Spinoza, and Kant, followed by the psychologists, including Wundt, James, McDougall, and Watson. Wundt

(1912/1924) and Titchener (1910) thought that emotion is a mental event. Watson (1919) said that emotion is behavior, and Wenger (1950) said that emotion is a type of physiological activity, specifically activity innervated by the autonomic nervous system. Virtually the same debate can be seen today when Solomon (1977) argued that emotion is a type of judgment (and hence a mental event) and Tomkins (1980) argued that emotions (or affects as they are now sometimes called) are "sets of muscular and glandular responses."[36]

Interestingly—not unlike Haidt's elephant and rider metaphor—Plato employed the metaphor of a charioteer (intellect) struggling to control two horses, one representing spirit or moral impulses and the other representing the passions or appetites.[37]

In the tangled lineage that stretches from contemporary research back to Plato, clear disciplinary tendencies are apparent. Biologists tend to treat emotion as a physiological state, for example, whereas psychologists treat it as a subjective drive state accompanied by some degree of cognitive awareness.[38] We can speak of feelings because we are cognitively aware of them, but emotion begins with processes of which we are unaware. It is a mistake, moreover, to think of the biophysical processes in which emotion originates as a single "emotion system." On the contrary, the body has evolved multiple physiological systems for accomplishing very different purposes that ultimately give rise to the states of awareness we experience as emotion. One of the most basic, perhaps, is the need to manage responses to danger. The limbic system, evolved to coordinate fight-or-flight responses, is also closely linked to the hippocampus, a brain structure involved in navigation and the consolidation and retention of memory. Animals that can remember and avoid sources of danger, after all, have an evolutionary advantage.[39] We experience the activation of these systems as fear. Fatigue, to take another example, is influenced by neurohormones regulated by the hypothalamus, along with other homeostatic emotions such as hunger and thirst.[40] And sexual desire, to take yet another example, is also regulated by the limbic system and by a variety of other brain structures—including the claustrum, anterior cingulate, putamen, and caudate nucleus.[41] Like our response to danger, homeostatic regulation and sexual reproduction are also crucial for species survival.

As these examples suggest, there is a certain functional basis for different categories of emotion. And the feelings that we consider to be emotions, along with our cognitive awareness of these feelings, are just the tip of a physiological iceberg involving many distinct neurochemical processes and neural structures. At the level of physiology, in fact, it may not even make sense to think of emotions as a single class of events. Joseph LeDoux argues that emotions are better viewed instead as distinct "biological functions of the nervous system."[42] LeDoux goes on to explain the physiological basis of emotion in this way:

> The brain . . . does not have a system dedicated to perception. The word "perception" describes in a general way what goes on in a number of specific neural systems—we see, hear, and smell the world with our visual, auditory, and olfactory systems. Each system evolved to solve different problems that animals face. In a similar vein, the various classes of emotions are mediated by separate neural systems that have evolved for different reasons. The system we use to defend against danger is different from the one we use in procreation, and the feelings that result from activating these systems—fear and sexual pleasure—do not have a common origin. There is no such thing as the 'emotion' faculty and there is no single brain system dedicated to this phantom function. If we are interested in understanding the various phenomena that we use the term 'emotions' to refer to, we have to focus on specific classes of emotions.[43]

Our conscious awareness of emotions and the meanings we assign to emotion are very different, then, from the biological systems that generate emotions. And yet, although LeDoux warns against treating emotion as a single category of physiological functioning, this does not prevent us from seeing emotion as a certain type of experience once we are cognitively aware of it.

Emotion as a cognitive phenomenon differs from emotion as a physiological response. Cognitively, we naturally distinguish between pleasure and pain, between positive and negative emotion. As Robert Zajonc has argued, based on a series of compelling experiments, we orient ourselves toward positive and negative experiences even before we have had a chance to interpret the experiences cognitively.[44] Our physiological capacity for emotion has already begun this process before we have time to think about it. Yet we do also think about our experiences. Beyond distinguishing among them according to valence—whether they are positive or negative—we can also make many other distinctions.

Some of these distinctions involve the social context of our experiences, as when we experience pride or humiliation. The social functioning of emotion introduces yet another layer of complexity. Although the roots of emotion may be physiological, the emotional plant grows upward from the individual into a much broader physical and social space. This social context, moreover, has many layers. The emotions aroused by our closest associates—parents, children, lovers—might be more intense than those evoked by more distant relationships. This distinction introduces a second aspect of emotion: not simply whether it is positive or negative but whether it produces a more or less intense drive state. Although individuals who are close to us may produce deep emotional reactions, intensity of emotion is not always a direct correlate of social distance. We may also experience passionate attachments to religious figures, strong patriotic feelings directed toward our country, and so on.[45]

These two dimensions of emotion—valence (positive or negative) and arousal (low to high intensity)—are widely discussed as the basis of emotions typologies.[46] It is along these axes that Silvan Tomkins, one of the best-known theorists of emotion, organizes emotions.[47] At the negative end of the valence spectrum, he places emotions such as distress–anguish, anger–rage, fear–terror, and shame–humiliation. At the positive end are enjoyment–joy and interest–excitement. Each of these emotion pairs ranges, moreover, from low to high arousal.[48] To take just one other example, James Russell's circumplex model of affect interprets emotion as arising from two neuro-physiological systems that create an orthogonal cognitive space. Like Tomkins, Russell organizes our cognitive awareness of emotion along the axes of valence and arousal.[49] These models of the simplest dimensional structure of emotions are not intended to capture the full complexity of emotion. In particular they do not suffice to account for the social context of emotion. Albert Mehrabian and James A. Russell thus introduce a third dimension of dominance/submissiveness in their pleasure–arousal–dominance (PAD) model of emotion precisely for this reason, in order to account for social hierarchy.[50]

The formation of images about countries is still further removed from basic social hierarchies. This is perhaps one reason that scholars such as Ross and Hall do not develop their accounts of emotion in international relations using a framework derived from one of these basic typologies. Although they do discuss many of the same emotions, such as anger and fear, they wisely refuse to commit themselves to a simple, interpersonal model of emotion. As Jonathan Mercer, another international relations scholar interested in the role of emotion, has argued, "individual and group-level emotions can feel the same, but the basis for the feeling is different."[51] This is especially so for emotions attached to group identities and state images. Mercer goes on to explain: "Identification requires a feeling of attachment; it is intrinsically social. Concern over my status involves a personal identity: it is social but individual. Concern over my country's status involves a social (or group) identity: it is social and depends upon a group."[52]

Ross's model of circulating affect is one way of accounting for this social context in order to describe the way emotion functions in the context of international relations. Another slightly different metaphor may be even more helpful here. Depth psychologists sometimes speak of emotional complexes as a way of describing emotions and attitudes that are locked together in distinctive patterns. Carl Jung sought to develop an account of these patterns.[53] Central to Jung's understanding of differences among people was the conviction that individuals are oriented primarily toward either an internal or external world. Because we are typically caught in some sort of tension between the two, in practice, psychological complexes represent different patterns of perceiving and evaluating these two worlds, built mostly on a bedrock of unconscious drive states and suppressed memories. These complexes give rise to patterned emotional behavior.

This notion of an *emotional complex* serves well to describe the more intricate patterns of emotional behavior that develop in specific social contexts. These patterns may have a foundation in the basic neuropsychology of emotion, relating for example to basic mechanisms such as fear. Yet they take on nuance depending on the social context. Even though Jung's ideas remain enormously influential among psychotherapists and even though the notion of a complex serves as useful shorthand for distinctive emotional patterns (e.g., the Oedipus or Elektra complex, the Napoleon complex, the god complex), few psychologists today would embrace this as an adequate general model of patterns in emotion and behavior.[54] Yet a general model of emotion is not what is needed to account for emotion in international relations.

In fact I do not intend to make a purely psychological argument at all. Rather, my interest in emotional states and complexes, like Jung's, is in the way they exist in tension between internal and external worlds—that is to say, between a world of internal emotional drives on one hand and external constraints of international relations on the other. Most constructivist scholars would find, in the interplay between these two sorts of worlds, a warrant for highly protean accounts of politics (or anything else). Yet, as Thomas Risse once observed, the fact that we can construct many and varied accounts of the world does not mean that we can plausibly construct any account whatsoever, or that all accounts are equally persuasive.[55] In fact we might hypothesize that the dominant emotional states of international relations take on certain stylized forms.

Between economic, political, or sociological accounts of external constraints on one hand and psychological accounts of emotional drives and cognitive predispositions on the other, there lies the emotional complex as an adaptive mechanism: a certain specific pattern of responses to internal needs and external constraints. Emotion usually gets well out in front of conscious efforts at adaptation.[56] We feel our response to political problems before we reason it out. Even though such emotional responses are rapid and instinctive—responses that Haidt might characterize as the "elephants" of System 1—they are nevertheless adaptive. They are not, in other words, purely a phenomenon of the *psyche* or of internal drives. In fact they may also serve as bridges among many people. At a somewhat higher level of abstraction, we may conceive of national emotional complexes as efforts by large groups of people to resolve the same sort of challenge—that is, to respond and adapt emotionally to the patterns of organized interaction at the level of international politics. These adaptive patterns vary considerably. Yet it is nevertheless possible to conceive of them as structured in certain basic ways.

As already noted, the simplest place to start—the place where psychologists of emotion start at the individual level—is with valence, denoting our basic emotional orientation toward things as either positive or negative, liking or disliking. Valence serves as a starting point for other categories of emotion. We know, almost instantly and before we have had a chance to refine our feelings, whether we like or dislike something. As Andrew Ortony, Gerald L. Clore, and Allan Collins point out, however, we do refine valence depending on its object. We can thus divide valence into several different kinds of emotional orientation: "being *pleased* vs. *displeased* (reaction to events), *approving* vs. *disapproving* (reaction to agents), and *liking* vs. *disliking* (reaction to objects)."[57]

Recall that the extensive literature on national image takes approving or disapproving reactions to other countries as its starting point. In his effort to develop a science of how we ascribe images to agents, Kenneth Boulding begins with whether or not we like them.[58] Applying the same logic to states, Boulding says that we must ask whether a given state is a force for good in the world or the opposite.[59] Hans Morgenthau also implicitly argued for the importance of valence in international relations when he distinguished between *status quo* and *revisionist* states, as did the foreign policy image theorists such as Richard Cottam who referred to this as the target country's *motivation*.[60]

Inasmuch as emotion serves as an adaptive mechanism in foreign policy, the first thing to which we must adapt is whether or not another country represents a threat or an opportunity. This judgment is accomplished by our valent reaction to it. The other crucial consideration in foreign policy is the other country's power relative to one's own. Unsurprisingly, therefore, assessments of *capability* constitute the second crucial judgment about other states for image theorists. Boulding and Cottam both point to capabilities as crucial for deciding what sort of threat or opportunity another state represents. Even weak states may represent threats, after all, and powerful states may be allies rather than enemies.

We should expect emotional states in foreign policy to respond primarily, therefore, to these two judgments: valence (or orientation) and relative power (or capability).[61] We may hypothesize, in other words, that our feelings about other countries will be organized at a fairly basic level in reaction to whether we see them as hostile or supportive, powerful or weak. Figure 6.1 depicts this two-dimensional emotional structure. The vertical axis of the graph represents the valent dimension ranging from like to dislike, and thus from generalized positive emotions such as trust to generalize negative emotion such as anger or hatred. The horizontal axis represents judgments about relative capabilities and ranges from generalized shame to generalized pride. Because this model rests on judgments along two dimensions—trust/anger and pride/shame, or T/A and P/S—we might for convenience call this the *TAPS model* of emotive imagery.

Specific emotional states result from combined judgments along these two dimensions. The simplest case, perhaps, occurs in the upper-right quadrant of the graph. When another country is seen in a positive light and as weaker than one's own, then there is no challenge to a positive national self-conception. One's own country is neither threatened nor inferior. *Sympathy* is an appropriate adaptive response to such countries, who are seen as supportive junior partners rather than as equals. When another country is

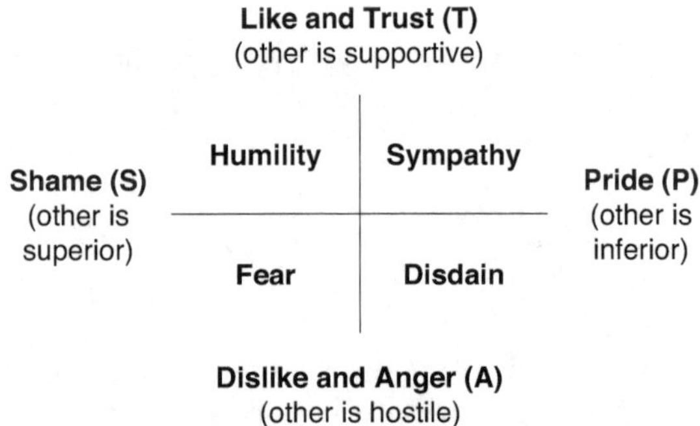

Figure 6.1. The TAPS Model of Emotive Images

more powerful than one's own but still seen positively, the picture is some-what more complicated. Although engagement with the other country may offer considerable benefit, this also highlights one's own vulnerability, producing an emotional politics of *humility* that is challenging even when it is necessary.[62]

In any case the two lower quadrants are far more problematic. If the other state is seen as both powerful and a threat to one's own, then it is usually understood as an *enemy*. Fear of what it may do is the adaptive response, just as it is when individuals are threatened, and this emotional state drives a national response that calls for one's compatriots to meet this challenge. If the other state is seen as weaker but still threatening, on the other hand, then *disdain* rather than fear is likely to dominate emotional politics. Such states (or their leaders) are usually held to be irrational or otherwise flawed. Otherwise, they would not presume to challenge a stronger power (one's own). In either case, the generalized negative response to threats from another state is likely to be anger.[63] But the fearful anger directed toward a powerful threat constitutes a very different emotional state than the dismissive or contemptuous anger that is directed toward weaker threats. Such contemptuous reactions are likely to provoke a much more aggressive response toward the threat than is the case when anger is accompanied by fear.

This simple typology is not meant to suggest that only four affective orientations suffice to describe the way emotion influences foreign policy. On the contrary, more subtle distinctions are both possible and likely. The burgeoning scholarship on national role conceptions, national identity, national branding, and national image certainly supports the claim that more than four images of other countries are likely to be at work in international relations. Just as with individuals, more nuanced emotions are to be expected in our reactions to foreign policy. Yet this four-fold typology represents an underlying emotional structure that, we might hypothesize, is likely to be pervasive in foreign policy.

One issue remains to be addressed before turning to the problem of assessing the way emotion informs images of Japan. In what sense can the four primary emotional patterns of the TAPS model—humility, sympathy, fear, and disdain—be described as *complexes*? They appear to be emotional ideal types constituting fairly basic emotional responses to other countries. Like emotion at the individual level, moreover, they serve an adaptive function, prompting and coordinating national responses to threats or opportunities. But the term "complex" is generally used to describe maladaptive behavior. The Napoleon complex, for example, describes not merely one's sense of self-worth but rather an exaggerated sense of self that might stem from an unconscious desire to compensate for perceived shortcomings. Complexes are far more likely to be derived from negative emotions. And so while it might be possible to have a humility complex or a sympathy complex—the two emotions on the top half of Figure 6.1—this seems unlikely to be a common concern. One could experience exaggerated humility or sympathy, of course, but the more typical problem is that these emotions are not felt keenly enough, especially in the political world.

The bottom half of Figure 6.1, on the other hand, is fertile ground for emotional complexes in foreign policy. Fear and disdain are also adaptive responses. Fear of a threatening state is an appropriate response when the threat is genuine, and it serves to prompt self-help in an international system that offers no other dependable source of aid. Similarly, disdain is a plausible reaction to the bad behavior of a vulnerable state. It sensitizes us to the prospect of dangerous behavior by potentially unpredictable leaders. Yet both of these reactions, fear and disdain, can also be exaggerated. It is this exaggerated fear or disdain that constitutes an emotional complex. The history of international relations is full of examples of such exaggerated emotions. In a recent study of US foreign policy and the politics of fear, for example, Trevor Thrall and Jane Cramer argue that the United States has routinely exaggerated threats, both big and small, contributing to just these two forms of hyperbolic emotion: outsized fear of threats seen as bigger than they really were, and overblown disdain for leaders seen as more irrational and unpredictable than they really were.[64] The so-called global war on terror has involved both, building up the notion of global terror networks into a far more dangerous bogeyman than it ever really was while simultaneously making distorted claims about national leaders—most notably Saddam Hussein—as a pretext for intervention or invasion.[65]

We might go all the way back to Thucydides, in fact, for examples of these problems. On one hand the military competition between Athens and Sparta is a classic example of an arms race in which exaggerated fears became a self-fulfilling prophecy. As Athens insisted on allegiance from previously independent polities within its sphere of influence, it justified the very responses that it feared. The archetype of this problem was Melos. Unlike Sparta, Melos was militarily insignificant from an Athenian perspective. The only threat it posed was that, by refusing to submit to Athenian demands, it set a bad example. Still, Athens had the power to compel Melos. Athens tellingly complains to the Melian delegation, "you will therefore show great blindness of judgment, unless, after allowing us to retire, you can find some counsel more prudent than this (that leads you to resist us)."[66] Consistent with the TAPS model, Athens experiences a *Sparta complex* of exaggerated fear. At the same time, when confronting weaker but still noncompliant powers, it experiences a *Melos complex* of exaggerated disdain, calling into question Melian leadership and dismissing its ill-fated protests.

ASSESSING THE EMOTIVE POLITICS OF JAPAN'S IMAGE

The next two chapters will test the hypothesis that our emotional response to a country is governed in important ways by our judgments about its orientation (positive/negative) and capabilities (superior/inferior). Ideally we might take a multimethod approach to evaluating this hypothesis, and to that end these chapters will review two different kinds of evidence. The first and more straightforward approach is to examine in more detail the language used by Chinese (Chapter 7) and South Korean (Chapter 8) leaders to describe Japan. We should expect them to speak in very different ways about a country they dislike than one they like. More importantly, however, we should also expect different emotions—and thus different statements about Japan—depending on whether they evaluate Japan as relatively strong or relatively weak in a given context. This approach will give us a first approximation of whether different emotional language is associated with different images of Japan. Then a somewhat more systematic test is made possible by extracting text from a sample of editorials in leading newspapers. This will allow us to study changes in emotional language in a more controlled fashion. The remainder of this chapter will describe how we might translate the relatively abstract argument about emotion in the context of foreign policy presented in the preceding section into something more concrete and measurable.

Because there is no well-established methodology for measuring emotion in foreign policy, it makes sense to begin "close to the ground" by looking at what national leaders actually say. Indeed it is likely that the different cultural and political contexts in China and South Korea will shape expressions of emotion toward Japan. For this reason as well, particularly in the early stages of developing a model of emotion in foreign policy discourse such as the TAPS model, it makes sense to temper expectations about the model's relevance with some sustained attention to the way leaders in different contexts speak about other countries in practice.[67] Ultimately, though, whether emotional attitudes toward other countries are guided more by the judgments identified by the TAPS model or whether they are defined by other vicissitudes of cultural context is an empirical question. The TAPS model is a prediction that there will be patterns in the way leaders talk about other countries, determined by emotional appraisals of geopolitical circumstances.

Each of the next chapters will start by reviewing some of the ways Chinese and South Korean leaders talk about Japan. The TAPS model presented in Figure 6.1 gives us some general expectations about what we will find. We do not need this model, of course, to anticipate that emotional language directed at Japan will be generally negative (and perhaps exaggerated). The preceding chapters have shown, however, that attitudes toward Japan—even in China and South Korea—are more variable than is widely appreciated. Emotional language directed toward Japan may change, therefore, depending on the time period and issues at stake. In the case of South Korea, in particular, we might even expect positive attitudes and more sympathetic language when the trilateral alliance with the United States is at issue.

The more interesting implication of the TAPS model is that negative attitudes toward Japan will take two very different forms depending on whether Japan's capabilities are assessed as high or low. In an area in which Japan has the upper hand, Japanese strength will translate into a fearful emotional reaction, perhaps combined with anger. This fear and anger will cause observers to stress Japan's power and the danger it poses. When the focus is on Japan's historical actions—again, a time when Japanese power was considerable—anger is likely to be the dominant emotion since fear has subsided. On the other hand, in areas of Japanese weakness, or when observers see their own country as overtaking Japan, negative attitudes will take a different form because the threats posed by a weaker adversary and the emotions these threats evoke are very different. The threat from a weaker adversary is that it will behave badly or irrationally, causing a danger to its own citizens as well as to other countries. Although this threat can be met effectively, since it comes from a weaker opponent, it should not come at all, and this provokes its own distinct form of disdainful anger as an emotional reaction.

When Japan's national capabilities or the delinquency of its leaders are exaggerated, moreover, this can give rise to an emotional complex portraying Japan as either a dangerous Spartan usurper or a reckless Melian intransigent. In either case, these exaggerations help to feed anger directed toward Japan as a threat. This anger will be expressed through a very different emotional pattern when the threat is Melian rather than Spartan. Anger directed at a weaker adversary provokes feelings of contempt toward a state that should "know better" than to threaten a stronger state. In fact, contempt in foreign policy is more likely to be directed toward a country's leadership than toward the country in general. Threats from weaker states call into question the sanity or maturity of their leaders. This kind of threat is likely to produce dismissive or disdainful reactions directed particularly at these leaders. On the other hand, stronger states constitute an existential threat, although not every strong state has this effect. The extensive literature on the democratic peace suggests, for example, that even strong democracies will not usually be seen by other democracies as threatening.[68] When a strong country is also seen as a threatening country, however, anger is likely to be directed at what it has already done (if it was a threat in the past) and fear is likely to be expressed about its future actions. Whether past or future, this combination of anger and fear is directed at the state in general as much as at its leaders. In a number of recent studies, in fact, Piotr Cap highlights this element of time and the fear of future acts as a key component of fear in public discourse.[69]

Cap relies heavily on the work of Paul Chilton, a British specialist in linguistics and political discourse who developed a formal model of discourse emphasizing the dimensions of space (from here to there, or self to other), time (from past to future), and modality (from uncertain to certain).[70] Chilton's formalism is the foundation of a much more ambitious approach to political discourse than is needed here, but it provides some helpful clues about how to undertake a second, more systematic way of analyzing emotive language.[71] In particular Cap and Chilton's work draws attention to the roles of time and distance in political discourse. Similarly, in a paper distinguishing fear from anger in political discourse, George Marcus also associates fear with "departures from the expected" and anger with "noxious threats on core values and practice."[72] Although he doesn't say so, this is also a distinction between the future where our expectations dwell and the past from which our anger emerges.

If the TAPS model is correct, then we can draw several inferences about the sort of emotive language that we will observe in different contexts. First, in discourse that focuses on the past—when Japan's power was relatively greater—we should expect to find more expressions of anger or outrage linked to (possibly exaggerated) statements about this power and the threat it posed. We might also find expressions of fear linked to the possibility of Japan's future action (militarization). When projected into the future, fear will be linked to what Chilton might call a modality of possibility rather than certainty. Finally we should expect that the target of fearful statements is likely to be the country as much or more than its leaders, since the country itself is seen as a threat. In contrast, in discourse that focuses on present circumstances in which China or South Korea have the upper hand (on China's growing power or South Korea's control over the Dokdo/Takeshima Islands), we should instead expect an emotional reaction of disdain. The modality in such cases is certainty, and Japan's failure to accommodate itself to present realities. More specifically, it is Japan's leaders who may be accused of ignoring these realities, and thus the nature of the threatening other in such situations is likely to shift from the country to its leaders, who will be seen as childish, immature, irrational, or untrustworthy.

Table 6.1 summarizes the different emotional patterns associated with negative images of Japan such as those that often dominate its relations with China and South Korea. To provide a more systematic test of this model, as noted previously, the next two chapters will examine a sample of editorials in leading Chinese and South Korean newspapers. Specifically, by compiling a list of adjectives used to describe Japan in different time periods and when different issues are at stake, we can observe more clearly how Japan's image changes over time and across different issue spaces. If descriptions of Japan change in the ways shown in Table 6.1, this will provide additional support for the TAPS model.

Andrew Ross laments that while "constructivists seem uniquely qualified to study emotion" given their interest in subjectivity, there nevertheless "remain significant obstacles preventing constructivism from taking emotions seriously."[73] One of these obstacles, he goes on to say, is that we have "no account of how norms, identities and other intellectual phenomena are sustained by deeper ranges of human expression."[74] An account of the way patterned emotional reactions sustain different country images will help to address this problem.

Another problem, which Ross does not mention, is that constructivists have not worked out empirical techniques for studying emotion. What Ross *does* say is that "the social world of emotion is a messy place. Emotions can fuel ordinary processes of socialization, but they can also surge, migrate, and blend in ways that disrupt business as usual."[75] This messy quality of emotions—the way fear blends into anger, anger into contempt, and so

Table 6.1: Emotional Content Associated with Negative Images of Japan

Dominant Emotion	Fear	Disdain
Emotional Target	State	Leaders
Target's Character	Rational	Irrational
Time Frame	Past or Future	Present
Modality	Certainty (of the past), or Uncertainty (about the future)	Certainty (about present circumstances)
Emotional Complex	"Sparta"	"Melos"

on—greatly complicates the empirical task. It is for this reason that it makes sense to look for a pattern of emotions such as that described in Table 6.1. There are other ways to study emotion, and many other emotions to study. But the patterns of the TAPS model should be fairly basic because they are strongly rooted in the most crucial distinctions that we make among states: their positive or negative orientation toward our own state, and their power relative to our own state. At the very least, these emotional patterns seem like promising places to start.

Notes

1. Sheidlower, *F-Word*, xvii.
2. Walt, *Origins of Alliances*; Waltz, *Theory of International Relations*.
3. Kowert, "Completing the Ideational Triangle."
4. See, e.g., Achen and Snidal, "Rational Deterrence Theory"; George and Smoke, "Deterrence and Foreign Policy"; Jervis, "Rational Deterrence"; Huth, "Deterrence and International Conflict"; Lebow, *Between Peace and War*; Lebow, "Deterrence Failure Revisited"; Lebow and Stein, "Rational Deterrence Theory"; Orme, "Deterrence Failures."
5. Marcus, Neuman, and MacKuen, *Affective Intelligence*.
6. Janis and Mann, *Decision Making*.
7. Janis and Mann's conflict model of decision proposes that decision making is mediated by stress induced by perceived risk, the availability of satisfactory solutions, and time pressure; see Janis and Mann, *Decision Making*. For a discussion of Janis and Mann's contribution in the broader context of research on stress and decision making, see Lazarus and Folkman, *Stress, Appraisal, and Coping*.
8. Levy, "Introduction to Prospect Theory"; Barberis, "Thirty Years of Prospect Theory." For a more detailed, technical treatment, see Wakker, *Prospect Theory*. *Uncertainty* is typically defined as a condition when the probabilities of different outcomes are unknown. *Risk*, on the other hand, describes a condition when probabilities can be assigned to different possible outcomes. We face risk when we know there is a 30 percent chance of rain tomorrow. We face uncertainty when we have not yet consulted the weather forecast.
9. Another interesting finding of prospect theory is that we tend to accept greater risks in order to avoid a loss than we do in order to make an equivalent gain; see Kahneman and Tversky, "Prospect Theory."
10. Stanovich and West, "Individual Differences in Reasoning," 658.
11. Kahneman, *Thinking, Fast and Slow*.
12. Haidt, *Happiness Hypothesis*; Haidt, *Righteous Mind*.
13. Haidt, *Happiness Hypothesis*, 4.
14. Haidt, *Righteous Mind*, 53–54.
15. Blight, *Shattered Crystal Ball*; Buzan, *People, States and Fear*; Isard, *Arms Races*; Smoker, "Fear in the Arms Race"; White, *Fearful Warriors*.
16. See Herrmann and Fischerkeller, "Beyond the Enemy Image."
17. Lebow, *Cultural Theory*.

18. Jervis, "Cooperation Under the Security Dilemma."

19. One of the first to call for a renewed focus on emotion was Neta Crawford, "Passion of World Politics." For discussions of this emotional turn, see also Ariffin, Coicaud, and Popovski, *Emotions in International Politics*; Brader and Marcus, "Emotion and Political Psychology"; Brodersen, *Emotional Motives*; Dolan, "Emotions and Foreign Policy"; Hoggett, *Politics, Identity and Emotion*; Hutchison and Bleiker, "Theorizing Emotions in World Politics"; Koschut, *Power of Emotions*; Marcus, "Emotions in Politics"; Marcus, "Psychology of Emotion and Politics"; Marcus and MacKuen, "Anxiety, Enthusiasm, and the Vote"; Marcus, Neuman and MacKuen, *Affective Intelligence*; McDermott, "Emotions in Foreign Policy Decision Making"; Mercer, "Feeling Like a State"; Moisi, *Geopolitics of Emotion*; Neuman, Marcus, Mackuen, and Crigler, *Affect Effect*; Wong, "Mapping the Repertoire of Emotions."

20. Koschut, *Power of Emotions*, 4.

21. Ross, *Mixed Emotions*.

22. Ross, *Mixed Emotions*, 6.

23. Goleman, Boyatzis, and McKee, *Primal Leadership*, 5.

24. Hall, *Emotional Diplomacy*. For a similar argument, see also Wong, "Mapping the Repertoire of Emotions."

25. Hall, *Emotional Diplomacy*, 4. A widely discussed example of the strategic use of anger occurred during the Cuban Missile Crisis, when both Kennedy and Khrushchev cultivated the perception that they risked losing control to hotheads within their own governments. For a discussion of the strategic cultivation of the "hothead" image, see Wong, "Stoics and Hotheads."

26. George and Smoke, *Deterrence in American Foreign Policy*.

27. Markwica, *Emotional Choices*.

28. Markwica, *Emotional Choices*, 2.

29. Markwica, *Emotional Choices*, 14.

30. Markwica, *Emotional Choices*, 19.

31. Dolan, "Emotions and Foreign Policy."

32. For a discussion of recent research on emotions and the management of risk in foreign policy decision making, see McDermott, "Emotions in Foreign Policy Decision Making."

33. An interesting study by Scott Clifford also finds that strong emotions such as anger tend to polarize political attitudes, which may further constrain bargaining opportunities; see Clifford, "How Emotional Frames Moralize."

34. Walt, *Origins of Alliances*.

35. Fehr and Russell, "Concept of Emotion," 464.

36. Fehr and Russell, "Concept of Emotion," 464–65. In this excerpt, Fehr and Russell cite Solomon, *Passions*; Titchener, *Text-book of Psychology*; Tomkins, "Affect as Amplification"; Watson, *Psychology*; Wenger, "Emotion as Visceral Action"; Wundt, *Introduction to Psychology*. For another good historical overview, see Calhoun and Solomon, *What Is an Emotion?*

37. See Ferrari, "Struggle in the Soul"; Zaborowski, "Plato's 'Phaedrus.'"

38. See, e.g., Plutchik, "Nature of Emotions." For a good overview of disciplinary tendencies in research on emotion, see LeDoux, *Emotional Brain*.

39. Paul D. MacLean's triune brain theory is a classic statement of this argument; see MacLean, "Some Psychiatric Implications." For an overview of MacLean's contributions, see Newman and Harris, "Scientific Contributions."

40. Gibson et al., "Conscious Perception." On homeostatic emotions (i.e., those emotions responsible for regulating the body's stable state), see Craig, "New View of Pain"; Paulus, "Neural Basis of Reward and Craving."

41. Arnow et al., "Brain Activation"; also see Argiolas and Melis, "Neurophysiology of the Sexual Cycle." Interestingly, the putamen also plays a role in the "hate circuit" of the brain as well; see Zeki and Romaya, "Neural Correlates of Hate."

42. LeDoux, *Emotional Brain*, 12.

43. LeDoux, *Emotional Brain*, 16.

44. Zajonc, "Feeling and Thinking."

45. See Bar Tal, "Patriotism as Fundamental Beliefs"; Druckman, "Nationalism, Patriotism"; Emmons, "Emotion and Religion."

46. See Marcus, "Hidden Affections."

47. Tomkins, *Affect Imagery Consciousness*.

48. Accompanying these emotions are one neutral emotional dimension (surprise–startle) and two physiologically specific feelings (disgust and its olfactory counterpart, dissmell); see Tomkins, *Affect Imagery Consciousness*.

49. Russell, "Circumplex Model of Affect." David Watson and Auke Tellegen developed a "positive activation, negative activation" (PANA) model that also occupies this two-dimensional space, but with the axes rotated 45 degrees from Russell's; see Watson and Tellegen, "Toward a Consensual Structure of Mood."

50. Mehrabian and Russell, *Approach to Environmental Psychology*.

51. Mercer, "Feeling Like a State," 517.

52. Mercer, "Feeling Like a State," 517.

53. Jung, *Psychologische Typen*.

54. See Singer and Kimbles, *Cultural Complex*.

55. Risse-Kappen, "Ideas Do Not Float Freely."

56. See Marcus, Neuman and MacKuen, *Affective Intelligence*; Zajonc, "Feeling and Thinking."

57. Ortony, Clore, and Collins, *Cognitive Structure of Emotions*, 33.

58. Boulding, *Image*.

59. Boulding, "National Images and International Systems."

60. Morgenthau, *Politics among Nations*; Cottam, *Foreign Policy Motivation*.

61. For some evidence supporting this expectation, see McAvene and Kowert, "Mapping the Emotional Terrain."

62. Humility and humiliation are often ignored in foreign policy. For an extended discussion of humiliation as well as fear and hope, however, see Moisi, *Geopolitics of Emotion*.

63. On the role of anger, specifically, in foreign policy, see Brodersen, *Emotional Motives*.

64. Thrall and Cramer, *American Foreign Policy*.

65. See Mearsheimer and Walt, "Unnecessary War."

66. Thucydides, *History of the Peloponnesian War*, Ch. XVII.

67. It is also possible that the linguistic (as well as cultural) context will affect emotional assessments of other countries. The tests of the TAPS model offered in Chapters 7 and 8 hold this constant by comparing statements about Japan in the same language (English), taken from prominent English-language newspapers. In many cases, though, these include or consist in their entirety of statements translated from a Chinese or Korean original text. One interesting way to extend tests of the TAPS model would be to compare assessments in different languages. McAvene and Kowert provide some

evidence, in any case, that the emotional structures of diplomacy cut across cultural and linguistic context; see McAvene and Kowert, "Mapping the Emotional Terrain."

68. The democratic peace literature is extensive. For a classic statement, see Doyle, "Kant, Liberal Legacies." For recent overviews, see Chernoff, "Study of Democratic Peace"; Rasler and Thompson, *Puzzles of the Democratic Peace*; Ish-Shalom, *Democratic Peace*; and Imai and Lo, "Robustness of Empirical Evidence."

69. Cap, *Language of Fear*.

70. Chilton, *Analysing Political Discourse*; Chilton, *Language, Space and Mind*.

71. For a discussion of the various elements of discourse that can be used to study emotion, see also Koschut, *Power of Emotions*, 9–12.

72. Marcus, "How Fear and Anger Impact Democracy."

73. Ross, "Coming in from the Cold," 198.

74. Ross, "Coming in from the Cold," 198–99.

75. Ross, *Mixed Emotions*, 60.

CHAPTER 7

The View from Beijing

In the twenty-first century, Chinese animosity toward Japan simmers at a slow boil, often kept at manageable levels but sometimes erupting into uncontainable outrage. The two countries trade diplomatic barbs but nonetheless find it convenient to cooperate, particularly on matters of joint economic interest. Still, two incidents that occurred early in the new century illustrate just how emotional, and how troubled, the relationship has become.

The first of these events began on September 16, 2003, when several hundred Japanese employees of the Osaka-based Kōki construction company arrived at the Zhuhai International Conference Centre Hotel for a company-sponsored vacation. Zhuhai was a boom town near Macau in southern China with a large red-light district and a reputation for sex tourism. Kōki managers evidently arranged with several members of the hotel staff to hire hundreds of local prostitutes. According to the Beijing *Youth Daily*, a two-day-long orgy ensued, sometimes spilling out into the hotel's public spaces.[1] The denouement came on September 18, which was significant for many observers, since this was the anniversary of the Mukden incident that served as a pretext for Japan's 1931 invasion and occupation of Manchuria. Online commentators swiftly condemned not only the incident but the Japanese in general: "'The Japanese are animals,' said one contribution to a chatroom. 'They deliberately selected the date to humiliate the Chinese people.'"[2] According to a reporter for the *South China Morning Post*, "threats to boycott Japanese products, to kill Japanese tourists and blow up the Zhuhai hotel sprinkled the angry electronic chatter."[3] Ultimately, two hotel employees were sentenced to life in prison for "organizing prostitution," and the Chinese government called for the arrest of three Japanese citizens on the same charge.[4]

Not quite a year later, another large Japanese delegation arrived in China, this time for the more benign purpose of competing in the Asian Football Confederation Asian Cup. The Japanese men's soccer team was the defending Asian Cup champion, and it once again made its way to the final, as did the Chinese hosts. On August 7 the Chinese and Japanese teams thus met in Beijing Workers Stadium to decide the 2004 Asian Cup winner. Japan scored first, but China responded with a goal of its own, and the first half ended in a 1–1 tie. At the 65-minute mark in the second half, Japan again pulled ahead with a controversial score from a corner kick that was directed into the goal off the arm of midfielder Nakata Kōji. This proved to be the winning goal. Japanese players had been the targets of abuse throughout the tournament, but for many Chinese fans the referee's error and China's subsequent loss were the last straw. Officials were compelled to broadcast static from stadium PA system after the game to drown out a torrent of obscenities from the crowd during the cup presentation ceremony, and 2,000 Japanese fans had to be detained in the stadium because the police could not guarantee their safety outside it.[5]

These two incidents illustrate many of the emotional themes in Sino-Japanese relations. Neither episode was initiated by any action on the part of CCP officials, and in fact the Chinese government actively tried to tamp down hostility directed at the Japanese soccer team in the second case.[6] These are situations in which popular emotional reactions depended, therefore, on something other than government manipulation. Moreover, neither case was caused by actions that were directly relevant to international security or to Japan's wartime behavior, and yet memories of past Japanese aggression swiftly came to mind for Chinese observers. Although it seems unlikely that mid-level managers at an Osaka construction firm would have intentionally chosen to commemorate the Mukden incident, this apparent coincidence of timing was nonetheless deeply felt as a form of humiliation by many Chinese citizens. Even in the case of the Asian Cup soccer riot, Chinese fans were quick to bring up the past. As one man interviewed by a Reuters reporter complained, "we're seeing their old fascism starting to come back a little. For example, they are sending troops abroad."[7]

To the extent that these events raised the specter of Japan's past behavior, anger dominated Chinese reactions. Past Chinese weakness was also directly associated with shame or humiliation, as suggested by the horizontal axis of the TAPS model presented in Chapter 6. The Zhuhai case recalled Japan's sexual enslavement of women in China and Korea along with notorious events such as the Rape of Nanjing. Unsurprisingly, an outraged editorial published in the *South China Morning Post* and entitled "Chinese Humiliation" asked: "Will history repeat itself? Does anyone remember the Nanjing slaughter? Who cares about Chinese women's position of privilege and dignity nowadays?"[8] The sexual domination symbolized by the Zhuhai incident calls into question national virility. So do losses in sports. Victor Cha argues, in fact, that "Japan's imperial past in Asia causes most former colonies to view every contest with Japan as a historical grudge match."[9] Complicating matters is the sense that performance in high-profile sporting competitions speaks not only to the past but also to the future. The 2004 Asian Cup was held only four years before Beijing was to host the Olympic Games, and the pressure on Team China was intense. When the focus shifts to the future, however, somewhat different emotions are at stake. From the Chinese perspective, Japan is cast in an inferior role not simply by the usual dynamics of sports fandom but also by a palpable sense that history is on China's side as Chinese power grows. A loss when history is on one's side suggests some form of treachery, and a bad call during the game benefiting Japan simply reinforced this predisposition. Events such as this may occur by chance, of course, but the TAPS model suggests that they are likely to be interpreted in patterned ways, shifting the focus to individuals who are irrational, deceitful, or untrustworthy in some other fashion.

If sports competitions stand in for political competitions, then we should expect to see the same dynamics at play in diplomatic relations between China and Japan. Lily Ling argues that this is especially the case in competition between former colonies and colonizers, leading both to embrace a hypermasculine state. "Colonizers have done so to maintain their status 'on top' while the colonized appropriated the same hypermasculine discourse to assert that they, too, are men."[10] To the extent that both of these cases call into question Chinese masculinity, they hit hard emotionally. This is just one example of a "political economy of emotion," in which certain emotional states (such as masculine pride) are valued and others are devalued. In a clever essay on the subject, Karl Gustafsson and Todd H. Hall argue that "the politics of emotional obligation is a politics of duty."[11] They go on to say:

> Its protagonists seek to impose a requirement on a target group or category of actors to feel a particular emotion. Where successful, it establishes the shared normative expectation that a given situation, context, or issue should induce a specific emotion in the actor in question, be it negative (e.g., anger or guilt) or positive (e.g., satisfaction and pride).[12]

Japan is thus supposed to feel a certain way (contrite), and China is entitled to feel another way (aggrieved). Japanese victory, and the Japanese pride that accompanies it, upsets this emotional economy.

We can imagine how intractable the emotional politics might be when Japan and China's current strategic interests are actually at stake. Consider, therefore, the emotional resonances of two prominent issues in East Asian geopolitics: territorial disputes and arms races. Each involves competition over scarce resources, either territory or security. These competitions are seen most often in constant-sum terms, so that Japan's gains represent a loss for China. For the most part, territorial and strategic competitions also create constant-sum dynamics in domestic politics. That is to say that politicians align themselves either with policies of national assertion (most often) or of deference (less often, though deference is sometimes embraced by the Japanese left). In an election, we can well imagine, national assertion has much greater appeal, and this has proven to be just as true in China's less democratic political environment. In domestic politics as in international politics, the strategic competition between a powerful country that is losing ground in relative terms (Japan) and a rising regional hegemon (China) is likely to generate strong emotions for the citizens of both countries. Emotions associated with the Second World War are also potent, more so today than during the Cold War era when they were held more tightly in check by the internal and external politics of both countries.[13]

That there should be strong emotions, therefore, is no surprise. What is less often appreciated is that the political economy of emotions in Sino-Japanese relations itself approximates a zero-sum game. As the emotional stakes of athletic contests show, it is hard for both countries to experience pride simultaneously. In addition to international and domestic competitions, therefore, there is often an emotional competition at work between the two countries. The argument developed in Chapter 6 and formalized in the TAPS model is that this emotional competition tends to be channeled down certain paths by judgments about valence and relative capabilities. In the case of contemporary Sino-Japanese relations, moreover, judgments about valence are already fairly circumscribed. A 2014 poll conducted by Genron NPO in Japan and the *China Daily* in China showed, for example, that 93 percent of Japanese respondents had an "unfavorable" impression of China, and 86.8 percent of Chinese respondents had an "unfavorable" impression of Japan, down slightly from 92.8 percent the previous year.[14] The way general antagonisms between Japan and China manifest themselves will also be associated, more specifically, with judgments about capabilities. To the extent that the other is understood to be inferior in some fashion, dislike manifests itself as *disdain*. Typically, disdain links another's inferior capabilities to other sorts of inferiority: poor judgment, moral failings, or malign intent. Thus the other is to blame for its own inferiority.

Alternatively, when the other's capabilities are great or seen as rising, then fear for the future is more likely, often accompanied with anger over past slights. The other has the capability to do harm (something it could not do so easily if it were weaker), and to do so would be unjust. Thus, focusing specifically on Chinese attitudes toward Japan, we might anticipate that China's rise will precipitate a shift from some blend of anger and fear to disdain. As Japan becomes weaker in relative terms (or to the extent that China is seen as stronger in the long run), expressions of dislike are likely to focus increasingly on moral failings that explain Japanese weakness, particularly the failings of Japanese leaders. Yet in domains where Japan remains strong—or when attention focuses on actions that might augment Japanese power, such as modification of the Japanese constitution in order to permit more extensive military armament—fear and anger are likely to figure more prominently in Chinese attitudes.

The TAPS model suggests the paths down which Chinese emotion toward Japan is most likely to be channeled. As shown in Figure 7.1, fear and anger are likely to dominate Chinese attitudes when events call to mind past Japanese aggression or when Japan is expected to pose a significant threat (as suggested, for example, by the possibility of Japanese rearmament). On the other hand, disdain is more likely in contexts that emphasize China's growing economic and military prowess and its general ascendancy within Asia. Moreover, when disdain creates a feedback loop that leads to exaggerated judgments about the irrationality or immaturity of Japanese leaders, a Melos complex may take hold. This will cause Chinese leaders to expect more deference from Japan than Japanese leaders can afford given their own domestic constraints. Conversely, in situations where Japan still has the upper hand, fear may even lead to exaggerated claims about Japanese capabilities and hostility, constituting a Sparta complex.

Fear of Japan is not evidence, *ipso facto*, of a Sparta complex. Aaron Friedberg and Thomas Christensen, among others, argue that Asia is an especially dangerous region characterized by intense security dilemmas.[15] According to Christensen, "Chinese analysts emphasize the advanced equipment that Japan has acquired, particularly since the late 1970s when it began developing a navy and air force designed to help the United States contain the Soviet Union's growing Pacific Fleet."[16] They are aware, moreover, "that Japan has practiced a great deal of self-restraint in eschewing weapons designed to project power far from the home islands."[17] Many of them, Christensen believes,

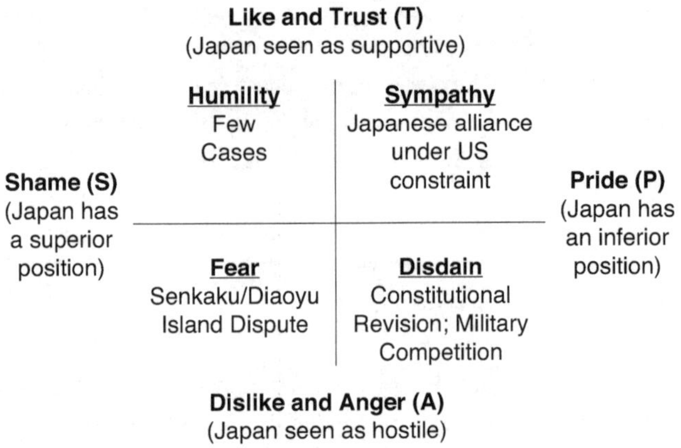

Like and Trust (T)
(Japan seen as supportive)

	Humility Few Cases	**Sympathy** Japanese alliance under US constraint	
Shame (S) (Japan has a superior position)			**Pride (P)** (Japan has an inferior position)
	Fear Senkaku/Diaoyu Island Dispute	**Disdain** Constitutional Revision; Military Competition	

Dislike and Anger (A)
(Japan seen as hostile)

Figure 7.1. Emotional Dynamics in China-Japan Relations

fear that this restraint is gradually eroding. This trend has continued since Christensen wrote, moreover, resulting in projects such as the conversion of Japan's *Izumo* class helicopter destroyers to permit deployment of F-35B V/STOL fighter aircraft, effectively making them light aircraft carriers.[18]

Still, Christensen's point is not that China is right to fear Japan but rather that there is a more significant debate among Chinese policymakers about how to react to Japan than is commonly appreciated in the West. To some extent, this ambivalence may be reflected in popular attitudes as well. That would explain why there are fluctuations in attitudes toward Japan even though they are generally negative overall. We would expect not only that attitudes would grow more negative when certain issues—such as disputes over contested territory or Japanese memorialization of war in ways that do not seem sufficiently contrite—inflame tensions. Such tendencies are all too apparent. What is less widely appreciated, however, is the way that different contexts evoke different emotional reactions. Angry fear is very different from disdain. Moreover, both emotions can become exaggerated, leading to distinctive emotional complexes.

OFFICIAL ATTITUDES

The period since Xi Jinping assumed office as the general secretary of the Chinese Communist Party in November 2012 has provided numerous opportunities to evaluate the TAPS model. Little more than a month later, in December 2012, Abe Shinzō returned to power after a brief and mostly unsuccessful first term in 2005–2006 as Japan's prime minister. The theme of Abe's second tenure as prime minister, echoing his own political fortunes, was that "Japan is back."[19] Despite this—or, in part, because of it—the ensuing eight years before Abe again left office in September 2020 saw relations between China and Japan plummet to some of their lowest depths. Abe's nationalism and its political efficacy with his electoral base undoubtedly contributed to this especially rocky patch in their relations.[20]

In the abstract we might expect that China's focus would be less on Abe's nationalism and more on economic matters. The years surrounding Abe's return to power coincided with China's rise to economic superpower status. In 2010 the Chinese economy surpassed Japan's to become the world's second-largest economy.[21] Just a few years later, in 2013, China overtook the United States as the world's largest goods trader (as well as the largest oil importer).[22] By this time, China's gross GDP was twice that of Japan.[23] With greater wealth at its disposal, China's military modernization program also accelerated steadily.[24] Increasingly the PLA has developed assets that go beyond territorial defense to permit force projection in regional and maritime conflicts.[25] Chinese ascendancy, combined with Japan's persistent economic malaise, should tend to foster dismissive attitudes toward Japan and an emotional politics of disdain. Just this sort of contemptuous attitude is readily apparent in many official Chinese statements. Even when combined with anger, this anger will tend to be directed more toward Japanese leaders who are seen as untrustworthy, immature, or irrational. On the other hand, when Chinese leaders look to the past, disdain will be filtered out by Japan's relatively greater capabilities, leaving only anger. Or, in areas where Japan still has the upper hand, this anger may be mixed with a degree of fear, particularly when Japanese capabilities are exaggerated.

We might begin, therefore, by considering the interactions of China and Japan's policymakers when dealing with issues that arise out of the general strategic relationship between the two countries, setting aside for the moment issues that specifically invoke their historical conflicts or territorial disputes. These are interactions in which China expects to have the upper hand due to the relative growth in its power. The TAPS model suggests that an emotional politics of disdain focusing specifically on Japanese leadership should dominate Chinese reactions to such issues.

In the first year following his return to the Kantei, Abe convened numerous security-related advisory councils. These included an Advisory Council on the Establishment of a National Security Council, an Advisory Panel on the Reconstruction of the Legal Basis for Security, and an Advisory Panel on National Security and Defense Capabilities.[26] Debates within Japan over possible revision or reinterpretation of the Japanese constitution's Article 9 constraints on the Self Defense Forces were closely followed in China. In the meetings of his advisory councils and in public speeches, Abe "repeatedly called attention to China's ongoing military modernization that included 10 percent increases in the defense budget for over 22 years."[27] Asked for comment, "Chinese Foreign Ministry spokesperson Hua Chunying charged the prime minster with repeatedly making 'provocative' remarks, showing 'once again that the Japanese politicians are deceiving themselves with arrogance and a guilty conscience.'"[28] Another spokesperson, Qin Gang, commenting on "Abe's charge that China is engaged in a military build-up . . . , expressed 'dissatisfaction with Japanese leaders' flagrant hype of the so-called China threat theory.'"[29] In comments such as these, as expected, Chinese officials castigate Japanese officials for conduct they view as provocative and irrational.

By December the Abe government had completed its defense review and issued a new Mid-Term Defense Plan and new National Security Strategy, both of which were approved by the Cabinet on December 17, 2013. These new plans called for an increased focus on air and sea defense capabilities in Japan's southwest region.[30] At this point, however, Sino-Japanese relations were overtaken by a new development. On December 26, as 2013 drew to a close, Prime Minister Abe elected to pay a controversial visit to Yasukuni Shrine, where Japan's war dead (including some classified as war criminals after World War II) are enshrined. This incident shifted the focus of emotions onto the past and thus provoked anger rather than disdain or contempt. At first, this may seem to be a curious response, and one might have expected more of the same sort of complaints Chinese officials were already making about provocative actions by Japanese leadership.

Because Yasukuni Shrine had become a symbol in China (and South Korea) of Japan's lack of true remorse for its wartime actions, however, Abe's shrine visit brought the past into the present, rekindling anger over Japan's imperial expansion. Anger dominated the resulting news coverage. The *Guardian* proclaimed: "Japan's Shinzo Abe Angers Neighbours and US by Visiting War Dead Shrine."[31] Bloomberg's story ran, "Abe Draws China Anger with Visit to Japan's Yasukuni War Shrine."[32] Agence France Press discerned an even more intense reaction: "Japan PM's Visit to Yasukuni War Shrine Infuriates China."[33] The BBC, likewise, described China's reaction as infuriated in its caption of Abe's photograph at the shrine.[34] And China's own English-language newspaper of record, the *China Daily*, was perhaps the most succinct of all: "Anger over Abe's Shrine Visit."[35]

Abe's visit to Yasukuni Shrine marked the first time a sitting Japanese prime minister visited the shrine since Koizumi Junichirō did so in 2006. Koizumi's visits also provoked intense reactions, including anti-Japanese riots in China.[36] Reacting to Abe's decision to resume prime ministerial visits to the shrine, China's Foreign Minister Wang Yi called it "a flagrant provocation against international justice . . . [that] treads arbitrarily on humanity's conscience." He went on to say, "Japan must bear 'full responsibility for the serious political consequences' of . . . [an] action [that] has pushed Japan in an 'extremely dangerous' direction."[37] Another representative of the Chinese Foreign Ministry, Qin Gang, proclaimed that "Abe's visit to the shrine whitewashes Japanese aggression and colonial rule, overthrows the international community's trial of Japanese militarism and challenges the post-war international order."[38] China's ambassador to Japan, Cheng Yonghua, labeled the visit a "political and diplomatic issue" bearing on "Japan's perception of the nature of the war of aggression and responsibility for that war."[39] Perhaps the most dramatic reaction came from China's ambassador to the United Kingdom, Liu Xiaoming, who wrote an op ed for the *Daily Telegraph* in which he resorts to fiction to find a suitably evil villain:

> In the Harry Potter story, the dark wizard Voldemort dies hard because the seven horcruxes, which contain parts of his soul, have been destroyed. If militarism is like the haunting Voldemort of Japan, the Yasukuni Shrine in Tokyo is a kind of horcrux, representing the darkest parts of that nation's soul.[40]

The choice of Voldemort as an analogy for Japanese militarism is telling. The other characters in J. K. Rowling's novel did not look down on Voldemort; they feared him.

Several things stand out about Chinese reactions to Abe's Yasukuni Shrine visit. One is the abrupt shift from disdainful comments about Abe as reckless or provocative to outright anger. At first blush, this is a curious reaction. It would seemingly have been easy for Chinese officials to condemn him for irresponsible behavior. By shifting the focus of attention to the past and to the acceptance of responsibility for Japan's wartime behavior, however, the shrine visits effectively shift the emotional landscape back into one in which China was the aggrieved victim rather than the rising power on the cusp of superpower status. This helps to explain why anger dominates Chinese reactions. It is also striking that Abe's actions are described as "dangerous" and incompatible with "international justice" and the "post-war international order." These are bold claims about what is at stake. Whether they are overblown is less the issue, for the present analysis, than what they require emotionally. When the stakes are this important, then it again seems likely that disdain must give way to outright anger.

The issue that bedevils Sino-Japanese relations more than any other, however, has to do with the future as much as the past: the ownership of a small group of islands in the East China Sea. Called the Pinnacle Islands by the British Navy in the nineteenth century, these uninhabited islands are located west of Okinawa, east of China, and northeast of Taiwan. After World War II the United States administered the islands until 1972, when control passed to Japan as part of the Okinawa Reversion Treaty. They are currently administered by Japan and called the Senkaku Islands, but they are also claimed by China and Taiwan and called the Diaoyu Islands in Chinese.[41] After the 1972 reversion to Japan, the descendants of a Japanese entrepreneur who had once constructed a bonito fish processing plant on one of the islands sold four of the islands to the Kurihara family. The crucial turning point came on September 11, 2012—just before Xi and Abe took office—when the Japanese government purchased three of these islands from the Kurihara family, nationalizing them in order to forestall a campaign to purchase and develop the islands led by Tokyo Governor Ishihara Shintarō. When activists from Hong Kong attempted to land on the islands in August 2012, while nationalization was still being considered, they were detained by Japanese authorities, which touched off the massive protests in China discussed in Chapter 5. Whatever the Japanese government's intent, this decision to nationalize the islands provoked a crisis and set off the downward spiral in Sino-Japanese relations that continued throughout Abe and Xi's first few years in office.

Because Japan effectively administers the islands, it has an advantageous position that we would expect to alter the emotional dynamics of this dispute. Rather than disdain provoked by the actions of an inferior but still-threatening state—one that has not learned the lessons of history—a territorial competition in which Japan holds the upper hand can be expected to provoke anger and, perhaps, even a degree of fear. This anger, moreover, is focused not on Japan's historical actions—although it would not be surprising for the past to be invoked as a way of justifying China's anger—but on the future and the question of whether Japan will remain a pacifist nation, live up to its obligations, and show suitable deference to those who formerly suffered at its hands.

After the Japanese decision to purchase the islands was announced, the Chinese Foreign Ministry proclaimed: "This is a serious infringement of China's sovereignty and has seriously hurt the feelings of 1.3 billion Chinese. . . .

The Chinese government and people express their resolute opposition and protest strongly."[42] Several weeks later, at a symposium marking the normalization of relations between China and Japan forty years earlier, Assistant Foreign Minister Le Yuchen again emphasized Chinese anger as well as the danger of the situation:

> Forty years after the normalization of their relations, China and Japan once again find themselves at a crossroads. The decision of the Japanese government to "purchase" Chinese islands, like an atomic bomb dropped on China, has aroused the anger of all Chinese and rallied the 1.3 billion people of China closely together. I want to make it as clear as possible to Japan: never expect China to accept the so-called "nationalization" of the Diaoyu Dao islands, never cherish the illusion for continued occupation of the islands, and never assume that the matter will simply disappear or be explained away by some kind of envoys. If Japan insists on having its own way and lurches down on its erroneous path, then the big ship of China-Japan relations may strike a rock and sink like the Titanic.[43]

Le concluded by admonishing Japan to "make a profound self-examination of its past mistakes, show political courage in making a resolute political decision to defuse the un-time bomb of the issue of Diaoyu Dao through credible measures, and call off all moves that jeopardize China's territorial sovereignty so as to bring China–Japan relations back to their correct track toward peace and friendship."[44] Le's comments are notable in just the ways anticipated by the TAPS model. They express anger and direct attention to the past. They also use dramatic images to stress the danger of the situation: Japan's action is likened to an "atomic bomb dropped on China" and to the sinking of the *Titanic*. Finally, they expressly look to the future as well, warning that the issue will never "simply disappear."

This mixture of anger and warnings of dire consequences in the future continued once Xi and Abe were in power. After Abe delivered his annual policy address on February 28, 2013, drawing a parallel between his administration and British Prime Minister Margaret Thatcher's defense of British sovereignty in the Falkland/Malvinas Islands, "China's Foreign Ministry spokesperson Hua Chunying responded to Abe's address by reasserting that 'the Daioyu Island and its affiliated islands have been China's inherent territory since ancient times.'"[45] Turning to the future, "Hua called on Japan to 'give up its illusion' with respect to the Diaoyu Islands and 'to face squarely history and reality.' If the relations are to improve, Japan should 'cease words and actions that insult China and by its actions make every effort to improve ties.'"[46] In the following year, China dramatically stepped up its own patrols around the disputed islands. "According to Japanese government figures, as of Sept. 9 (2014), a total of 208 Chinese government ships had entered Japan's territorial waters on 62 separate days in the year since nationalization. Japanese Coast Guard figures put days spent in Japan's sovereign waters and contiguous zone at 260 since nationalization."[47] Chinese figures were about the same, setting "the number at 59 days spent in the area of the Senkakus/Diaoyus. China's State Oceanic Administration, commenting on the patrols, issued a statement that said 'China is building a strong maritime nation. All actions undermining China's interests in sovereignty, security and development will face strong opposition and firm resistance.'"[48] The forcefulness of China's response, combined with the use of dramatic imagery such as the atomic bombing, suggests not only anger but perhaps an instance of the Sparta complex in which an exaggerated threat from Japan justifies an equally robust response from China.

As 2014 began, Abe attended the World Economic Summit in Davos, where he used a press conference to compare Japan and China to Britain and Germany a century earlier and warned that their economic interdependence had not been enough to prevent the first world war.[49] Asked to comment on this analogy, Chinese Foreign Minister Wang Yi replied, "Abe's remarks struck me as total disorder of time and space, making no sense at all."[50] Wang then launched into a disquisition about Japan's own history as a colonial aggressor before concluding: "Since history is the subject here, we advise the Japanese leader to fully reflect on history and learn its lessons. Only by doing so can Japan create a better future and win the trust of its neighboring countries."[51] As in previous Chinese commentary, Wang thus moves from the past to the future and the danger Japan poses as a potential aggressor.

From the nadir of Sino-Japanese relations, capped off by Abe's Yasukuni Shrine visit in 2013, the relationship slowly began to improve. Abe sought a summit with Xi at the November 2014 Asia–Pacific Economic Cooperation (APEC) meeting in Beijing, and Xi finally, reluctantly agreed. Their meeting culminated in a notoriously awkward handshake.[52] Somehow this awkward moment managed to break the ice, however, and the two leaders had a slightly warmer exchange five months later in Bandung, Indonesia, on the sidelines of the Asian–African summit commemorating the 60th anniversary of the Bandung Conference.[53] The question of whether to look forward or backward continued to complicate matters as the seventieth anniversary of the end of hostilities in the Pacific War approached. On August 14, 2015, Abe delivered a speech to mark the occasion that delivered much of what even his critics wanted. According to Robert Manning, "Abe's Cabinet-approved speech was an amply dignified and contrite effort that attempted to 'squarely face up to history' as leaders in China and South Korea demanded."[54]

From this point the anger expressed by Chinese officials began to revert back to a more typical pattern of mistrust. Chinese leaders questioned Abe's sincerity but scaled back their warnings of a dire Japanese threat. Even the passage of new security legislation in September 2015 allowing the Japanese military to engage in overseas operations for the purposes of "collective self-defense" mostly prompted complaints that Japan was shifting toward right-wing nationalism under Abe. Bonnie Glaser and Brittney Farrar characterized "remarks by Chinese officials on the updated U.S.-Japan defense guidelines . . . [as] relatively mild."[55] The following spring, at a press conference coinciding with the National People's Congress in March 2016, Chinese foreign minister Wang Yi complained that "Japan was guilty of 'double dealing.'"[56] He continued, "On the one hand, Japanese government leaders say nice things about wanting to improve relations, on the other hand, they are making trouble for China at every turn. . . . This is what I would call a typical case of double dealing."[57] As it happens Wang made his remarks at about the same time that Japan announced new Self-Defense Forces (SDF) deployments tasked with monitoring its southern islands, including "a 160-man Ground Self-Defense Force (GSDF) observation unit on Yonaguni Island" and plans to "spend $107 million to rebuild an observation post on Okinotorishima."[58] That these developments were met with exasperation more than anger and alarm signals that China had returned its focus to the general military balance and to its ongoing diplomatic goals. Consistent with the TAPS model, emotions shifted back to contempt directed, in particular, at Japanese leaders.

EDITORIALIZING IN BEIJING

There is much more to the war of words between Beijing and Tokyo's top officials than mere dislike. This itself is an important corrective to the blasé assertion that Japan's wartime actions have simply produced an unshakable hatred toward Japan in China and South Korea. On the contrary something more interesting is going on in China (and, as the next chapter will argue, in South Korea). Statements by Chinese officials display a recognizable pattern, shifting toward anger when Japan has the upper hand and even reflecting a degree of hyperbolic fear about Japanese capabilities and the prospect of future militarization. Anger also dominates official discourse when the conversation shifts to the legacy of the Pacific War, during which Japan's power was relatively greater. On the other hand, when Chinese officials turn to the topic of contemporary Asian security, their emotional language seems to shift from anger to derision and a critical appraisal of the choices of specific Japanese leaders, such as Koizumi and Abe.

This pattern is consistent with the TAPS model, but the statements presented in the preceding section—while suggestive—do not constitute much of a test. One problem is that it is difficult to find statements that discuss only a single issue in isolation. Instead Chinese leaders often discuss Japan's contemporary security decisions, its historical behavior, and the prospect of future militarization all in the same breath. When Japan announced its revised guidelines for defense cooperation with the United States and passed the necessary legislation to authorize "collective self-defense" in May 2015, for example, Chinese officials mostly dismissed the move as an outdated application of Cold War logic. Yang Jiechi, one of the principal architects of China's foreign policy under Xi, linked the past to the future by complaining that "the Japanese side runs against the tide of the times and the general trend of the world by accelerating the build-up of its military muscles and significantly changing its military security policy, which cannot but raise concern and questions from its neighboring countries."[59] And when Japan released a defense white paper blaming China for Japan's worsening security environment, Chinese officials again looked backward and forward in time. Chinese Foreign Ministry spokesperson Lu Kang complained that "Japan once again ignores facts . . . [and] makes irresponsible remarks."[60] Lu went on to note that "the Diaoyu Islands have been China's inherent territory since ancient times" before proclaiming that "China will continue to take necessary measures and stay firm in safeguarding territorial sovereignty."[61] It is not surprising that past actions, the ongoing islands dispute, and Japan's future military strategy are all linked in statements such as these. We should expect emotional reactions in China to be "blended" as well, although this complicates the task of studying the way different circumstances give rise to different emotions.

To undertake a somewhat more systematic test of the TAPS model, we might attempt to compensate for this problem by searching for instances in which Chinese leaders focus on a single issue. One way to do so is by sampling articles in the *People's Daily Online*—the official English-language online newspaper of the CCP—in the years before and after specific Japanese policy changes. The *People's Daily* maintains a searchable archive of articles published since 2009. Although this archive represents only a small fraction of Chinese commentary, it is nevertheless very useful. Many of the indexed articles are either partially or entirely translated from

Chinese articles. They represent, moreover, a self-conscious effort on the part of Communist Party officials to present a quasi-official Chinese perspective on daily events to the world. In this sense they may constitute an even better distillation of elite Chinese views than would a more diverse range of commentary available in Chinese sources. Sampling articles from this database between 2010 and 2015 is thus a good way to capture sentiment before, during, and after the Senkaku/Diaoyu Islands imbroglio, which is a good test case for an issue that places Japan in an advantageous position. In contrast, searching for articles on constitutional revision in Japan during the same time span allows us to highlight the general military balance between China and Japan, which places China in an increasingly favorable position.

To control for bias in the selection of statements, the following discussion analyzes a sample of *People's Daily* articles from each year on the relevant topic, excluding articles that extensively discuss multiple issues in Sino-Japanese relations and following the detailed procedures described in the Appendix. Because the TAPS model is at an early stage of development, carefully studying a smaller sample of text is more useful than a circumscribed analysis of a larger sample. This analysis extracts all adjectives referring to Japan, the Japanese government, Japanese leaders, or the state of Sino-Japanese relations from each article. Contrasting an issue in which Japanese capabilities are in relative decline compared to those of China (the overall military balance) with an issue over which Japan still holds considerable sway (the islands dispute) permits a comparison of emotional patterns. As an additional test of the extent to which adjectives describing China constitute a mirror image of those describing Japan, adjectives describing China were also coded separately. I have no preconceived formal theory of the way adjectives describing Japan will necessarily relate to a given emotion such as fear, anger, or disdain. But the work of Piotr Cap and Paul Chilton, discussed in Chapter 6, offers some general guidance about what to expect. Table 7.1 offers an overview of the different expectations we might have for the two cases.

In general, in the case of constitutional revision, we would expect the focus of China's emotional reaction to be on the character or rationality of Japanese leaders, both of which will be seen as lacking. And although one might expect irrationality to result in unpredictable behavior, Chinese dominance should nevertheless lead to an emotional confidence about the ultimate outcome: that Japan will have to acknowledge China's true position of dominance and exhibit proper deference. The contrast between the seemingly irrational (from Beijing's perspective) efforts to resist China's rise and

Table 7.1: Emotional Content and Chinese Discourse on Japan

Case	Constitutional Revision	Islands Dispute
Japan's Position	Relatively Disadvantageous	Relatively Advantageous
Dominant Emotion	Disdain	Fear or Anger
Emotional Target	Leaders	State
Target's Character	Irrational, Untrustworthy	Rational, Dangerous
Time Frame	Present	Past (Anger) / Future (Fear)
Modality	Predictable	Unpredictable (in the future)

its inevitability is precisely the source of Chinese attitudes of disdain. On the other hand, in the specific case of the Senkaku/Diaoyu Islands dispute, where Japan currently maintains an advantageous position in part because of support from the United States, the focus is instead on the danger posed by the Japanese state itself, its unwillingness to learn from past mistakes, and its potential for reckless behavior in the future.

Constitutional Revision and Military Competition

In July 2014 Japanese Prime Minister Abe Shinzō announced his government's reinterpretation of Article 9 of the Japanese Constitution. Previously, the Liberal Democratic Party (LDP) had interpreted the constitution to allow for self-defense. As discussed in the preceding section, however, Abe extended this line of reasoning to refer to "collective self-defense" as well, thus permitting Japan to use its SDF in support (defense) of alliance partners outside of Japanese territory. Although this may appear to be the incremental extension of a logic that has long been commonplace in Japanese discussions of constitutional defense issues, it has nevertheless appeared to others—both outside Japan and also within—as crossing an important Rubicon. For the first time since occupation, it claims formal justification to deploy armed Japanese personnel in military operations outside of, and not explicitly linked to the defense of, Japanese territory. Although the issue is one of constitutional interpretation, it serves as a good proxy for the general issue of East Asian security and the military balance between China and Japan.

To assemble a list of adjectives associated in Chinese discourse with Japan's constitutional reinterpretation and plans for collective self-defense, I coded *People's Daily* articles that mention "Japan" and "constitution" for each year from 2010 to 2015. The Appendix presents the complete list of all adjectives describing Japan identified in these articles, divided into those prior to Abe's constitutional reinterpretation and those after it. Between 2010 and 2013, articles in the *People's Daily Online* described Japan in many different ways. The adjectives used are overwhelmingly, though not entirely, negative. Japan is seen as *aggressive, alarming, anti-China, backwards, dangerous, fraught, intolerable, malicious, provocative, untrustworthy,* and even *villainous.* On the valence dimension (like to dislike), these adjectives clearly indicate an overall negative rather than positive attitude toward Japan. The few positive adjectives—such as *active, advanced, bold,* or *pacifist*—were typically qualified in some way. That is, they referred to one aspect of the Japanese state's activities (its *advanced* economy), to the (*pacifist, decent*) sentiments of the people in contrast to the activities of the state, or to a particular (*active* or *bold*) behavior that, itself, might not be desirable, even if *boldness* in general might have positive connotations.

Beyond the generally negative tone, however, the more interesting aspect of Chinese emotions pertains to the shame/pride dimension related to capabilities and China's growing power relative to Japan. To the extent that references to Japan's peace constitution and to the prospect that it might be revised are, implicitly, references to the military balance between the two countries, China's growing power is expected to create attitudes of disdain for a country that fails to understand and accept the new reality. The target of such emotions is more likely to be Japan's leaders rather than the Japanese state in general, and adjectives are likely to express various forms of contempt for their flaws and failure to "reflect properly" on the lessons of the Second World War. The vast majority of adjectives observed in the 2010–2013 articles, including several of the generally negative adjectives already mentioned, are adjectives of this type: *backwards, brazen, deliberate, hawkish, impenitent, irresponsible, perverse, repugnant, rightist, rightwing, secretive, short-sighted, unreasonable, unrepentant, untrustworthy, villainous,* and *willful.* Such adjectives are not merely negative. They all express condemnation of actors or behavior that is regarded as flawed, petty, or irrational. They express the judgment, in other words, that Japan is acting without proper regard even for its own interests, much less for China's. These are not the adjectives one would use to describe a state that is threatening because it is a powerful commercial or even strategic rival. We may have harsh words for the latter sort of state as well, but we understand why it behaves as it does (because we also seek economic or strategic advantage).

We might also consider how often specific adjectives are used rather than the range of adjectives. Figure 7.2 shows all adjectives used more than once in the articles coded for 2010–2013. What stands out is that nearly *all* of the most frequently used adjectives—*rightwing* (or *rightist*), *militarist, unpopular,* and *controversial*—specifically refer to deficiencies in Japanese decision making. Only one, *dangerous,* could be taken as a more generally negative reaction to perceived Japanese threat.

Generally speaking, Chinese adjectives describing the strategic competition with Japan can be expected to adopt a condescending and judgmental tone. We should keep in mind, moreover, that these are adjectives appearing in articles that discuss the general prospect of Japanese constitutional revision *before* Abe's specific proposal in 2014. It may also be instructive to see whether there is any difference after this event. Constitutional revision conceivably allows for the expansion of a technologically sophisticated Japanese military with greater capability for power projection than is currently the case. It seems unlikely that Chinese policymakers would expect this to call into question the general historical shift toward Chinese advantage. Yet Abe's 2014 reinterpretation is notable in one other way: it specifically focuses on collective self-defense, presumably in coordination with the United States. By linking Japanese capabilities to American capabilities, this does create a more threatening prospect for China. So, although we might continue to expect critical appraisals of Japanese leaders during this later period (again, it is likely that Chinese officials continue to assess Japan as a regional power in relative decline compared with China), it would not be surprising to find some expressions of anger or even fear regarding the threat posed by this alliance and the prospect of future Japanese militarization within it.

The adjectives used by the *People's Daily Online* in late 2014 and 2015 do exhibit some apparent changes compared with the earlier period (see the

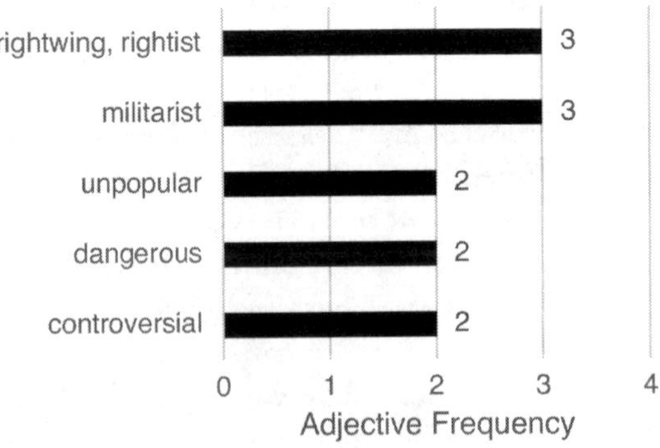

Figure 7.2. Frequency of Adjectives Referring to Japan and Constitutional Reform, 2010–phy 13

Appendix for the complete list). As in 2010–13, they include expressions of general negativity (e.g., *alarming, flagrant, offensive, reprehensible*). And they do continue to include many expressions of contempt for Japan and, in particular, for Abe and other Japanese leaders: *ambitious, bigoted, blatant, deliberate, militarist, nationalistic, reprehensible, right-wing,* and *unpopular,* among others. Yet after 2014 there are also more adjectives—such as *alarming, dangerous, expansionist, hegemony-seeking,* and *offensive*—expressing fears linked directly to the prospect of increasing Japanese capabilities, perhaps in concert with the United States. These are sentiments less likely to be attached to an adversary seen as inferior but instead to one that is seen as dangerous. They are more likely to provoke anger or fear rather than disgust or disdain.

A frequency analysis of adjectives (Figure 7.3) also reveals some changes. Not only *dangerous* but also *alarming* appear this time among the most frequently used adjectives. The other most-frequently used adjectives—*right-wing* (and its synonyms), *provocative, isolated,* and *irresponsible*—continue to signal a critique of Japanese leadership as extreme, out of step (isolated), and irrational. So, although there is some evidence of a shift in the pattern of adjectives used to describe Japan in the pages of the *People's Daily Online* after Abe announced his administration's constitutional reinterpretation, the general pattern of adjectives remains fairly consistent and as predicted. Overwhelmingly, adjectives applied to Japan reflect the sentiment that Japan (and, specifically, its leadership) is retrograde, inferior, and characterized by some sort of moral failing. This sentiment is often associated with

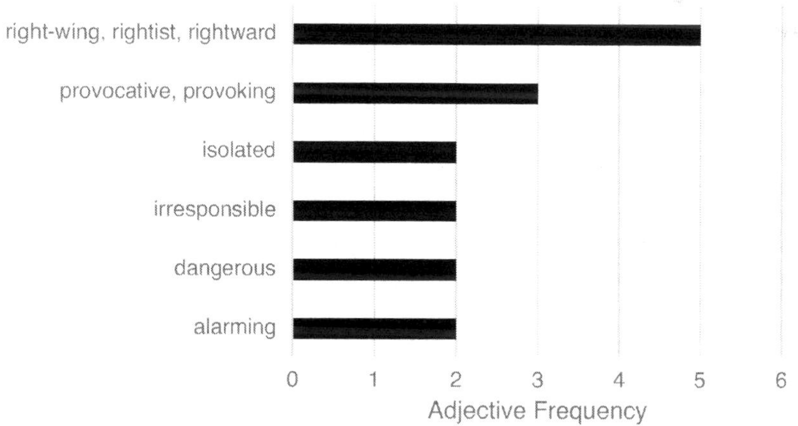

Figure 7.3. Frequency of Adjectives Referring to Japan and Constitutional Reform, 2014–15

a rightward shift by Japanese leaders such as Abe and with remonstrations about Japanese failures to reflect properly on the country's war responsibility. In some cases these criticisms are coupled with unfavorable comparisons to Germany. The headline of one *People's Daily* editorial proclaimed, "Historically Cowardly Abe Needs a Good Dose of German Bravery."[62]

Students of national role conceptions and foreign policy images, such as those discussed at some length in Chapter 3, hypothesize that our judgments about other countries often serve as an important mirror for our "national selves."[63] Thus if Japan is characterized as inferior and morally failing, we might expect accompanying descriptions of China to stress the latter's moral rectitude and virtues. This is indeed generally the case with adjectives referring to China in the coded articles referring to Japan and its constitution. China is described as *courageous, defensive, peaceful,* and *peace-loving.* It is not a *threat.* There are also several adjectives that paint a much different picture of China, describing it as *bullied, humiliated,* or *insulted.* These are the sorts of self-descriptions we might expect from an emotional context that presents an adversary as a strong threat rather than a (relatively) weak but problematic country. Sparta can bully, to put this another way, but not Melos. A closer look at the articles containing these adjectives shows that, in each case, the adjective was used in the context of a discussion of Japan's historical actions. The point was that China might have been bullied or humiliated in the past, but that this is no longer possible.

In general, therefore, the adjectives used to describe both Japan and China are consistent with the TAPS model of emotive politics. In articles that focus on the basic strategic calculus of East Asian geopolitics and the military balance between the two countries, perceptions in China of a gradually improving strategic position should lead to an emotional account of Japan that is dismissive more than angry. Of course Japan retains not only considerable economic importance but also substantial military potential. There are occasions when Chinese politicians and pundits do tend to sound alarmed and angry rather than dismissive or condescending. The dispute over the Senkaku/Diaoyu Islands is just such a case.

Island Disputes

A search for articles in the *People's Daily Online* including the terms *Japan* and *Diaoyu* reveals a marked upsurge in attention beginning in Fall 2012, when Ishihara Shintarō's plan to purchase the islands began to gain notice, ultimately prompting the central government's move to nationalize them instead. In the two years prior, an average of 15 articles a year mentioned these two terms. In the immediate aftermath of Japan's decision to nationalize the islands, attention increased by an order of magnitude. In 2012 and 2013 the same terms were mentioned in an average of 172 articles a year. Thereafter (in 2014 and 2015) attention began to subside, but the terms are still mentioned in an average of a hundred articles a year. It makes sense, therefore, to divide an analysis of these articles into three phases: before nationalization of the islands (2010–11); immediately after nationalization, corresponding to the lowest point in Sino-Japanese relations (2012–13); and the subsequent two years during which the relationship slowly recovered (2014–15). As with the previous analysis of articles pertaining to constitutional revision, articles were sampled from each of these six years to produce lists of adjectives describing Japan, its leaders, its policies, and its relations with China (see the Appendix for the complete list of adjectives).

The first period (2010–11) serves as a baseline. We might expect the adjectives used to describe Japan during this interval to be somewhat less dismissive of Japan, given Japan's advantageous position on the islands, compared with those in the articles describing the general military balance or constitutional revisions plans discussed previously. With China's focus divided among a variety of issues, however, it would not be surprising for China's more generally disdainful attitudes to be present in these articles as well. In the second period (2012–13) after the decision to nationalize the islands, however, we should expect Beijing's attention to be focused on what it perceives as a direct challenge. Given Japan's de facto administrative control of the islands, China's reaction is more likely to tend toward anger than disdain, and criticism is more likely to focus on the aggressive policies of the Japanese state rather than the unrepentant attitudes of its leaders. Finally, in the third period (2014–15), we might expect expressions of outrage to subside somewhat while a more complex emotional picture takes shape, one torn between competing images of Japan as a powerful threat (perhaps even an exaggerated threat, i.e., the Sparta complex) and a weak but corrupt threat (the Melos complex).

Not only was there far more attention to the islands dispute in the Chinese media after 2012, but a sample of the same number of articles yields considerably more adjectives: 23 different adjectives in 2010–11, compared with 38 different adjectives in 2012–13. The adjectives in the latter period are also much more negative. In 2010 and 2011, as expected, the adjectives used describe Japan and its leaders as *clueless, extremist, hawkish, irresponsible,* and *restless.* Sino-Japanese relations are sometimes described as *beneficial, cooperative,* and even *friendly,* but at other times as *simmering, strained,* and *troubled.* References to Japanese capabilities are similarly uncertain; Japan is seen as *major* but also increasingly *dependent* and *once-dynamic.* In general, then, the pattern is similar to that seen in articles that refer to Japan and its constitution in these years—with negative references that mostly express disdain (Japan is *clueless* and *irresponsible*)—but also with some adjectives reflecting a deeper concern, including descriptions of Japan's policies as *invalid* and *offensive* and relations with China as *strained* or *troubled* as a result.

After Japanese nationalization of the disputed islands, the picture changes dramatically. Not only is the tone of references to Japan far more negative, but condescending references are almost entirely replaced by adjectives depicting Japan as a more potent threat. Japan is described as *dangerous, imperialist,* and *provocative.* Its actions are *baseless, deliberate, illegal, inflammatory,* and *wrong.* Direct references to Japan's capabilities describe the country as *influential, hegemonic,* and *strong* (in notable contrast to the descriptions of Japan as *dependent* and *once-dynamic* in the earlier period). When adjectives refer specifically to Japanese leaders, they tend to emphasize their hawkishness rather than their inferior reason. They are described as *hardline, inflammatory,* and *recidivist* and as *troublemakers,* and terms such as *reckless* and *unreasonable* (markers of irrationality) are offset by others such as *bold, rational,* and *smarty-pants.* In general, the nature of the Japanese threat appears to have been inflated, Japanese leaders are taken more seriously, and the emotional response in China has shifted from disdain to anger as expected. In descriptions such as *dangerous* and *serious,* there is even a hint of fear.

Over the subsequent two years (2014–15), the more usual pattern of moral judgment and disdain partially reasserts itself. As the decision to nationalize the islands faded slightly into the background, Japanese leaders were seen as *knavish, militaristic, nationalistic, revisionist, unapologetic ultra-rightists* who were *flagrant* and *deliberate* in their *provocative* behavior. Even though the rhetoric remained far stronger than during the years preceding the nationalization decision, the emotional tone mostly reverted to form. Descriptions of relations between the two countries took on a different character, however, being described as *frozen, icy, rocked,* and *strained.* The damage to their relations thus seems to reflect a more serious judgment than did the disdainful adjectives used prior to 2012.

A frequency analysis of adjectives is less revealing than was the case for the issue of constitutional revision. Although more adjectives were used to describe Japan in articles on the islands dispute than on constitutional revision, relatively few were repeated. In the first period (2010–11), in fact, only three adjectives—*beneficial, cooperative,* and *hawkish*—were repeated (each was used twice). In the second period (2012–13), five adjectives were repeated (again, each was used twice): *groundless, hidden, provocative, unreasonable,* and *wrong.* Finally, in the third period (2014–15), *provocative* and *unilateral* were used twice, *rightist* (or *rightward*) were used three times, and references to cold relations (*freezing, frosty, icebound, icy,* etc.) were made six times. Figure 7.4 shows the frequency of adjectives used across the entire six-year period and is somewhat more helpful. References to cold relations were the most commonly used adjectives. Other adjectives stressing the seriousness of the issue—*provocative, wrong,* and *strained*—are also in evidence. So are adjectives indicating a harsh judgment of Japan's leaders: *rightist, unreasonable, unilateral, reckless, hawkish,* and *baseless.* The only adjectives

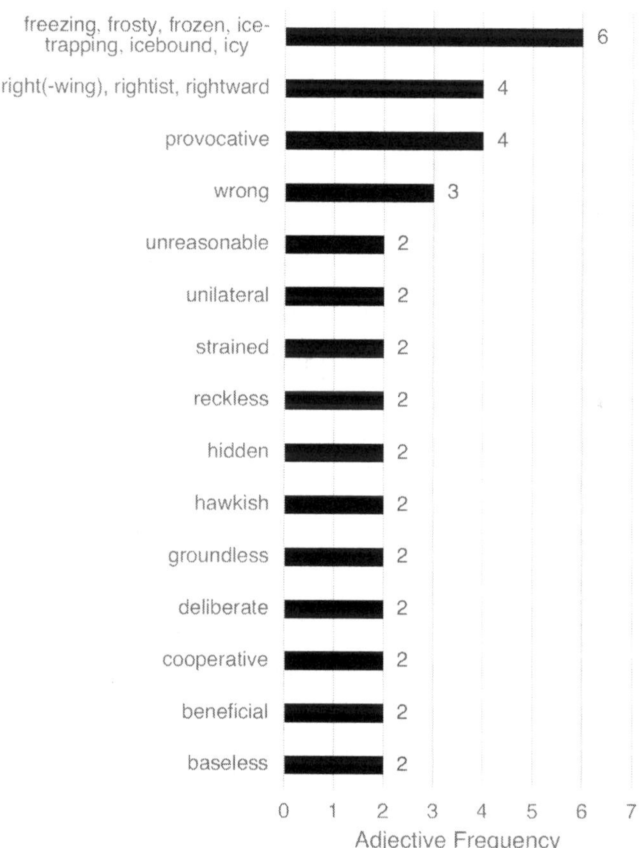

Figure 7.4. Frequency of Adjectives Referring to Japan and Diaoyu Islands, 2010–15

of this sort used more than twice, however, were descriptions of Japan's leadership as *right-wing*, which is often used in *People's Daily* articles to suggest an unrepentant attitude toward the past, and thus perhaps a greater threat than descriptions emphasizing recklessness.

Adjectives describing China are also markedly different in articles published before Japan's decision to nationalize the islands (2010–11) and those published after the decision (2012–15). If the image of Japan shifts toward that of a more serious threat, then China's self-image should also shift from that of a country embodying the virtues lacking in an inferior opponent to that of a country determinedly resisting the power of a more serious threat. When the adversary is seen as more nearly an equal, then it becomes a Sparta-like enemy (rather than an object of scorn like Melos). China's self-image thus becomes more of a true mirror image (each state is the enemy of the other).

Before 2012, adjectives describing China stressed its strength (*large, largest, strong*) and its virtue (China was *stern* but not a *threat*). After Japan nationalized the islands, however, China was *defensive, determined,* and *firm* but also *normal, peaceful,* and a *ready partner, supporting* the "pillars of security." It is notable—and consistent with the phenomenon of mirror imaging—that even as China's rhetoric directed against Japan grew far harsher as Japan became a more significant threat, China's self-image was moderated. Put another way, one can envision partnering with an enemy in order to avoid a mutually destructive conflict, but it is much harder to justify partnering with an inferior country that is irrational or untrustworthy.

EMOTIONAL STALEMATES?

The way history relates to capabilities is underappreciated. Usually, the "history problem" in Japan's relations with other countries is taken simply to mean that memories of the Pacific War, combined perhaps with a desire to repress unpleasant memories of this history in Japan, function at best as an irritant and at worst as a profound impediment to efforts to promote stable security regimes in East Asia.[64] Japan's image and role within the region are so constrained by its past, according to this line of reasoning, that it is difficult even to promote mutually beneficial trade agreements between the two largest Asian economies. Yet the history problem is not this simple.

The preceding analysis suggests that contemporary Sino-Japanese relations are not merely a case of old hatreds manifesting themselves in new ways. As noted in Chapter 2, Japan did not figure prominently in the Chinese imagination at all, for the most part, until its rise as a modern power. And then Chinese views were mixed, at first more admiring than fearful. Historian Lu Yan points out that "the recognition of Japan's success as well as the desire to learn its secret motivated many Chinese to journey east. Going to study in Japan became a 'passage to a world of new ideas' originating from the West. Indeed, high-ranking officials and popular writers at the time shared the view that Japan, by its modern success, its cultural affinity, and its geographical proximity, provided a convenient bridge to the West."[65] In the decades following the first Sino-Japanese War, of course, attitudes soured. Yet after China's communist revolution, relations again improved under Mao Zedong, in large part because Communist Party leaders were eager to project a narrative of victory over the feudal institutions to which they attributed China's downfall.[66] They were less inclined, as a result, to single out Japan as a particular evil. Comparatively good relations persisted through what Ezra Vogel, Ming Yuan, and Akihiko Tanaka called the "golden age" of the US–China–Japan triangle up to 1989, before another precipitous decline.[67]

History is less a neutral container, serving up evidence that countries are a certain way because that is how the past reveals them to be, and instead more a repository for source material that is used to construct narratives that change over time. To put this differently, the stakes of history are always in the present as much as the past, as we make ongoing choices about which narratives of the past to emphasize. National capabilities are a crucial part of these narratives. We may choose to tell stories about the past that emphasize our own national strength or weakness, as well as that of others, acting out the part of naïve historians in order to construct particular national images, reinforcing our own identities in the process. Narratives may also change from one issue to another, as is evident in the shift in Chinese attitudes regarding the Senkaku/Diaoyu Islands dispute compared with the more general character of Sino-Japanese security relations. But in both cases, the stakes are high.

Just how high is made plain by the updated textbooks for China's compulsory junior high school course on "Morals and Rule of Law." In the aftermath of the Tiananmen uprising, patriotic education took center stage within China's school curriculum. Under Xi Jinping this tendency has accelerated while turning away from the notion of a multiethnic China and emphasizing "5,000 years of glorious Chinese culture" as part of a single tradition instead.[68] The Morals textbook makes the emotional stakes of China's status very clear: "When the country prospers, I share in its glory; when the country declines, I am humiliated."[69] Edward Vickers thus argues, "the ideal citizen is a 'self-confident Chinese person' . . . whose confidence derives from, and in turn enhances, national power and status."[70] Perhaps this is one reason why Chinese leaders so often pointedly refer to "the feelings of Chinese people." After all, as Peter Gries has argued, "a humiliating past . . . can be the source of anxiety and anger in the present."[71] This is something Beijing usually seeks to avoid, lest this anger be reflected back at the ruling party, and its program of patriotic education has been very effective at crafting a more positive emotional narrative. The ironic consequence, according to Jessica Chen Weiss, is that having set the stage so effectively, the government cannot simply "stage manage" Chinese nationalism.[72] It has been too effective in teaching its citizens to take pride in Chinese power for that.

Notes

1. *Sydney Morning Herald*, "Furious Chinese." The coverage of the incident that appeared in the *Youth Daily* is no longer available online. For a thoughtful discussion of the way this incident was covered and, more generally, the way it served as an important emotional performance in China, see Hall, "Three Approaches to Emotion."
2. *Sydney Morning Herald*, "Furious Chinese." Todd Hall suggests that the growth of online chatrooms in China at exactly this time played an important role in inflaming passions regarding the Zhuhai incident and in prompting the Chinese government to act; see Hall, "Extremely Obnoxious," 33–35.
3. McNeill, "China Fumes."
4. NBC News, "China Jails 14."
5. CNN, "Chinese Riot."
6. CNN, "Chinese Riot."
7. CNN, "Chinese Riot."
8. *South China Morning Post*, "Chinese Humiliation."
9. Cha, *Beyond the Final Score*, 25. Cha argues that sport is political everywhere but "arguably more political in Asia than elsewhere in the world"; see Cha, *Beyond the Final Score*, 23.
10. Ling, "Decolonizing the International," 580.
11. Gustafsson and Hall, "Politics of Emotions," 975.
12. Gustafsson and Hall, "Politics of Emotions," 975.
13. See Vogel, Yuan, and Tanaka, *Golden Age*.
14. Genron NPO and China Daily, "10th Japan-China Public Opinion Poll."
15. Friedberg, "Ripe for Rivalry"; Christensen, "China, the US-Japan Alliance."
16. Christensen, "China, the US-Japan Alliance," 55.
17. Christensen, "China, the US-Japan Alliance," 56.
18. See Cannon and Rossiter, "Unraveling Japan's Aircraft Carrier Puzzle."
19. Shad, "Japan's Back."
20. Berger, "Abe's Perilous Patriotism"; Doak, "Abe's Civic Nationalism"; Nakahara, "Deconstructing Abe."
21. Barboza, "China Passes Japan."
22. Anderlini and Hornby, "China Overtakes US."
23. Zhang, "China's Perceptions."

24. Cooper, *PLA Military Modernization*; Cordesman, Hess, and Yarosh, *Chinese Military Modernization*; Wuthnow and Saunders, *Chinese Military Reform*.

25. Cooper notes that the CCP's "current guidance, as revealed in China's 2015 defense white paper, directs the PLA to 'win informatized local wars' with emphasis on struggle in the maritime domain"; see Cooper, *PLA Military Modernization*, 4.

26. Summaries of the meetings of each of these advisory panels are available on the website of the Japanese Prime Minister's Office, in a section on "The Prime Minister in Action." This section is divided into subsections for each Cabinet; the relevant section covering December 2012 through December 2014, Japan's ninety-sixth postwar cabinet, is https://japan.kantei.go.jp/96_abe/actions/index.html.

27. Przystup, "Can We Talk?," 100. The following discussion makes extensive use of James Przystup's summaries of Japanese and Chinese interactions published in the Pacific Forum's *Comparative Connections* online journal of bilateral relations in the Indo-Pacific, which serves as an excellent source of relevant events data. Przystup's summaries give an extensive, detailed account of high-level diplomatic interactions between China and Japan.

28. Przystup, "Can We Talk?," 101.

29. Przystup, "Can We Talk?," 101.

30. See Przystup, "Can We Talk?," 103.

31. Guardian, "Japan's Shinzo Abe Angers Neighbours."

32. Hirokawa, "Abe Draws China Anger."

33. Ozawa, "Japan PM's Visit."

34. BBC, "Japan PM Shinzo Abe Visits Yasukuni."

35. China Daily, "Anger over Abe's Shrine Visit."

36. See, e.g., BBC, "Koizumi Shrine Visit Stokes Anger."

37. China Daily, "Anger over Abe's Shrine Visit."

38. Xinhua, "China Scathes Abe's Yasukuni Visit."

39. Przystup, "Past as Prologue," 115.

40. Liu, "Comments."

41. Interestingly, the Japanese term *senkaku-shotō* is itself indirectly derived from a translation of the English name, via Chinese, into Japanese. For a more detailed discussion of naming issues associated with these islands, see Shaw, "Diaoyutai/Senkaku Islands Dispute," 10.

42. Takenaka and Wee, "Japan Infuriates China."

43. Le, "Remarks."

44. Le, "Remarks."

45. Przystup, "Treading Troubled Waters," 112.

46. Przystup, "Treading Troubled Waters," 112–13.

47. Przystup, "Can We Talk?," 99.

48. Przystup, "Can We Talk?," 99–100.

49. Takenaka, "Abe Sees World War One Echoes."

50. Zhang, "Transcript of Interview."

51. Zhang, "Transcript of Interview."

52. Schiavenza, "Awkward—and Productive—Exchange."

53. Sieg and Kapoor, "Japan PM Abe Meets China's Xi."

54. Manning, "Abe Speech."

55. Glaser and Farrar, "Through Beijing's Eyes."

56. Przystup, "Staying on a Test Course," 106.

57. Przystup, "Staying on a Test Course," 106.

58. Przystup, "Staying on a Test Course," 108.

59. Yang, "Yang Jiechi Voices Solemn Stance." Xi himself similarly described Japan's move as "the outdated thinking of [the] Cold War"; see Tiezzi, "China Decries."

60. Xinhua, "China Strongly Dissatisfied."

61. Xinhua, "China Strongly Dissatisfied."

62. Du and Yao, "Commentary"; also see, e.g., Liu, "High Time"; Reuters, "China Uses D-Day Anniversary."

63. Cottam, *Foreign Policy Motivation*; Herrmann, *Perceptions and Behavior*; Neumann, *Uses of the Other*. One of the classic studies of the mirror image in foreign policy was Urie Bronfenbrenner's account of US and Soviet mirror images; see Bronfenbrenner, "Mirror Image."

64. See, e.g., Ikenberry, "Japan's History Problem."

65. Lu, *Re-understanding Japan*, 248.

66. Gries, *China's New Nationalism*, 109.

67. Vogel, Yuan, and Tanaka, *Golden Age*. This "golden age" persisted, they argue, from the normalization of Sino-Japanese relations in 1972 to the Tiananmen Square uprising in 1989.

68. Vickers, "Smothering Diversity," 160. Also see Carrico, *Great Han*.

69. Vickers, "Smothering Diversity," 163.

70. Vickers, "Smothering Diversity," 163.

71. Gries, "Nationalism, Indignation," 107. Gries also sees the relationship between national capabilities and emotion as crucial to the formation of national identity; see Gries, *China's New Nationalism*.

72. See Weiss, "How Hawkish."

CHAPTER 8

The View from Seoul

Places stir emotions. The majesty of the Sierra Nevadas prompted Theodore Roosevelt to proclaim: "There can be nothing in the world more beautiful than the Yosemite, the groves of the giant sequoias and redwoods, the Canyon of the Colorado, the Canyon of the Yellowstone, the Three Tetons; and our people should see to it that they are preserved for their children and their children's children forever, with their majestic beauty all unmarred."[1] In Roosevelt's imagination, encounters with natural spaces defined the American spirit. Their importance famously prompted him to create the US Forest Service and to establish numerous national parks and wildlife preserves. For the Japanese, Mount Fuji's centrality—culturally even more than geographically—is such that D. T. Suzuki opined: "The Japanese love of Nature, I often think, owes much to the presence of Mount Fuji in the middle part of the main island of Japan."[2] This "love of nature" is such a ubiquitous trope in Japan that Suzuki's claim about Fuji-san's centrality is tantamount for Japanese myth-making to Frederick Jackson Turner's frontier thesis for American mythology.[3] Both peoples, it is said, derive their national character from their attitude toward the natural environment. For Koreans, Mount Paektu occupies a similar place in heart and mind as the birthplace of Dangun, the legendary founder of the first Korean kingdom. Not coincidentally, North Korean hagiography also locates Kim Jong-Il's birthplace on Mount Paektu.[4]

The importance of place is amplified, in Korea, by a tradition of geomancy applying ideas of harmony with the natural world. It remains common to consult a practitioner of *pungsu-jiri* (Korean geomancy, roughly equivalent to Chinese *feng shui*) before siting a building or grave. Yoon Hong-Key argues that "the impact of geomancy on Chinese and Korean culture has been so large for so long that it is almost impossible to understand East Asian culture without it. Much of the Chinese and Korean landscapes are a product of the implementation of geomantic ideas."[5] Even for contemporary South Koreans who might associate pungsu-jiri with premodern superstition, geomantic concerns were propelled into the forefront of national consciousness by the decision to tear down the Government-General Building (GGB) in central Seoul.

The GGB was constructed by imperial Japanese authorities on the southern portion of the site of Gyeongbokgung, the primary royal palace of the Joseon Dynasty. Many of the structures of Gyeongbokgung were destroyed for this purpose, and the GGB served as the administrative seat of Japanese rule in Korea from its completion in 1926 until 1945. The Joseon rulers are supposed to have selected this site for Gyeongbokgung because of its auspicious location along an axis from Mount Bugak in the north to the Han River in the south. The Japanese decision to locate the GGB here is widely interpreted in Korea not only as the imprimatur of Japanese authority over Korean dynastic rule but as an attempt to block the very flow of national "energy."[6] The GGB was damaged during the Korean War, and such was its notoriety that Syngman Rhee left it derelict rather than remodeling it to use as the seat of his government. That task fell to Park Chung-hee, who refurbished it to provide offices for the national government. After these offices were moved to the nearby Central Government Complex in 1970, the GGB took on a new function as the National Museum of Korea. Finally, the election of Kim Young-sam in 1993 brought a proclamation that the GGB would be demolished in 1995 on the fiftieth anniversary of the end of Japan's colonial rule over Korea. This decision set off a protracted national debate over the symbolism of the GGB and the wisdom of its demolition.

Preservationists noted the building's architectural and historical significance and held that it should be preserved as a symbol of Korea's past. The majority view, however, was that it should be destroyed. The reasons given for this preference are telling. Historian Han Jung-Sun argues that the GGB "was widely seen as symbolizing 'national shame'" in South Korea:

This was linked to a widespread public perception that the GGB had been part of a Japanese colonial plot specifically aiming to "distort national spirit" or "block national energy (*gi*)". For example, a 1992 poll carried out by the College of Urban Science, University of Seoul, found that 71.3 per cent of Seoul citizens supported the idea of dismantling or relocating the building (dismantle 43.4 per cent; relocate 27.9 per cent). The reasons were that: (1) the building was a national shame (71.8 per cent); (2) the building was blocking national energy (19.4 per cent); and (3) the building was spoiling the scenery (4.3 per cent).[7]

As one Seoul resident put it in a 1993 interview, summing up what many others evidently thought, "it is humiliating to preserve such a shameful historic site."[8] Even the preservationists recognized how emotion-laden the decision had become. "If the building is destroyed," they argued, "Japan remains the same, but Korea will have squandered over 200 billion won and ended up with one less place to put the national treasures. To them, it was a matter of reason versus national hysteria."[9] What debate there was ended in 1995 with the demolition of the GGB. Today a reconstructed version of Gyeongbokgung has risen in its place, restoring the national spirit.

The removal of the GGB helped to crystallize ideas about shame and national redemption for a new generation of South Koreans. Yet it was far from the only symbol of Korea's colonial subjugation to evoke these sentiments. A plaque in Seoul on an exhibit about Japanese colonial rule contains these words:

> During the 5,000 years of history this nation has recovered wisely from many foreign aggressors and national crises. However, in 1910 we left a shameful page in history by letting the Japanese infringe upon our nation. Through activities of the righteous armies, independence movements on foreign soil, the national independence movement, the feeling of unified national sentiment, and various resistance movements, we ultimately achieved the long awaited liberation from the Japanese occupation of this country.[10]

As Cooney and Scarbrough go on to note, "This simple but powerful message expresses the attitude of many South Koreans toward the Japanese occupation: feelings of shame and victimization."[11] In contrast, South Korea's economic ascendancy and the new prominence of Korean cultural exports—the hallyu phenomenon—is a source of great pride.

The intricate fabric of contemporary Japanese–South Korean relations is woven from these emotions. Yet as we have seen in the case of Sino-Japanese relations, the complexity of Korean attitudes toward Japan belies simplistic assertions about colonial wounds, Korean resentment, and Japanese pride. Resentment and pride are certainly part of the story. So is a degree of anger and fear that sometimes seems wildly out of place, particularly among two members of an ostensibly trilateral alliance with the United States. And so are feelings of contempt and derision that are manifest when some topics are discussed and conspicuously absent in other settings. In short, the emotional structure of Korea–Japan relations—like that of China–Japan relations—is more complex than simple verities about wartime memories would suggest.

EXPLAINING SOUTH KOREAN ATTITUDES

The general expectation among scholars of international relations, reviewed in Chapter 4, is that the degree of South Korea's strategic cooperation with Japan should have less to do with emotions and more to do with geopolitics. Despite any lingering sentiments of outrage at Korea's treatment in the first half of the twentieth century, we would anticipate that the gradual restoration of Chinese power should compel Korea and Japan to form a cooperative defensive alliance. For a time, as Chinese scholars such as Zheng Bijian proclaimed China's peaceful rise, it may have seemed that such an alliance would be unnecessary.[12] In this moment of optimism, David Kang suggested that South Korea could safely ignore pressures to either "bandwagon" with China or to join Japan and the United States in "balancing" against it, instead walking a middle road.[13] Yet soon enough, and particularly after the leadership transition in China that brought Xi Jinping to power, a more assertive China quickly brought the challenge to other Asian powers into sharper focus.[14] Even those who argue that China's policies have not drastically changed nevertheless express concern that the appearance of assertiveness exacerbates the security dilemma for the United States, Japan, and South Korea.[15] Furthermore, David Kang and Bang Jiun argue, the threat posed by North Korea is also likely to drive South Korea and Japan together.[16]

South Korea should have little choice but to deepen its security cooperation with the United States in the first instance, and with Japan secondarily, or so this argument goes. As Scott Snyder explains, "despite sharper debates and increasing friction over South Korea's future direction, the U.S.–South Korea alliance will remain an essential instrument for assuming South Korea's security given its relative weakness compared to its neighbors."[17] Examining the complementarities between South Korea and Japan's security interests within this US-led system, Tae-hyo Kim and Brad Glosserman find a strong rationale for deepening the ongoing security cooperation among these three allies.[18] "By taking advantage of their strengths and convergent characteristics," Ryo Hinata-Yamaguchi similarly concludes, "a Japan-ROK partnership to complete the trilateral alliance with the United States would be an essential and logical step forward to deal with future uncertainties."[19] And in a study of cooperation between Japan and South Korea within multilateral fora from 2011 to 2015, Van Jackson shows that the two US allies did indeed manage to cooperate despite generally poor bilateral relations during this period.[20] Of course, Jackson's study also highlights the puzzle: even as the two countries found ways to cooperate, Japan–South Korean relations remained notoriously poor.

One of the most prominent and clever explanations for this chronically bad relationship from a realist perspective was advanced by Victor Cha. Because South Korea and Japan both exited their midcentury wars enmeshed in an American-led alliance system, they were spared the necessity of coming to terms first with Russian power and then with China's rise. Anti-Japanese sentiment was allowed to flourish in South Korea precisely because it had little cost so long as American power held communist threats in check. When the US security commitment to South Korea and Japan is strong, Cha argues, poor relations between South Korea and Japan are likely to be the norm rather than an anomaly.[21] Conversely, when US commitment appears weak, South Korea and Japan are more likely to draw together. Cha calls this arrangement a *quasi-alliance* and argues that "the end of the Cold War has effectively made fears of U.S. abandonment structurally inherent in the quasi-alliance triangle, thus leading to greater levels of Japan-ROK [Republic of Korea] cooperation."[22] A case in point, he goes on to say, "occurred in November 1992 when Japanese and ROK leaders responded to the election of the first Democratic administration since Carter with unusually intimate and informal summit meetings in Kyoto, producing a joint statement communicating the two governments' abandonment fears and pledging closer Japan-ROK cooperation."[23] Tongfi Kim extended the same argument to fears about the depth of the Trump administration's commitment to US allies in Asia, suggesting that the time was again ripe for rapprochement between South Korea and Japan.[24]

The challenge of such broad-brush structural explanations is suggested by the contrast between Cha's argument and the more typical Waltzian anticipation of alliance balancing. If South Korea draws closer to Japan, it is to be expected because of the threat posed by China and North Korea. If South Korea fails to draw close to Japan, it is also to be expected because the United States buffers the threats they both face. Perhaps it is true that the end of the Cold War raised the specter of US disengagement and propelled South Korea and Japan into a closer embrace. Yet it is also true that the South Korea–Japan relationship has experienced numerous and deep ruptures since the Cold War ended. In general it is hard to accept the claim that the tenor of relations between Seoul and Tokyo can be accounted for solely by the structural imperatives of China's rise or of fluctuating American commitment.[25]

Domestic political incentives, discussed at greater length in Chapter 5, also contribute to tensions between South Korea and Japan. Ralph Cossa is one of several prominent observers to denounce the tendency of politicians on both sides to "pander" to nationalists in order to score easy political points.[26] Robert Kelly argues, in a similar vein, that the democratization of South Korea has exacerbated the problem since it simultaneously makes politicians more sensitive to popular animosities and, at the same time, gives them incentives to stir up trouble to win points from nationalist constituents due to rally-round-the-flag effects.[27] A thoughtful review of South Korean presidential approval ratings from 1993 to 2016, conducted by Wonjae Hwang, Wonbin Cho, and Krista Wiegand, lends support to these hypotheses. Hwang, Cho, and Wiegand find that South Korea's bilateral spats with Japan do, in fact, boost presidential approval ratings. They conclude, "nationalist sentiments can easily mobilize people and boost internal solidarity around political leadership in Korea, as the rally-round-the-flag effect theory explains."[28] A clever variation on the argument that electoral populism is undermining South Korea–Japan relations has been offered by Melanie Barry, who suggests that voters' disgust with corruption and mistrust of the political establishment in South Korea have also undermined efforts to strike a deal with Japan, notably in South Korea's repudiation of the agreement Park Geun-hye struck with Abe Shinzō for reparations to South Korea's comfort women.[29] It is worth noting, moreover, that similar dynamics operate in Japan.[30] And even when they are not pursuing their own rally-around-the-flag advantage, Jennifer Lind argues that many Japanese politicians prefer to say nothing rather than to engage in a dialogue on history with Korea since Japan's apologies tend to inflame the more nationalist portions of the Japanese electorate so much.[31]

To the extent that there are domestic incentives for South Korean leaders to demonize Japan—and for Japanese leaders to pay them back in kind—these incentives still don't provide a good explanation for the cycles of upheaval and rapprochement in Japan–South Korean relations. Domestic political incentives undoubtedly have an impact on South Korean–Japanese relations. Yet there are two problems with an explanation that stops here. First, these incentives are more or less constant, and yet the South Korea–Japan bilateral relationship has experienced many ups and downs. And second, even to the extent that electoral opinion does affect the relationship, popular opinion is not inflamed solely at the will of politicians. Even in China, as argued in Chapters 5 and 7, the CCP does not completely control public opinion but must often respond to it. Still less are South Korean politicians in the driver's seat. Often, as with the abortive 2012 effort to sign an intelligence-sharing pact with Japan, South Korea's leaders are stymied by public opinion rather than acting as puppet-masters. The question of what inflames passions among South Korean citizens thus remains an important one.

This chapter asks whether there is an independent emotional logic that informs South Korea's relations with Japan. It asks, in other words, what a psychopolitik of emotions—distinct from both realpolitik and innenpolitik—can contribute to our understanding of the rocky South Korea–Japan relationship. The argument developed in Chapter 6 is that emotional reactions in international relations are driven by judgments on at least two dimensions: (1) a valent dimension ranging from trust (T) to animosity (A), and (2) a comparative dimension of national capability. When the valent dimension is negative, attitudes toward another country will vary in the other dimension depending on whether that country is seen as comparatively weak, generating pride (P), or powerful, generating shame (S). A powerful and threatening other is more likely to elicit fearful anger, whereas a weaker country is more likely to elicit contempt or disdain.

Applied to the case of South Korean–Japanese relations, the two-dimensional TAPS model suggests that we should expect a different emotional landscape depending on what political issues are at stake. In particular, points of contention in which South Korea has the upper hand will tend to generate disdain, whereas disputes in which Japan has the upper hand will be more likely to generate fear and anger. These two alternatives constitute the two lower quadrants of Figure 8.1.

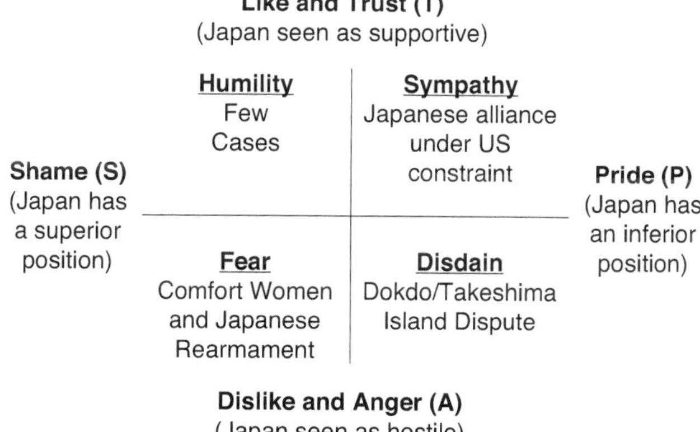

Figure 8.1. Emotional Dynamics in South Korea–Japan Relations

Chapter 7 mapped out a similar pattern for China. China and South Korea have both experienced economic ascendancy, while Japan has experienced relative economic decline (particularly with respect to its expectations a generation earlier). Unlike China, however, South Korea is a partner in an alliance relationship with the United States and Japan. China and North Korea represent the primary strategic threat to both of them, and so there are also circumstances in which Japan plays a supportive rather than hostile role, particularly in the context of the alliance with the United States. These circumstances occupy the upper-right quadrant of Figure 8.1. Although Japan should appear less threatening and relatively more powerful to South Korea than to China, cases in the upper-left quadrant remain unlikely. This is particularly so because the United States has never been able to institutionalize cooperation within the trilateral alliance in a way that has made South Korea dependent on specific Japanese capabilities. As a result, and as a result of South Korea's economic rise in general, South Korea is unlikely to exhibit much humility toward Japan.

Territorial disputes highlight the contrast between Chinese and South Korean attitudes toward Japan. In the case of the Senkaku/Diaoyu Islands dispute, Japan administers the islands and thus has the upper hand in a way that it does not in many other Sino-Japanese issues. Whereas China's rise to great power status may allow it to consider Japan relatively inferior in many other cases (and to exhibit disdain as a result), this is not the case in their territorial dispute. As Chapter 7 demonstrates, expressions of anger, even tinged with fear, are much more common in this case. In South Korea, on the other hand, the expectations are reversed. Because South Korea administers the Dokdo/Takeshima Islets, it has the upper hand. In fact, combined with the growth of South Korean economic, cultural, and political clout, we might therefore expect disdain to be the most common emotional refrain in South Korean attitudes toward Japan in almost all contemporary cases.

Instances of alliance cooperation with the United States and Japan, however, are a partial exception to this rule. Whether because of US encouragement or because of Chinese or North Korean action, the trilateral alliance is one context in which different emotions might emerge. Those familiar with the history of American efforts to get South Korea and Japan to work together will be rightly skeptical about whether South Korean emotions will really differ much in these cases. For the most part, South Korea's economic and political growth seems to have moved it along the horizontal axis of Figure 8.1 from left to right—from anger and resentment to contempt—and not much up the vertical axis toward more cooperative attitudes. Victor

Cha's argument about quasi-alliances, moreover, would suggest that situations invoking the alliance with the United States might actually free up South Koreans to embrace even *more* negative emotions. The emotional complexes model predicts, however, that to the extent the alliance really does offer benefits to all parties while highlighting mutual threats, it will tend to draw South Korea and Japan together emotionally. In these circumstances we should be more likely to find some evidence of positive or sympathetic South Korean emotions toward Japan born not out of deference (the upper-left quadrant of Figure 8.1) but rather out of appreciation for Japan's actual or potential assistance.

The other exception to a general expectation that disdain will dominate South Korean attitudes toward Japan—and perhaps even that a Melos complex will take hold in Seoul—occurs when issues of historical fault come to the fore. Japan's treatment of "comfort women" (women sexually enslaved by the Japanese army), its forced conscription of Korean laborers, and periodic denials of its wartime record from some quarters in Japan all constitute a past that is still very much present. And in this "present past," Japan remains a colonial oppressor. These are the sorts of issues that cast Japan in a dominant role and invite it, as a matter of acknowledging Korean sensibilities, to renounce its former dominance. Of course, this invitation has gone largely ignored in Japan, particularly at a time when Japanese leaders are sensitive to their country's economic stagnation and the shift from "Japan-bashing" to "Japan-passing." It is hard for them to show grace and forbearance to Korea when they are so occupied by the problem of how to restore Japan's momentum. On issues such as the comfort women, therefore, we should expect to see the greatest levels of acrimony and an emotional tableau that incorporates outright anger, hostility, and perhaps even some residual fear.

In general, therefore, the TAPS model suggests that the question to be asked about South Korean attitudes toward Japan is not why they are so negative or whether they are destined to remain so. It does not simply invite us to muse about the long shadow Japan's occupation of Korea continues to cast over the two countries' relations. Rather the model encourages us to look for variations in South Korean attitudes toward Japan from one issue area to another. It suggests that problems over which Japan holds sway (or which involve Japan's former colonial domination) are likely to generate different emotions than issues in which South Korea is dominant. And it further suggests that the US may be more able to play a mediating role by highlighting areas of mutual strategic advantage than is commonly acknowledged. At the very least, such interactions should generate more positive attitudes.

OFFICIAL ATTITUDES

Several episodes in the recent history of South Korea–Japanese relations serve to illustrate the predictions of the TAPS model. To demonstrate the general condition of the relationship, the series of flare-ups over the Dokdo/Takeshima Islets serve particularly well. What South Korea calls "Dokdo" and Japan calls "Takeshima"—and what Wikipedia, to avoid giving offense, calls the Liancourt Rocks after European practice based on the name (*Le Liancourt*) of a French whaling ship that nearly ran aground there—consist of a small group of rocky islets located east of the Korean Peninsula and north of Japan's Shimane Prefecture, a little more than 200 kilometers from either. The islands are barely 46 acres (roughly 18.7 hectares) and have been administered by South Korea since it declared a marine boundary line in 1952 (the Syngman Rhee Line) that placed the islets within South Korean territory. As with many such territorial disputes, there is conflicting evidence in the form of historical maps dating back for many centuries that variously name the islets as Korean or Japanese territory. The oldest claims belong to Korea. Japan maintains that the islets were *terra nullius* (unclaimed territory) in 1905, however, when it incorporated them into Shimane Prefecture. Several times Japan has proposed that the International Court of Justice (ICJ) arbitrate the issue. South Korea holds that such colonial-era claims are void and that there should be no dispute, either historically or currently, about the islets' ownership. For this reason, it has rejected ICJ arbitration (the same tactic that Japan has taken in its dispute with China over the Senkaku/Diaoyu Islands).[32]

What is not in dispute is that South Korean emotions run high when Japan takes steps to press its claim. When Shimane Prefecture declared a Takeshima Day in March 2005, the reaction was swift. Massive protests erupted in front of the Japanese Embassy in Seoul. The *New York Times* reported that, caught up in the moment, "a mother and son each cut off a finger; a man whose father had been brutally forced to serve in the Japanese Imperial Army, Heo Kyung Wook, 54, set himself on fire."[33] Tellingly, Mr. Heo explained (as he recuperated), "my father passed away 20 years ago, but he used to tell us stories about how the Japanese treated him, and my anger built up over the years. . . . When I saw the news about Tokdo on television, I couldn't contain my anger."[34] Taken at face value, this reaction seems inconsistent with the argument that emotional responses to the Dokdo/Takeshima dispute should take the form of contempt rather than anger since Korea actually controls the islets. Mr. Heo places Japan's actions in the context of its imperial past, however, and so anger is precisely the emotion we would expect. South Korea's secretary for public information,

Lee Baek-man, excoriated Japan in the following terms: "Exactly 100 years after its occupation of Korea, Japan is again attempting to rob us of our history. The key to the Dokdo issue is the liquidation of the war of the Japanese imperialists' aggression. In that sense, Dokdo stands at the center of our efforts to rectify a history distorted by a war of aggression."[35] Again specifically invoking the past, a mix of anger and fear of Japanese aggression are the dominant motifs. Nor were Mr. Heo and Mr. Lee alone in their reactions. After the incident, "in April 2005, only eight percent of respondents in a public opinion poll said they had a positive view of Japan, compared to 63 percent that had a negative view of Japan."[36]

When South Korean officials concentrate on Japanese actions in the present, however, their language takes on a different, though still negative, tone. The following year, after Japan proposed to undertake a maritime survey of the islands, South Korea dispatched twenty ships and surveillance planes to the area and threatened "to use force and seize any Japanese ships in the vicinity of the islands."[37] On April 24 South Korean President Roh Moo-hyun delivered an emotional televised address to condemn the Japanese. He spoke at length about Japan and its actions. In the first part of the speech, he addressed Japan's historical aggressions and condemned a "painful history."[38] Turning to Japan's 2006 behavior and the South Korean response, however, he called Japan's actions "unjust" and "wrongdoings" that "offend" and "detract from the dignity of the Korean people."[39] "I believe the Japanese people are well aware," he went on, "of the truth that actions, which jeopardize friendly relations between Korea and Japan as well as peace in East Asia, are by no means righteous or in Japan's own interests."[40] He then addressed the "people and leaders of Japan" directly:

We are no longer demanding renewed apologies. We are simply calling for actions that would do justice to the apologies which have repeatedly been made. We are asking for the cessation of actions of seeking to glorify or legitimize its unjust history, which offend Korea's sovereignty and the dignity of its people. We are not demanding any special treatment for Korea but actions keeping with the universal values and standards of the international community. We are asking for honesty and humility in the face of historical truth and the conscience of humanity. It is when Japan comports itself in conformity with these standards towards its neighbors and the international community as well that it will finally stand as a nation of maturity that befits its economic size and as a nation that can assume a leading role in the international community.[41]

As the speech moves into the present, the emotional tone moves away from anger at the past and toward repeated expressions that Japan's current leadership is behaving in a dishonest, undignified, and shameful manner. These are not adjectives associated with coercion and fear but rather with disdain. This section of Roh's remarks concludes by specifically invoking standards of "maturity" that would allow Japan to assume a leading international role.

Several years later, in August 2012, Roh's successor Lee Myung-bak became the first serving South Korean president to visit the disputed island, provoking another crisis. In response, Japan withdrew its ambassador to South Korea and attempted to bring the case to the ICJ for the first time since 1964. Lee was mired in corruption scandals at the time, and it is easy enough to interpret his decision to visit the islets as an effort to distract public attention.[42] Whatever the underlying reason, Lee's rhetoric is consistent with the TAPS model. In a speech delivered after arriving on the islets by helicopter, Lee said, "Japan should sincerely apologize as it started a bad war, but it has not done so. That's why pent-up grievances are not resolved."[43] Later, during dinner with the group who accompanied him to the islets, he went on: "I have no intentions to provoke Japan or create a standoff too much, but Japan has been too insincere about the issues."[44] Here, as with Roh, Lee is focused on Japanese sincerity.

These examples illustrate two tendencies in South Korean emotional reactions to the Dokdo/Takeshima issue. When the dispute is cast as an unresolved wartime issue, we would expect to see straightforward expressions of anger consistent with the TAPS model and provoked by recollections of Japan's coercive power during the colonial era. On the other hand, when the topic is Japan's recent action—Takeshima Day celebrations, proclamations by Japanese politicians, or other actions meant to assert a claim to the islets—we should expect the shift in relative power to prompt an emotional shift as well. A challenge issued by a comparatively weak party is either irrational or insincere, and these are precisely the complaints levied by South Koreans against Japanese leadership.

When Lee came to power in 2008, most observers expected South Korea's relations with Japan to improve after a period of deterioration under Roh and Japanese Prime Minister Koizumi Junichirō. In his first year in office, Lee paid a visit to Tokyo, and the relationship seemed to be on the mend. Yet four years later, as Lee prepared to leave office in 2012, the relationship was at another low point. In fact, just weeks before Lee's helicopter trip to the islets, a military intelligence sharing agreement with Japan had also fallen apart. The General Security of Military Information Agreement (GSOMIA) was strongly pushed by the United States, which, without it, was compelled to serve as a conduit for intelligence on North Korea between South Korea and Japan. The Lee administration had negotiated the agreement in secret, and just moments before the signing ceremony was to have taken place, South Korea backed out in the face of public pressure and complaints from opposition party politicians.

Because the GSOMIA issue involved the alliance with the United States, and because it implicitly invokes the strategic advantage of cooperation with Japan, it serves as another interesting test of the TAPS model. Although South Korea's decision to delay signing the agreement occurred at roughly the same time as Lee's Dokdo/Takeshima visit, we would expect the different context to produce a different emotional reaction. Prior to the failed attempt to sign the pact, Yonhap News Agency cited an unnamed government official who explained: "Japan has a lot of intelligence on North Korea and the GSOMIA with Japan will benefit us a lot. . . . Our network will expand under this deal."[45] As the prospective agreement became politicized by the approaching South Korean elections, news coverage increasingly turned to the wisdom of signing an agreement with a former colonial oppressor, and emotions swung predictably toward an angrier tone with newspapers (particularly on the left) citing concerns that the agreement would somehow "open the sluice gate of Japan's militaristic ambitions."[46] In fact, analyzing coverage of the topic, a study by the Korean Broadcasting System later determined that "only 5% of all media reports covered the actual contents of the agreement."[47]

The agreement was not finally signed until 2016 under President Park Geun-hye and Japanese Prime Minister Abe Shinzō. Ironically, relations between the two countries had continued to deteriorate between Park's hard line on Japan (motivated, in part, by a desire to distance herself from her father's pro-Japan image) and Abe's nationalist proclamations.[48] Somehow, though, the pact was finally signed on November 23, 2016, and South Korea's Ministry of National Defense (MND) released a statement that was undoubtedly one of the nicest things officials in Seoul had said about Japan in some time: "Japan possesses surveillance and detection assets which are superior in both quality and quantity as it spends far more money on national defense expenditure."[49] Consistent with the emotional complexes model, the context of defense cooperation did ratchet down the negative emotional rhetoric to a degree.

Of course, such rhetoric did not subside entirely. Park was, by this time, already embroiled in an influence-peddling scandal that would soon lead to her impeachment. Political opponents gleefully seized on the agreement as evidence not only of her corruption but also lack of character. The agreement itself, they proclaimed, was "unpatriotic and humiliating."[50] Park's more liberal successor Moon Jae-in quickly moved to improve relations with North Korea after his election in 2017—he even climbed Mount Paektu together with Kim Jong-il—and to repudiate the GSOMIA.[51] As progress with North Korea stalled and pressure from the US mounted, however, Moon ultimately relented on the intelligence-sharing pact and reversed his earlier decision to leave the agreement.[52]

Moon went even further to undermine the other key agreement his predecessor had managed to strike with Japan. In December 2015 Park and Abe reached an agreement whereby Japan would make an official apology for having enslaved Korean women and set up a 1 billion yen fund, to be administered by the South Korean government, to support "projects for recovering the honour and dignity and healing the psychological wounds."[53] Abe expressed "his most sincere apologies and remorse to all the women who underwent immeasurable and painful experiences and suffered incurable physical and psychological wounds as comfort women."[54] South Korea, meanwhile, promised to consider the matter "finally and irreversibly" resolved. On its face, the agreement gave both countries much of what they wanted.

A January 2016 poll in South Korea showed, however, that "only 26 percent of respondents supported the accord, while 56 percent opposed it. A full 72 percent of respondents believed the accord did not represent a sincere apology by the Japanese government."[55] Moon Jae-in declared the agreement "defective" and announced that his administration would review it.[56] Although he ultimately decided not to renegotiate the deal itself, he did dissolve the foundation set up to disburse the Japanese funds, making it effectively impossible to implement the terms of the agreement.[57] Then, in October 2018, a South Korean court held Nippon Steel responsible for having used forced Korean labor and ordered it to pay 100 million won to each of four plaintiffs. Japan retaliated by tightening export controls and "questioning South Korea's trustworthiness in handling sensitive security-related products."[58] As relations continued to deteriorate, "people marched on the Japanese Embassy. They boycotted Japanese clothes, beers, cosmetics, and cars. They curtailed tourist travel to Japan. Two men in their 70s died after setting themselves on fire near the embassy."[59] And so South Korea–Japan relations again tumbled to a low point. "The comfort women movement is still going on," Moon proclaimed. "The victims' wounds have not been completely healed as a true apology and reconciliation are still out of reach."[60]

The situation changed once more in 2022 with the return to power of South Korea's conservatives under Yoon Suk Yeol. As part of a program to improve relations with Japan, Yoon moved to set up a new South Korean foundation to compensate those subjected by Japan to forced labor during the war.[61] Yoon also traveled to Tokyo to meet Japanese Prime Minister Kishida in 2023, the first visit by a Korean leader to Tokyo in twelve years. Striking a very different tone from his predecessor during this meeting, Yoon praised Japan for having "expressed deep remorse and heartfelt apology in regard to its past colonial rule."[62] Relations between the two countries have thus once again thawed notably, though further progress is called into question by Yoon's impeachment.

As these statements by South Korean leaders illustrate, attitudes toward Japan have fluctuated—over time and across issues—more than is commonly acknowledged. In general, they seem consistent with the TAPS model that anticipates anger when Japan's past actions come to the fore (as with the comfort women issue), disdain when Japan challenges Korea's advantageous position on the Dokdo/Takeshima islets, and even a limited degree of sympathy when the need for cooperation is highlighted by North Korean threats and US alliance pressures. For a more systematic review of South Korean attitudes, however, the next section documents differences in South Korean newspaper coverage across each of these issue areas.

EDITORIALIZING IN SEOUL

To test the claims developed in the previous section, I undertake a content analysis of newspaper coverage of several issues involving Japan. The first of these issues, Japan's apology and reparations for the sexual enslavement of Korean women (the comfort women issue) provides a general measure of Korean attitudes on backward-looking historical issues related to Japan's imperial past. Because such issues recall a time when Japan exerted its power over Korea, the emotional complexes model predicts that anger will feature prominently in the Korean emotional response. In contrast, the dispute over the Dokdo/Takeshima islets has often involved contemporary Japanese actions, such as celebrations of Takeshima Day in Japan, declarations by Japanese leaders, and actions taken (or proposed) by the Japanese Coast Guard. Because Korean news coverage often casts the islands dispute as a legacy of Japan's colonial past, we would still expect expressions of anger. Even so, Korea has the upper hand since it administers the islands, and thus—particularly when coverage turns to recent Japanese action—we would expect this issue to generate a second emotional reaction of disdain rather than anger. Since it may seem irrational to pursue what Koreans regard as a settled matter, we would particularly expect to find expressions of contempt directed at Japanese leaders characterized as childish, unreasonable, and reactionary. Finally, because Korea also differs from China in having an alliance with the United States, we would expect that discussions of the alliance would result in more moderate language and even some expressions of sympathy toward Japan. This last prediction is perhaps the hardest test of the model since observers in the United States have so often bemoaned the complete absence of sympathetic reactions in South Korea toward Japan even when the two countries seem to have mutual interests.

To measure the difference in emotional reactions, and following the same procedure as that employed in Chapter 7, I recorded all adjectives referring to Japan in a sample of articles on each topic in editorials and news articles appearing between 2010 and 2016 in the most prominent South Korean newspaper, *Chosun Ilbo*.[63] This time span includes the years before and after Lee Myung-bak's visit to the disputed islands, deterioration of relations with the intensification of the comfort women issue and the dramatic 2012 collapse of the GSOMIA, and improvement in relations with the 2015 agreement between Park and Abe on the comfort women and the 2016 signing of the GSOMIA. Holding the time period roughly constant, therefore, all three issues are highly salient within this window. Moreover, this period also includes a transition from the government of Lee Myung-bak to that of Park Geun-hye in South Korea and from Noda Yoshihiko to Abe Shinzō in Japan (as well as the very end of the Kan Naoto administration in 2010). This is also roughly the same time span that was coded for China in Chapter 7.

For each year, and for each of the three issue areas, a sample of articles containing the term *Japan* and a key word related to the issue area (*comfort women*, *Dokdo*, or *alliance*) were selected using the searchable English-language *Chosun Ilbo* website.[64] Articles that did not deal primarily with the selected topic were eliminated from the sample, as were articles that dealt with more than one of the topics.[65] Adjectives referring to Japan, to Japanese leaders, or to Japanese policies or actions were compiled from each selected article. Adjectives referring to China (as well as Japan) were also compiled in the analysis of the *People's Daily*. Perhaps owing to differences in editorial tone, however, the sampled *Chosun Ilbo* articles contained very few adjectives describing South Korea, and so these were not coded.

To guide interpretation of the adjectives identified in *Chosun Ilbo* articles, Table 8.1 summarizes the expectations we might have based on Piotr Cap and Paul Chilton's analysis of language and emotion, discussed in

Table 8.1: Emotional Content and South Korean Discourse on Japan

Case	Comfort Women	Islands Dispute	Alliance
Japan's Position	Relatively Advantageous	Relatively Disadvantageous	Partner
Dominant Emotion	Anger	Disdain	Sympathy
Emotional Target	State	Leaders	State
Target's Character	Rational, Dangerous	Irrational, Untrustworthy	Rational, Helpful
Time Frame	Past	Present	Present / Future
Modality	Historical	Predictable	Unpredictable

Chapter 6. Because the comfort women issue directs attention to a past in which Japanese power was great, expressions of anger should dominate (whereas Japanese dominance in the present would be more likely to mingle fear with anger). The islands dispute, on the other hand, places South Korea in a more advantageous position, and so expressions of disdain should particularly target Japanese leaders. Finally, discussions of Japan's trilateral alliance with South Korea and the United States reframe Japanese power as a benefit rather than a threat and should thus produce more sympathetic emotions (something that is sorely lacking, according to many observers).

Comfort Women

It is no surprise that adjectives describing Japan and its leaders are overwhelmingly negative in Korean articles about the comfort women issue. As previously noted, we would expect that an issue highlighting Japan's wartime conduct would lead to expressions of anger linked to descriptions of its coercive power, and this is seen in adjectives such as *illegal, imperialist, forced* (*forceful, forcible*), *foul, unprecedented,* and *unspeakable.* At the same time, discussions of Japan's current leadership and its decisions regarding reparations and apologies do also lead to more disdainful emotional reactions. This is apparent in adjectives such as *blind, conservative, convicted, discredited, extreme, militarist, revisionist,* (far) *right, rightwing,* and *sincere* (questioning whether Japan is sincere). These adjectives reflect a judgment that either extremism or irrationality pushes Japan and its leaders to behave inappropriately. Overall, there is a mixture of anger and disdain adjectives (see the Appendix for the complete list of adjectives).

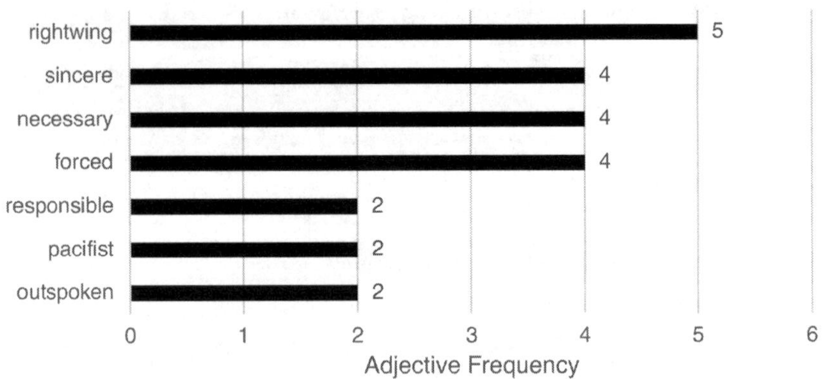

Figure 8.2. Frequency of Adjectives Referring to Japan and Comfort Women, 2010–16

Because Prime Minister Abe claimed in 2007 to find no evidence that comfort women had been coerced into sexual servitude, we might also expect the already-critical descriptions of Japanese leadership to intensify and change after his reelection.[66] This is easier to see when we consider not only the types of adjectives used but also their frequency. The most frequently used adjectives describing Japan in *Chosun Ilbo* coverage of the comfort women issue are shown in Figure 8.2. One might expect that Abe's more nationalist rhetoric and comfort women denials would increase the prominence of disdain adjectives. Indeed, many of the adjectives in Figure 8.2 call into question the sincerity, responsibility, and political character of Japanese leaders. To the extent that South Koreans associate Abe with a more assertive and remilitarized foreign policy, and also with denials of Japan's wartime actions, we might also expect anger to be displayed. Although the most common adjective used to describe Japan or its leaders was *rightwing*, four of the five occurrences of this term were in articles from the period before Abe's reelection, as were three of the four incidences of *sincere* (generally in demands for a sincere apology). In contrast, nearly all the references to force (*forced, forceful, forcible*) occurred after Abe returned to office.

So, although there were indeed many disdainful references to Japanese leadership in the Abe-era as well (as *extreme, revisionist,* etc.), there was, if anything, a shift toward angry complaints about Japan's forcible conquest of Korea, perhaps stemming from the sense that Abe had failed to acknowledge Japan's history. In general, there are perhaps somewhat more expressions of disdain in articles dealing with comfort women than predicted, but there are also many expressions of anger (as expected).

Island Disputes

The territorial dispute between South Korea and Japan should generate a different emotional response than the comfort women issue given South Korea's advantageous position. In contrast to the articles on comfort women, South Korean articles on the disputed islands overwhelmingly contain adjectives expressing disdain, describing Japan and Japanese leaders in terms such as *absurd, angry, childish, ignorant, ill-informed, militarist* (*militaristic*), *nationalist* (*nationalistic*), *rightwing, rash, silly, unrepentant*, and *wrongheaded*. Japanese policies or actions are described as being in *disarray, dubious, flimsy, noisy, populist, provocative, regressive* (*retrogressive*), and *spurious*. Descriptions such as *childish, ignorant, ill-informed, silly*, and *wrongheaded* perfectly illustrate the expected condescending and disdainful character of South Korean attitudes. If we consider the pre-Abe and Abe periods separately, there are again some differences. In the earlier period (and in contrast to articles focusing on the comfort women issue), there are only a few adjectives (*colonial, imperial, sinister*) that appear to reflect anger. In the Abe era, on the other hand, adjectives reflecting anger again become somewhat more common. One reason for this, perhaps, is that articles increasingly referred to Japan's "flimsy, colonial-era claim" to the islands. By putting the islands dispute in the context of Japan's colonial policies, we would expect to find more indications of anger in the second period, and this is the case when Japan and its policies are described as *brutal, colonial, imperialist, resurgent*, and *unilateral*.

A frequency analysis further clarifies the picture. Figure 8.3 shows all adjectives used more than once during the pre-Abe period. Once again, adjectives reflecting disdain are prominent. Indeed, the two most frequently used adjectives are *rightwing* and *dubious*. The term *colonial* is also used, generally in reference to Japan's "colonial claim," but only five times in this period.

In contrast, in the period during Abe's time in office shown in Figure 8.4, *colonial* is the most frequently used adjective. Along with *resurgent*, the adjectives reflect not just dismissive attitudes but greater underlying concern about a more assertive or threatening Japan. Adjectives indicating contempt, such as *flimsy* and *rightwing*, are still present as one would expect. But South Korean attitudes do appear to have shifted once Abe took office.

In general, then, two things stand out about the array of emotions on display in South Korean articles about the islands dispute. First, overall, the tone of South Korean newspaper coverage of this topic is far more condescending or disdainful in its descriptions of Japan than is its coverage of

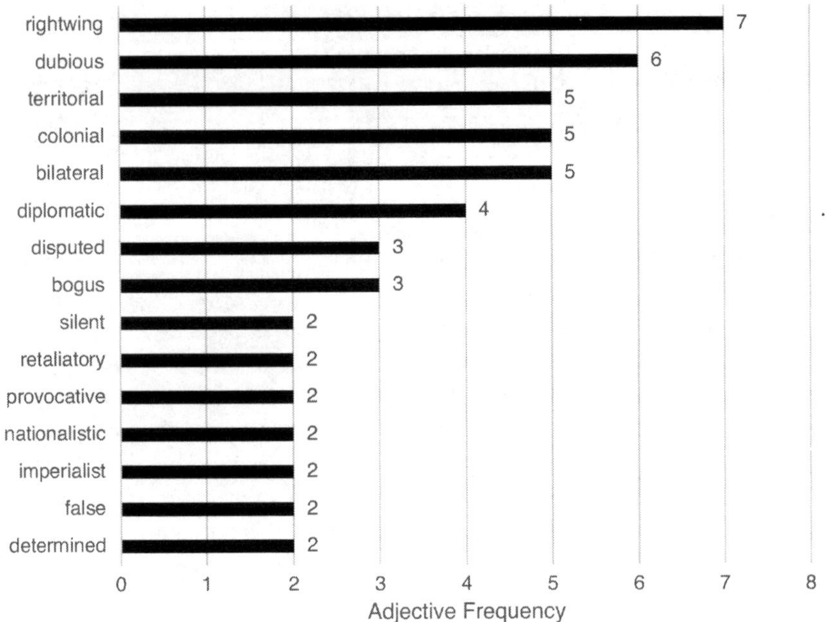

Figure 8.3. Frequency of Adjectives Referring to Japan and Dokdo, 2010–12

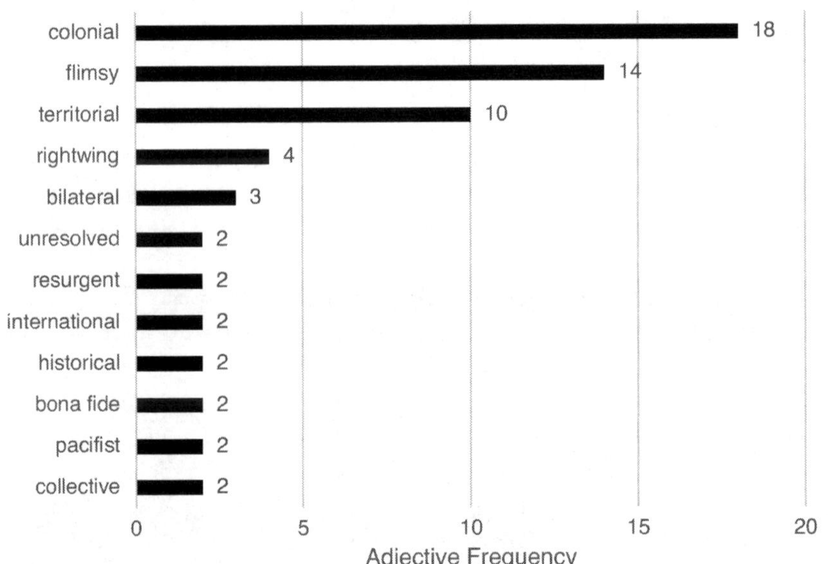

Figure 8.4. Frequency of Adjectives Referring to Japan and Dokdo, 2013–16

the comfort women issue. Another aspect of this reporting that reflects the same tendency is the dutiful coverage, in *Chosun Ilbo*, of Korean government protests against Japanese actions in a way that emphasizes Japanese subservience. These excerpts from a November 4, 2013, article are typical: "The Foreign Ministry on Friday again summoned the chief of mission at the Japanese Embassy in Seoul to lodge a protest against an English-language video promoting Tokyo's colonial claim to Korea's Dokdo islets. The Foreign Ministry first summoned Takashi Kurai on Oct. 23. . . . Foreign Ministry Spokesman Cho Tae-yong said the Korean government 'strongly protests' against the clips and wants them removed immediately."[67] In this article, and in many others using similar wording, it is Korea that does the summoning and the demanding. These articles are frequently accompanied by an unflattering photo of a meek- or flustered-looking Japanese diplomat, further reinforcing the theme of disdain.

A second general point is that the tone of *Chosun Ilbo*'s coverage of the islands dispute shifts somewhat after Abe's return to power. At the beginning of the decade, coverage in *Chosun Ilbo* was fairly dry and matter of fact, mostly consisting of occasional stories about research uncovering maps that showed the islands to be Korean rather than Japanese territory. By the middle of the decade, in response to Abe's intensifying campaign to assert a claim to the islands, South Korean coverage not only became more overtly emotional but was also increasingly likely to put the issue of the islands in the context of other issues such as Japan's treatment of comfort women.[68] A February 2014 editorial typifies this trend:

> The administration of Japanese Prime Minister Shinzo Abe is threatening the very basis of Seoul-Tokyo relations. After constant denials that the Japanese government had anything to do with forcing women to serve as sex slaves for the Imperial Army during World War II and paying homage at a shrine honoring war criminals, Abe has now said he wants to take his country's flimsy colonial claim to Korea's Dokdo islets to the International Court of Justice.[69]

Whereas articles in 2010 would refer to "Japan's territorial claim to Dokdo," references were consistently rendered as "Japan's flimsy colonial claim" beginning in 2013. This is why *colonial* and *flimsy* top the list of adjectives in the second period. Phrases such as this continue to reflect a dismissive attitude regarding Japan's "flimsy" reasoning. Yet perhaps as a result of increasing references to the colonial past, descriptions of Japanese policies as *brutal* and *unilateral* also begin to show up, signifying a degree of anger.

Alliance

Given the rapid deterioration in South Korean–Japanese relations during this seven-year period, it is unsurprising that the GSOMIA fell apart in 2012. Relations went from bad to worse under Park and Abe. Yet, as previously noted, these two leaders who had barely seemed to be on speaking terms somehow managed to conclude an agreement on the comfort women issue in 2015 followed by an agreement to sign the long-delayed GSOMIA in 2016.[70] Most analysts, reflecting on this history, would expect few South Korean expressions of sympathy during these years, even during the moments when Park and Abe managed to paper over their differences. Yet adjectives describing Japan in articles containing the terms *Japan* and *alliance* between 2010 and 2016 reveal a more complex picture.

Although there are certainly some adjectives expressing negative and generally angry judgments (*brutal, harsh*), what is striking about this list is how different it is from the previous ones (see the Appendix for the complete list). Descriptions of Japan, its leaders, and its policies include *active, beneficial, bilateral, bona-fide, close* (*closer*), *compromise, cooperative, dynamic, essential, joint, mutual, pacifist, prepared, proactive, proud, splendid, strengthened,* and *strong*. To be sure, some of these adjectives were conditional. References to Japan's *pacifist* constitution, for example, usually came in the context of concern about the Abe administration's policies. Still, overall, this is a remarkably positive set of descriptors spanning the entire period from 2010 to 2016. Even adjectives reflecting tension—*strained, tense,* or *thorny*—are far more nuanced than those in the cases discussed previously. When the topic was Japan's alliance with the United States, South Korean commentators were thus more sympathetic toward Japan as the TAPS model predicts. It is entirely possible, of course, that the *Chosun Ilbo*'s rightward editorial tilt influences this finding, but the contrast with the comfort women and Dokdo/Takeshima cases is nevertheless striking.

The picture is even clearer when focusing on the most frequently used adjectives. For the 2010–12 period, these are shown in Figure 8.5. Remarkably, all of these adjectives are positive. This is certainly not what one might expect in a period that is generally considered a low point in the countries' bilateral relations.

The most frequent adjectives from the latter period, representing Abe's time in power, are shown in Figure 8.6. Once again, the most commonly used adjectives—such as *pacifist, collective, active, strong,* and *joint*—are generally positive. The single most commonly used adjective, *military*, is neither positive nor negative since it mostly just refers to factual matters (e.g., "military

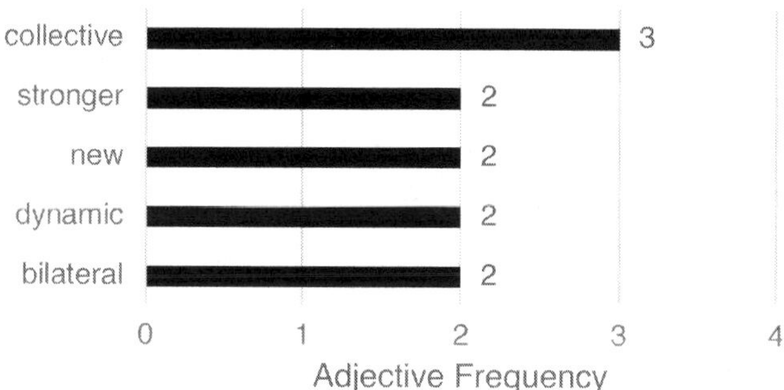

Figure 8.5. Frequency of Adjectives Referring to Japan and Alliance, 2010–12

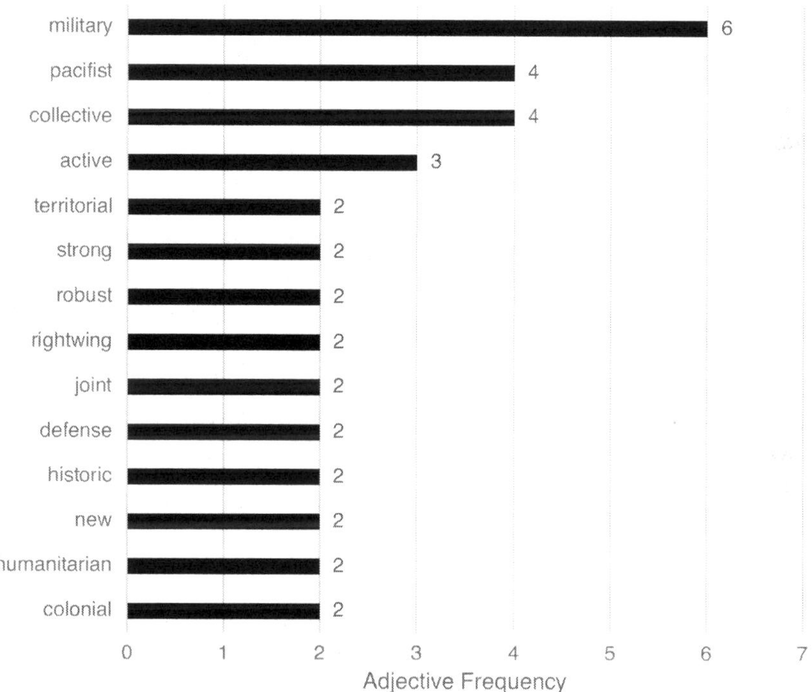

Figure 8.6. Frequency of Adjectives Referring to Japan and Alliance, 2013–16

issues, "military posture," "military operations") and is not a description of Japan as *militarist*. *Rightwing* does appear on this list as an example of more disdainful rhetoric, as does *colonial* as an example of more angry rhetoric. It is perhaps unsurprising that such terms make an appearance during the Abe years. Even so, however, it is noteworthy that the Park–Abe years did not produce especially negative descriptions of Japan when alliance matters were the topic of discussion.

Overall, the difference in emotional tone between the set of articles focused on alliance matters and those focused on disputes over comfort women and Dokdo/Takeshima is profound. Based on the TAPS model, this is exactly what we would expect, and it is reassuring to find that typical characterizations of South Korean attitudes toward Japan during this period are perhaps more bleak than is warranted. This is not to underestimate the depth of South Korean anger, resentment, and disdain for Japan and particularly for its leaders. Indeed, another general lesson of the South Korean case is that leadership does matter. This can be seen in the shifts in emotional tone, particularly in the islands dispute, once Park and Abe took office. But the overarching lesson seems to be that South Korean attitudes toward Japan do vary across issue areas more than is commonly recognized.

OFF THE CHARTS?

The question usually posed about South Korea's relations with Japan is why the relationship remains so troubled, and why emotion runs so high, when the two countries have so much to gain from their trilateral alliance with the United States. As Robert Kelly recently put it in the pages of *The Diplomat*: "the issue is not why does Korea dislike Japan. Japan's imperial behavior and continued ambivalence all but ensures that. The real question is why Korean animosity is so off-the-charts."[71] The resulting "Korean tension with Japan," Kelly goes on to say, "is a major stumbling block to a more coherent American posture in East Asia. It is arguably the single most important reason for the lack of an Asian NATO."[72] In a similar vein, Kevin Cooney and Alex Scarbrough ask, almost plaintively, "can Japan and South Korea work together?"[73]

Kelly is absolutely right that the acrimony in this relationship creates numerous problems for Japan, the United States, and for South Korea itself. But what the foregoing analysis of emotional language has sought to show is that asking about generalized South Korean antipathy toward Japan somewhat misses the point. Korean attitudes toward Japan are not unrelentingly negative, regardless of time period or issue area. Rather, there are several distinct patterns of emotional response at work. They are animated by different concerns, and they are provoked by different sorts of behavior on Japan's part.

So Cooney and Scarbrough's question might better be phrased not to ask whether Japan and South Korea can work together but instead to ask, *when* and *on what* can Japan and South Korea work together? On matters of military cooperation, for all the fits and starts, they have generally found ways to cooperate when needed, and particularly when under threat from China or North Korea. And even on the most contentious issues, such as Japan's acknowledgment of its imperial past and the Dokdo/Takeshima dispute, it is important for the two countries' diplomats to recognize that different emotions are at play in different contexts.

The Japanese public and even many Japanese leaders have often seemed mystified by the reaction in other countries to policies that would seem unremarkable as a matter of realpolitik when practiced by a country other than Japan. Of course, Japan is not any other country, and its past has left a deep imprint on its neighbors. Symbolic steps such as tearing down the GGB and rebuilding Gyeongbokgung won't easily change this picture or erase the past. Yet the past is not immutable. Efforts to change perceptions and improve Japan's image must begin with an understanding of what perceptions are at issue and what emotions sustain them.

Notes

1. Roosevelt, *Outdoor Pastimes*, 353.
2. Suzuki, *Zen and Japanese Culture*, 331. See also Earhart, *Mount Fuji*.
3. Cf. Asquith and Kalland, *Japanese Images of Nature*; Turner, *Frontier*.
4. Smith and Shin, "North Korean History."
5. Yoon, *Culture of Fengshui*, 8.
6. See, inter alia, Kang, "Kyŏngbok Palace."
7. Han, "Japan in the Public Culture," 9. For the 1992 poll data, Han cites an interview with Kim Seung-kon, the president of the Korean Liberation Association, in the *Kyunghyang Newspaper*, September 2, 1993.
8. Han, "Japan in the Public Culture," 9; Han cites Choi, "Let's Demolish the GGB."
9. Kang, "Kyŏngbok Palace," 30.
10. Cooney and Scarbrough, "Japan and South Korea," 174. Cooney and Scarbrough cite Thomas, "Capitol, Seoul," 62.
11. Cooney and Scarbrough, "Japan and South Korea," 174.
12. Zheng, "China's Peaceful Rise."
13. Kang, "Between Balancing and Bandwagoning."
14. See Christensen, "Advantages of an Assertive China"; Moore, "Bismarck or Wilhelm?"; Yahuda, "China's New Assertiveness."
15. Johnston, "How New and Assertive."
16. Kang and Bang, "North Korean Leadership Change."
17. Snyder, *South Korea at the Crossroads*. See also Ikenberry, "Between the Eagle and the Dragon"; Park, "Pattern of Cooperation."
18. Kim and Glosserman, *Future of US–Korea–Japan Relations*. Also see Nam, "Alliance Transformation"; Jo and Mo, "Does the United States Need a New East Asian Anchor?"

19. Hinata-Yamaguchi, "Completing the US–Japan–Korea Alliance Triangle," 400.
20. Jackson, "Buffers, Not Bridges." Wonjae Hwang finds a similar congruence in South Korean and Japanese voting behavior within the United Nations; see Hwang, *South Korea's Changing Foreign Policy*, 92–3.
21. Cha, *Alignment Despite Antagonism*. See also Cha, "Abandonment, Entrapment."
22. Cha, "Abandonment, Entrapment," 284.
23. Cha, "Abandonment, Entrapment," 284.
24. Kim, "Can Donald Trump Save South Korea–Japan Relations?"
25. Indeed, running somewhat counter to Cha's argument, the end of the Cold War initially seemed to bring with it greater US involvement in Asia, notably the Obama administration's "pivot to Asia." See, e.g., Clinton, "America's Pacific Century." Also ironically, the Trump administration's intensification of rivalry with China was accompanied by a turn away from engagement with the United States' Asian allies.
26. Cossa, "Japan–South Korea Relations." For a detailed discussion of the way nationalist rhetoric about the Korea–Japan relationship can be used as a tool of national identity formation, see Seo, "Diagnosing Korea–Japan Relations."
27. Kelly, "Three Hypotheses."
28. Hwang, Cho, and Wiegand, "Korean–Japanese Historical Disputes," 705.
29. Berry, "Historical Memory."
30. See, e.g., Hwang and Nishikawa, "Diversionary Incentives."
31. Lind calls this phenomenon "backlash." See Lind, *Sorry States*, 183–6.
32. On the proposals for ICJ arbitration, see Miller, "ICJ and the Dokdo/Takeshima Dispute." For a more scholarly and far more detailed treatment, see Van Dyke, "Legal Issues."
33. Onishi, "Dispute over Islets Frays Ties."
34. Onishi, "Dispute over Islets Frays Ties."
35. Baek-man Lee, quoted in Weinstein, "South Korea–Japan Dokdo/Takeshima Dispute."
36. Wiegand and Choi, "Nationalism, Public Opinion," 235; Wiegand and Choi cite Moon and Suh, "Identity Politics."
37. Wiegand and Choi, "Nationalism, Public Opinion," 234.
38. Roh, "Special Message."
39. Roh, "Special Message."
40. Roh, "Special Message."
41. Roh, "Special Message."
42. After the visit, Lee did enjoy a 10-point boost in his overall approval rating, and approval within South Korea of his visit to the islets went as high as 83.6 percent; see Hwang, Cho, and Wiegand, "Korean–Japanese Historical Disputes," 699.
43. Korea Times, "Lee Criticizes Japan."
44. Korea Times, "Lee Criticizes Japan."
45. Korea Times, "Korea, Japan to Sign Military Accord."
46. Shin, "Seoul Under Fire." Also see Hankyoreh, "Don't Just Delay." Public opinion data show that a sizable majority of South Koreans opposed the GSOMIA agreement even though many regarded it as necessary; see Chung, *Pride, Not Prejudice*, chap. 7.
47. Klingner, "Washington Should Urge"; Klingner cites a report prepared by Jiyoon Kim, Karl Friedhoff, and Chungku Kang for the Asan Institute for Policy Studies (see Kim, Friedhoff, and Kang, "Asan Monthly Opinion Survey").
48. Moon and Hur, "South Korean Perspective."
49. Ji, "S. Korea, Japan Sign."

50. Agence France Press, "South Korea, Japan Sign."
51. Shin and Lee, "Fulfilling a Dream."
52. Chappell, "South Korea Says."
53. BBC, "Comfort Women."
54. BBC, "Comfort Women."
55. Moon and Hur, "South Korean Perspective."
56. Arrington, "South Korea Ended Its Review."
57. Japan Times, "Seoul Guts the 'Comfort Women' Agreement."
58. Choe, "Embattled at Home."
59. Choe, "Embattled at Home."
60. Lee, "Moon Says Campaign."
61. Kim, "Yoon."
62. McCurry, "Yoon Arrives in Japan."
63. Three newspapers dominate the news landscape in South Korea: *Chosun Ilbo*, *Joongang Ilbo*, and *Dong-a Ilbo*. Each of these has a circulation of over 2 million, with *Chosun Ilbo* the largest by a small margin and generally seen as the most influential. Each of the three largest newspapers leans center-right, and so editorially the *Chosun Ilbo* might be thought of as resembling the *Wall Street Journal*. The most prominent newspaper of the left, *Hankyoreh Shinmun*, has a circulation of about 450,000. See Press Reference, "South Korea."
64. I am grateful to my research assistant, Kristin Hynes, for her assistance in compiling the samples of articles to be coded. *Chosun Ilbo*'s English-language website (english.chosun .com) contains English translations of prominent *Chosun Ilbo* news articles and editorials. A sample of ten articles per year was necessary to provide sufficient adjectives to analyze, whereas five articles per year sufficed in the case of the *People's Daily* editorials analyzed in Chapter 7.
65. Particularly after Lee's 2012 visit to the disputed islands, articles often referred to the visit, to Japanese reactions, and to the comfort women issue. These articles were excluded. See the Appendix for more details of article selection.
66. Onishi, "Japan Stands by Declaration."
67. Chosun Ilbo, "Japan Continues Dokdo Land-Grab Campaign."
68. Note that these articles were removed from the sample since they involved both topics (comfort women and the islands). Had they been included, adjectives in the second period would have shown an even greater tendency toward anger in addition to disdain.
69. Chosun Ilbo, "How Much Further." Following the coding protocol, such articles, referring to multiple topics such as comfort women and the territorial dispute, are not coded for either topic. But the increasing tendency to mix together these issues is itself telling.
70. On the state of Park and Abe's relationship in 2013, see Fackler and Choe, "Growing Chill."
71. Kelly, "Three Hypotheses."
72. Kelly, "Three Hypotheses."
73. Cooney and Scarbrough, "Japan and South Korea," 174.

CHAPTER 9

Conclusion: The View from Tokyo

The view from Tokyo is not the same as the view from Beijing or Seoul. The difference is not so much a matter of disputing facts, although there are certainly concrete disputes among Japanese, Chinese, and South Korean leaders over how to interpret the past, where to draw territorial lines in the present, and what policies should be embraced to ensure a peaceful future. Even where matters of fact are at issue, the symbolic, emotional value of disputes among these countries is often what weighs most heavily on their diplomacy. Although the territorial disputes that divide these countries involve islands with some limited strategic value, for example, few of their leaders would suggest privately that the land itself is essential to their country's commercial or strategic success. Despite this, even fewer would dismiss the importance of their own country's claims. Above all these claims have emotional rather than material value.

Emotions weigh heavily in the international relations of East Asia. Not only there but in the Balkans, the Middle East, and along the fault zones of many other persistent international conflicts, it is widely assumed that hatred and mistrust are "baked in" to the historical context. As Andre Gerolymatos says of the Balkan wars, "the history of the Balkan states is replete with heroes, villains, and most important, martyrs who offer an example of self-sacrifice for each succeeding generation."[1] These stories of the past are ever-present. "At the heart of all the Balkan wars," Gerolymatos suggests, "is the clarion call of ethnic hatred served up as cultural heritage."[2] Even when leaders wish to back away from historical animosities, there is little they can do to resist the popular emotional tide. All too often, instead, they allow themselves to be swept up by nationalist passions, stoking the flames rather than offering leafy olive branches. It often seems there is nothing anyone can do to resist the "clarion call of ethnic hatred."

One of the central claims of this book is that the emotional politics of East Asian international relations offer room for hope as well as fear and hatred.[3] Even in cases of deep-seated mistrust based on a historical record of wartime brutality, of suspicions and perceived slights that have bedeviled Japan's relations with China and South Korea for seventy-five years, the "emotional record" is not an unbroken refrain of negativity. It is obvious that attitudes toward Japan have changed in some of its former adversaries, not least in the United States. The preceding chapters have also sought to establish that attitudes in China and South Korea periodically undergo shifts as well. At its lowest points, Japan's image in these countries could hardly have gotten much worse if they were actually at war. Yet there have also been moments when tempers have cooled and even been replaced by a degree of sympathy.

Perhaps the most obvious occasions for sympathy come in the moments after a natural disaster. When the Great Wenchuan Earthquake struck Sichuan in May 2008, killing nearly 70,000 and leaving almost 5 million people homeless, Japan sent the first foreign search and rescue team to arrive in China.[4] Hu Jintao later met with members of Japanese medical and search and rescue teams, praised their humanitarian spirit, and declared, "your actions fully exhibited the Japanese people's friendly sentiment toward the Chinese people."[5] Later, after the 2011 earthquake, tsunami, and radiological disaster in Japan, an editorial by Liu Jiangyong in the *People's Daily* proclaimed, "we can never forget the aid provided by Japan during 2008's enormous Wenchuan earthquake."[6] Another unsigned statement released by Xinhua News avowed, "the willingness and readiness to help each other is just a natural reflection of the time-honored friendly bond between the two neighboring Oriental civilizations."[7] China sent its own disaster relief, millions clicked on internet links to "pray for Japan," and Chinese citizens expressed admiration for the orderly conduct and bravery of many Japanese during and after the Triple Disaster.[8] In a meeting with Chinese Premier Wen Jiabao, Japanese Prime Minister Kan Naoto "expressed gratitude for expressions of condolences and assistance from the Chinese government and people in the wake of the disaster" and went on to say that their actions "helped improve friendship between the two nations."[9]

Wen and Kan's remarks occurred at a trilateral summit of Chinese, South Korean, and Japanese leaders held in Japan a little more than a week after the triple disaster. Commenting on the summit and the prospect of a "new era in China-Japan relations," Amy King points out that "disaster diplomacy" is often short-lived, but she also acknowledges "the regularity of ups and downs in the Sino-Japanese relationship over the long-term."[10] The evidence presented in Chapters 7 and 8 suggests that she is correct, and disaster diplomacy—or another such sporadic impetus for sympathy—is unlikely to serve as an adequate explanation for the pattern of warming and cooling relations between China and South Korea on one hand and Japan on the other.

In fact there is probably no single explanation that neatly ties together all the threads of emotional politics in diplomacy. It would be hard to dismiss out of hand the relevance of the international environment, and the US–Japan alliance has tended to weigh heavily on Japan's relations with both China and South Korea. Yet alliance politics clearly doesn't suffice as an explanation of attitudes toward Japan. If it did, we would expect South Koreans to have more positive attitudes than they do. Nor does historical conflict suffice to explain the way attitudes in China or South Korea have changed over time, as argued in Chapter 4. Rather, past actions and ongoing shifts in strategic capabilities serve as raw material that can be deployed in emotional discourse for different purposes, sometimes ratcheting up animosity and sometimes tamping it down.

If we suspect that emotion can be manipulated, this suggests in turn that domestic political considerations might drive attitudes. Clearly, innenpolitik does matter in both China and South Korea. Yet Chapter 5 shows that leaders in both countries also respond to public pressure as much as—or perhaps even more than—they manipulate it. Public attitudes toward other countries also possess their own emotional dynamics that leaders can ill afford to ignore. Many scholars have sought to explain the forces that drive these public attitudes. Gries proposed, as discussed in Chapter 2, that a persistent righteous anger in China is linked to a cosmology that places Japan in a subordinate role with respect to its Chinese "elder."[11] Zhang Yongjin argues, to take another example, that a sense of alienation from international society might account for some part of Chinese attitudes.[12] Extending this line of argument, Shogo Suzuki suggests that a sense of victimization by Japan offers a convenient target to those who perceive and resent China's exclusion from contemporary liberal international society.[13] Leo T. S. Ching also surmises that anticolonial awareness still shapes Chinese attitudes, not only when Japan's own economic and cultural successes evoke its erstwhile colonial power but also through its association with American dominance.[14] And several commentators, including Ching, direct our attention to the profound gendering of East Asian diplomacy and the way defending Chinese and Korean masculinity makes the tropes of comfort women and the Rape of Nanjing so important.[15] At the more positive end of the spectrum, meanwhile, the attractiveness of Japanese popular culture undoubtedly exerts some influence, particularly on younger Chinese and South Koreans.

Rather than proposing another monocausal account of what serves as the foundation for attitudes in China and South Korea toward Japan, I have instead proposed a model of how emotion is channeled down certain pathways. Returning for a moment to the metaphor borrowed from Andrew Ross and discussed in Chapter 6, it helps to conceive of emotion at the social level as a fluid that circulates within the body politic. Ross calls this the *circulation of affect*.[16] Changing the metaphor slightly, emotion may spring from many headwaters. Thus it may not make sense to conceive of one source as the "true" origin of emotions in politics. Still, we can profitably study the way emotions are guided by social context, and the TAPS model gives us one way of looking at this process. Specifically, the TAPS model assumes that two elements of social context are crucial for guiding political emotions: valence and capability. The first of these, *valence*, depends on whether we have a positive or negative relationship with the object of our emotions. The second dimension, *capability*, defines the sort of political relationship we might have, depending on whether the object of our emotions is powerful or weak (relative to ourselves). The first dimension ranges, therefore, from attitudes of trust (T) to anger (A); the second ranges from pride (P) in our own strength to shame (S) at our own weakness. There is no reason to suppose that only the emotions defined by this two-dimensional space are relevant to politics. But these emotions—humility, sympathy, fear, and disdain along with the axial emotions of trust, anger, pride, and shame—do seem to cover a great deal of the emotional landscape in politics, and in international politics specifically. Figure 9.1 summarizes the TAPS model in its generic form, as applied to Japan.

The TAPS model helps to explain how different international contexts channel emotion in different ways. It gives us a baseline for expectations about the way popular sentiment will manifest itself toward Japan, or any other country for that matter. From this perspective, it is not surprising that Japan can be seen in more than one way. Nor is it surprising that attitudes toward Japan sometimes change, depending on the context. For this reason, one further implication of the TAPS model is that Japan is not fated indefinitely to be an object of intense dislike in China and South Korea. We may acknowledge the acrimony directed at Japan as being genuine and heartfelt while also recognizing that circumstances do change. Certainly this was the case with American attitudes toward Japan. In China, on the other hand, the transition from communist internationalism under Mao to post-Tiananmen

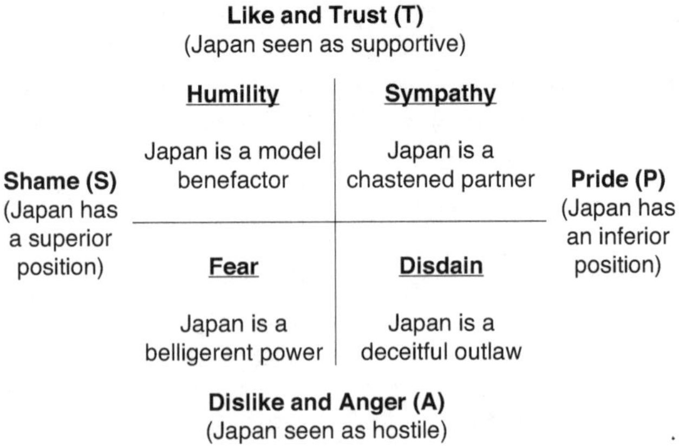

Like and Trust (T)
(Japan seen as supportive)

	<u>Humility</u>	<u>Sympathy</u>	
Shame (S) (Japan has a superior position)	Japan is a model benefactor	Japan is a chastened partner	**Pride (P)** (Japan has an inferior position)
	<u>Fear</u>	<u>Disdain</u>	
	Japan is a belligerent power	Japan is a deceitful outlaw	

Dislike and Anger (A)
(Japan seen as hostile)

Figure 9.1. The TAPS Model of Attitudes toward Japan

nationalism has meant a shift in the opposite direction. And in South Korea, there are halting steps toward cooperation and understanding in some areas, coexisting with persistent anger and frustration in others. The evidence suggests that attitudes depend on emotion in complex ways, sometimes shifting and sometimes enduring.

Undoubtedly Japan wishes to promote a better image in both China and South Korea. Before turning to the question of how its own diplomacy might foster improved relationships, however, one other matter deserves at least brief attention. To this point I have paid almost no attention to the way Japanese citizens perceive China and South Korea. It seems clear that episodes of perceived anti-Japanese sentiment in those countries weigh heavily on Japanese attitudes. Equally, it will not help matters in Beijing or Seoul if people perceive hostility emanating from Tokyo.

SEEING CHINA AND KOREA

Andrew Ross has paid special attention to the circulation of affect in the postconflict reconciliation process. Focusing on Rwanda, he sums up the emotional stakes for former aggressors in the following way: "I fear revenge when I categorize others as potential aggressors whom I suspect of having a clear perception of me as responsible for their injuries."[17] Scholars of ontological security point out that, even more than revenge, we also fear continued criticism, shame, and other assaults on our self-image.[18] In either case Chinese and Koreans would surely argue that it is not their responsibility to assuage Japan's fears. Yet history still inflects Japanese attitudes just as it does in China and Korea. The palpable sense in Tokyo that no amount of apologizing will ever lead to forgiveness from China or Korea increasingly seems to be hardening attitudes toward Japan's closest neighbors. And indeed at least one cross-national study of intergroup forgiveness, conducted in China, Taiwan, the Philippines, France, Russia, and Poland, found that mainland Chinese were significantly less forgiving than any of these other groups.[19] One thing that does *not* appear to explain this difference is the act of apologizing itself. In the twenty years preceding their 2013 study, Hanke et al. count twenty-nine formal Japanese apologies directed at China or Asian countries in general, whereas Germany issued one formal apology (to Poland) in the same time span.[20] Hanke and her associates found instead that Chinese reluctance to forgive was particularly associated with a sense in China that Japan's historical actions remain relevant today and that forgiveness would have various costs (depriving China of sympathy, encouraging Japanese revisionists, etc.). A 2019 study by Suzuki Shogo makes a similar point about Korean attitudes, speculating that contemporary feedback loops keep war memories alive. Koreans fear giving succor to Japanese revisionists, and at the same time conservatives in Japan thus feel that a positive Japanese self-image is undermined by critiques from abroad.[21]

Such reciprocal fears—that "Japan is unrepentant" and that "China and Korea are unforgiving"—suggest that worsening attitudes toward Japan will track along with negative attitudes in Japan toward other countries. To determine whether this is indeed the case, we might look once again to the opinion surveys conducted in both China and Japan since 2005 by Genron NPO and *China Daily*. The Genron NPO/*China Daily* data already discussed in Chapter 2 show a fair amount of fluctuation in Chinese attitudes. For example, only about 37 percent of Chinese expressed negative attitudes about Japan in 2007, whereas 93 percent had negative attitudes in 2013.[22] Figure 9.2 compares the Chinese attitude data with corresponding survey data on Japanese attitudes. The first decade of the twentieth century saw shifts in attitudes that do not seem obviously reciprocal. In 2007, for example, attitudes in China toward Japan improved markedly, while in Japan negativity toward China increased from 36 percent to 66 percent in a year-on-year comparison with 2006. On the other hand, negativity in China toward Japan increased from 41 percent in 2008 to 65 percent in 2009, while negativity in Japan toward China decreased slightly in the same period (from 76 percent to 73 percent).

Broadly speaking, from that time (2009) onward to about 2015, attitudes in Japan and China did begin to track together. For the most part, they became increasingly negative in both countries, with the biggest jump

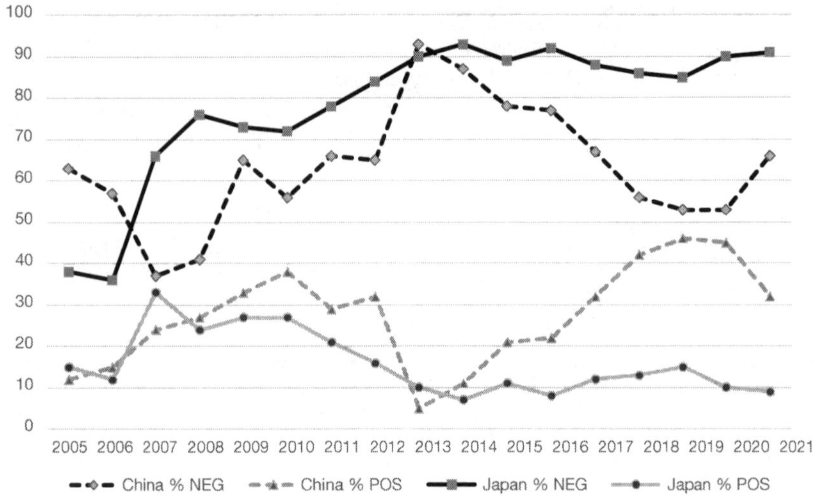

Figure 9.2. Reciprocal Attitudes in China and Japan, 2005–21
(Data from Genron NPO, "Japan-China Public Opinion Survey 2021.")

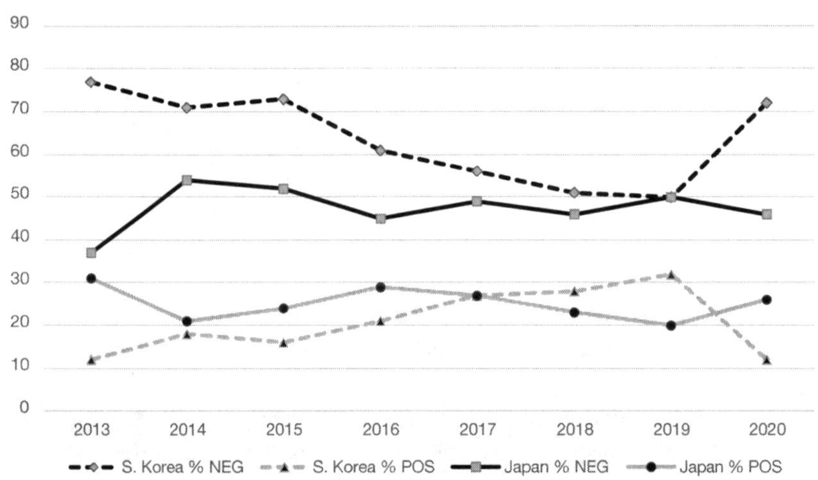

Figure 9.3. Reciprocal Attitudes in South Korea and Japan, 2013–20
(Data from Kudo, "South Korean Attitudes.")

occurring in 2013 after the Senkaku/Diaoyu Islands nationalization crisis. Then they began to diverge once again. This time, whereas attitudes toward Japan began to improve in China, attitudes toward China in Japan remained consistently negative.

Longitudinal opinion data are even more limited in the case of Japan–South Korean relations, but Genron NPO has conducted public opinion surveys in these two countries as well since 2013. Japan–South Korean relations were at a low point that year after disputes over history, territory, and the collapse of the General Security of Military Information Agreement (GSOMIA). The Genron NPO polling data, shown in Figure 9.3, indicate that relations improved thereafter and the percentage of South Koreans with negative attitudes gradually declined in subsequent years from 2013 (77 percent negative) to 2018 (51 percent negative).[23] Meanwhile, in Japan, attitudes shifted abruptly from relatively positive (only 37 percent negative) in 2013 to relatively negative (54 percent negative) in 2014 and then remained fairly constant, though showing some slight improvement (to 46 percent negative) by 2018. In 2020, South Korean attitudes toward Japan made a strongly negative shift, but the same did not occur in Japan.[24] In general, over this time span, it would appear that South Korean attitudes toward Japan have been more variable, whereas Japanese attitudes toward South Korea have been more consistent and somewhat, though not overwhelmingly, negative (typically 40–50 percent negative and 20–30 percent positive).[25]

We should be wary of generalization based on such limited longitudinal data. As Chapter 2 showed, looking only at a few, well-chosen opinion polls might support the conclusion that attitudes toward Japan in China and South Korea are implacably hostile, whereas a longer time span reveals more variability.[26] The Genron NPO data are too limited, therefore, to draw any firm conclusions about how Chinese, South Korean, and Japanese citizens respond to one another's attitudes. The available data do suggest, however, that the picture is probably more complicated than simplistic arguments about hurt feelings or generalized dislike would suggest. It may be that perceptions of negative attitudes elsewhere do sometimes lead to reciprocal hard feelings. Indeed, a very interesting series of experiments conducted by Eunbin Chung in Japan, China, and South Korea finds that affirmation of one's own identity helps to produce a more positive image of other countries and more generous actions toward their citizens.[27] Yet in the case of Japanese attitudes, a lack of external affirmation is probably not the only factor at work. It seems likely that increasing Chinese power and assertiveness under Xi Jinping, for example, have also led to a greater ongoing sense of threat in Japan.[28] In fact, this is one of the emotional outcomes that the TAPS model might lead us to expect in Japan as Chinese power grows, and it would explain why Japanese attitudes have remained persistently negative. It is equally possible, as Chinese authorities allege, that the Liberal Democratic Party (LDP) in particular has sought to capitalize on the "China threat" to advance its own national security priorities.[29]

PERCEIVING ONESELF

It should not be too surprising to find at least some evidence of Suzuki's "feedback loops" in East Asian public opinion. After all, Chapter 5 found evidence that external enemies can indeed pay domestic political dividends. Even if this were not the case, it is all too easy to blame others for the same flaws that one ignores among one's own compatriots. The biblical wisdom of Matthew 7:3—"why beholdest thou the mote that is in thy brother's eye, but considerest not the beam that is in thine own eye?"—finds a ready parallel in Asia. In the *Dhammapada*, a collection of Buddhist aphorisms in verse form, the Buddha observes: "Easily seen is the fault of others, but one's own fault is difficult to see. Like chaff one winnows another's faults, but hides one's own, even as a crafty fowler hides behind sham branches."[30] While we ignore our own faults, moreover, we stand ready to correct anyone who might think to point them out.

The Japanese interest in the way Japan is perceived by outsiders arguably rises to an unusual level. "One finds a similar preoccupation and insecurity of identity in many other countries," Kenneth Pyle says, "but the Japanese case seems unique in its intensity and its persistence."[31] And even more than with Americans or Russians—two other peoples preoccupied with their own national distinctiveness—concern among Japanese with their own national distinctiveness has given rise to an enormous literature on "theories of Japaneseness," or nihonjinron.[32] This is not the place to rehearse the many and varied claims that make up the corpus of nihonjinron. My point is simply that Japan displays a particular, intense sensitivity to the way the country is perceived by outsiders.

Masao Miyoshi, the eminent scholar of Japanese literature and culture, felt this preoccupation so keenly that he was compelled to write an essay declaring, tongue firmly in cheek, that "Japan is not interesting." In his essay of this title, Miyoshi declared, "the overwhelming majority of the Japanese place excessive importance on their collective identity, which is presented as 'singular' in the sense of both single/homogeneous and unique/exceptional."[33] Echoing Benedict Anderson, Miyoshi argues that the notion of a shared community was "invented and promoted" in Japan, as elsewhere, because it served a variety of elite interests within the broader context of capitalist and imperialist incentive structures.[34] Perhaps, he says, "in the case of Japan, the discourse of national identity preceded the project of constructing a modern nation-state. Partly because of the insularity of the Japanese archipelago along the rim of the Asian continent, the Japanese elites seem to have always felt acutely the hegemony of Sino and Indian civilizations.

Nativism was also a function of the Tokugawa policy of closure, which nearly isolated Japan from international circulation."[35] Yet the nihonjinron preoccupation was not solely a function of feudal isolation or nation-building. It was further reinforced among Japanese, he says, "during the six years of the U.S. occupation, by the presence of the visible dominant other in their midst."[36] At this point,

> The wartime slogans of "national unity" (*kyokoku itchi*) and "one hundred million deaths for the fatherland" (*ichioku gyokusai*) were switched to the postwar "unanimous penitence" (*ichioku sozange*), preparing the public opinion for the national ideal of "economic superpower" (*keizai taikoku*)—via "peace nation" (*heiwa kokka*), "culture nation" (*bunka kokka*), and now even "atom-bombed nation" (*hibakukoku*) in which everyone is an atom bomb victim.[37]

Many and varied have been the catchphrases that signal Japan's distinctiveness.

Miyoshi's objection to the fetish of Japanese national uniqueness is not that it lacks historical foundation. On the contrary it has many such foundations: one can take one's pick, and the nihonjinron literature is correspondingly vast. Rather, Miyoshi's complaint is that an obsession with one's own distinctiveness serves as a perpetual tool for misrepresentation and disenfranchisement, for obscuring difference and exerting totalizing rule. It masks the reality of diversity among Japanese while simultaneously hindering awareness of interests and vulnerabilities held in common with others. The former has predictable effects for those who do not fit in within Japan, while the latter compounds the problem of Japan's foreign policy. As Miyoshi puts it,

> Obviously, the representation of others is hazardous, because it nearly always ends in misrepresentation. Yet, one cannot forget that self-representation is not guaranteed to be right or authoritative either. Furthermore, even self-representation inevitably involves the representations of others. One should of course avoid deliberate misrepresentation of the other, which is rampant in both the media and academia. And yet the bond with all the exploited is the precondition of one's own liberation. All ethnic and social groups have internal minorities who need the support of the outside world.[38]

The mythology of Japanese distinctiveness, in Miyoshi's view, shuts down important conversations. During the war, invocations to national unity worked to suppress dissent. In postwar Japan, where dissent is possible, it is instead made mostly irrelevant. Harry Harootunian says of Miyoshi that "everywhere he looked he saw nothing but the signs of somnolent stagnation and cultural self-satisfaction."[39]

Miyoshi was not alone. Others have complained that the strong impetus to see Japan as unique has deprived the Japanese of ways to engage the rest of the world. Tamamoto Masaru illustrates the same point by highlighting the contrast between the two twentieth-century Japanese recipients of the Nobel Prize in Literature.[40] Kawabata Yasunari devoted his Nobel lecture, entitled "Japan, the Beautiful, and Myself," to the way Zen Buddhism captures a distinctively Japanese awareness of the beauty of minimalism, of "the emptiness, the nothingness, of the Orient."[41] Kawabata approvingly looked to the poetry of Dōgen and Myōe for its spare minimalism capturing the "spiritual foundation" and true beauty of Japan.[42] A quarter-century later, Ōe Kenzaburō took what he saw as Kawabata's parochialism to task in his own Nobel lecture, "Japan, the Ambiguous, and Myself."[43] The ambiguity of Kawabata's Zen mysticism, Ōe felt, had been a recipe for totalitarianism and suffering. "What I call Japan's 'ambiguity,'" Ōe said, "is a kind of chronic disease that has been prevalent throughout the modern age."[44] Instead, Ōe "identified himself with the humanism of William Yeats, William Blake, W. H. Auden, George Orwell, Milan Kundera, and others, stressing decency, innocence and sanity as desirable values of humanity."[45] "This identification was not made as an equal," Tamamoto points out, but rather "by depicting himself as a writer from the world's periphery."[46] Like Miyoshi, Ōe finds that "Japan is not interesting" so long as it embraces a commitment to its own sublime but ultimately ambiguous distinctiveness.

Since Tamamoto wrote, a third Nobel-laureate author of Japanese ancestry has completed this evolution toward worldliness. Born in Nagasaki, Kazuo Ishiguro grew up in the UK and became a British citizen in 1983. The masterpiece that brought him fame, *The Remains of the Day*, is a quintessentially English novel about the misplaced loyalties of a British butler coming to terms with his squandered opportunities. In it, according to Salman Rushdie, "Ishiguro turned away from the Japanese settings of his first two novels and revealed that his sensibility was not rooted in any one place, but capable of travel and metamorphosis."[47] Ishiguro delivered his Nobel lecture, "My Twentieth Century Evening—and Other Small Breakthroughs," in 2017.[48] He recognized that, as a young author, he had been "busily constructing in my mind a richly detailed place called 'Japan'—a place to which I in some way belonged, and from which I drew a certain sense of my identity and my confidence."[49] Gradually, Ishiguro faces up to the realization, delivered in the twilight of his own "twentieth century evening," that he had "been living for some years in a bubble."[50] This was not because he still maintained the "fragile" image of Japan that he had painstaking crafted as a young man, but because racism, "tribal nationalisms," and the persistence of "enormous inequalities" and "savage meritocracies that resemble apartheid" all combined in the new century to destroy his faith in a vision of "liberal democracies living in near-borderless friendship."[51]

Ishiguro realized Ōe's vision of identifying with a broader, humanistic consciousness, but at the cost of leaving behind his imagined vision of Japanese distinctiveness and searching instead for a "new idea, a great humane vision, around which to rally."[52] Whatever this idea might be, it will not be an idea of Japan but, instead, one of some more cosmopolitan grouping. Meanwhile, for those who wonder what Japan might contribute to this vision, Tamamoto points out the "great discrepancy between Japan's intellectual ambiguity, on the one hand, and its social achievements and economic power in the world, on the other."[53] Japan is no longer isolated or peripheral, but it remains ambiguous. And the cost of this ambiguity is a lack of international trust. "A Japan without core values," Tamamoto fears, is "a Japan which can swing from liberal internationalism to militarism and imperialism, then to politically isolationist economics—which is a rough description of the swings in Japan's orientation in the world during the twentieth century."[54] Tamamoto worries that a country with an ambiguous identity can never be welcomed fully into the community of nations. An ambiguous identity means an ambiguous foreign policy.

MANAGING PERCEPTIONS

Many contemporary Japanese authors bemoan the lack of a compelling national identity in modern Japan. Tamamoto points out that there is not quite even a word for *identity* in Japanese: some use the English-derived neologism *aidentiti*, while others refer to *shutaisei*, which connotes individuality, independence, and subjectivity.[55] "Most Japanese thinkers are agreed that Japan lacks shutaisei," Tamamoto says, and yet "nobody seems to have a satisfactory idea of what a Japan with shutaisei may be, or what it takes to bring shutaisei to Japan."[56] Conservative commentators and politicians seem to feel that the problem is mostly one of having sufficient national pride. The priority of neoconservative groups such as Nippon Kaigi (Japan Conference), therefore, has been to replace a "masochistic" remorse for Japan's wartime record with a sense of patriotism.[57] Meanwhile, efforts on the left to counter nationalism with an internationalist commitment to liberal values seem to founder on the rocks of "ambiguity." And so, gradually, the calls have increased for Japan to cast off its special status as a "peace nation" (*heiwa kokka*), to revise its constitution, and to become a "normal country" (*futsu no kuni*).[58]

What discussions of Japan's identity often leave out, but what conservative politicians in Japan appreciate very well, is that image management is a problem of emotions as well as cognitive content involving goals, creed, or aspirational values. David Leheny makes the same point in his own recent study of hope in the Japanese emotional landscape.

> The social dimensions of emotion—how we communicate our feelings to others, how we experience them together—clearly have political consequences, whether in the ways in which actors creatively deploy them in the fraught circumstances of post-conflict situations or truth-and-reconciliation commissions, or in the ways in which shared experiences of trauma are used to establish collective identities.[59]

Leheny's book is a superb illustration of the way Japanese politicians use emotions such as hopefulness to manage both domestic and international expectations about Japan's global role. The TAPS model presented in this book is an effort to organize our accounts of the same problem by placing the discussion of emotion within the context of two core elements of image construction, valence and capability. In the first instance, emotion management in diplomacy depends on encouraging a shift toward the positive end of the valence dimension in the way others view one's own country, but it also requires attention to the implications of national power.

Starting with the first of these problems, the basic challenge is a familiar one to specialists in national branding: encouraging a positive national image. International politics is largely a game of putting out fires, if not wars. There is always a crisis of some sort to be managed, and this works against long-term policies intended to build up a reservoir of positive emotions such as trust and goodwill. On the contrary, the usual instruments of diplomacy—coercion and deterrence—involve the manipulation of negative emotions through the threat of inflicting pain on one's adversary. The instruments of pleasure are less often tried.[60] Perhaps one reason the carrot is employed less frequently than the stick is that the former can so easily seem self-serving. The challenge of using positive inducements in diplomacy is akin to the challenge of producing an appealing viral video as part of a.

marketing campaign. Corporate advertisers would like to take advantage of the enormous reach enjoyed by so-called internet influencers. The most visible social media influencers rival and, by some measures, far exceed the popularity of well-known musicians, movie stars, and politicians, who are themselves obliged to have a large social media presence.[61] Unfortunately, it is difficult to produce a video that mimics successful viral videos while serving the intended advertising purpose. It is not impossible, however, and viral advertising campaigns have become increasingly sophisticated.[62]

National branding presents its own challenges. Not only does a parallel problem of authenticity affect national branding campaigns in the same way that viral marketing can appear contrived, but nation branding must contend with two very different audiences, one domestic and one foreign. The LDP's efforts to promote patriotism illustrate the problem nicely. Its efforts to encourage national pride at home often seem to intensify criticism from abroad. One might object that this is because LDP efforts to honor Japan's own wartime sacrifices are too often clumsy at best and downright insensitive to the suffering of Japan's former adversaries at worst, particularly when they seem intended to whitewash the wartime record through campaigns such as Nippon Kaigi's efforts to rewrite history textbooks.[63]

Perhaps these challenges are one reason that efforts at national self-promotion are often channeled through proxy competitions such as sporting events. As briefly discussed in Chapter 3, the Olympic Games are a particularly visible example of this sort of competition. Judging from the enormous efforts at national pageantry expended by host nations in recent iterations of the Olympics, it seems clear that positive branding is a desired outcome. Yet one study found that American concern for human rights violations in China actually increased immediately after the 2008 Beijing Olympics.[64] Another interesting study of reactions to the 2012 London Games found that the more time people spent watching televised coverage, the more their own feelings of patriotism and nationalism were amplified.[65] Even when one can negotiate the difficult challenge of managing both internal and external audience expectations, therefore, it is by no means certain that demonstrations of national prowess actually confer a positive international image.

It may well be that, as with viral marketing online, the best way to promote a positive image abroad is to make no obvious effort to do so at all, instead relying on aspects of soft power that are transferrable to the country's image. In this way, the Cool Japan campaign promotes a positive international image not by directly advancing national symbolism but instead by promoting cultural products that others will nevertheless associate with Japan. There is some limited evidence that these campaigns work, particularly with younger audiences, just as blue jeans and jazz music once advanced American diplomatic interests.[66] Another lesson from the world of online marketing, however, is that their success may be short-lived given the perpetual desire for novelty among brand consumers. There is undoubtedly much more to be said about how best to manipulate a nation's image—and Japan's image specifically—to positive effect. Yet how to do so is not specifically the topic of this book, which is instead concerned with the way emotion shapes different aspects of national images.

Emotion also affects the second dimension of a country's international image that, following the TAPS model, involves estimations of relative power. Although relative power is not a valence dimension—that is, it is not the case that either relative strength or relative weakness is a good (or bad) thing for a country's image in principle—there are nevertheless particular dangers associated with either end of the relative power spectrum. The principal danger of being seen as relatively powerful, one can readily appreciate, is that a country also risks being seen as a threat. Many national leaders have felt, on the other hand, that projecting an image of national power was essential to forestall challenges. Steve Chan argues, for example, that a key element of the Chinese strategy of "soft deterrence" has been to avoid direct confrontation with the United States while nevertheless "projecting an image of being too big to swallow and too tough to mess with."[67]

At the other end of the spectrum, perceptions of weakness would appear to invite challenges. Although a weaker state may well be seen as a helpful junior partner in diplomacy, weakness quickly gives rise to scorn when valence turns negative.[68] No one enjoys being on the receiving end of contemptuous or scornful behavior, but in international relations such attitudes are especially dangerous. Consider the way the United States treats the countries it labels "rogue states" or "outlaw states."[69] Unlike enemies, whose power is mostly checked, if it can be resisted at all, through policies of containment, rogue states are potentially targets for interventionist policies.[70] At the very least this may entail interference in their domestic affairs. Particularly since the advent of its so-called war on terror, moreover, the United States has seemed increasingly willing to use more direct, military forms of intervention.[71]

The ironic implication for Japanese foreign policy is that efforts to reduce the Chinese sense of threat by limiting expressions of Japanese power may actually backfire. Inasmuch as they shift an emotional politics of fear and enmity to one of contempt and disdain, they may actually make Chinese challenges more likely. This is not to say that Japanese leaders should be indifferent to Chinese sensibilities. Japan's image in China must be managed in terms of valence, however, while giving due attention to relative power. Increasing Japanese capabilities and shifts in its military doctrine will undoubtedly prompt objections in Beijing, but actions that emphasize Japan's orientation—visits to Yasukuni and textbook revisions—may actually prompt a bigger response than Japan's evolution toward military self-sufficiency. This conclusion is at odds with the expectations of realist theories that treat power more or less as a synonym for threat. Yet the premise of the TAPS model is that, when it comes to national imagery, the dimensions of threat (valence) and power (capabilities) are distinct.

Efforts to improve Japan's international image are complicated precisely because image management is a multidimensional problem. The problem is further compounded by the extent to which different issue areas evoke different sorts of emotional responses. Chapters 7 and 8 show that China and South Korea are both inclined to see Japan as relatively weak and flawed in certain contexts and as strong and cunning in others. It does not help that Japan's own policies exhibit a certain schizophrenia, vacillating between assertiveness on some occasions and deference on others.[72] One reason for these oscillations is that different leaders in Japan proceed from different assumptions, particularly about China and the United States. Some believe that CCP leaders are mostly reacting to their own problems, managing the growing expectations of a population that is large and diverse while also contending with growing pressures from Washington. Others evidently consider China a regional bully whose provocations must be resisted. Many prominent LDP politicians seem to fall into the latter camp. In a 2013 interview with the *Wall Street Journal*, Prime Minister Abe argued that "Japan is expected to exert leadership not just on the economic front, but also in the field of security in the Asia-Pacific," and that it must be more assertive with China as a result.[73] Several months later, at the World Economic Forum in Davos, Abe appealed for international support by arguing that "we must restrain military expansion in Asia . . . which otherwise could go unchecked."[74] Abe was not alone, and his assassination in 2022 will not change the broader political calculus within the LDP. It is now well established in Japan that a platform of hawkishness on regional security matters can pay political dividends.[75] As the Japanese Diet prepared to pass new security legislation reinterpreting the constitution to allow for collective self-defense in 2015, for example, conservative Diet member Yuriko Koike, who was soon to run for the governorship of Tokyo, crowed: "at last, Japan stands up."[76]

It is hard to say whether the more conservative LDP factions actually believe this "China threat" rhetoric, or whether they simply find it useful as a campaign talking point or a means of advancing their own domestic political agendas. David Leheny inclines toward the latter position, arguing that the emotional politics driving Japanese foreign policy today are rooted firmly in domestic priorities.[77] Leheny contends that apprehension about the evolution of Japanese family structures and sexual mores is the real driving force behind conservative advocacy for constitutional revision. Thus, antiterror legislation and normalization of the status of the SDF are part of a package along with constraints on pornography and prostitution, all of which serve as vehicles to increase state surveillance and control over society. Japanese politicians thus "think global," Leheny says, but "fear local." This is a plausible argument, and yet not all Japanese fears are local.

On the contrary the emotional politics of Japanese foreign policy has its own incentives and its own patterns. Particularly at a moment when China's rise is transforming the balance of power in East Asia, it should come as no surprise that the emotional landscape of Japanese foreign policy is unsettled. Just as China was once able to play Americans and Russians against each other, Japan is now in a position to hedge quietly against demands from either China or the United States.[78] Skeptics might point out that it is never easy to negotiate the shifting terrain between two superpowers. Doing so will be a protracted exercise in policy calibration as well as image management. And this is only one of the reasons why it matters how Japan is seen. The international image that Japan cultivates will affect the roles it plays in international organizations and its prospects for gaining a long-sought permanent seat on the UN Security Council. It will determine whether or not Japan has a say in the evolving architecture of Asia's regional institutions in the twenty-first century. Needless to say, Japan's image remains important to the United States, which counts Japan as a crucial ally. And it matters in China and South Korea, not only because of Japan's strategic importance to both of those states but also because Japan has played and continues to play an important role in the way their own national identities are defined.

Indeed, Japan's importance for Chinese and South Korean identity is precisely what raises the stakes of emotional politics in East Asian international relations. Not only have emotions been channeled down pathways leading toward anger and fear at some times and disdain at others, but there is always a danger that the image of Japan produced by these emotions could become ossified in strategically dangerous ways. One of the main findings presented in this book is that Japan's image in China and South Korea is more variable than many observers realize. Chapter 6 also argued that emotions can give rise to a national image that becomes exaggerated and fixed as a caricature of a dangerous other. The Sparta and Melos complexes represent the dangers of exaggerated fear on one hand and exaggerated condescension on the other.

Japan cannot afford complacency about the way it is seen because it is always possible for the exaggerated negative attitudes that sometimes flourish in China and South Korea to take root in ways that make them more resistant to change than in the past.

Above all, though, the way Japan is seen matters to the Japanese themselves. Well over a century ago, in 1905, Japanese journalist Kiyoshi Kawakami issued this *cri de cœur* on behalf of his compatriots.

> The Japanese of New Japan are anxious almost to a man, if I mistake not, to see their country cease to be regarded as a land inhabited by dear little doll-like people, as the land of miniature landscape gardens, of quaint tea-houses, and of weird temples. Who is to blame, even after our victories over the Great Northern Power, for that popular misconception that we are only pretty weaklings, and how shall we force the foreigner to believe that 'the steam-whistle, the newspaper, the voting-tablet, the postal-box at every street-corner and even in remote villages, the clerk in shop and bank and public office hastily summoned from our side to answer the ring of the telephone bell, the railway replacing the palanquin, the iron-clad replacing the war-junk,—that these and a thousand other startling changes testify that Japan is transported ten thousand miles away from her former moorings?[79]

Kawakami was himself a complex figure whose own life nicely illustrates the extent to which identity can be plastic.[80] He grew up in poverty but found sponsors to finance his legal studies in Tokyo. He became a Christian social-ist and was so influenced by Karl Marx that he took on "Karl" as a pen name. When the Social Democratic Party he helped found was dissolved by the police in 1901, he left for the United States, where he accepted a postgrad-uate scholarship at the University of Iowa. Kawakami married an American and became a prominent contributor to American newspapers while also traveling widely in Asia as a correspondent for major Japanese dailies. He was deeply impressed by American democracy but also distressed by its racial animosities. He wrote extensively on Japanese contributions to Hawaii and California and eventually became an apologist for Japan's militarism in the 1930s. Still in the United States after the Pearl Harbor attack, Kawakami was incarcerated in an internment camp but also later assisted the US gov-ernment in devising its own propaganda urging Japanese soldiers to surren-der.[81] In the volatility of Kawakami's life, one finds a metaphor for the vola-tility of Japan's international image.

Kawakami cared passionately about his Japanese identity and longed for his country to attain its due recognition on the global stage. To the extent that nationality plays a role in defining our sense of self, we care how our country is seen because we care how we are seen. This is the surest testimony to the relevance of emotion in foreign policy. We can no more dispense with emotion in foreign policy than we can dispense with emotion in interpersonal relations. It is also helpful to remember that emotion serves an adaptive function. It is not merely an impediment to reasoned calculation, representing an ever-present danger during international crises as an earlier generation of scholars tended to see it. It alerts us to dangers and compels us to act. More fundamentally, however, it helps to define the way we see ourselves and others.

Notes

1. Gerolymatos, *Balkan Wars*, 4.
2. Gerolymatos, *Balkan Wars*, 5.
3. Indeed, David Leheney argues that hope is *the* central theme in contemporary Japanese political discourse; see Leheney, *Empire of Hope*.
4. See CBC News, "Almost 5 Million Chinese Homeless."
5. Hu, "Hu Jintao Meets."
6. Blanchard, "Japan's Hour of Need."
7. Richburg, "Japan Quake."
8. Lim, "China Acts Fast."
9. Wen and Kan, "Premier Wen Jiabao Holds Talks."
10. King, "Trilateral Summit." Chung and Rhee also find that the attitudes of disaster victims themselves toward out-groups tend to become more negative; see Chung and Rhee, "Disasters and Intergroup Peace."
11. Gries, *China's New Nationalism*.
12. Zhang, *China in International Society*.
13. Suzuki, "Importance of 'Othering.'"
14. Ching, *Anti-Japan*.
15. Ching, *Anti-Japan*, chap. 3; Louie, *Chinese Masculinities*; Seo, "Politics of Memory."
16. Ross, *Mixed Emotions*.
17. Ross, *Mixed Emotions*, 148.
18. Kinnvall, "Globalization and Religious Nationalism"; Mitzen, "Ontological Security"; Steele, *Ontological Security*. On Japan–South Korea relations specifically, see Suzuki, "Japanese Revisionists"; and on Japan–China relations, see Gustafsson, "Memory Politics and Ontological Security."
19. Hanke et al., "When the Past Haunts the Present."
20. Hanke et al., "When the Past Haunts the Present," 293. Indeed, although the evidence is limited, Hanke et al. find that the number of apologies is negatively associated with forgiveness. They speculate that this is because Japan is responding to requests for

apologies and that the resulting statements, when delivered, are not perceived as sincere; see Hanke et al., "When the Past Haunts the Present," 299.

21. Suzuki, "Japanese Revisionists."

22. Genron NPO, "Japan–China Public Opinion Survey 2021."

23. Kudo, "South Korean Attitudes."

24. Kudo, "South Korean Attitudes."

25. Tamaki offers one way to explain this consistency, arguing that Japan has never been able to get beyond the narrative of its own natural leadership when it comes to Korea, leading to a persistent dismissiveness that parallels contemporary Chinese attitudes toward Japan; see Tamaki, *Deconstructing Japan's Image*.

26. As shown in Figure 2.5, for example, only 29 percent of Chinese were reported to have negative attitudes toward Japan in 1992. This figure jumped to 73 percent in 2000, dropped back to 48 percent in 2002, and later peaked at 93 percent in 2013.

27. Chung, *Pride, Not Prejudice*. Chung's well-conceived studies provide further evidence, in any case, that identity-affirming emotion helps to shape the images of other countries.

28. Conversely, Sasaki argues that Chinese perceptions of threat have increased because of Japan's defense build up beginning in the late 1980s, coupled with closer defense ties to the United States beginning in the mid-1990s; see Sasaki, "China Eyes the Japanese Military."

29. Hagström and Jerdén, "Understanding Fluctuations"; Hughes, "Japan's 'Resentful Realism'"; Liff and Ikenberry, "Racing toward Tragedy?"; Mochizuki, "Japan's Shifting Strategy." The strategic advantage created by manipulating emotions is one reason that Gustafsson and Hall encourage further study of the political economy of emotions; see Gustafsson and Hall, "Politics of Emotions."

30. *Dhammapada* 18:252; see Buddharakkhita, *Dhammapada*.

31. Pyle, "Japanese Self-Image," 2.

32. For a thoughtful overview of nihonjinron by a Japanese scholar, see Oguma, *Tan'itsu Minzoku Shinwa no Kigen*. A sampling of Japanese studies of the way outsiders, specifically, perceive Japan includes Kawatake et al., *Gaikoku Media no Nihon Imēji*; Kase, *Kagami no nai Kuni*; Miyamoto and Nagasawa, *Amerikajin no Nihonjin Kan*; Murakami, *Gaikokujin ni Yoru Sengo Nihonron*; Satō, *Okiwasure Nihongaku*.

33. Miyoshi, "Japan Is Not Interesting," 196. On Miyoshi's importance, see Harootunian, "As We Saw Him."

34. Miyoshi, "Japan Is Not Interesting," 196. See Anderson, *Imagined Communities*.

35. Miyoshi, "Japan Is Not Interesting," 196.

36. Miyoshi, "Japan Is Not Interesting," 197.

37. Miyoshi, "Japan Is Not Interesting," 197.

38. Miyoshi, "Japan Is Not Interesting," 204.

39. Harootunian, "As We Saw Him," 15.

40. Tamamoto, "Ambiguous Japan."

41. Kawabata, "Japan, the Ambiguous, and Myself."

42. Kawabata, "Japan, the Ambiguous, and Myself." Prime Minister Abe Shinzō later embraced the notion of "beautiful Japan" (*utsukushii nihon*) as a political rallying cry. For an extended discussion of this aspect of Abe's nationalism, see Kolmaš, *National Identity*.

43. Ōe, "Japan, the Ambiguous, and Myself."

44. Ōe, "Japan, the Ambiguous, and Myself."

45. Tamamoto, "Ambiguous Japan," 199–200.

46. Tamamoto, "Ambiguous Japan," 200.

47. Rushdie, "Salman Rushdie on Kazuo Ishiguro."

48. Ishiguro, "My Twentieth Century Evening."

49. Ishiguro, "My Twentieth Century Evening," 6.

50. Ishiguro, "My Twentieth Century Evening," 14.

51. Ishiguro, "My Twentieth Century Evening," 14, 15.

52. Ishiguro, "My Twentieth Century Evening," 16.

53. Tamamoto, "Ambiguous Japan," 200.

54. Tamamoto, "Ambiguous Japan," 202. Cf. Ashizawa, "When Identity Matters," who argues that claims about values in foreign policy are intrinsically bound up with state identity.

55. Tamamoto, "Ambiguous Japan," 204–5.

56. Tamamoto, "Ambiguous Japan," 205.

57. McNeill, "Nippon Kaigi."

58. Kitaoka, *Futsū no Kuni e*; Ozawa, "Futsu no Kuni ni Nare"; Hagström, "'Abnormal' State"; Soeya, Welch, and Tadokoro, *Japan as a "Normal Country"?*

59. Leheny, *Empire of Hope*, 10.

60. Breslin reminds us that pleasure of all sorts—bribery, flattery, sexual favors, and other gifts—has always been a part of the diplomatic repertoire; see Breslin, *Beyond Pain*.

61. See, e.g., Time, "30 Most Influential People"; Gómez, "Digital Fame."

62. Audrezet, de Kerviler, and Moulard, "Authenticity under Threat."

63. McNeill, "Nippon Kaigi." Fukuoka notes that "joint history writing projects with China (2006–10) and South Korea (2002–5, 2007–10) largely failed, which left a sense of disappointment and weariness among the participating parties"; see Fukuoka, "Japanese History Textbook Controversy," 313. The unfortunate result may be to cede the playing field to groups such as Nippon Kaigi, which remain strongly motivated to rewrite Japan's textbooks. In an interesting study, Yinan He contrasts the failure of Sino-Japanese efforts to develop a common historical narrative with German–Polish initiatives to produce jointly written textbooks. Successes in the latter case, she argues, have worked to "demythify" history and to create a much less fraught emotional politics between the two countries; see He, *Search for Reconciliation*.

64. Heslop, Nadeau, and O'Reilly, "China and the Olympics."

65. Billings et al., "From Pride to Smugness."

66. On the United States's musical diplomacy, see Davenport, *Jazz Diplomacy*. On the efficacy of the Cool Japan campaign and other Japanese efforts to use cultural exports to enhance soft power, see Kimura and Harris, *Exporting Japanese Aesthetics*; Otmazgin, "Chrysanthemum and the Cool"; Valaskivi, "Brand New Future?"; and Watanabe and McConnell, *Soft Power Superpowers*. For a more skeptical view, see Groot, "Cool Japan."

67. Chan, "Soft Deterrence," 77.

68. There have been comparatively few studies of the "junior partner" image in international relations. See, however, Rodkiewicz, *China's Junior Partner*; Schmitt, *Allies that Count*.

69. Henriksen, "Rise and Decline of Rogue States"; Hoyt, "'Rogue State' Image"; Klare, *Rogue States*; O'Reilly, "Rogue Doctrine?"; Tanter, *Rogue Regimes*.

70. Herrmann and Fischerkeller, "Beyond the Enemy Image"; Hoyt, "'Rogue State' Image"; Miles, *US Foreign Policy*; O'Reilly, "Rogue Doctrine?" Even Robert Litwak, who mostly advocates modified policies of containment against rogue states, argues that "the

development of an appropriate strategy is contingent on an accurate 'image' of the target state"; see Litwak, *Rogue States*, 245.

71. Chomsky, *Rogue States*; O'Reilly, "Rogue Doctrine?"

72. Chalmers Johnson identifies just this pattern in Japanese attitudes toward China, arguing that they have tended to fluctuate between flattery and contempt; see Johnson, "Patterns of Japanese Relations with China."

73. Abe, quoted in Baker and Nishiyama, "Abe Says Japan Ready."

74. Abe, quoted in MacKinnon, "Japan Tells World to Stand Up."

75. See Catalinac, *Electoral Reform*.

76. Koike, "Commentary." Koike served as Abe's secretary of defense in 2007.

77. Leheny, *Think Global, Fear Local*.

78. Cf. Foot and King, "China's World View"; Koga, "Concept of 'Hedging' Revisited"; Matsuda, "Engagement and Hedging"; Nagy, "Japan's Proactive Pacifism."

79. Kawakami, *Japan and the Japanese*, x.

80. For a well-researched study of Kawakami's life and thought, see Gavin, "Meiji Christian Socialist."

81. I am indebted to Gavin, "Meiji Christian Socialist," for many of these details.

Coding Newspapers for Emotion

In Chapters 7 and 8, I study the language used to describe Japan in two newspapers: *The People's Daily* in China, and *Chosun Ilbo* in South Korea. This Appendix describes the procedures I used to identify a sample of articles from each newspaper and to code adjectives within each selected article. It also contains the complete lists of adjectives extracted from these articles for each issue area studied in Japan's relations with China and South Korea.

People's Daily Analysis

A search of the *People's Daily Online* database for articles containing the terms *Japan* and *constitution* identified a list of articles to be coded for each year from 2010 to 2015 (a total of six years). Another search for the terms *Japan* and *Diaoyu* produced a second list of articles in the same time frame. The searches returned articles in reverse chronological order for each year, and the coded sample includes the first five articles with adjectives referring to Japan, the Japanese government, Japanese leaders, or Sino-Japanese relations. Not every year contained such articles, so that a total of twenty-one articles pertaining to Japan's constitution were coded, yielding seventy-eight distinct adjectives describing Japan. Thirty articles pertaining to the Diaoyu Islands were coded, yielding eighty-nine distinct adjectives describing Japan. References to Japan's self-perceptions (e.g., "Japan is campaigning as a victim" or "Japan wants to be seen as a normal country") were excluded, as were articles found to contain no references to the relevant topics. The searches also excluded articles that refer to the topic only in passing and articles that extensively discuss multiple issues in Sino-Japanese relations. Only adjectives, rather than other descriptions of Japan, were coded. Thus, the adjective "strained" (referring to Sino-Japanese relations) is coded, whereas the prepositional phrase "under strain" is not. Descriptions of Japanese leaders themselves are coded, but not descriptions of their actions, views, and so on. Finally, adjectives describing China in these articles were also coded, resulting in a list of eighteen adjectives describing China in articles on the Japanese constitution and fourteen adjectives describing China in articles on the Diaoyu Islands.

Adjectives describing Japan in articles prior to Japan's constitutional reinterpretation (2010–13) are as follows: *active, advanced, aggressive, alarming, anti-China, backwards, blatant, bold, brazen, dangerous, deliberate, detrimental, fraught, gloomy, grim, hawkish, hidden, impenitent, intolerable, irresponsible, isolated, lost, malicious, marginalized, not smooth, pacifist, pawn, perverse, provocative, rampant, regrettable, repugnant, rightist, right-wing, rocky, secretive, shortsighted, squeezed, troubling, unreasonable, unrepentant, untrustworthy, villainous,* and *willful.* Adjectives describing Japan after its constitutional reinterpretation (which include all articles selected for 2014 as well as those in 2015) are: *alarming, ambitious, arbitrary, bigoted, blatant, chilly, chronic, clumsy, Cold War* (used as an adjective, e.g., a "Cold War mindset"), *controversial, dangerous, decent, deliberate, distorting, eccentric, expansionist, export-dependent, flagrant, frozen, hegemony-seeking, icy, inappropriate, invalid, lost, low, militarist, nationalistic, offensive, peace-loving, persistent, pitiful, provocative, publicly-repelled, regrettable, repeated, reprehensible, right-wing, rightist, rightward, struggling, thawing, unpopular,* and *unprecedented.*

In the sampled articles on Japan's constitution from 2010 to 2015, there were eighteen adjectives describing China: *alarmed, assumed enemy,* (formerly) *bullied,* (not a) *bully, claimant, concerned, courageous, defensive, foreign trade* (used as an adjective, e.g., a "foreign trade country"), *humiliated, insulted, peaceful, peace-loving,* (not a) *rival, second-largest, target,* (not a) *threat,* and *world power.*

Adjectives describing Japan in *People's Daily* articles referencing *Japan* and *Diaoyu* in 2010–11 are as follows: *beneficial, clueless, coldest, controversial, cooperative, dependent, extremist, fearful, friendly, hawkish, invalid, irresponsible, major, offensive, once-dynamic, positive, promising, reciprocal, restless, simmering, strained, strategic,* and *troubled.* In 2012–13, Japan was described in coded articles referencing *Diaoyu* as: *baseless, bold, close, dangerous, deadlocked, deliberate, embarrassed, flaring, groundless, grudging, half-dead, hardline, hegemonic, hidden, illegal, imperialist, inflammatory, influential, intentional, interdependent, intransigent, jolted, normal, provocative, rational, recidivist, reckless, right(-wing), serious, shadowed, smarty-pants, strong, troublemaker, unacceptable, unreasonable, unscrupulous, vehement,* and *wrong.* And in 2014–15, Japan was described in coded articles referencing *Diaoyu* as: *baseless, deliberate, detrimental, fearless, flagrant, forced, freezing, frosty, frozen, humiliated, icebound, ice-trapping, icy, intertwined, knavish, militaristic, nationalistic, negative, provocative, restrained, revisionist, rightist, rightward, rocked, strained, superior, tense, thawing, ultra-rightist, unapologetic, undeclared, unilateral,* and *wrong.*

In the sampled articles referencing *Diaoyu,* there were six adjectives describing China in the years (2010–11) before the islands were nationalized: *equal, large, largest, stern, strong,* (not a) *threat.* There were nine adjectives describing China in the years (2012–15) after nationalization: *defensive, determined, firm, normal, peaceful, ready* (partner), *solemn, supporting,* (not a) *threat.*

Chosun Ilbo Analysis

A search of the *Chosun Ilbo* English-language website for articles from 2010 to 2016 containing the term *Japan* and another term related to the issue area—*comfort women, Dokdo,* or *alliance*—yielded a list of articles from which a sample was selected. As in the *People's Daily* analysis, articles containing references to multiple issue areas were excluded, as were articles that did not deal primarily with the selected issue area and articles of fewer than 500 words (a necessary constraint to ensure sampling articles with sufficient content). The first articles meeting these criteria in each year were selected for analysis, up to a maximum of ten articles per year. A total of twenty-five articles referencing *Japan* and *comfort women* were coded for analysis, and a total of thirty-one distinct adjectives describing Japan were identified within them. On *Japan* and *Dokdo,* thirty-eight articles were coded, yielding 116 distinct adjectives. And on *Japan* and *alliance,* thirty-two articles were coded, yielding seventy-eight distinct adjectives.

The twelve adjectives describing Japan in *Chosun Ilbo* articles referencing *Japan* and *comfort women* in 2010–12 (before Abe's return to power) are as follows: *blind, convicted, grave, humility, illegal, imperialist, militarist, pacifist, rightwing, shocked,* (not) *sincere,* and *unprecedented.* The twenty-two adjectives describing Japan in *Chosun Ilbo* articles referencing *Japan* and *comfort women* in 2013–16 (after Abe's return to power) are as follows: *conservative, contradictory, discredited, extreme, fair, forced, forceful, forcible, foul, guilty, inevitable, necessary, outspoken, pacifist, responsible, revisionist,* (far) *right, rightwing*, (not) *sincere, undeniable, unspeakable*, and *vague*. Three adjectives (*pacifist, rightwing*, and *sincere*) appeared in both time periods.

The eighty-two adjectives describing Japan in *Chosun Ilbo* articles referencing *Japan* and *Dokdo* in 2010–12 are as follows: *absurd, administrative, afraid, angry, bent, bilateral, bogus, bona fide, childish, claimed, clear, clever, closer, colonial, comprehensive,* (not) *content, contested, convicted, determined, difficult, diplomatic, disappointed, disappointing, disarray, disputed, dubious, due, explicit, false, flimsy, forceful, formal, future-oriented, guilty, ignorant, imperialist, inaccurate, isolated, long, lower* (priority), *militarist, militaristic, nationalist-flavored, nationalist-minded, nationalistic, nearsighted, new, noisy, opposed, past, patient, peaceful, perennial, permanent, persistent, poised, populist, prone, provocative, rare, regressive, renewed, retaliatory, rightwing, serious, shy, silent, silly, sinister, sovereign, stealthy, strange, strongest, territorial, ugly, unconditional, unfounded, unprecedented, upset, welcome, worse,* and *wrongheaded*. The forty-seven adjectives describing Japan in *Chosun Ilbo* articles referencing *Japan* and *Dokdo* in 2013–16 are as follows: *absurd, accurate, anachronistic, bilateral, bona fide, broader, brutal, collective, colonial, colonial-era, consistent, distorted, dubious, educational, erroneous, false, far-right, flimsy, groundless, historical, ill-informed, imperialist, inaccurate, international, new, official, opposed, pacifist, proper, rash, regrettable, regular, resurgent, retrogressive,* (far) *right, rightwing, security, self-defense, so-called, spurious, tantamount, territorial, transparent, unilateral, unrepentant, unresolved,* and *unwilling*. Thirteen adjectives appear in both time periods: *absurd, bilateral, bona fide, colonial, dubious, false, flimsy, imperialist, inaccurate, new, opposed, rightwing,* and *territorial*.

The thirty-three adjectives describing Japan in *Chosun Ilbo* articles referencing *Japan* and *alliance* in 2010–12 are as follows: *active, bilateral, brutal, closer, collective, committed, compromise, cooperative, critical, defense, defensive, determined, disputed, dynamic, essential, expanded, half, harsh, illegal, joint, military, multilateral, new, permanent, proactive, rapid,* (no more) *sophisticated, strained, stronger, tense, thorny, together,* and *trilateral*. The fifty-four adjectives describing Japan in *Chosun Ilbo* articles referencing *Japan* and *alliance* in 2012–16 are as follows: *active, assertive, beneficial, bona-fide, close, collective, colonial, continued, defense, defensive, determined, diplomatic, effective, flimsy, good, healthy, helpful, historic, humanitarian, icy, joint, latent, limited, military, mutual, new, occupied, ordinary, pacifist, poised, popular, postwar, prepared, proud, ready, rightwing, robust, security, self-defense, sincere, splendid, stabilizing, strained, strengthened, strong, surprising, territorial, threatened, trading, transparent, unfettered, unprecedented, wartime,* and *weak*. Nine adjectives appear in both time periods: *active, collective, defense, defensive, determined, joint, military, new,* and *strained*.

BIBLIOGRAPHY

Abdelal, Rawi, Yoshiko M. Herrera, Alastair Iain Johnston, and Rose McDermott. "Identity as a Variable." *Perspectives on Politics* 4, no. 4 (2006): 695–711.

Abe, Shinzō. "Japan Is Back: A Conversation with Shinzo Abe." *Foreign Affairs* 92 (2013): 2–8.

Abney, David L. "Japan Bashing: A History of America's Anti-Japanese Acts, Attitudes, and Laws." PhD diss., University of Arizona, 1995.

Achen, Christopher H., and Duncan Snidal. "Rational Deterrence Theory and Comparative Case Studies." *World Politics* 41, no. 2 (1989): 143–69.

Acheson, Dean. *Present at the Creation: My Years at the State Department.* New York: Norton, 1969.

Agence France Press. "South Korea, Japan Sign Controversial Intelligence Deal." *Daily Sun*, November 23, 2016. http://www.daily-sun.com/amp/post/186296, accessed July 26, 2022.

Akaha, Tsuneo. "'Soft Power' in Japan's Security Policy: Implications for Alliance with the United States." *Pacific Focus* 20, no. 1 (2005): 59–91.

Akhavi, Shahrough. "In Memoriam: Richard Cottam." *MESA Bulletin* 31, no. 2 (1997): 203–5.

Alcock, Rutherford. *The Capital of the Tycoon: A Narrative of Three Years Residence in Japan,* vol. 1. New York: Harper and Brothers, 1863.

Alemán, José, and Dwayne Woods. "Inductive Constructivism and National Identities: Letting the Data Speak." *Nations and Nationalism* 24, no. 4 (2018): 1023–45.

Alexander, Michele G., Shana Levin, and Peter J. Henry. "Image Theory, Social Identity, and Social Dominance: Structural Characteristics and Individual Motives Underlying International Images." *Political Psychology* 26, no. 1 (2005): 27–45.

Alexandrov, Maxym. "The Concept of State Identity in International Relations: A Theoretical Analysis." *Journal of International Development and Cooperation* 10, no. 1 (2003): 33–46.

Ambrose, Stephen E. "Comparing and Contrasting Ike and Dick." In *Richard M. Nixon: Politician, President, Administrator,* edited by Leon Friedman and William F. Levantrosser, 15–22. New York: Greenwood, 1991.

Anderlini, Jamil, and Lucy Hornby. "China Overtakes US as World's Largest Goods Trader." *Financial Times,* January 10, 2014.

Anderson, Benedict. *Imagined Communities: Reflections on the Origin and Spread of Nationalism.* London: Verso, 1991; originally published 1983.

Anholt, Simon. "Brand Africa: What Is Competitive Identity?" *African Analyst* 2, no. 2 (2007): 72–81.

Anholt, Simon. *Competitive Identity: The New Brand Management for Nations, Cities and Regions*. London: Palgrave Macmillan, 2007.

Anno, Tadashi. *National Identity and Great-Power Status in Russia and Japan: Non-Western Challengers to the Liberal International Order*. London: Routledge, 2018.

Anthias, Floya, and Nira Yuval-Davis. *Racialized Boundaries: Race, Nation, Gender, Colour and Class and the Anti-Racist Struggle*. London: Routledge, 1992.

Argiolas, Antonio, and M. R. Melis. "The Neurophysiology of the Sexual Cycle." *Journal of Endocrinological Investigation* 26, no. 3 Suppl (2003): 20–22.

Ariffin, Yohan, Jean-Marc Coicaud, and Vesselin Popovski, eds. *Emotions in International Politics: Beyond Mainstream International Relations*. Cambridge, United Kingdom: Cambridge University Press, 2016.

Arnow, Bruce A., John E. Desmond, Linda L. Banner, Gary H. Glover, Ari Solomon, Mary Lake Polan, Tom F. Lue, and Scott W. Atlas. "Brain Activation and Sexual Arousal in Healthy, Heterosexual Males." *Brain* 125, no. 5 (2002): 1014–23.

Arrington, Celeste. "South Korea Ended Its Review of Its 'Comfort Women' Deal with Japan. Here's What You Need to Know." *Washington Post*, January 11, 2018.

Ashizawa, Kuniko. "When Identity Matters: State Identity, Regional Institution-Building, and Japanese Foreign Policy." *International Studies Review* 10, no. 3 (2008): 571–98.

Asō, Tarō. "A New Look at Cultural Diplomacy: A Call to Japan's Cultural Practitioners." *Japanese Ministry of Foreign Affairs Website*, April 28, 2006. http://www.mofa.go.jp/announce/fm/aso/speech0604-2 .html; accessed May 9, 2022.

Asquith, Pamela J., and Arne Kalland, eds. *Japanese Images of Nature: Cultural Perspectives*. London: Curzon, 1997.

Atanassova-Cornelis, Elena. "Chinese Nation Building and Foreign Policy: Japan and the US as the Significant 'Others' in National Identity Construction." *East Asia* 29, no. 1 (2012): 95–108.

Audrezet, Alice, Gwarlann de Kerviler, and Julie Guidry Moulard. "Authenticity under Threat: When Social Media Influencers Need to Go beyond Self-presentation." *Journal of Business Research* 117 (2020): 557–69.

Auer, James E. "Article Nine of Japan's Constitution: From Renunciation of Armed Force Forever to the Third Largest Defense Budget in the World." *Law and Contemporary Problems* 53, no. 2 (1990): 171–87.

Baji, Tomohito. *International Thought of Alfred Zimmern: Classicism, Zionism and the Shadow of Commonwealth*. New York: Palgrave Macmillan, 2021.

Baker, Gerard, and George Nishiyama. "Abe Says Japan Ready to Counter China's Power." *Wall Street Journal*, October 26, 2013.

Balibar, Etienne, and Immanuel Wallerstein. *Race, Nation, Classe: Les Identités Ambiguës*. Paris: Editions La Découverte, 1988.

Ball, W. Macmahon. *Japan: Enemy or Ally?* New York: John Day, 1949.

Barberis, Nicholas C. "Thirty Years of Prospect Theory in Economics: A Review and Assessment." *Journal of Economic Perspectives* 27, no. 1 (2013): 173–96.

Barboza, David. "China Passes Japan as Second-Largest Economy." *New York Times*, August 15, 2010.

Barnett, Michael. "Historical Sociology and Constructivism: An Estranged Past, a Federated Future?" In *Historical Sociology of International Relations*, edited by Stephen Hobden and John M. Hobson, 99–119. Cambridge, United Kingdom: Cambridge University Press, 2002.

Bar-Tal, Daniel. "Patriotism as Fundamental Beliefs of Group Members." *Politics and the Individual* 3, no. 2 (1993): 45–62.

Baryshev, Eduard B. *Nichiro Dōmei no Jidai 1914–1917 Nen: "Reigaiteki na Yūkō" no Shinsō* [The Epoch of Russo-Japanese Alliance, 1914–1917: The Truth about an "Exceptional Friendship"]. Fukuoka: Hanashoin, 2007.

Baxter, Kylie, and Shahram Akbarzadeh. *US Foreign Policy in the Middle East: The Roots of Anti-Americanism*. London: Routledge, 2012.

Baycroft, Timothy, and David Hopkin. *Folklore and Nationalism in Europe during the Long Nineteenth Century*. Leiden: Brill, 2012.

BBC. "2011 BBC Country Rating Poll." *BBC World Service*, March 7, 2011. https://worldpublicopinion .net/wp-content/uploads/2017/12/BBCEvalsUS_Mar11_rpt.pdf; accessed February 4, 2025.

BBC. "2012 BBC Country Rating Poll." *BBC World Service*, May 10, 2012. https://worldpublicopinion.net /wp-content/uploads/2017/12/BBCEvals_May12_rpt.pdf; accessed February 4, 2025.

BBC. "2013 BBC Country Rating Poll." *BBC World Service*, May 22, 2013. https://globescan.com/wp-content /uploads/2013/05/2013_country_rating_poll_bbc_globescan.pdf; accessed February 4, 2025.

BBC. "'Comfort Women': Japan and South Korea Hail Agreement." *BBC News*, December 28, 2015. http:// www.bbc.com/news/world-asia-35190464, accessed July 26, 2022.

BBC. "Japan PM Shinzo Abe Visits Yasukuni WW2 Shrine." *BBC News*, December 26, 2013. http://www .bbc.com/news/world-asia-25517205, accessed July 1, 2022.

BBC. "Koizumi Shrine Visit Stokes Anger." *BBC News*, August 15, 2006. http://news.bbc.co.uk/2/hi/asia -pacific/4789905.stm, accessed July 1, 2022.

BBC. "South Korea's Lee Myung-bak Visits Disputed Islands" *BBC News*, August 10, 2012. http://www.bbc .com/news/world-asia-19204852, accessed July 16, 2022.

BBC. "Twitter User Numbers Overtaken by China's Sina Weibo." *BBC News*, May 17, 2017. http://www .bbc.com/news/technology-39947442, accessed July 18, 2022.

Befu, Harumi. *Hegemony of Homogeneity: An Anthropological Analysis of* Nihonjinron. Melbourne: Trans Pacific, 2001.

Befu, Harumi, and Manabe Kazufumi. "Empirical Status of Nihonjinron: How Real Is the Myth?" *Kwansei Gakuin University Annual Studies* 36 (1987): 97–111.

Bell, Daniel A. *The China Model: Political Meritocracy and the Limits of Democracy.* Princeton: Princeton University Press, 2015.

Benedict, Ruth. *The Chrysanthemum and the Sword.* Boston: Houghton Mifflin, 1946.

Benedict, Ruth. *Patterns of Culture.* New York: Houghton, Mifflin, 1934.

Berenskoetter, Felix. "Identity in International Relations." *Oxford Research Encyclopedia of International Studies* (2017). https://doi.org/10.1093/acrefore/9780190846626.013.218.

Berger, Thomas U. "Abe's Perilous Patriotism: Why Japan's New Nationalism Still Creates Problems for the Region and the U.S.-Japanese Alliance." *CSIS Japan Chair Platform*, October 3, 2014. http://www.csis .org/analysis/abe's-perilous-patriotism-why-japan's-new-nationalism-still-creates-problems-region -and-us, accessed June 23, 2022.

Berger, Thomas U. *Cultures of Antimilitarism: National Security in Germany and Japan.* Baltimore: Johns Hopkins University Press, 1998.

Berger, Thomas U. "From Sword to Chrysanthemum: Japan's Culture of Anti-militarism." *International Security* 17, no. 4 (Spring 1993): 119–50.

Berger, Thomas U. "The Triumph of Hope over Experience: The False Promise of Japanese Soft Power in East Asia." In *Japan's Foreign Relations in Asia*, edited by James D. J. Brown and Jeff Kingston, 114–30. London: Routledge, 2018.

Berger, Thomas U., and Youngshik Bong. "To Apologize and to Forgive: Lessons for Asia from Europe's Struggle with History." Issue Brief, Asan Institute for Policy Studies, No. 34, November 22, 2012. http://en.asaninst.org/contents/issue-brief-no-34-to-apologize-and-to-forgive-lessons-for-asia-from -europes-struggle-with-history, accessed January 21, 2024.

Berry, Melanie C. "Historical Memory and Domestic Civic Trust in Japan-South Korea Security Relations." PhD diss., Georgetown University, 2018.

Berton, Peter. "From Enemies to Allies: The War and Russo-Japanese Relations." In *The Impact of the Russo-Japanese War*, edited by Rotem Kowner, 98–108. London: Routledge, 2007.

Best, Antony. *British Engagement with Japan, 1854–1922: The Origins and Course of an Unlikely Alliance.* Abingdon: Routledge, 2021.

Billings, Andrew C., Natalie A. Brown, Kenon A. Brown, Guoqing, Mark A. Leeman, Simon Ličen, David R. Novak, and David Rowe. "From Pride to Smugness and the Nationalism between: Olympic Media Consumption Effects on Nationalism across the Globe." *Mass Communication and Society* 16, no. 6 (2013): 910–32.

Bisley, Nick. "The Japan-Australia Security Declaration and the Changing Regional Security Setting: Wheels, Webs and Beyond?" *Australian Journal of International Affairs* 62, no. 1 (2008): 38–52.

Blanchard, Ben. "Japan's Hour of Need Prompts Show of Chinese Goodwill." *Reuters*, March 13, 2011. http://www.reuters.com/article/us-japan-quake-china/japans-hour-of-need-prompts-show-of-chinese-goodwill-idUSTRE72C2SK20110313; accessed August 7, 2022.

Blight, James G. *The Shattered Crystal Ball: Fear and Learning in the Cuban Missile Crisis*. Lanham, MD: Rowman and Littlefield, 1992.

Boulding, Kenneth. *The Image: Knowledge in Life and Society*. Ann Arbor: University of Michigan Press, 1956.

Boulding, Kenneth. "National Images and International Systems." *Journal of Conflict Resolution* 3, no. 2 (1959): 120–31.

Boxer, Charles Ralph. *The Christian Century in Japan: 1549–1650*. Berkeley: University of California Press, 1951.

Bozdağlıoğlu, Yücel. *Turkish Foreign Policy and Turkish Identity: A Constructivist Approach*. New York: Routledge, 2003.

Brader, Ted, and George E. Marcus. "Emotion and Political Psychology." In *The Oxford Handbook of Political Psychology*, edited by Leonie Huddy, David O. Sears, and Jack S. Levy, 165–204. Oxford: Oxford University Press, 2013.

Bradley, Robert N. *Racial Origins of English Character*. London: Kennikat Press, 1971; originally published 1926.

Brady, Anne-Marie. "The Beijing Olympics as a Campaign of Mass Distraction." *China Quarterly* 197 (2009): 1–24.

Breslin, Thomas A. *Beyond Pain: The Role of Pleasure and Culture in the Making of Foreign Affairs*. Westport, CT: Praeger, 2002.

Breuning, Marijke. "Role Theory in Foreign Policy." *Oxford Research Encyclopedia of Politics* (2017). https://doi.org/10.1093/acrefore/9780190228637.013.334.

Brodersen, Rupert, ed. *Emotional Motives in International Relations: Rage, Rancour and Revenge*. London: Routledge, 2018.

Bronfenbrenner, Urie. "The Mirror Image in Soviet-American Relations: A Social Psychologist's Report." *Journal of Social Issues* 17, no. 3 (1961): 45–56.

Brook, Timothy. *Documents on the Rape of Nanking*. Ann Arbor: University of Michigan, 1999.

Browning, Christopher S. *Constructivism, Narrative and Foreign Policy Analysis: A Case Study of Finland*. Bern: Peter Lang, 2008.

Browning, Christopher S. "Nation Branding and Development: Poverty Panacea or Business as Usual?" *Journal of International Relations and Development* 19 (2016): 50–75.

Browning, Christopher S. "Nation Branding, National Self-Esteem, and the Constitution of Subjectivity in Late Modernity." *Foreign Policy Analysis* 11, no. 2 (2015): 195–214.

Brummer, Klaus, and Cameron G. Thies. "The Contested Selection of National Role Conceptions." *Foreign Policy Analysis* 11, no. 3 (2015): 273–93.

Brysk, Alison, Craig Parsons, and Wayne Sandholtz. "After Empire: National Identity and Post-colonial Families of Nations." *European Journal of International Relations* 8, no. 2 (2002): 267–305.

Brzezinski, Zbigniew. *The Fragile Blossom: Crisis and Change in Japan*. New York: Harper and Row, 1972.

Bucher, Bernd, and Ursula Jasper. "Revisiting 'Identity' in International Relations: From Identity as Substance to Identifications in Action." *European Journal of International Relations* 23, no. 2 (2017): 391–415.

Buddharakkhita, Acharya, trans. *The Dhammapada: The Buddha's Path of Wisdom*. Kandy, Sri Lanka: Buddhist Publication Society, 1985. http://www.buddhanet.net/pdf_file/scrndhamma.pdf, accessed August 10, 2022.

Bukh, Alexander. *Japan's National Identity and Foreign Policy: Russia as Japan's "Other."* London: Routledge, 2010.

Buruma, Ian. "A Dangerous Rift between China and Japan." *Wall Street Journal*, May 10, 2013.

Bush, Richard C. "China–Japan Tensions, 1995–2006: Why They Happened, What to Do." *Brookings Policy Paper* 16 (June 2009). http://www.brookings.edu/wp-content/uploads/2016/06/06_china_japan _bush.pdf, accessed July 16, 2022.

Buzan, Barry. *People, States and Fear: The National Security Problem in International Relations*. London: Wheatsheaf Books, 1983.

Búzás, Zoltán I. "The Color of Threat: Race, Threat Perception, and the Demise of the Anglo-Japanese Alliance (1902–1923)." *Security Studies* 22, no. 4 (2013): 573–606.

Cahan, Jean Axelrad. "National Identity and the Limits of Constructivism in International Relations Theory: A Case Study of the Suez Canal." *Nations and Nationalism* 25, no. 2 (2019): 478–98.

Cairns, Christopher, and Allen Carlson. "Real-World Islands in a Social Media Sea: Nationalism and Censorship on Weibo during the 2012 Diaoyu/Senkaku Crisis." *China Quarterly* 225 (2016): 23–49.

Calhoun, Cheshire, and Robert C. Solomon, eds. *What Is an Emotion? Classic Readings in Philosophical Psychology*. Oxford: Oxford University Press, 1984.

Callahan, William A. *China: The Pessoptimist Nation*. Oxford: Oxford University Press, 2010.

Callahan, William A. "History, Identity, and Security: Producing and Consuming Nationalism in China." *Critical Asian Studies* 38, no. 2 (2006): 179–208.

Callahan, William A. "Identity and Security in China: The Negative Soft Power of the China Dream." *Politics* 35, no. 3–4 (2015): 216–29.

Calleo, David. *Beyond American Hegemony: The Future of the Western Alliance*. New York: Basic, 1987.

Cannon, Brendon J., and Ash Rossiter. "Offensive or Defensive: The Debate over Japan's 'Aircraft Carrier' Upgrade." *East Asia Monitor* 2, no. 1 (February 3, 2019): 5–6.

Cannon, Brendon J., and Ash Rossiter. "Unraveling Japan's Aircraft Carrier Puzzle: Leveraging Carriers' Symbolic Value." *Asian Security* 18, no. 1 (2022): 20–37.

Cantir, Cristian, and Juliet Kaarbo. "Contested Roles and Domestic Politics: Reflections on Role Theory in Foreign Policy Analysis and IR Theory." *Foreign Policy Analysis* 8, no. 1 (2012): 5–24.

Cantir, Cristian, and Juliet Kaarbo, eds. *Domestic Role Contestation, Foreign Policy, and International Relations*. New York: Routledge, 2016.

Cap, Piotr. *The Language of Fear: Communicating Threat in Public Discourse*. London: Palgrave Macmillan, 2017.

Carlson, Allen. "A Flawed Perspective: The Limitations Inherent within the Study of Chinese Nationalism." *Nations and Nationalism* 15, no. 1 (2009): 20–35.

Carlson, Allen. "It Should Not Only Be about Nationalism: China's Pluralistic National Identity and Its Implications for Chinese Foreign Relations." *International Studies* 48, no. 3–4 (2013): 223–236.

Carr, Edward Hallett. *The Twenty Years' Crisis, 1919–1939: An Introduction to the Study of International Relations*. London: Macmillan, 1939.

Carrico, Kevin. *The Great Han: Race, Nationalism and Tradition in China Today*. Berkeley: University of California Press, 2017.

Castano, Emanuele, Alain Bonacossa, and Peter Gries. "National Images as Integrated Schemas: Subliminal Primes of Image Attributes Shape Foreign Policy Preferences." *Political Psychology* 37, no. 3 (2016): 351–366.

Catalinac, Amy L. *Electoral Reform and National Security in Japan: From Pork to Foreign Policy*. New York: Cambridge University Press, 2016.

Catalinac, Amy L. "Identity Theory and Foreign Policy: Explaining Japan's Responses to the 1991 Gulf War and the 2003 US War in Iraq." *Politics & Policy* 35, no. 1 (2007): 58–100.

Caudill, William, and Harry A. Scarr. "Japanese Value Orientations and Culture Change." *Ethnology* 1, no. 1 (January 1962): 53–91.

CBC News. "Almost 5 Million Chinese Homeless after Quake: Officials." *CBC News*, May 16, 2008. http://www.cbc.ca/news/world/almost-5-million-chinese-homeless-after-quake-officials-1.725907, accessed August 7, 2022.

Cerutti, Furio, and Sonia Lucarelli, eds. *The Search for a European Identity: Values, Policies and Legitimacy of the European Union*. London: Routledge, 2008.

Cha, Victor D. "Abandonment, Entrapment, and Neoclassical Realism in Asia: The United States, Japan, and Korea." *International Studies Quarterly* 44, no. 2 (2000): 261–91.

Cha, Victor D. *Alignment Despite Antagonism: The US–Korea–Japan Security Triangle.* Stanford: Stanford University Press, 1999.

Cha, Victor D. *Beyond the Final Score: The Politics of Sport in Asia.* New York: Columbia University Press, 2009.

Cha, Victor D. "Bridging the Gap: The Strategic Context of the 1965 Korea–Japan Normalization Treaty." *Korean Studies* 20, no. 1 (1996): 123–60.

Chae, Haesook, and Steven Kim. "Conservatives and Progressives in South Korea." *Washington Quarterly* 31, no. 4 (2008): 77–95.

Chamberlain, Basil Hall. *Things Japanese.* London: Kegan Paul, 1890.

Chan, Steve. "Soft Deterrence, Passive Resistance: American Lenses, Chinese Lessons." In *Hegemony Constrained: Evasion, Modification, and Resistance to American Foreign Policy,* edited by Davis B. Bobrow, 62–80. Pittsburgh: University of Pittsburgh Press, 2008.

Chapman, David, and Carol Hayes, eds. *Japan in Australia: Culture, Context and Connections.* New York: Routledge, 2020.

Chappell, Bill. "South Korea Says It Won't Pull Out of Japan Intel-Sharing Pact—For Now." *NPR,* November 22, 2019. http://www.npr.org/2019/11/22/781945244/south-korea-says-it-wont-pull-out-of -japan-intel-sharing-pact-for-now, accessed July 26, 2022.

Chang, Richard T. *From Prejudice to Tolerance: A Study of the Japanese Image of the West, 1826–1864.* Tokyo: Sophia University, 1970.

Chen, Ni. "Branding National Images: The 2008 Beijing Summer Olympics, 2010 Shanghai World Expo, and 2010 Guangzhou Asian Games." *Public Relations Review* 38, no. 5 (2012): 731–45.

Cheng, Joseph Y. S. *China's Japan Policy: Adjusting to New Challenges.* Singapore: World Scientific, 2014.

Cheng, Joseph Y. S. "China's Peaceful Rise—Speeches of Zheng Bijian, 1997–2005." *Journal of Contemporary Asia* 37, no. 1 (2007): 132–134.

Cheong, Sung-Hwa. *The Politics of Anti-Japanese Sentiment in Korea: Japanese–South Korean Relations under American Occupation, 1945–1952.* New York: Greenwood Press, 1991.

Chernoff, Fred. "The Study of Democratic Peace and Progress in International Relations." *International Studies Review* 6, no. 1 (2004): 49–77.

Cheung, Mong. "Political Survival and the Yasukuni Controversy in Sino-Japanese Relations." *The Pacific Review* 23, no. 4 (2010): 527–48.

Chiba, Hiromi. "From Enemy to Ally: American Public Opinion and Perceptions about Japan, 1945–1950." PhD diss., University of Hawai'i at Manoa, 1990.

Chilton, Paul. *Analysing Political Discourse: Theory and Practice.* London: Routledge, 2004.

Chilton, Paul. *Language, Space and Mind: The Conceptual Geometry of Linguistic Meaning.* Cambridge, United Kingdom: Cambridge University Press, 2014.

China Daily. "Anger over Abe's Shrine Visit." *China Daily,* December 27, 2013. http://www.chinadaily.com .cn/world/2013-12/27/content_17199569.htm, accessed July 1, 2022.

Chinese View of Japan Editorial Committee. *Chūgokujin no Nihon Kan: Kodai Kara Nijūichi-kajō Yōkyū Made* [The Chinese View of Japan: From Antiquity to the Twenty-One Demands], vols. 1 and 2. Tōkyō: Shakai Hyōronsha, 2016.

Ching, Leo T. S. *Anti-Japan: The Politics of Sentiment in Postcolonial Asia.* Durham: Duke University Press, 2019.

Chiozza, Giacomo. *Anti-Americanism and the American World Order.* Baltimore: Johns Hopkins University Press, 2009.

Choe, Sang-Hun. "Embattled at Home, South Korea's Leader Turns on Japan, Stoking Old Hostilities." *New York Times,* August 30, 2019.

Choe, Sang-Hun. "South Koreans Now Dislike China More than They Dislike Japan." *New York Times,* August 20, 2021.

Choi, B. "Let's Demolish the GGB, the Offensive Remains of Japanese Rule." *Kyonghang Sinmun,* May 21, 1993.

Chomsky, Noam. *Rogue States: The Rule of Force in World Affairs*. Chicago: Haymarket Books, 2015.

Chosun Ilbo. "How Much Further Can Abe Go?" *Chosun Ilbo*, February 3, 2014.

Chosun Ilbo. "Japan Continues Dokdo Land-Grab Campaign." *Chosun Ilbo*, November 4, 2013.

Christensen, Asger Rojle. "Cool Japan, Soft Power." *Global Asia* 6, no. 1 (2011): 76–81.

Christensen, Thomas J. "Advantages of an Assertive China: Responding to Beijing's Abrasive Diplomacy." *Foreign Affairs* 90, no. 2 (2011): 54–67.

Christensen, Thomas J. "China, the US-Japan Alliance, and the Security Dilemma in East Asia." *International Security* 23, no. 4 (1999): 49–80.

Christensen, Thomas J. "Chinese Realpolitik." *Foreign Affairs* 75, no. 5 (September–October 1996): 37–52.

Chung, Eunbin. *Pride, Not Prejudice: National Identity as a Pacifying Force in East Asia*. Ann Arbor: University of Michigan Press, 2022.

Chung, Eunbin, and Inbok Rhee. "Disasters and Intergroup Peace in Sub-Saharan Africa." *Journal of Peace Research* 59, no. 1 (2022): 58–72.

Clifford, Scott. "How Emotional Frames Moralize and Polarize Political Attitudes." *Political Psychology* 40, no. 1 (2019): 75–91.

Clinton, Hillary. "America's Pacific Century." *Foreign Policy* 189 (2011): 56–63.

CNN. "Chinese Riot after Japan Win Final." *CNN.com*, August 7, 2004. http://www.cnn.com/2004/SPORT/football/08/07/china.japan/; accessed June 15, 2022.

Cole, Allan B. "American Professors on Postwar Japan." *Public Opinion Quarterly* 8, no. 4 (Winter, 1944–1945): 530–536.

Connaughton, Richard, John Pimlott, and Duncan Anderson. *The Battle for Manila*. London: Bloomsbury, 1995.

Constantino, Renato, ed. *Southeast Asian Perceptions of Japan*. Tokyo: Zensei, 1991.

Cooney, Kevin J., and Alex Scarbrough. "Japan and South Korea: Can These Two Nations Work Together?" *Asian Affairs* 35, no. 3 (2008): 173–92.

Cooper, Cortez A. *PLA Military Modernization: Drivers, Force Restructuring, and Implications*; testimony presented before the U.S.–China Economic and Security Review Commission, February 15, 2018. Santa Monica: RAND, 2018.

Cordesman, Anthony H., Ashley Hess, and Nicholas S. Yarosh. *Chinese Military Modernization and Force Development: A Western Perspective*. Lanham: Rowman & Littlefield, 2013.

Coser, Lewis A. *The Functions of Social Conflict*. New York: Free Press, 1956.

Cossa, Ralph A. "Japan–South Korea Relations: Time to Open Both Eyes." *Current Issues in US–ROK Relations*. Washington, DC: Council on Foreign Relations, 2012. http://www.cfr.org/report/japan-south-korea-relations-time-open-both-eyes.

Côté, James E. *Adolescent Storm and Stress: An Evaluation of the Mead-Freeman Controversy*. New York: Routledge, 1994.

Cottam, Martha, and Chih-yu Shih, eds. *Contending Dramas: A Cognitive Approach to International Organization*. New York: Praeger, 1992.

Cottam, Richard. *Foreign Policy Motivation: A General Theory and a Case Study*. Pittsburgh: University of Pittsburgh Press, 1977.

Cox, Michael, ed. *E. H. Carr: A Critical Appraisal*. London: Palgrave, 2000.

Craig, Arthur D. "A New View of Pain as a Homeostatic Emotion." *Trends in Neurosciences* 26, no. 6 (2003): 303–7.

Crawford, Neta C. "The Passion of World Politics: Propositions on Emotion and Emotional Relationships." *International Security* 24, no. 4 (2000): 116–56.

Creighton, Millie. "Japanese Surfing the Korean Wave: Drama Tourism, Nationalism, and Gender via Ethnic Eroticisms." *Southeast Review of Asian Studies* 31 (2009): 10–38.

Curtis, William E. *The Yankees of the East: Sketches of Modern Japan*. New York: Stone and Kimball, 1896.

Daase, Christopher, Stefan Engert, Michel-André Horelt, Judith Renner, and Renate Strassner, eds. *Apology and Reconciliation in International Relations: The Importance of Being Sorry*. London: Routledge, 2016.

Dale, Peter N. *The Myth of Japanese Uniqueness.* London and Sydney: Croom Helm and Nissan Institute for Japanese Studies, 1986.

Davenport, Lisa E. *Jazz Diplomacy: Promoting America in the Cold War Era.* Jackson: University Press of Mississippi, 2010.

Davidann, Jon Thares. *Cultural Diplomacy in U.S.–Japanese Relations, 1919–1941.* New York: Palgrave Macmillan, 2007.

Day, Beth Feagles. *The Philippines: Shattered Showcase of Democracy in Asia.* New York: M. Evans, 1974.

Demertzis, Nicolas. *The Political Sociology of Emotions: Essays on Trauma and Ressentiment.* New York: Routledge, 2020.

Deng, Iris. "Tencent's WeChat Hits 1 Billion Milestone as Lunar New Year Boosts Monthly Active Users." *South China Morning Post,* March 5, 2018.

Deng, Qingbo. "Why Taiwanese Are Pro-Japan but Anti-China." *Think China,* October 19, 2020. http://www.thinkchina.sg/why-taiwanese-are-pro-japan-anti-china.

Deng, Yong. "Chinese Relations with Japan: Implications for Asia-Pacific Regionalism." *Pacific Affairs* 70, no. 3 (Autumn 1997): 373–91.

Denyer, Simon. "China's Scary Lesson to the World: Censoring the Internet Works." *Washington Post,* May 23, 2016.

Diamond, Larry. "No More Mr. Nice China: Beijing's 'Peaceful Rise' No Longer Serves the Country's Rulers. Instead They Have Adopted 'Sharp Power.'" *Hoover Digest* 1 (2021): 79–86.

Dickinson, Fred R. "The Idea of Japan: Western Images, Western Myths." *Orbis* 41, no. 3 (Summer 1997): 489–499.

Dickson, Bruce. *The Dictator's Dilemma: The Chinese Communist Party's Strategy for Survival.* New York: Oxford University Press, 2016.

Doak, Kevin. "Abe's Civic Nationalism." *CSIS Japan Chair Platform,* May 15, 2013. http://csis.org/publication/Japan-chair-platform-shinzo-abes-civic-nationalism, accessed June 23, 2022.

Doi, Takeo. *Amae no Kōzō* [The Anatomy of Dependence]. Tokyo: Kodansha, 1971; published in English in 1973.

Dolan, Thomas. "Emotions and Foreign Policy." In *Oxford Research Encyclopedia of Politics,* edited by William R. Thompson. Oxford: Oxford University Press, 2018. http://doi.org/10.1093/acrefore/9780190228637.013.417.

Doyle, Michael W. "Kant, Liberal Legacies, and Foreign Affairs." *Philosophy & Public Affairs* 12, no. 3 (1983): 205–35.

Dower, John W. *War without Mercy: Race and Power in the Pacific War.* New York: Pantheon, 1986.

Dower, John W., and Patrick Lawrence. "Japan and the United States: Reflections on War, Empire, Race and Culture." *Asia-Pacific Journal: Japan Focus* 17, no. 2 (January 15, 2019).

Downs, Erica Strecker, and Phillip C. Saunders. "Legitimacy and the Limits of Nationalism: China and the Diaoyu Islands." *International Security* 23, no. 3 (1998/99): 114–46.

Dreyer, June Teufel. "The Japan–Taiwan Relationship: An Unstable Stability." *Asia Policy* 26, no. 1 (2019): 161–6.

Dreyer, June Teufel. *Middle Kingdom and Empire of the Rising Sun: Sino-Japanese Relations, Past and Present.* Oxford: Oxford University Press, 2016.

Druckman, Daniel. "Nationalism, Patriotism, and Group Loyalty: A Social Psychological Perspective." *Mershon International Studies Review* 38, no. 1 (1994): 43–68.

Du, Mingming, and Yao Chun. "Commentary: Historically Cowardly Abe Needs a Good Dose of German Bravery." *People's Daily Online,* March 9, 2015. http://english.people.com.cn//n/2015/0309/c90777-8860195.html, accessed July 6, 2022.

Du Bois, Cora. *The People of Alor: A Social-Psychological Study of an East Indian Island.* Minneapolis: University of Minnesota Press, 1944.

Earhart, H. Byron. *Mount Fuji: Icon of Japan.* Columbia: University of South Carolina Press, 2011.

Economist. "A World of Hurt." *Economist,* February 4, 2016.

Eden, Lynn. *Whole World on Fire: Organizations, Knowledge, and Nuclear Weapons Devastation.* Ithaca: Cornell University Press, 2004.

Edström, Bert. *Japan's Quest for a Role in the World: Roles Ascribed to Japan Nationally and Internationally, 1969–1982*. Stockholm: Institute of Oriental Languages, University of Stockholm, 1988.

Elfstrom, Manfred. *Workers and Change in China: Resistance, Repression, Responsiveness*. Cambridge, United Kingdom: Cambridge University Press, 2021.

Elfstrom, Manfred, and Sarosh Kuruvilla. "The Changing Nature of Labor Unrest in China." *ILR Review* 67, no. 2 (2014): 453–80.

Elgström, Ole, and Michael Smith. *The European Union's Roles in International Politics: Concepts and Analysis*. London: Routledge, 2006.

Eliade, Mircea. *The Sacred and the Profane: The Nature of Religion*. Translated by Willard R. Trask. New York: Harvest/HBJ Publishers, 1957.

Emmons, Robert A. "Emotion and Religion." In *Handbook of the Psychology of Religion and Spirituality*, edited by Raymond F. Paloutzian and Crystal L. Park, 235–52. New York: Guilford, 2005.

Evans, Peter. *Embedded Autonomy: States and Industrial Transformation*. Princeton: Princeton University Press, 1995.

Fackler, Martin, and Choe Sang-Hun. "A Growing Chill between South Korea and Japan Creates Problems for the U.S." *New York Times*, November 23, 2013.

Fearon, James. "What Is Identity (As We Now Use the Word)?" unpublished manuscript, 1999. http://fearonresearch.stanford.edu, accessed April 14, 2022.

Fehr, Beverley, and James A. Russell. "Concept of Emotion Viewed from a Prototype Perspective." *Journal of Experimental Psychology: General* 113, no. 3 (1984): 464–86.

Ferrari, Giovanni R. F. "The Struggle in the Soul: Plato, Phaedrus 253c7-255a1." *Ancient Philosophy* 5, no. 1 (1985): 1–10.

Fewsmith, Joseph. "The Challenges of Stability and Legitimacy." In *China in the Era of Xi Jinping: Domestic and Foreign Policy Challenges*, edited by Robert S. Ross and Jo Inge Bekkevold, 92–114. Washington: Georgetown University Press, 2016.

Fitzpatrick, Michael. "Japan Has a Major International Image Problem." *Fortune*, February 21, 2014.

Flamm, Patrick. *South Korean Identity and Global Foreign Policy: Dream of Autonomy*. New York: Routledge, 2019.

Fogel, Joshua A. *Articulating the Sinosphere: Sino-Japanese Relations in Space and Time*. Cambridge, MA: Harvard University Press, 2009.

Fogel, Joshua A. *Sagacious Monks and Bloodthirsty Warriors: Chinese Views of Japan in the Ming-Qing Period*. Norwalk, CT: EastBridge, 2002.

Foot, Rosemary, and Amy King. "China's World View in the Xi Jinping Era: Where Do Japan, Russia and the USA Fit?" *British Journal of Politics and International Relations* 23, no. 2 (2021): 210–27.

Fougner, Tore. "The State, International Competitiveness and Neoliberal Globalisation: Is There a Future beyond the 'Competition State'?" *Review of International Studies* 32, no. 1 (2006): 165–85.

Fouse, David. "Japan–Taiwan Relations: A Case of Tempered Optimism." Asia-Pacific Center for Security Studies, October 2004. Defense Technical Information Center, https://apps.dtic.mil/sti/citations/ADA592231.

Fox, William T. R. *The Super-Powers*. New York: Harcourt, Brace & Co., 1944.

Freedom House. "Silencing the Messenger: Communication Apps under Pressure." Report on *Freedom on the Net 2016*, November 2016. http://freedomhouse.org/report/freedom-net/freedom-net-2016, accessed July 19, 2022.

Freyburg, Tina, and Solveig Richter. "National Identity Matters: The Limited Impact of EU Political Conditionality in the Western Balkans." *Journal of European Public Policy* 17, no. 2 (2010): 263–81.

Friedberg, Aaron L. "Ripe for Rivalry: Prospects for Peace in a Multipolar Asia." *International Security* 18, no. 3 (Winter 1993/94): 5–33.

Friedhoff, Karl, and Kang Chungku. "Rethinking Public Opinion on Korea–Japan Relations." Asan Institute for Policy Studies, *Issue Brief* 73 (October 15, 2013): 1–12. http://en.asaninst.org/contents/issue-brief-no-73-rethinking-public-opinion-on-korea-japan-relations.

Friedrichs, Gordon M. *US Global Leadership Role and Domestic Polarization: A Role Theory Approach*. New York: Routledge, 2020.

Fukuda, Madoka. "Recent Developments in Japan–Taiwan Relations." In *Japan–Taiwan Relations: Opportunities and Challenges*, edited by Yuki Tatsumi and Pamela Kennedy, 12–21. Washington: Stimson Center, 2021.

Fukuoka, Kazuya. "Japanese History Textbook Controversy at a Crossroads? Joint History Research, Politicization of Textbook Adoption Process, and Apology Fatigue in Japan." *Global Change, Peace & Security* 30, no. 3 (2018): 313–34.

Funabashi, Yoichi. "Japan and the New World Order." *Foreign Affairs* 70, no. 5 (Winter 1991): 58–74.

Gallup. "Country Ratings." *News.gallup.com*. http://news.gallup.com/poll/1624/perceptions-foreign -countries.aspx, accessed January 31, 2022.

Gartzke, Erik, and Kristian Skrede Gleditsch. "Identity and Conflict: Ties that Bind and Differences that Divide." *European Journal of International Relations* 12, no. 1 (2006): 53–87.

Gasiorowski, Mark J. "The 1953 Coup d'Etat in Iran." *International Journal of Middle East Studies* 19, no. 3 (1987): 261–86.

Gavin, Masako. "A Meiji Christian Socialist Becomes a Spokesperson for Japan: Kawakami Kiyoshi's 'Pilgrimage in the Sacred Land of Liberty.'" *East Asia: An International Quarterly* 33, no. 3 (2016): 175–96.

Gellman, Barton, and Laura Poitras. "US, British Intelligence Mining Data from Nine US Internet Companies in Broad Secret Program." *Washington Post*, June 7, 2013.

Gentzkow, Matthew A., and Jesse M. Shapiro. "Media, Education and Anti-Americanism in the Muslim World." *Journal of Economic Perspectives* 18, no. 3 (2004): 117–33.

Genron NPO. "Japan-China Public Opinion Survey 2021." *Genron-npo.net*, October 2021. http://www .genron-npo.net/en/pp/docs/211025.pdf.

Genron NPO and China Daily. "The 10th Japan-China Public Opinion Poll: Analysis Report on the Comparative Data." *Genron-npo.net*, September 9, 2014. http://www.genron-npo.net/en/pp/docs/10th _Japan-China_poll.pdf; accessed June 17, 2022.

George, Alexander L., and Richard Smoke. *Deterrence in American Foreign Policy: Theory and Practice*. New York: Columbia University Press, 1974.

George, Alexander L., and Richard Smoke. "Deterrence and Foreign Policy." *World Politics* 41, no. 2 (1989): 170–82.

Gerolymatos, Andre. *The Balkan Wars: Conquest, Revolution, and Retribution from the Ottoman Era to the Twentieth Century and Beyond*. New York: Basic, 2002.

Geuens, Robin. "How Many Users Does X (Twitter) Have?" *Soax.com*, February 19, 2025. http:// soax .com/research/twitter-active-users, accessed February 25, 2025.

Geuens, Robin. "What Are the Top Social Media Platforms in 2024." *Soax.com*, February 19, 2025. http:// soax.com/research/top-social-media-platforms, accessed February 25, 2025.

Gibson, Alan St. Clair, Denise A. Baden, Mike I. Lambert, E. Vicki Lambert, Yolande X. R. Harley, Dave Hampson, Vivienne A. Russell, and Tim D. Noakes. "The Conscious Perception of the Sensation of Fatigue." *Sports Medicine* 33, no. 3 (2003): 167–76.

Gilbert, W. S., and Arthur Sullivan. "The Mikado." Gilbert and Sullivan Archive. https://www.gsarchive.net /mikado/webopera/mk101.html, accessed November 9, 2021.

Glaser, Bonnie, and Brittney Farrar. "Through Beijing's Eyes: How China Sees the U.S.–Japan Alliance." *National Interest*, May 12, 2015.

Glazer, Nathan. "From Ruth Benedict to Herman Kahn: The Postwar Japanese Image in the American Mind." In *Mutual Images: Essays in American Japanese Relations*, edited by Akira Iriye, 138–68. Cambridge, MA: Harvard University Press, 1975.

Glosserman, Brad, and Scott A. Snyder. *The Japan–South Korea Identity Clash*. New York: Columbia University Press, 2015.

Goffman, Erving. *The Presentation of Self in Everyday Life*. Edinburgh: University of Edinburgh, 1956.

Goldstein-Gidoni, Ofra. "Producers of 'Japan' in Israel: Cultural Appropriation in a Non-colonial Context." *Journal of Anthropology Museum of Ethnography* 68, no. 3 (2003): 365–90.

Goleman, Daniel, Richard E. Boyatzis, and Annie McKee. *Primal Leadership: Unleashing the Power of Emotional Intelligence*. Boston: Harvard Business Review Press, 2013.

Gómez, Alexandra Ruiz. "Digital Fame and Fortune in the Age of Social Media: A Classification of Social Media Influencers." *aDResearch: Revista Internacional de Investigación en Comunicación* 19 (2019): 8–29.

Gorer, Geoffrey. *The American People: A Study in National Character.* New York: W. W. Norton, 1948.

Gorer, Geoffrey. *The People of Great Russia: A Psychological Study.* London: Cresset Press, 1949.

Green, Michael J. *By More than Providence: Grand Strategy and American Power in the Asia Pacific since 1783.* New York: Columbia University Press, 2017.

Greenwald, Glenn, and Ewen MacAskill. "NSA Prism Program Taps in to User Data of Apple, Google and Others." *Guardian,* June 7, 2013.

Gries, Peter Hays. *China's New Nationalism: Pride, Politics, and Diplomacy.* Berkeley: University of California Press, 2005.

Gries, Peter Hays. "China's Rise: A Review Essay." *Asian Security* 4, no. 1 (2008): 101–5.

Gries, Peter Hays. "Nationalism, Indignation and China's Japan Policy." *SAIS Review of International Affairs* 25, no. 2 (2005): 105–14.

Gries, Peter Hays, Derek Steiger, and Tao Wang. "Popular Nationalism and China's Japan Policy: The Diaoyu Islands Protests, 2012–2013." *Journal of Contemporary China* 25, no. 98 (2016): 264–76.

Groot, Gerry. "Cool Japan versus the China Threat: Does Japan's Popular Culture Success Mean More Soft Power?" In *Japanese Language and Soft Power in Asia,* edited by Hashimoto Kayoko, 15–41. Singapore: Springer, 2018.

Grossman, Michael. "Role Theory and Foreign Policy Change: The Transformation of Russian Foreign Policy in the 1990s." *International Politics* 42, no. 3 (2005): 334–51.

Gruhl, Werner. *Imperial Japan's World War Two: 1931–1945.* New Brunswick: Transaction Publishers, 2010.

Guardian. "Japan's Shinzo Abe Angers Neighbours and US by Visiting War Dead Shrine." *Guardian,* December 26, 2013.

Gustafsson, Karl. "Memory Politics and Ontological Security in Sino-Japanese Relations." *Asian Studies Review* 38, no. 1 (2014): 71–86.

Gustafsson, Karl, Linus Hagström, and Ulv Hanssen. "Japan's Pacifism Is Dead." *Survival* 60, no. 6 (2018): 137–58.

Gustafsson, Karl, Linus Hagström, and Ulv Hanssen. "Long Live Pacifism! Narrative Power and Japan's Pacifist Model." *Cambridge Review of International Affairs* 32, no. 4 (2019): 502–20.

Gustafsson, Karl, and Todd H. Hall. "The Politics of Emotions in International Relations: Who Gets to Feel What, Whose Emotions Matter, and the 'History Problem' in Sino-Japanese Relations." *International Studies Quarterly* 65, no. 4 (2021): 973–84.

Gustafsson, Karl, and Nina C. Krickel-Choi. "Returning to the Roots of Ontological Security: Insights from the Existentialist Anxiety Literature." *European Journal of International Relations* 26, no. 3 (2020): 875–95.

Hackett, Roger F. *Yamagata Aritomo in the Rise of Modern Japan, 1838–1922.* Cambridge, MA: Harvard University Press, 1971.

Hagström, Linus. "The 'Abnormal' State: Identity, Norm/Exception and Japan." *European Journal of International Relations* 21, no. 1 (2015): 122–45.

Hagström, Linus, and Björn Jerdén. "Understanding Fluctuations in Sino-Japanese Relations: To Politicize or to De-politicize the China Issue in the Japanese Diet." *Pacific Affairs* 83, no. 4 (2010): 719–39.

Hagström, Linus, and Marie Söderberg. "Taking Japan–North Korea Relations Seriously: Rationale and Background." *Pacific Affairs* 79, no. 3 (2006): 373–85.

Haidt, Jonathan. *The Happiness Hypothesis: Finding Modern Truth in Ancient Wisdom.* New York: Basic, 2006.

Haidt, Jonathan. *The Righteous Mind: Why Good People Are Divided by Politics and Religion.* New York: Pantheon, 2012.

Hall, Ian, and Frank Smith. "The Struggle for Soft Power in Asia: Public Diplomacy and Regional Competition." *Asian Security* 9, no. 1 (2013): 1–18.

Hall, Rodney Bruce. *National Collective Identity: Social Constructs and International Systems.* New York: Columbia University Press, 1999.

Hall, Todd H. *Emotional Diplomacy: Official Emotion on the International Stage.* Ithaca: Cornell University Press, 2015.

Hall, Todd H. "'An Extremely Obnoxious and Illegal Case': Three Approaches to Affect, Emotion and Discourse in the Aftermath of the Zhuhai Incident." In *The Power of Emotions in World Politics,* edited by Simon Koschut, 31–47. London: Routledge, 2020.

Hall, Todd H. "Three Approaches to Emotion and Affect in the Aftermath of the Zhuhai Incident." *International Studies Review* 19, no. 3 (2017): 487–91.

Hammond, Phil, ed. *Cultural Difference, Media Memories: Anglo-American Images of Japan.* London: Cassell, 1997.

Han, Jung-Sun. "Japan in the Public Culture of South Korea, 1945–2000s: The Making and Remaking of Colonial Sites and Memories." *Asia-Pacific Journal* 12–15, no. 2 (2014): 1–19.

Han, Seung-Mi. "Consuming the Modern: Globalization, Things Japanese, and the Politics of Cultural Identity in Korea." In *Globalizing Japan: Ethnography of the Japanese Presence in Asia, Europe, and America,* edited by Harumi Befu and Sylvia Guichard-Anguis, 216–30. New York: Routledge, 2001.

Hanke, Katja, James H. Liu, Denis J. Hilton, Michal Bilewicz, Ilya Garber, Li-Li Huang, Cecilia Gastardo-Conaco, and Feixue Wang. "When the Past Haunts the Present: Intergroup Forgiveness and Historical Closure in Post World War II Societies in Asia and in Europe." *International Journal of Intercultural Relations* 37, no. 3 (2013): 287–301.

Hankyoreh. "Don't Just Delay, Scrap Military Agreement with Japan." *Hankyoreh,* June 30, 2012.

Harnisch, Sebastian. "Conceptualizing in the Minefield: Role Theory and Foreign Policy Learning." *Foreign Policy Analysis* 8, no. 1 (2012): 47–69.

Harnisch, Sebastian, Cornelia Frank, and Hanns Walter Maull, eds. *Role Theory in International Relations: Approaches and Analyses.* Abingdon: Routledge, 2011.

Harootunian, Harry. "As We Saw Him: Masao Miyoshi and the Vocation of Critical Struggle." *boundary 2* 46, no. 3 (2019): 5–22.

Hartshorne, Thomas L. *The Distorted Image: Changing Conceptions of the American Character since Turner.* Cleveland: Case Western Reserve University Press, 1968.

Hartz, Louis. *The Liberal Tradition in America: An Interpretation of American Political Thought since the Revolution.* New York: Harcourt, Brace & World, 1955.

Hatch, Walter. *Ghosts in the Neighborhood: Why Japan Is Haunted by Its Past and Germany Is Not.* Ann Arbor: University of Michigan Press, 2023.

Hayashi, Keiichi. "China Risks Becoming Asia's Voldemort." *Daily Telegraph,* January 5, 2014.

Hayden, Craig. *The Rhetoric of Soft Power: Public Diplomacy in Global Contexts.* Lanham, MD: Lexington Books, 2012.

Hayman, John G. "Notions on National Characters in the Eighteenth Century." *Huntington Library Quarterly* 35, no. 1 (November 1971): 1–17.

He, Yinan. "History, Chinese Nationalism and the Emerging Sino-Japanese Conflict." *Journal of Contemporary China* 16, no. 50 (2007): 1–24.

He, Yinan. "Identity Politics and Foreign Policy: Taiwan's Relations with China and Japan, 1895–2012." *Political Science Quarterly* 129, no. 3 (Fall 2014): 469–500.

He, Yinan. "Remembering and Forgetting the War: Elite Mythmaking, Mass Reaction, and Sino-Japanese Relations, 1950–2006." *History & Memory* 19, no. 2 (2007): 43–74.

He, Yinan. *The Search for Reconciliation: Sino-Japanese and German–Polish Relations since World War II.* New York: Cambridge University Press, 2009.

Hearn, Lafcadio. *The Japanese Letters of Lafcadio Hearn.* Edited by Elizabeth Bisland. Boston: Houghton Mifflin, 1910.

Heere, Cees. *Empire Ascendant: The British World, Race, and the Rise of Japan, 1894–1914.* Oxford: Oxford University Press, 2020.

Heider, Fritz. *The Psychology of Interpersonal Relations.* New York: Wiley, 1958.

Heisig, James W., and John C. Maraldo. *Rude Awakenings: Zen, the Kyoto School, and the Question of Nationalism.* Honolulu: University of Hawai'i Press, 1994.

Hemmer, Christopher, and Peter J. Katzenstein. "Why Is There No NATO in Asia? Collective Identity, Regionalism, and the Origins of Multilateralism." *International Organization* 56, no. 3 (2002): 575–607.

Heng, Yee-Kuang. "Mirror, Mirror on the Wall, Who Is the Softest of Them All? Evaluating Japanese and Chinese Strategies in the 'Soft' Power Competition Era." *International Relations of the Asia-Pacific* 10, no. 2 (2010): 275–304.

Henning, Joseph M. *Outposts of Civilization: Race, Religion, and the Formative Years of American–Japanese Relations.* New York: New York University Press, 2000.

Henriksen, Thomas H. "The Rise and Decline of Rogue States." *Journal of International Affairs* 54, no. 2 (2001): 349–73.

Hernandez, Alvaro David Hernandez, and Taiki Hirai. "The Reception of Japanese Animation and Its Determinants in Taiwan, South Korea and China." *Animation: An Interdisciplinary Journal* 10, no. 2 (2015): 154–69.

Herrick, Christopher, Zheya Gai, and Surain Subramaniam, eds. *China's Peaceful Rise: Perceptions, Policy and Misperceptions.* Manchester: Manchester University Press, 2016.

Herrmann, Richard K. *Perceptions and Behavior in Soviet Foreign Policy.* Pittsburgh: University of Pittsburgh Press, 1985.

Herrmann, Richard K. "Perceptions and Image Theory in International Relations." In *The Oxford Handbook of Political Psychology*, edited by Leonie Huddy, David O. Sears, and Jack S. Levy, 334–63. Oxford: Oxford University Press, 2013.

Herrmann, Richard K. "The Soviet Decision to Withdraw from Afghanistan: Changing Strategic and Regional Images." In *Dominoes and Bandwagons: Strategic Beliefs and Great Power Competition in the Eurasian Rimland*, edited by Robert Jervis and Jack Snyder, 220–49. New York: Oxford University Press, 1991.

Herrmann, Richard K., and Michael Fischerkeller. "Beyond the Enemy Image and Spiral Model: Cognitive-Strategic Research after the Cold War." *International Organization* 49, no. 3 (1995): 415–50.

Heslop, Louise A., John Nadeau, and Norm O'Reilly. "China and the Olympics: Views of Insiders and Outsiders." *International Marketing Review* 27, no. 4 (2010): 404–33.

Hinata-Yamaguchi, Ryo. "Completing the US–Japan–Korea Alliance Triangle: Prospects and Issues in Japan-Korea Security Cooperation." *Korean Journal of Defense Analysis* 28, no. 3 (2016): 383–402.

Hirokawa, Takashi. "Abe Draws China Anger with Visit to Japan's Yasukuni War Shrine." *Bloomberg News US Edition*, December 26, 2013. http://www.bloomberg.com/news/articles/2013-12-26/abe-visits -japanese-war-shrine-yasukuni-in-risk-to-china-ties, accessed July 1, 2022.

Hiyama, Hiroshi. "Japan to Get First Post-WWII Aircraft Carriers." *Agence France Press*, December 18, 2018. http://sg.news.yahoo.com/japan-approves-defence-plan-including-two-aircraft-carriers-041214905 .html.

Hobbes, Thomas. *Leviathan.* Edited by Richard Tuck. Cambridge, United Kingdom: Cambridge University Press, 1991; originally published 1651.

Hobden, Stephen, and John M. Hobson, eds. *Historical Sociology of International Relations.* Cambridge, United Kingdom: Cambridge University Press, 2001.

Hobsbawm, Eric J. *Nations and Nationalism since 1780: Programme, Myth, Reality.* Cambridge, United Kingdom: Cambridge University Press, 1990.

Hoffman, Michael. "Cultures Combined in the Mists of Time: Origins of the China–Japan Relationship." *Asia Pacific Journal: Japan Focus* 4, no. 2 (February 3, 2006): 1–9.

Hoggett, Paul. *Politics, Identity and Emotion.* New York: Routledge, 2016; originally published 2009.

Holmes, Colin, and A. H. Ion. "Bushidō and the Samurai: Images in British Public Opinion, 1894–1914." *Modern Asian Studies* 14, no. 2 (1980): 309–29.

Holsti, Kal J. "National Role Conceptions in the Study of Foreign Policy." *International Studies Quarterly* 14 (1970): 233–309.

Hopf, Ted. "Making Identity Count: Constructivism, Identity, and IR Theory." In *Making Identity Count: Building a National Identity Database*, edited by Ted Hopf and Bentley Allan, 3–19. Oxford: Oxford University Press, 2016.

Hopf, Ted. "The Promise of Constructivism in International Relations Theory." *International Security* 23, . no. 1 (1998): 171–200.

Hopf, Ted. *Social Construction of International Politics: Identities and Foreign Policies, Moscow, 1955 and 1999.* Ithaca: Cornell University, 2002.

Hopf, Ted, and Bentley Allan, eds. *Making Identity Count: Building a National Identity Database.* Oxford: Oxford University Press, 2016.

Hotta, Eri. *Pan-Asianism and Japan's War 1931–1945.* New York: Palgrave Macmillan, 2007.

Howe, Paul. "The Utopian Realism of E. H. Carr." *Review of International Studies* 20, no. 3 (July 1994): 277–97.

Hoyt, Paul D. "The 'Rogue State' Image in American Foreign Policy." *Global Society* 14, no. 2 (2000): 297–310.

Hu, Jintao. "Hu Jintao Meets with Representatives of Japanese Rescue, Medical Teams." *Chinese Ministry of Foreign Affairs website,* July 8, 2008. http://www.mfa.gov.cn/ce/cein//eng/zgbd/t455356.htm, accessed August 7, 2022.

Huemer, Michael. *Skepticism and the Veil of Perception.* Lanham: Rowman & Littlefield, 2001.

Hughes, Christopher W. "Japan's 'Resentful Realism' and Balancing China's Rise." *Chinese Journal of International Politics* 9, no. 2 (2016): 109–50.

Human Rights Watch. "China: Events of 2015." *World Report 2016,* Human Rights Watch website, 2016. http://www.hrw.org/world-report/2016/country-chapters/china-and-tibet, accessed July 19, 2022.

Hume, David. *A Treatise of Human Nature.* Edited by Lewis Amherst Selby-Bigge. Oxford: Clarendon Press, 1896; originally published 1739 and 1740. http://archive.org/details/treatiseofhumann01humeuoft.

Huntington, Samuel P. "The Clash of Civilizations?" *Foreign Affairs* 72, no. 3 (1993): 22–49.

Hutchinson, Andrew. "Here's Why Twitter Is So Important, to Everyone." *Social Media Today,* March 18, 2016. http://www.socialmediatoday.com/social-networks/heres-why-twitter-so-important-every-one, accessed July 18, 2022.

Hutchinson, Rachael. *Nagai Kafu's Occidentalism: Defining the Japanese Self.* Albany: State University of New York Press, 2011.

Hutchison, Emma, and Roland Bleiker. "Theorizing Emotions in World Politics." *International Theory* 6, no. 3 (2014): 491–514.

Huth, Paul K. "Deterrence and International Conflict: Empirical Findings and Theoretical Debates." *Annual Review of Political Science* 2 (1999): 25–48.

Hwang, Wonjae. *South Korea's Changing Foreign Policy: The Impact of Democratization and Globalization.* London: Lexington Books, 2017.

Hwang, Wonjae, and Misa Nishikawa. "Do Diversionary Incentives Affect Korea–Japan Historical Disputes?" *Korea Observer* 48, no. 4 (2017): 733–64.

Hwang, Wonjae, Wonbin Cho, and Krista Wiegand. "Do Korean–Japanese Historical Disputes Generate Rally Effects?" *Journal of Asian Studies* 77, no. 3 (2018): 693–711.

Hyun, Ki Deuk, and Jinhee Kim. "The Role of New Media in Sustaining the Status Quo: Online Political Expression, Nationalism, and System Support in China." *Information, Communication & Society* 18, no. 7 (2015): 766–81.

Ikenberry, G. John. "Between the Eagle and the Dragon: America, China, and Middle State Strategies in East Asia." *Political Science Quarterly* 131, no. 1 (2016): 9–43.

Ikenberry, G. John. "Japan's History Problem." *Washington Post,* August 17, 2006.

Imai, Kosuke, and James Lo. "Robustness of Empirical Evidence for the Democratic Peace: A Nonparametric Sensitivity Analysis." *International Organization* 75, no. 3 (2021): 901–19.

Ingram, David. "Facebook Hits 2 Billion-User Mark, Doubling in Size since 2012." *Reuters,* June 27, 2017. http://www.reuters.com/article/us-facebook-users/facebook-hits-2-billion-user-mark-doubling-in-size-since-2012-idUSKBN19I2GG, accessed July 18, 2022.

Inkeles, Alex, and Raymond A. Bauer. *The Soviet Citizen: Daily Life in a Totalitarian Society.* Cambridge, MA: Harvard University Press, 1959.

Iriye, Akira, ed. *Mutual Images: Essays in American Japanese Relations*. Cambridge, MA: Harvard University Press, 1975.

Isaacs, Harold R. *Scratches on Our Minds: American Images of China and India*. New York: John Day, 1958.

Isard, Walter. *Arms Races, Arms Control and Conflict Analysis: Contributions from Peace Science and Peace Economics*. New York: Cambridge University Press, 1989.

Ishiguro, Kazuo. "My Twentieth Century Evening—and Other Small Breakthroughs." Nobel Lecture, December 7, 2017. http://www.nobelprize.org/uploads/2018/06/ishiguro-lecture_en-1.pdf, accessed August 11, 2022.

Ishihara, Shintarō. *The Japan That Can Say No: Why Japan Will Be First among Equals*. New York: Simon and Schuster, 1991.

Ishii, Akio. "Gaikokujin no Mita Nihon: Kūru Japan to Sono Genryū o Motomete" [Japan as Seen by Foreigners: In Search of Cool Japan and its Origins]. *Hospitality Management* 8, no. 1 (2017): 143–55.

Ish-Shalom, Piki. *Democratic Peace: A Political Biography*. Ann Arbor: University of Michigan Press, 2013.

Jackson, Peter, and Jan Penrose, eds. *Constructions of Race, Place, and Nation*. London: University College of London Press, 1993.

Jackson, Van. "Buffers, Not Bridges: Rethinking Multilateralism and the Resilience of Japan-South Korea Friction." *International Studies Review* 20, no. 1 (2018): 127–51.

Jacob, Frank, and Sepp Linhart. *War and Stereotypes: The Image of Japan's Military Abroad*. Leiden: Brill, 2020.

Jain, Purnendra. "Japan–India Relations: Peaks and Troughs." *Round Table* 99, no. 409 (2010): 403–12.

Janis, Irving, and Leon Mann. *Decision Making: A Psychological Analysis of Conflict, Choice, and Commitment*. New York: Free Press, 1977.

Japan, National Diet, House of Representatives. "Resolution to Renew the Determination for Peace on the Basis of Lessons Learned from History." June 9, 1995. http://www.mofa.go.jp/announce/press/pm/murayama/address9506.html.

Japan–Taiwan Exchange Association. "Public Opinion Poll of Taiwan: Results of Sixth Survey." Japan–Taiwan Exchange Association website, February 14–27, 2019. http://www.koryu.or.jp/business/poll.

Japan Times. "Seoul Guts the 'Comfort Women' Agreement." *Japan Times*, November 23, 2018.

Japan Tourism Agency. "Ōbātsūrizumu no Nizen Bōshi Yokusei ni Muketa Torikumi" [Efforts to Prevent and Control Overtourism]. Japan Tourism Agency, March 22, 2024. https://www.mlit.go.jp/kankocho/seisaku_seido/kihonkeikaku/jizoku_kankochi/jizokukano_taisei/overtourism.html, accessed January 4, 2025.

Jepperson, Ronald L., Alexander Wendt, and Peter J. Katzenstein. "Norms, Identity, and Culture in National Security." In *The Culture of National Security: Norms and Identity in World Politics*, edited by Peter J. Katzenstein, 33–75. New York: Columbia University, 1996.

Jervis, Robert. "Cooperation under the Security Dilemma." *World Politics* 30, no. 2 (1978): 167–214.

Jervis, Robert. "Rational Deterrence: Theory and Evidence." *World Politics* 41, no. 2 (1989): 183–207.

Ji, Dagyum. "S. Korea, Japan Sign Intelligence Sharing Pact against N. Korea: MND." *NKNews*, November 23, 2016. http://www.nknews.org/2016/11/s-korea-japan-sign-intelligence-sharing-pact-against-n-korea-mnd, accessed July 26, 2022.

Jin, Shuai. *Politics of Economic Inequality in China: Unbalanced Responsiveness*. London: Routledge, 2023.

Jo, Eun A. "Memory, Institutions, and the Domestic Politics of South Korean–Japanese Relations." *International Organization* 76, no. 4 (2022): 767–98.

Jo, Hyeran, and Jongryn Mo. "Does the United States Need a New East Asian Anchor? The Case for U.S.–Japan–Korea Trilateralism." *Asia Policy* 9 (2010): 67–100.

Johnson, Chalmers. "How China and Japan See Each Other." *Foreign Affairs* 50, no. 4 (July 1972): 711–21.

Johnson, Chalmers. Japan: Who Governs? An Essay on Official Bureaucracy." *The Journal of Japanese Studies* 2, no. 1 (1975): 1–28.

Johnson, Chalmers. "The Patterns of Japanese Relations with China, 1952–1982." *Pacific Affairs* 59, no. 3 (Autumn 1986): 402–28.

Johnson, Sheila K. *The Japanese through American Eyes*. Stanford: Stanford University Press, 1988.

Johnston, Alastair Iain. "How New and Assertive Is China's New Assertiveness?" *International Security* 37, no. 4 (2013): 7–48.

Johnston, Alastair Iain. "Is Chinese Nationalism Rising? Evidence from Beijing." *International Security* 41, no. 3 (Winter 2016/17): 7–43.

Jones, Charles. *E. H. Carr and International Relations: A Duty to Lie.* Cambridge, United Kingdom: Cambridge University Press, 1998.

Jordan, Paul. *The Modern Fairy Tale: Nation Branding, National Identity and the Eurovision Song Contest in Estonia.* Tartu: University of Tartu Press, 2014.

Jung, Carl G. *Psychologische Typen* [Psychological Types]. Zurich: Rascher Verlag, 1921.

Jung, Eun-Young. "Transnational Korea: A Critical Assessment of the Korean Wave in Asia and the United States." *Southeast Review of Asian Studies* 31 (2009): 69–80.

Kahn, Joseph. "If 22 Million Chinese Prevail at U.N., Japan Won't." *New York Times*, April 1, 2005.

Kahneman, Daniel. *Thinking, Fast and Slow.* New York: Farrar, Straus and Giroux, 2011.

Kahneman, Daniel, and Amos Tversky. "Prospect Theory: An Analysis of Decision under Risk." *Econometrica* 47, no. 2 (1979): 263–92.

Kajima, Morinosuke. *The Emergence of Japan as a World Power, 1859–1925.* Rutland, VT: C. E. Tuttle, 1968; first published in 1938 as *Teikoku Gaiko no Kihon Seisaku* [Fundamentals of Imperial Diplomacy].

Kanaoka, Hirofumi. "Tourism Surges to Japan's No. 2 'Export,' behind Cars." *Nikkei Asia*, June 26, 2024. https://asia.nikkei.com/Economy/Tourism-surges-to-Japan-s-No.-2-export-behind-cars, accessed January 4, 2025.

Kaneva, Nadia. "Nation Branding: Toward an Agenda for Critical Research." *International Journal of Communication* 5 (2011): 117–41.

Kang, David C. "Between Balancing and Bandwagoning: South Korea's Response to China." *Journal of East Asian Studies* 9, no. 1 (2009): 1–28.

Kang, David C., and Jiun Bang. "Japan–Korea Relations: Groundhog Day in Foreign Policy." *Comparative Connections* 15, no. 1 (May 2013): 127–36.

Kang, David C., and Jiun Bang. "Japan–Korea Relations: North Korean Leadership Change Overshadows All." *CSIS Comparative Connections* 14, no. 4 (2012). http://csis.org/files/publication/1103qjapan_korea.pdf.

Kang, David C., and Jiun Bang. "Japan–Korea Relations: What Goes Up, Must Come Down." *Comparative Connections* 18, no. 3 (January 2017): 91–101.

Kang, Min Soo. "Kyŏngbok Palace: History, Controversy, Geomancy." *Mānoa* 11, no. 2 (1999): 23–39.

Karim, Moch Faisal. "Role Conflict and the Limits of State Identity: The Case of Indonesia in Democracy Promotion." *Pacific Review* 30, no. 3 (2017): 385–404.

Kase, Hideaki. *Kagami no nai Kuni: Sekai no Chishikijin ga Mita Nihon* [A Mirrorless Country: Japan as Seen by Intellectuals around the World]. Tokyo: Yamate Shobō, 1981.

Kataoka, Takichi. "Takayama Ukon." *Monumenta Nipponica* 1, no. 2 (July 1938): 451–64.

Katzenstein, Peter J., ed. *Between Power and Plenty: Foreign Economic Policies in Advanced Industrial States.* Madison: University of Wisconsin Press, 1978.

Katzenstein, Peter J., ed. *The Culture of National Security: Norms and Identity in World Politics.* New York: Columbia University Press, 1996.

Katzenstein, Peter J. *Small States in World Markets: Industrial Policy in Europe.* Ithaca: Cornell University Press, 1985.

Katzenstein, Peter J. *A World of Regions: Asia and Europe in the American Imperium.* Ithaca: Cornell University Press, 2005.

Katzenstein, Peter J., and Nobuo Okawara. *Japan's National Security: Structures, Norms, and Policy Responses in a Changing World.* Ithaca: Cornell University Press, 1993.

Katzenstein, Peter J., and Robert O. Keohane, eds. *Anti-Americanisms in World Politics.* Ithaca: Cornell University Press, 2007.

Kawabata, Yasunari. "Japan, the Ambiguous, and Myself." Nobel Lecture, December 12, 1968. http://www.nobelprize.org/prizes/literature/1968/kawabata/lecture/, accessed August 11, 2022.

Kawakami, Karl Kiyoshi. *Japan and the Japanese as Seen by Foreigners Prior to the Beginning of the Russo-Japanese War*. Tokyo: Keiseisha, 1905.

Kawatake, Kazue, Hara Yumiko, Sugiyama Akiko, and Sakurai Takeshi, *Gaikoku Media no Nihon Imēji: 11-kagoku Chōsa kara* [Japan's Image in the Foreign Media: From Surveys in 11 Countries]. Tokyo: Gakubunsha, 2000.

Kelly, Robert E. "Three Hypotheses on Korea's Intense Resentment of Japan." *The Diplomat*, March 13, 2014. https://thediplomat.com/2014/03/three-hypotheses-on-koreas-intense-resentment-of-japan, accessed July 18, 2022.

Kennedy, Paul. *The Rise and Fall of the Great Powers: Economic Change and Military Conflict from 1500 to 2000*. New York: Random House, 1987.

Kennedy, Trevor, and Misato Nagakawa. "Public Divided over 'Comfort Women' Agreement." *East Asia Forum*, January 22, 2016. http://www.eastasiaforum.org/2016/01/22/public-divided-over-comfort -women-agreement, accessed July 16, 2022.

Kim, J. James, and Kang Chungku. "South Korean Attitudes about ROK-Japan Relations on the Rocks." Asan Institute for Policy Studies, *Issue Brief* (October 2019): 1–11. http://en.asaninst.org/contents /south-korean-attitudes-about-rok-japan-relations-on-the-rocks.

Kim, Ji Young. "Escaping the Vicious Cycle: Symbolic Politics and History Disputes between South Korea and Japan." *Asian Perspective* 38, no. 1 (2014): 31–60.

Kim, Jiyoon, Karl Friedhoff, and Chungku Kang. "Asan Monthly Opinion Survey." *Asan Institute for Policy Studies*, July 2012.

Kim, Jongtae. "The West and East Asian National Identities: A Comparison of the Discourses of Korean Seonjinguk, Japanese Nihonjinron, and Chinese New Nationalism." In *Globalization and Development in East Asia*, edited by Jan Nederveen Pieterse and Jongtae Kim, 92–109. New York: Routledge, 2012.

Kim, Samuel Seongseop, Jerome Agrusa, Heesung Lee, and Kaye Chon. "Effects of Korean Television Dramas on the Flow of Japanese Tourists." *Tourism Management* 28, no. 5 (2007): 1340–53.

Kim, Seung-Hwan. "Anti-Americanism in Korea." *Washington Quarterly* 26, no. 1 (2002): 109–22.

Kim, Tae-hyo, and Brad Glosserman. *The Future of US–Korea–Japan Relations: Balancing Values and Interests*. Washington, DC: Center for Strategic and International Studies, 2004.

Kim, Tongfi. "Can Donald Trump Save South Korea–Japan Relations?" *IES Policy Brief* 4, April 2019. http://aei.pitt.edu/100403/1/KFVUB_Policy-Brief-2019-04.pdf, accessed July 25, 2022.

Kim, Tong-hyung. "Yoon: Forced Labor Plan Crucial for Better Ties with Japan." *AP News*, March 7, 2023. http://apnews.com/article/south-korea-japan-forced-labor-world-war-ii -3d78fe07258b0458df8258825cd6851c.

Kimura, Hiroshi. *Japanese-Russian Relations under Brezhnev and Andropov*. Armonk, NY: M. E. Sharpe, 2000.

Kimura, Hiroshi. *Japanese-Russian Relations under Gorbachev and Yeltsin*. Armonk, NY: M. E. Sharpe, 2000.

Kimura, Tets, and Jennifer Harris, eds. *Exporting Japanese Aesthetics: Evolution from Tradition to Cool Japan*. Brighton: Sussex Academic Press, 2020.

King, Amy. "Hurting the Feelings of the Chinese People." *Sources and Methods: A Blog of the History and Public Policy Program*, Wilson Center, February 15, 2017. http://www.wilsoncenter.org/blog-post/hurting -the-feelings-the-chinese-people.

King, Amy. "The Trilateral Summit: A New Era in China–Japan Relations." *East Asia Forum*, June 2, 2011. http://www.eastasiaforum.org/2011/06/02/the-trilateral-summit-a-new-era-in-china-japan -relations/, accessed August 7, 2022.

Kinnvall, Catarina. "Globalization and Religious Nationalism: Self, Identity, and the Search for Ontological Security." *Political Psychology* 25, no. 5 (2004): 741–67.

Kinnvall, Catarina, and Jennifer Mitzen. "Anxiety, Fear, and Ontological Security in World Politics: Thinking with and beyond Giddens." *International Theory* 12, no. 2 (2020): 240–56.

Kipling, Rudyard. *Departmental Ditties and Ballads and Barrack-Room Ballads*. Garden City, NY: Doubleday, Page and Co., 1910.

Kitaoka, Shōichi. *Futsū no Kuni e* [Towards a Normal Country]. Tokyo: Chūō Kōron Shinsha, 2000.

Kizelbach, Urzula. *The Pragmatics of Early Modern Politics: Power and Kingship in Shakespeare's History Plays.* Amsterdam: Rodopi, 2014.

Klare, Michael T. *Rogue States and Nuclear Outlaws: America's Search for a New Foreign Policy.* New York: Macmillan, 1995.

Klien, Susanne. *Rethinking Japan's Identity and International Role: Tradition and Change in Japan's Foreign Policy.* New York: Routledge, 2002.

Klingner, Bruce. "Washington Should Urge Greater South Korean–Japanese Military and Diplomatic Cooperation." *Report Asia,* September 24, 2012. http://www.heritage.org/asia/report/washington-should-urge-greater-south-korean-japanese-military-and-diplomatic, accessed July 26, 2022.

Ko, Sung-Bin. "South Korea's Search for an Independent Foreign Policy." *Journal of Contemporary Asia* 36, no. 2 (2006): 258–73.

Kobayashi, Yoshiki. "Chūgoku ni okeru 'Tainichi Kanjō' ni Kan Suru Kōsatsu: Kakushu Seron Chōsa Kekka no Fukugōteki Bunseki" [An Examination of Chinese Perceptions of Japan: A Complex Analysis of Various Opinion Poll Results]. *Ajia Kenkyū* [Asian Studies] 54, no. 4 (2008): 87–108.

Kobayashi, Yoshiki. "'Chūgoku ni okeru Tainichi Kanjō' no Jittai to Akka Yōin ni Kan Suru Kenkyū" [The Current State of 'Chinese Attitudes toward Japan' and Research on the Causes of Their Deterioration]. PhD diss., Waseda University, 2009.

Koga, Kei. "The Concept of 'Hedging' Revisited: The Case of Japan's Foreign Policy Strategy in East Asia's Power Shift." *International Studies Review* 20, no. 4 (2018): 633–60.

Koh, Tommy. "Japan, Singapore and 50 Years of Post-War Friendship." *Straits Times,* April 26, 2016.

Kohno, Masaru. "Limits of Neoliberal Institutionalism: Learning from the Failure of Multilateral Institutions in East Asian Security." Paper presented at the joint meeting of the Japan Association of International Studies and the International Studies Association, Makuhari, Japan, September 20–22, 1996.

Koike, Yuriko. "Commentary: At Last, Japan Stands Up." *Japan Times,* June 28, 2015.

Kokami, Shoji. *Kūru Japan!? Gaikokujin ga Mita Nippon* [Cool Japan!? Japan as Seen by Foreigners]. Tokyo: Kodansha, 2015.

Kolmaš, Michal. *National Identity and Japanese Revisionism: Abe Shinzō's Vision of a Beautiful Japan and Its Limits.* London: Routledge, 2019.

Konno, Shigemitsu. "Sofuto Pawā to Nihon no Senryaku" [Soft Power and Japanese Strategy]. In *Imēji no Naka no Nihon: Sofuto Pawā Saikō* [Japan in the Image: Rethinking Soft Power], edited by Ōishi Yutaka and Yamamoto Nobuto. Tokyo: Keiō Gijuku Daigaku Shuppankai, 2008.

Koo, Bon Sang, and Jun Young Choi. "Who Takes the Japanese Threat Seriously? A Survey-Based Analysis of South Koreans' Perceptions." *Pacific Focus* 37, no. 2 (2022): 289–315.

Korea Times. "Korea, Japan to Sign Military Accord on Intelligence Exchange: Source." *Korea Times,* June 27, 2012.

Korea Times. "Lee Criticizes Japan for Lack of Efforts to Resolve Colonial-Era Issues." *Korea Times,* August 13, 2012.

Koschut, Simon, ed. *The Power of Emotions in World Politics.* London: Routledge, 2020.

Kowert, Paul A. "Completing the Ideational Triangle: Identity, Choice, and Obligation in International Relations." In *Psychology and Constructivism in International Relations: An Ideational Alliance,* edited by Vaughn P. Shannon and Paul A. Kowert, 30–53. Ann Arbor: University of Michigan Press, 2011.

Kowert, Paul A. "Foreign Policy and the Social Construction of State Identity." In *The International Studies Encyclopedia,* edited by Robert A. Denemark, 2479–98. Oxford: Blackwell, 2010.

Kowert, Paul A. "National Identity: Inside and Out." *Security Studies* 8, no. 2 (Winter 1998/99): 1–34.

Kowert, Paul A., and Cameron G. Thies. "(Babylonian) Lions, (Asian) Tigers, and (Russian) Bears: A Statistical Test of Three Rivalrous Paths to Conflict." *Journal of International Relations and Development* 16, no. 3 (2013): 406–33.

Kowner, Rotem, ed. *The Impact of the Russo-Japanese War.* London: Routledge, 2007.

Kristof, Nicholas D. "The Problem of Memory." *Foreign Affairs* 77, no. 6 (November–December 1998): 37–49.

Krueger, Brian S. "Government Surveillance and Political Participation on the Internet." *Social Science Computer Review* 23, no. 4 (2016): 439–52.

Ku, Minseon. "The Role of Identity in South Korea's Policies towards Japan." *Korean Social Science Journal* 43 (2016): 75–94.

Ku, Yangmo. "Irreparable Animosity? Centripetal versus Centrifugal Force in South Korea-Japan Mutual Perceptions, 1998–2015." *Asian Journal of Peacebuilding* 4, no. 1 (2016): 53–76.

Kudo, Yasushi. "South Korean Attitudes toward Japan Have Worsened Dramatically, Annual Survey Finds." Genron NPO (2020). http://www.genron-npo.net/en/20201018_3.pdf.

LaCapra, Dominick. *History and Memory after Auschwitz*. Ithaca: Cornell University Press, 1998.

LaFeber, Walter. *The Clash: US–Japanese Relations throughout History*. New York: Norton, 1998.

Lazarus, Richard S., and Susan Folkman. *Stress, Appraisal, and Coping*. New York: Springer, 1984.

Le, Yucheng. "Remarks by Assistant Foreign Minister Le Yucheng at Symposium Marking the 40th Anniversary of the Normalization of Relations between China and Japan." *Chinese Ministry of Foreign Affairs Website*, September 28, 2012. http://www.mfa.gov.cn/mfa_eng/topics_665678/diaodao_665718/201209/t20120928_701838.html, accessed July 5, 2022.

Lebow, Richard Ned. *Between Peace and War: The Nature of International Crisis*. Baltimore: Johns Hopkins University Press, 1981.

Lebow, Richard Ned. *A Cultural Theory of International Relations*. Cambridge, United Kingdom: Cambridge University Press, 2008.

Lebow, Richard Ned. "Deterrence Failure Revisited." *International Security* 12, no. 1 (1987): 197–213.

Lebow, Richard Ned. *National Identities and International Relations*. Cambridge, United Kingdom: Cambridge University Press, 2016.

Lebow, Richard Ned. *The Politics and Ethics of Identity: In Search of Ourselves*. Cambridge, United Kingdom: Cambridge University Press, 2012.

Lebow, Richard Ned, and Janice Gross Stein. "Rational Deterrence Theory: I Think, Therefore I Deter." *World Politics* 41, no. 2 (1989): 208–24.

Lebra, Takie Sugiyama. *Japanese Patterns of Behavior*. Honolulu: University of Hawaii Press, 1976.

LeDoux, Joseph. *The Emotional Brain: The Mysterious Underpinnings of Emotional Life*. New York: Simon and Schuster, 1998.

Lee, Chi-dong. "Moon Says Campaign for 'Comfort Women' Should Go on Despite Recent Controversy." *Yonhap News Agency*, June 8, 2020. http://en.yna.co.kr/view/AEN20200608006951315, accessed July 26, 2022.

Lee, Claire Seungeun. "Remembering 'Winter Sonata,' the Start of Hallyu." *Korean Herald*, December 30, 2011. http://www.koreaherald.com/view.php?ud=20111230000497, accessed July 16, 2022.

Lee, Claire Seungeun. *Soft Power Made in China: The Dilemmas of Online and Offline Media and Transnational Audiences*. London: Palgrave Macmillan, 2018.

Lee, Eun-Jeung. "The 1960s in South Korea: Modernisation, Nationalism and the Pursuit of Democratisation." *International Quarterly for Asian Studies* 52, no. 3–4 (2021): 187–205.

Lee, Hyunjung. "The Female Body as the Site of Historical Controversy: Ghostly Reappearance in South Korean Historical Fiction." In *Asia and the Historical Imagination*, edited by Jane Yeang Chui Wong, 109–26. Singapore: Palgrave Macmillan, 2018.

Leerssen, Joep, and Eric Storm, eds. *World Fairs and the Global Moulding of National Identities: International Exhibitions as Cultural Platforms, 1851–1958*. Leiden: Brill 2021.

Leheny, David R. *Empire of Hope: The Sentimental Politics of Japanese Decline*. Ithaca: Cornell University Press, 2018.

Leheny, David R. "A Narrow Place to Cross Swords: Soft Power and the Politics of Japanese Popular Culture in East Asia." In *Beyond Japan: The Dynamics of East Asian Regionalism*, edited by Peter J. Katzenstein and Takashi Shiraishi, 211–34. Ithaca: Cornell University Press, 2006.

Leheny, David R. *Think Global, Fear Local: Sex, Violence, and Anxiety in Contemporary Japan*. Ithaca: Cornell University Press, 2006.

Lehmann, Jean-Pierre. *The Image of Japan: From Feudal Isolation to World Power 1850–1905*. London: Allen & Unwin, 1978.

Lehmann, Jean-Pierre. "Old and New Japonisme: The Tokugawa Legacy and Modern European Images of Japan." *Modern Asian Studies* 18, no. 4 (1984): 757–68.

Leichtova, Magda. *Misunderstanding Russia: Russian Foreign Policy and the West*. London: Routledge, 2016.

Leigh, James H., and Terrance G. Gabel. "Symbolic Interactionism: Its Effects on Consumer Behavior and Implications for Marketing Strategy." *Journal of Consumer Marketing* 9, no. 1 (1992): 27–38.

Le Prestre, Philippe G., ed. *Role Quests in the Post–Cold War Era: Foreign Policies in Transition*. Montreal: McGill-Queen's University Press, 1997.

Levada Center. "Rossiysko-Yaponskiye Otnosheniya." [Russian–Japanese Relations]. November 30, 2018. http://www.levada.ru/2018/11/30/rossijsko-yaponskie-otnosheniya, accessed January 20, 2022.

LeVine, Robert A. "Culture and Personality Studies, 1918–1960: Myth and History." *Journal of Personality* 69, no. 6 (2001): 803–18.

Levy, Jack S. "The Diversionary Theory of War: A Critique." In *Handbook of War Studies*, edited by Manus I. Midlarsky, 259–88. Boston: Unwin Hyman, 1989.

Levy, Jack S. "An Introduction to Prospect Theory." *Political Psychology* 13, no. 2 (1992): 171–86.

Li, Cheng. "China's New Politburo and Politburo Standing Committee." *Brookings Interactive*, October 26, 2017. http://www.brookings.edu/interactives/chinas-new-politburo-standing-committee, accessed July 18, 2022.

Li, Xiang, and Kyriaki Kaplanidou. "The Impact of the 2008 Beijing Olympic Games on China's Destination Brand: A US-Based Examination." *Journal of Hospitality & Tourism Research* 37, no. 2 (2013): 237–61.

Li, Xin, and Verner Worm. "Building China's Soft Power for a Peaceful Rise." *Journal of Chinese Political Science* 16, no. 1 (2011): 69–89.

Liao, Ning. "Presentist or Cultural Memory: Chinese Nationalism as Constraint on Beijing's Foreign Policy Making." *Asian Politics & Policy* 5, no. 4 (2013): 543–65.

Liff, Adam P., and G. John Ikenberry. "Racing toward Tragedy? China's Rise, Military Competition in the Asia Pacific, and the Security Dilemma." *International Security* 39, no. 2 (2014): 52–91.

Lim, Louisa. "China Acts Fast in Aiding Japan Post-Earthquake." *NPR.org*, March 15, 2011. http://www.npr.org/2011/03/15/134567659/china-acts-fast-in-aiding-japan-post-earthquake, accessed August 7, 2022.

Lim, Susanna Soojung. *China and Japan in the Russian Imagination, 1685–1922: To the Ends of the Orient*. London: Routledge, 2013.

Lim, Tai Wei. *The Merlion and Mt. Fuji: 50 Years of Singapore–Japan Relations*. Singapore: World Scientific Publishing, 2017.

Lind, Jennifer M. "Pacifism or Passing the Buck? Testing Theories of Japanese Security Policy." *International Security* 29, no. 1 (2004): 92–121.

Lind, Jennifer M. *Sorry States: Apologies in International Affairs*. Cornell University Press, 2008.

Lindgren, Y. Wrenn, and Petter Y. Lindgren. "Identity Politics and the East China Sea: China as Japan's 'Other.'" *Asian Politics & Policy* 9, no. 3 (2017): 378–401.

Ling, Lily H. M. "Decolonizing the International: Towards Multiple Emotional Worlds." *International Theory* 6, no. 3 (2014): 579–83.

Littlewood, Ian. *The Idea of Japan: Western Images, Western Myths*. Chicago: Ivan R. Dee, 1996.

Litwak, Robert S. *Rogue States and US Foreign Policy: Containment after the Cold War*. Washington, DC: Woodrow Wilson Center Press, 2000.

Liu, Jieyi. "Comments in the 7105th Meeting of the United Nations Security Council." *Security Council Report S/PV.7105*, January 29, 2014. http://www.securitycouncilreport.org/atf/cf/%7B65BFCF9B-6D27-4E9C-8CD3-CF6E4FF96FF9%7D/s_pv_7105.pdf, accessed July 12, 2022.

Liu, Tian. "High Time for Japan to Learn from Germany's Reflection on History." *People's Daily Online*, March 9, 2015. http://en.people.cn/n/2015/0309/c90780-8860301.html, accessed July 8, 2022.

Liu, Xiaoming. "China and Britain Won the War Together." *Daily Telegraph*, January 1, 2014.

Lobell, Steven E., Norrin M. Ripsman, and Jeffrey W. Taliaferro, eds. *Neoclassical Realism, the State, and Foreign Policy*. Cambridge, United Kingdom: Cambridge University Press, 2009.

Louie, Kam. *Chinese Masculinities in a Globalizing World*. London: Routledge, 2014.

Lu, Yan. *Re-understanding Japan: Chinese Perspectives, 1895–1945*. Honolulu: University of Hawaii Press, 2004.

MacArthur, Douglas. "Farewell Address to Congress." April 19, 1951. http://www.americanrhetoric.com/speeches/douglasmacarthurfarewelladdress.htm, accessed July 12, 2022.

MacKinnon, Angus. "Japan Tells World to Stand Up to China or Face Consequences." *Agence France Presse*, January 22, 2014. http://sg.news.yahoo.com/japan-appeals-world-restrain-39-military-expansion-39-173227252.html, accessed August 12, 2022.

MacLean, Paul D. "Some Psychiatric Implications of Physiological Studies on Frontotemporal Portion of Limbic System (Visceral Brain)." *Electroencephalography and Clinical Neurophysiology* 4, no. 4 (1952): 407–18.

Malici, Akan, and Stephen G. Walker. *Role Theory and Role Conflict in US–Iran Relations: Enemies of Our Own Making*. New York: Routledge, 2016.

Mandler, Peter. *The English National Character: The History of an Idea from Edmund Burke to Tony Blair*. New Haven, CT: Yale University Press, 2006.

Manning, Robert A. "Abe Speech May Exorcize the Ghosts of History." *Atlantic Council*, August 14, 2015. http://www.atlanticcouncil.org/blogs/new-atlanticist/japan-abe/, accessed June 23, 2022.

Manyin, Mark E. "North Korea–Japan Relations: The Normalization Talks and the Compensation/Reparations Issue." Congressional Research Service, U.S. Congress, June 13, 2001. http://digital.library.unt.edu/ark:/67531/metacrs3109/m1/1/high_res_d/RS20526_2002Sep12.pdf, accessed July 13, 2022.

Marcus, George E. "Emotions in Politics." *Annual Review of Political Science* 3 (2000): 221–50.

Marcus, George E. "Hidden Affections: Presumptions that Continue to Misshape the Measurement of Emotion." *Advances in Politics and Economics* 5, no. 1 (2022): 73–98. http://dx.doi.org/10.22158/ape.v5n1p73.

Marcus, George E. "How Fear and Anger Impact Democracy." *Items: Insights from the Social Sciences*. Brooklyn: Social Science Research Council, 2019. http://items.ssrc.org/democracy-papers/how-fear-and-anger-impact-democracy/, accessed June 10, 2022.

Marcus, George E. "The Psychology of Emotion and Politics." In *Oxford Handbook of Political Psychology*, edited by David O. Sears, Leonie Huddy, and Robert Jervis, 182–221. Oxford: Oxford University Press, 2003.

Marcus, George E., and Michael B. MacKuen. "Anxiety, Enthusiasm, and the Vote: The Emotional Underpinnings of Learning and Involvement during Presidential Campaigns." *American Political Science Review* 87, no. 3 (1993): 672–85.

Marcus, George E., W. Russell Neuman, and Michael MacKuen. *Affective Intelligence and Political Judgment*. Chicago: University of Chicago Press, 2000.

Markwica, Robin. *Emotional Choices: How the Logic of Affect Shapes Coercive Diplomacy*. Oxford: Oxford University Press, 2018.

Marra, Michael F. ed. *The Poetics of Motoori Norinaga: A Hermeneutical Journey*. Honolulu: University of Hawaii Press, 2007.

Marx, Anthony W. "Race-Making and the Nation-State." *World Politics* 48, no. 2 (1996): 180–208.

Marx, Karl. *The Eighteenth Brumaire of Louis Napoleon*. Translated by Daniel De Leon. Chicago: Charles H. Kerr, 1907; originally published 1852.

Maslow, Sebastian. "China and Japan: Partner, Rival, and Enemy." In *China's International Roles: Challenging or Supporting International Order?* edited by Sebastian Harnisch, Sebastian Bersick, Jörn-Carsten Gottwald, 189–206. New York: Routledge, 2016.

Matsuda, Yasuhiro. "Engagement and Hedging." *SAIS Review of International Affairs* 32, no. 2 (2012): 109–19.

Matthews, Chris. *Hardball: How Politics Is Played Told by One Who Knows the Game*. New York: Simon and Schuster, 1988.

McAvene, Stephen E., and Paul A. Kowert. "Mapping the Emotional Terrain of Foreign Policy." *International Politics* (2024): 1–26. https://doi.org/10.1057/s41311-024-00617-1.

McClory, Jonathan. "Soft Power 30: A Global Ranking of Soft Power 2019." Portland and USC Center on Public Diplomacy. London: Portland, 2019. http://softpower30.com/wp-content/uploads/2019/10/The-Soft-Power-30-Report-2019-1.pdf.

McClory, Jonathan, and Olivia Harvey. "The Soft Power 30: Getting to Grips with the Measurement Challenge." *Global Affairs* 2, no. 3 (2016): 309–19.

McCourt, David M. *Britain and World Power since 1945: Constructing a Nation's Role in International Politics.* Ann Arbor: University of Michigan Press, 2014.

McCourt, David M. "The Roles States Play: A Meadian Interactionist Approach." *Journal of International Relations and Development* 15, no. 3 (2012): 370–92.

McCurry, Justin. "Kyoto Bans Tourists from Parts of Geisha District amid Reports of Bad Behavior." *Guardian*, March 7, 2024.

McCurry, Justin. "Yoon Arrives in Japan for Historic Talks with Kishida—and Beloved Omurice." *Guardian*, March 16, 2023.

McDermott, Rose. "Emotions in Foreign Policy Decision Making." In *Oxford Research Encyclopedia of Politics*, edited by William R. Thompson. Oxford: Oxford University Press, 2017. https://doi.org/10.1093/acrefore/9780190228637.013.418.

McGrath, Jason, Moriya Frankel, and Kimberly Leidel. "Nation Brands Index 2023: Japan Takes the Lead for the First Time in NBI History." *Ipsos.com*, November 1, 2023. https://www.ipsos.com/en-us/nation-brands-index-2023, accessed January 4, 2025.

McGray, Douglas. "Japan's Gross National Cool." *Foreign Policy* 130 (2002): 44–54.

McNeill, David. "As China Fumes, Japan Turns Up Nose at Orgy." *South China Morning Post*, October 8, 2003.

McNeill, David. "Nippon Kaigi and the Radical Conservative Project to Take Back Japan." *Asia-Pacific Journal: Japan Focus* 13(50), no. 4 (December 14, 2015): 1–5.

McPherson, Alan L., and Philip Zelikow. *Yankee No! Anti-Americanism in US–Latin American Relations.* Cambridge, MA: Harvard University Press, 2003.

Mead, George Herbert. *Mind, Self, and Society.* Edited by Charles W. Morris. Chicago: University of Chicago Press, 1934.

Mead, Margaret. *Coming of Age in Samoa: A Psychological Study of Primitive Youth for Western Civilization.* New York: Morrow Quill Paperbacks, 1928.

Mead, Margaret. *And Keep Your Powder Dry! An Anthropologist Looks at America.* New York: William Morrow, 1942.

Mead, Margaret. "Preface." In *Patterns of Culture*, edited by Ruth Benedict, xiii–xvi. New York: Houghton, Mifflin, 1934.

Mead, Margaret. "The Swaddling Hypothesis: Its Reception." *American Anthropologist* 56, no. 3 (1954): 395–409.

Mearsheimer, John J., and Stephen M. Walt. "An Unnecessary War." *Foreign Policy* 134 (January–February 2003): 50–59.

Mehrabian, Albert, and James A. Russell. *An Approach to Environmental Psychology.* Cambridge, MA: MIT Press, 1974.

Mei, Bing, and Gavin T. L. Brown. "Conducting Online Surveys in China." *Social Science Computer Review* 36, no. 6 (2018): 721–34.

Mercer, Jonathan. "Feeling like a State: Social Emotion and Identity." *International Theory* 6, no. 3 (2014): 515–35.

Mettler, Meghan Warner. *How to Reach Japan by Subway: America's Fascination with Japanese Culture, 1945–1965.* Lincoln: University of Nebraska Press, 2018.

Michishita, Narushige. "Japan, Singapore, and 70 Years of Post-War Ties." *Straits Times*, February 11, 2015. http://www.straitstimes.com/opinion/japan-singapore-and-70-years-of-post-war-ties.

Mihara Ryūtarō. "Kūru Japan wa Naze Kirawareru no ka" [Why Is Cool Japan Hated?]. Tokyo: Chūō-kōron Shinsha, 2014.

Mikami, Takanori. "Nihon Oranda Denmāku no Sofuto Pawā Hikaku" [Comparison of Soft Power between Japan, the Netherlands and Denmark]. *Shudo Law* 33, no. 2 (2011): 53–77.

Mikhailova, Yulia. "Japan's Place in Russian and Soviet National Identity: From Port Arthur to Khalkhingol." *Japanese Slavic and East European Studies* 23 (2002): 1–32.

Mikhailova, Yulia. "Representations of Japan and Russian–Japanese Relations in Russian Newspapers: 1906–1910." *Acta Slavica Iaponica* 30 (2011): 43–62.

Mikhailova, Yulia, and M. William Steele, eds. *Japan and Russia: Three Centuries of Mutual Images*. Folkestone, England: Global Oriental, 2008.

Mikhailova, Yulia, and Sergei Torchinov. "Images at an Impasse: Anime and Manga in Contemporary Russia." In *Japan and Russia: Three Centuries of Mutual Images*, edited by Yulia Mikhailova and M. William Steele, 175–91. Folkestone, UK: Global Oriental, 2008.

Miles, Alex. *US Foreign Policy and the Rogue State Doctrine*. New York: Routledge, 2012.

Miller, J. Berkshire. "The ICJ and the Dokdo/Takeshima Dispute." *Diplomat*, May 13, 2014. http://thediplomat.com/2014/05/the-icj-and-the-dokdotakeshima-dispute, accessed July 26, 2022.

Minami, Hiroshi. *Nihonjinron: Meiji kara Konnichi made* [Theories of the Japanese: From the Meiji Era to Today]. Tokyo: Iwanami Shoten, 1994.

Minegishi, Hiroshi. "Yoon Era Stokes Hope in Japan for Better South Korea Relations." *Nikkei Asia*, May 11, 2022. http://asia.nikkei.com/Politics/International-relations/Yoon-era-stokes-hope-in-Japan-for-better-South-Korea-relations, accessed July 18, 2022.

Mitter, Rana. "Behind the Scenes at the Museum: Nationalism, History and Memory in the Beijing War of Resistance Museum, 1987–1997." *China Quarterly* 161 (2000): 279–93.

Mitzen, Jennifer. "Ontological Security in World Politics: State Identity and the Security Dilemma." *European Journal of International Relations* 12, no. 3 (2006): 341–70.

Miyamoto, Michiko, and Nagasawa Makoto. *Amerikajin no Nihonjin Kan: 240-Nin no Amerikajin to no Intabyū* [American Views of the Japanese: Interviews with 240 Americans]. Tokyo: Sōshisha, 1982.

Miyoshi, Masao. "Japan Is Not Interesting." In *Trespasses: Selected Writings*, edited by Miyoshi Masao, 189–204. Durham: Duke University Press, 2010; essay originally published 2000.

Mochizuki, Mike M. "Japan's Shifting Strategy toward the Rise of China." *Journal of Strategic Studies* 30, no. 4–5 (2007): 739–76.

Mochizuki, Mike M., and Samuel Parkinson Porter. "Japan under Abe: Toward Moderation or Nationalism?" *Washington Quarterly* 36, no. 4 (2013): 25–41.

Moisi, Dominique. *The Geopolitics of Emotion: How Cultures of Fear, Humiliation, and Hope Are Reshaping the World*. New York: Anchor, 2010.

Montaigne, Michel de. *Essais de Messire Michel Seigneur de Montaigne*, livre premier et second. Bordeaux: S. Millanges, 1580. http://gallica.bnf.fr/ark:/12148/btv1b8609579f.

Moon, Chung-in, and Seung-Won Suh. "Identity Politics, Nationalism, and the Future of Northeast Asian Order." In *The United States and Northeast Asia: Debates, Issues, and New Order*, edited by G. John Ikenberry and Chung-in Moon, 193–229. Lanham, MD: Rowman & Littlefield, 2008.

Moon, Chung-in, and Won-young Hur. "A South Korean Perspective: Trilateral Co-operation: The Devil's in Domestic Politics." *Global Asia* 12, no. 1 (2017). http://www.globalasia.org/v12no1/cover/a-south-korean-perspective-trilateral-co-operation-the-devils-in-domestic-politics_chung-in-moon-won-young-hur, accessed July 26, 2022.

Moore, Gregory J. "Bismarck or Wilhelm? China's Peaceful Rise vs. Its South China Sea Policy." *Asian Perspective* 42, no. 2 (2018): 265–83.

Moran, J. F. *The Japanese and the Jesuits: Alessandro Valignano in Sixteenth Century Japan*. London: Routledge, 1993.

Morgenthau, Hans J. *Politics among Nations: The Struggle for Power and Peace*. New York: Knopf, 1948.

Morikawa, Jun. "Japan and Africa after the Cold War." *African and Asian Studies* 4, no. 4 (2005): 485–508.

Morita, Akio, and Ishihara Shintarō. *"NO" to Ieru Nihon* [The Japan that Can Say "No"]. Tokyo: Kōbunsha, 1989.

Morris, Narrelle. *Japan-Bashing: Anti-Japanism since the 1980s*. London: Routledge, 2010.

Morris-Suzuki, Tessa. *Re-inventing Japan: Time, Space, Nation*. Armonk, NY: M. E. Sharpe, 1998.

Mosse, George L. "Racism and Nationalism." *Nations and Nationalism* 1, no. 2 (1995): 163–73.

Mouer, Ross, and Yoshio Sugimoto. *Images of Japanese Society*. London: Kegan Paul, 2002.

Murakami, Katsutoshi. *Gaikokujin ni Yoru Sengo Nihonron: Benedikuto kara Worufuren made* [Postwar Japan as Seen by Foreigners: From Benedict to Wolferen]. Tokyo: Madosha, 1997.

Muramatsu, Michio, and Ellis S. Krauss. "Bureaucrats and Politicians in Policymaking: The Case of Japan." *American Political Science Review* 78, no. 1 (1984): 126–46.

Murayama, Tomiichi. "Prime Minister's Address to the Diet." House of Representatives, National Diet of Japan, June 9, 1995. http://www.mofa.go.jp/announce/press/pm/murayama/address9506.html.

Murayama, Tomiichi. "Statement by Prime Minister Tomiichi Murayama 'On the Occasion of the 50th Anniversary of the War's End.'" August 15, 1995. http://www.mofa.go.jp/announce/press/pm/murayama/9508.html.

Naff, William E. "Reflections on the Question of 'East' and 'West' from the Point of View of Japan." *Comparative Civilizations Review* 13, no. 13 (1985): 215–32.

Nagatani, Keizo, and David W. Edgington. *Japan and the West: The Perception Gap.* Brookfield, VT: Ashgate, 1998.

Nagel, Thomas. *The View from Nowhere.* New York: Oxford University Press, 1986.

Nagy, Stephen R. "Japan's Proactive Pacifism: Investing in Multilateralization and Omnidirectional Hedging." *Strategic Analysis* 41, no. 3 (2017): 223–35.

Nagy, Stephen R. "Nationalism, Domestic Politics, and the Japan Economic Rejuvenation." *East Asia* 31, no. 1 (2014): 5–21.

Nakahara, Junki. "Deconstructing Abe Shinzo's 'Take Back Japan' Nationalism." *Asia-Pacific Journal: Japan Focus* 19, 24, no. 1 (2021): 1–13.

Nakajima, Mineo. "Mao and His Career as Seen by Japanese Writers." Paper presented to the Association for Asian Studies Annual Meeting, Chicago, April 2, 1982.

Nam, Chang-hee. "The Alliance Transformation and US–Japan–Korea Security Network: A Case for Trilateral Cooperation." *Pacific Focus* 25, no. 1 (2010): 34–58.

NBC News. "China Jails 14 over 'Japanese Orgy.'" *NBCNews.com*, December 12, 2003. http://www.nbcnews.com/id/wbna3691590, accessed June 14, 2022.

Neuman, W. Russell, George E. Marcus, Michael Mackuen, and Ann N. Crigler, eds. *The Affect Effect.* Chicago: University of Chicago, 2007.

Neumann, Birgit. "Towards a Cultural and Historical Imagology: The Rhetoric of National Character in 18th-Century British Literature." *European Journal of English Studies* 13, no. 3 (2009): 275–91.

Neumann, Iver. *Uses of the Other: "The East" in European Identity Formation.* Minneapolis: University of Minnesota, 1999.

Newman, John D., and James C. Harris. "The Scientific Contributions of Paul D. MacLean (1913–2007)." *Journal of Nervous and Mental Disease* 197, no. 1 (2009): 3–5.

Ngai, Mae M. *Impossible Subjects: Illegal Aliens and the Making of Modern America.* Princeton: Princeton University Press, 2014.

Nisbet, Robert. "Tocqueville's Ideal Types." In *Reconsidering Tocqueville's Democracy in America*, edited by Abraham Eisenstadt, 171–91. New Brunswick: Rutgers University Press, 1988.

Nish, Ian. "An Overview of Relations between China and Japan, 1895–1945." *China Quarterly* 124 (December 1990): 601–23.

Nitobe, Inazō. *Bushidō: The Soul of Japan.* Philadelphia: Leeds and Biddle, 1900.

Nitobe, Inazō. *The Japanese Nation: Its Land, Its People, and Its Life.* New York: Knickerbocker Press, 1912.

Nosco, Peter. *Remembering Paradise: Nativism and Nostalgia in Eighteenth-Century Japan.* Cambridge, MA: Harvard University Press, 1990.

Nye, Joseph S. Jr. *Bound to Lead: The Changing Nature of American Power.* New York: Basic, 1990.

Nye, Joseph S. Jr. "Get Smart: Combining Hard and Soft Power." *Foreign Affairs* 88, no. 4 (July–August 2009): 160–63.

Nye, Joseph S. Jr. "The Soft Power of Japan." *Gaiko Forum* 4, no. 2 (2004): 3–7.

Nye, Joseph S. Jr. *Soft Power: The Means to Success in World Politics.* New York: Public Affairs, 2004.

Nye, Joseph S. Jr. "Soft Power: The Origins and Political Progress of a Concept." *Palgrave Communications* (February 21, 2017). https://doi.org/10.1057/palcomms.2017.8.

Ōe, Kenzaburō. "Japan, The Ambiguous, and Myself." Nobel Lecture, December 7, 1994. http://www.nobelprize.org/prizes/literature/1994/oe/lecture/, accessed August 11, 2022.

Ogata, Sadako. "The Business Community and Japanese Foreign Policy: Normalization of Relations with the People's Republic of China." In *The Foreign Policy of Modern Japan*, edited by Robert A. Scalapino, 175–203. Berkeley: University of California Press, 1977.

Oguma, Eiji. *Tan'itsu Minzoku Shinwa no Kigen: "Nihonjin" no Jigazō no Keifu* [Origin of the Myth of the Homogenous Nation: A Genealogy of "Japanese" Self-Images]. Tokyo: Shinyōsha, 1995.

O'Hagan, Jacinta. "Civilisational Conflict? Looking for Cultural Enemies." *Third World Quarterly* 16, no. 1 (1995): 19–38.

Ōishi, Yutaka, and Yamamoto Nobuto, eds. *Imēji no Naka no Nihon: Sofuto Pawā Saikō* [Japan's Image: Revisiting Soft Power]. Tokyo: Keiō Gijuku Daigaku Shuppankai, 2008.

Okakura, Kakuzō. *The Ideals of the East: With Special Reference to the Art of Japan*. London: J. Murray, 1920. First published 1903.

Onishi, Norimitsu. "Dispute Over Islets Frays Ties between Tokyo and Seoul." *New York Times*, March 22, 2005.

Onishi, Norimitsu. "Japan Stands by Declaration on 'Comfort Women,'" *New York Times*, March 16, 2007.

Onuf, Nicholas. "World-Making, State-Building." In *Semantics of Statebuilding: Language, Meanings and Sovereignty*, edited by Nicolas Lemay-Hébert, Nicholas Onuf, Vojin Rakić, and Petar Bojanić, 31–48. London: Routledge, 2013.

Onuf, Nicholas, and Peter Onuf. *Nations, Markets and War: Modern History and the American Civil War*. Charlottesville: University of Virginia Press, 2006.

Oppermann, Kai, Ryan Beasley, and Juliet Kaarbo. "British Foreign Policy after Brexit: Losing Europe and Finding a Role." *International Relations* 34, no. 2 (2020): 133–56.

Orbach, Danny. *Curse on This Country: The Rebellious Army of Imperial Japan*. Ithaca: Cornell University Press, 2017.

O'Reilly, K. P. "Perceiving Rogue States: The Use of the 'Rogue State' Concept by U.S. Foreign Policy Elites." *Foreign Policy Analysis* 3, no. 4 (2007): 295–315.

O'Reilly, K. P. "A Rogue Doctrine? The Role of Strategic Culture on US Foreign Policy Behavior." *Foreign Policy Analysis* 9, no. 1 (2013): 57–77.

Organski, A. F. K. *World Politics*. New York: Alfred A. Knopf, 1960.

Orme, John. "Deterrence Failures: A Second Look." *International Security* 11, no. 4 (1987): 96–124.

Ortony, Andrew, Gerald L. Clore, and Allan Collins. *The Cognitive Structure of Emotions*. Cambridge, United Kingdom: Cambridge University Press, 1988.

Otmazgin, Nissim. "Contesting Soft Power: Japanese Popular Culture in East and Southeast Asia." *International Relations of the Asia-Pacific* 8, no. 1 (2008): 73–101.

Otmazgin, Nissim. "A Tail that Wags the Dog? Cultural Industry and Cultural Policy in Japan and South Korea." *Journal of Comparative Policy Analysis: Research and Practice* 13, no. 3 (2011): 307–325.

Otmazgin, Nissim Kadosh. "The Chrysanthemum and the Cool: Cultural Diplomacy and Soft Power in Japan's Foreign Policy." In *Routledge Handbook of Japanese Foreign Policy*, edited by Mary M. McCarthy, 55–70. London: Routledge, 2018.

Otmazgin, Kadosh Nissim, and Nissim Otmazgin. "Japan Imagined: Popular Culture, Soft Power, and Japan's Changing Image in Northeast and Southeast Asia." *Contemporary Japan* 24, no. 1 (2012): 1–19.

Olins, Wally. "Branding the Nation: The Historical Context." In *Destination Branding: Creating the Unique Destination Proposition*, edited by Nigel Morgan, Annette Pritchard, and Roger Pride, 17–25. Oxford: Elsevier Butterworth-Heinemann, 2002.

Ozawa, Harumi. "Japan PM's Visit to Yasukuni War Shrine Infuriates China." *Agence France Presse*, December 25, 2013. http://sg.news.yahoo.com/japan-pm-abe-visits-yasukuni-war-shrine-035900997.html, accessed July 1, 2022.

Ozawa, Ichirō. "Futsu no Kuni ni Nare" [On Becoming a Normal Country]. In *Sengo Nihon Gaikō Ronshū: Kōwa Ronsō kara Wangan Sensō made* [Postwar Japanese Diplomacy: From the Peace Controversy to the Gulf War], edited by Kitaoka Shin'ichi, 461–81. Tokyo: Chūō Kōronsha, 1995.

Pamment, James. "'Putting the GREAT Back into Britain': National Identity, Public–Private Collaboration & Transfers of Brand Equity in 2012's Global Promotional Campaign." *British Journal of Politics and International Relations* 17 (2015): 260–83.

Panda, Ankit. "The 'Final and Irreversible' 2015 Japan-South Korea Comfort Women Deal Unravels." *Diplomat*, January 9, 2017. http://thediplomat.com/2017/01/the-final-and-irreversible-2015-japan-south-korea-comfort-women-deal-unravels, accessed July 18, 2022.

Park, Cheol-Hee. "Cooperation Coupled with Conflicts: Korea–Japan Relations in the Post–Cold War Era." *Asia-Pacific Review* 25, no. 3 (2008): 13–35.

Park, Cheol-Hee. "Historical Memory and the Resurgence of Nationalism: A Korean Perspective." In *East Asia's Haunted Present: Historical Memories and the Resurgence of Nationalism*, edited by Tsuyoshi Hasegawa and Kazuhiko Togo, 190–203. Westport, CT: Praeger, 2008.

Park, Cheol-Hee. "The Pattern of Cooperation and Conflict between Korea and Japan: Theoretical Expectations and Empirical Realities." *Japanese Journal of Political Science* 10, no. 3 (2009): 247–65.

Park, Han S. *North Korea: The Politics of Unconventional Wisdom*. New York: Lynne Rienner, 2002.

Park, Sang-Hyun. *Kankokujin wa Nihonjin o Dō Omotte Iru no ka: Itsu made Tatte mo Tokenai Gokai wa Kōshite Umareta* [What Do Koreans Think of the Japanese? How the Unresolvable Misunderstanding Was Born]. Tokyo: Shin Jinbutsu Ōraisha, 2010.

Patriarca, Silvana, and Lucy Riall, eds. *The Risorgimento Revisited: Nationalism and Culture in Nineteenth-Century Italy*. New York: Palgrave Macmillan, 2012.

Paulus, Martin P. "Neural Basis of Reward and Craving—A Homeostatic Point of View." *Dialogues in Clinical Neuroscience* 9, no. 4 (2022): 379–387.

Pempel, T. J. "The Bureaucratization of Policymaking in Postwar Japan. *American Journal of Political Science* 18, no. 4 (1974): 647–64.

Penney, Matthew, and Bryce Wakefield. "Right Angles: Examining Accounts of Japanese Neo-nationalism." *Pacific Affairs* 81, no. 4 (2008): 537–55.

Pew Research Center. "How Asians View Each Other." *Pewresearch.org*, July 14, 2014. http://www.pewresearch.org/global/2014/07/14/chapter-4-how-asians-view-each-other/, accessed January 19, 2022.

Pew Research Center. "How Asia-Pacific Publics See Each Other and Their National Leaders." *Pewglobal.org*, September 2, 2015. http://www.pewglobal.org/2015/09/02/how-asia-pacific-publics-see-each-other-and-their-national-leaders/; accessed January 19, 2022.

Pew Research Center. "Japanese Public's Mood Rebounding, Abe Highly Popular." *Pewresearch.org*, July 11, 2013. http://www.pewresearch.org/global/2013/07/11/japanese-publics-mood-rebounding-abe-strongly-popular, accessed July 13, 2022.

Pham, P. L. "On the Edge of the Orient: English Representations of Japan, circa 1895–1910." *Japanese Studies* 19, no. 2 (1999): 163–81.

Phillips, Joe, Wondong Lee, and Joseph Yi. "Future of South Korea–Japan Relations: Decoupling or Liberal Discourse." *Political Quarterly* 91, no. 2 (2020): 448–56.

Piesse, Edmund L. "Japan and Australia." *Foreign Affairs* 4, no. 3 (April 1926): 475–88.

Place Brand Observer. "Anholt Nation Brands Index (NBI) 2024: Key Highlights and Trends." *Placebrandobserver.com*, December 17, 2024. https://placebrandobserver.com/anholt-nation-brands-index-nbi-2024/, accessed January 4, 2025.

Plutchik, Robert. "The Nature of Emotions." *American Scientist* 89, no. 4 (2001): 344–50.

Pollock, John L., and Joseph Cruz. *Contemporary Theories of Knowledge*. 2nd ed. Lanham, MD: Rowman and Littlefield, 1999.

Poole, Steven. *Trigger Happy: Videogames and the Entertainment Revolution*. New York: Arcade Publishing, 2004.

Popkin, Richard Henry. *The History of Scepticism: From Savonarola to Bayle*. Oxford: Oxford University Press, 2003.

Potter, David M. *People of Plenty: Economic Abundance and the American Character*. Chicago: University of Chicago Press, 1954.

Press Reference. "South Korea," *pressreference.com*, no date. http://www.pressreference.com/Sa-Sw/South-Korea.html, accessed July 26, 2022.

Przystup, James J. "Japan–China Relations: Can We Talk?" *Comparative Connections* 15, no. 3 (2014): 99–109.

Przystup, James J. "Japan–China Relations: Past as Prologue." *Comparative Connections* 16, no. 1 (2014): 115–28.

Przystup, James J. "Japan–China Relations: Staying on a Test Course." *Comparative Connections* 18, no. 1 (2016): 105–15.

Przystup, James J. "Japan–China Relations: Treading Troubled Waters." *Comparative Connections* 15, no. 1 (2013): 111–26.

Pufendorf, Samuel. *Of the Law of Nature and Nations.* 4th ed., Translated by Basil Kennett. Clark, NJ: Law Book Exchange, 2005; originally published 1672.

Pyle, Kenneth B. "The Japanese Self-Image." *Journal of Japanese Studies* 5, no. 1 (1979): 1–4.

Qiu, Jin. "The Politics of History and Historical Memory in China–Japan relations." *Journal of Chinese Political Science* 11, no. 1 (Spring 2006): 25–53.

Rabb, Kate Milner. *National Epics.* Chicago: A. C. McClurg, 1896.

Raizman, David, and Ethan Robey, eds. *Expanding Nationalisms at World's Fairs: Identity, Diversity, and Exchange, 1851–1915.* London: Routledge, 2018.

Ranke, Leopold von. "Zur Geschichte Deutschlands und Frankreichs im 19. Jahrhundert." In *Sämtliche Werke,* edited by Alfred Dove, vol. 49–50. Leipzig: Duncker and Humblot, 1887.

Rasler, Karen, and William Thompson. *Puzzles of the Democratic Peace: Theory, Geopolitics, and the Transformation of World Politics.* New York: Palgrave Macmillan, 2005.

Reilly, James. *Strong Society, Smart State: The Rise of Public Opinion in China's Japan Policy.* New York: Columbia University Press, 2012.

Reinhart, R. J. "On Eve of Summit, Americans Still View Japan Positively." *Gallup Blog,* April 14, 2021. http://news.gallup.com/opinion/gallup/347090/eve-summit-americans-view-japan-positively.aspx, accessed January 31, 2022.

Reischauer, Edwin O. "The Broken Dialogue with Japan." *Foreign Affairs* 39, no. 1 (1960): 11–26.

Reuters. "China Uses D-Day Anniversary to Praise Germany, Slam Japan." *Reuters,* June 6, 2014. http://www.reuters.com/article/us-dday-anniversary-china-japan/china-uses-d-day-anniversary-to-praise-germany-slam-japan-idINKBN0EH0Y020140606, accessed July 13, 2022.

Reynolds, Gary. "U.S. Prisoners of War and Civilian American Citizens Captured and Interned by Japan in World War II." Congressional Research Service, Library of Congress, December 17, 2002. http://www.history.navy.mil/research/library/online-reading-room/title-list-alphabetically/u/us-prisoners-war-civilian-american-citizens-captured.html#bib, accessed October 26, 2021.

Richburg, Keith B. "Japan Quake: China Sets Aside Disputes, Offers Help." *Washington Post,* March 12, 2011.

Rieker, Pernille. *Europeanization of National Security Identity: The EU and the Changing Security Identities of the Nordic States.* London: Routledge, 2005.

Riesman, David. *The Lonely Crowd: A Study of the Changing American Character Type.* New Haven, CT: Yale University Press, 1950.

Riesman, David. "Psychological Types and National Character: An Informal Commentary." *American Quarterly* 5, no. 4 (Winter 1953): 325–43.

Ringmar, Erik. *Identity, Interest and Action: A Cultural Explanation of Sweden's Intervention in the Thirty Years' War.* Cambridge, United Kingdom: Cambridge University, 1996.

Ripsman, Norrin M., Jeffrey W. Taliaferro, and Steven E. Lobell. *Neoclassical Realist Theory of International Politics.* New York: Oxford University Press, 2016.

Risse-Kappen, Thomas. "Ideas Do Not Float Freely: Transnational Coalitions, Domestic Structures, and the End of the Cold War." *International Organization* 48, no. 2 (1994): 185–214.

Rodkiewicz, Witold. *China's Junior Partner: Russia's Korean Policy.* Warsaw: Ośrodek Studiów Wschodnich im. Marka Karpia, 2018.

Roger, Philippe. *The American Enemy: The History of French Anti-Americanism*. Chicago: University of Chicago Press, 2005.

Roh, David S., ed. *Techno-Orientalism: Imagining Asia in Speculative Fiction, History, and Media*. New Brunswick: Rutgers University Press, 2015.

Roh, Moo-hyun. "Special Message by President Roh Moo-hyun on Korea–Japan Relations." *NewsWire*, April 25, 2006. http://www.newswire.co.kr/newsRead.php?no=145520, accessed July 26, 2022.

Roosevelt, Theodore. *Outdoor Pastimes of an American Hunter*. New York: Charles Scribner's Sons, 1906.

Rose, Gideon. "Neoclassical Realism and Theories of Foreign Policy." *World Politics* 51, no. 1 (1998): 144–72.

Rosen, Stanley. "Public Opinion and Reform in the People's Republic of China." *Studies in Comparative Communism* 22, no. 2–3 (Summer–Autumn 1989): 153–70.

Rosenstone, Robert A. *Mirror in the Shrine: American Encounters with Meiji Japan*. Cambridge, MA: Harvard University Press, 1988.

Ross, Andrew A. G. "Coming in from the Cold: Constructivism and Emotions." *European Journal of International Relations* 12, no. 2 (2006): 197–222.

Ross, Andrew A. G. *Mixed Emotions: Beyond Fear and Hatred in International Conflict*. Chicago: University of Chicago Press, 2014.

Ross, Andrew, and Kristin Ross, eds. *Anti-Americanism*. New York: New York University Press, 2004.

Ross, Michael. "Nakasone Apologizes for Occupation of Korea." *UPI Archive*, September 7, 1984. http://www.upi.com/Archives/1984/09/07/Nakasone-apologizes-for-occupation-of-Korea/3316000633477, accessed July 16, 2022.

Rummel, Rudolph J. *Statistics of Democide: Genocide and Mass Murder since 1900*. Münster: Lit Verlag, 1998.

Rushdie, Salman. "Salman Rushdie on Kazuo Ishiguro: His Legendary Novel *The Remains of the Day* Resurges." *Globe and Mail*, August 15, 2014.

Russell, Bertrand. *Human Knowledge: Its Scope and Limits*. New York: Simon and Schuster, 1948. http://archive.org/details/humanknowledgeit00russ.

Russell, James. "A Circumplex Model of Affect." *Journal of Personality and Social Psychology* 39, no. 6 (1980): 1161–78.

Saaler, Sven, and J. Victor Koschmann, eds. *Pan-Asianism in Modern Japanese History: Colonialism, Regionalism and Borders*. London: Routledge, 2007.

Said, Edward W. *Orientalism*. New York: Pantheon Books, 1978.

Saitō, Shirō. *Omoiyari Jidai no Shūen: Yureru Beikoku no Tainichi Kanjō* [The End of the Era of Compassion: Shifting US Sentiment toward Japan], (1st ed.). Tokyo: Nihon Keizai Shinbunsha, 1990.

Sakaki, Alexandra. "Japan–South Korea Relations—A Downward Spiral: More than 'Just' Historical Issues." *SWP Comment* 35, Deutsches Institut für Internationale Politik und Sicherheit, August 2019. http://www.ssoar.info/ssoar/handle/document/64095, accessed July 18, 2022.

Salter, Mark B. *Barbarians and Civilization in International Relations*. London: Pluto Press, 2002.

Samuels, Richard J. *"Rich Nation, Strong Army": National Security and the Technological Transformation of Japan*. Ithaca: Cornell University Press, 1994.

Sasaki, Tomonori. "China Eyes the Japanese Military: China's Threat Perception of Japan since the 1980s." *China Quarterly* 203 (2010): 560–80.

Satō, Keiko. *Okiwasure Nihongaku: Gaikokujin ga Mitsuketa Nihon no Kokoro* [Misplaced Japanology: The Heart of Japan as Discovered by Foreigners]. Tōkyō: Ningen to Rekishisha, 1986.

Saveliev, Igor R., and Yuri S. Pestushko. "Dangerous Rapprochement: Russia and Japan in the First World War, 1914–1916." *Acta Slavica Iaponica* 18 (2001): 19–41.

Schafer, Mark, and Stephen G. Walker. *Operational Code Analysis and Foreign Policy Roles: Crossing Simon's Bridge*. New York: Routledge, 2021.

Schiavenza, Matt. "An Awkward—and Productive—Exchange between China and Japan." *Atlantic*, November 11, 2014.

Schonberg, Karl. *Constructing 21st Century US Foreign Policy: Identity, Ideology, and America's World Role in a New Era*. New York: Palgrave Macmillan, 2009.

Schmitt, Olivier. *Allies that Count: Junior Partners in Coalition Warfare*. Washington, DC: Georgetown University Press, 2018.

Schulze, Hagen. *States, Nations and Nationalism: From the Middle Ages to the Present*. Translated by William E. Yuill. Oxford: Blackwell, 1996.

Schuman, Frederick. *International Politics*. 3rd ed. New York: McGraw-Hill, 1941.

Seo, Jungmin. "Diagnosing Korea–Japan Relations through Thick Description: Revisiting the National Identity Formation Process." *Third World Quarterly* 45, no. 6 (2024): 1106–21.

Seo, Jungmin. "Politics of Memory in Korea and China: Remembering the Comfort Women and the Nanjing Massacre." *New Political Science* 30, no. 3 (2008): 369–92.

Serazio, Michael. "Branding Politics: Emotion, Authenticity, and the Marketing Culture of American Political Communication." *Journal of Consumer Culture* 17, no. 2 (2017): 225–41.

Shad, Nadeem. "Japan's Back and So Is Nationalism." *Diplomat*, December 14, 2014. http://thediplomat.com/2014/12/japans-back-and-so-is-nationalism, accessed June 23, 2022.

Shakespeare, William. *King Henry IV, Part 2*, ed. David Scott Kastan. London: Arden Shakespeare, 2002.

Shambaugh, David. *China's Future*. Cambridge, United Kingdom: Polity, 2016.

Shambaugh, David. "Contemplating China's Future." *Washington Quarterly* 39, no. 3 (2016): 121–30.

Shambaugh, David. "The Soldier and the State in China: The Political Work System in the People's Liberation Army." *China Quarterly* 127 (September 1991): 527–68.

Shannon, Vaughn P., and Paul A. Kowert, eds. *Psychology and Constructivism in International Relations: An Ideational Alliance*. Ann Arbor: University of Michigan Press, 2012.

Shaw, Han-yi. "The Diaoyutai/Senkaku Islands Dispute: Its History and an Analysis of the Ownership Claims of the P.R.C., R.O.C., and Japan." *Occasional Papers/Reprints Series in Contemporary Asian Studies* 3, no. 152. Baltimore: University of Maryland School of Law, 1999.

Sheidlower, Jesse. *The F-Word* (3rd ed.). New York: Oxford University Press, 2009.

Shi, Jinkai. "Ekkyō Suru Bunka kara Miru 'Kūru Japan'" [Cool Japan as Seen from Transborder Culture]. Sōka University Graduate School Bulletin 41 (2020): 99–120.

Shibusawa, Naoko. *America's Geisha Ally: Reimagining the Japanese Enemy*. Cambridge, MA: Harvard University Press, 2006.

Shigemitsu, Mamoru. "Address before the United Nations General Assembly on the Occasion of Japan's Admission to the United Nations." Japanese Ministry of Foreign Affairs website, December 18, 1956. http://www.mofa.go.jp/policy/un/address5612.html.

Shih, Chiy-yu. "National Role Conception as Foreign Policy Motivation: The Psychocultural Bases of Chinese Diplomacy." *Political Psychology* 9, no. 4 (1988): 599–631.

Shimko, Keith L. *Images and Arms Control*. Ann Arbor: University of Michigan Press, 1991.

Shin, Hyon-hee. "Seoul under Fire for Tokyo Military Pact." *Korea Herald*, June 28, 2012.

Shin, Hyonhee, and Joyce Lee. "Fulfilling a Dream, South Korea's Moon Visits Sacred North Korean Mountain with Kim." *Reuters*, September 20, 2018. http://www.reuters.com/article/us-northkorea-southkorea-summit-mountain/fulfilling-a-dream-south-koreas-moon-visits-sacred-north-korean-mountain-with-kim-idUSKCN1M006F, accessed July 26, 2022.

Shin, Hyunjoon. "Reconsidering Transnational Cultural Flows of Popular Music in East Asia: Transbordering Musicians in Japan and Korea Searching for 'Asia.'" *Korean Studies* 33 (2009): 101–23.

Shinano, Yūjin, *Shinajin no Mita Nihonjin* [The Japanese as Seen by the Chinese]. Tokyo: Seinen Shobō, 1940.

Shirk, Susan. *China: Fragile Superpower. How China's Internal Politics Could Derail Its Peaceful Rise*. Oxford: Oxford University Press, 2007.

Sieg, Linda, and Kanupriya Kapoor. "Japan PM Abe Meets China's Xi, Says to Work for Better Ties." *Reuters*, April 21, 2015. http://www.reuters.com/article/uk-asia-africa-japan/japan-pm-abe-meets-chinas-xi-says-to-work-for-better-ties-idUKKBN0ND04M20150422, accessed July 5, 2022.

Simmel, Georg. *Conflict*. Translated by Kurt H. Wolff. Glencoe: Free Press, 1955.

Singer, Thomas, and Samuel L. Kimbles, eds. *The Cultural Complex: Contemporary Jungian Perspectives on Psyche and Society*. Hove, UK: Brunner-Routledge, 2004.

Slobogin, Christopher. *Privacy at Risk: The New Government Surveillance and the Fourth Amendment*. Chicago: University of Chicago Press, 2007.

Smith, Josh, and Hyonhee Shin. "The North Korean History behind Kim Jong Un's Mountain Horse Ride." *Reuters*, October 17, 2019. http://www.reuters.com/article/us-northkorea-kimjongun-explainer /the-north-korean-history-behind-kim-jong-uns-mountain-horse-ride-idUSKBN1WW1J9, accessed July 25, 2022.

Smith, Rogers M. "Beyond Tocqueville, Myrdal, and Hartz: The Multiple Traditions in America." *American Political Science Review* 87, no. 3 (September 1993): 549–66.

Smoker, Paul. "Fear in the Arms Race: A Mathematical Study." *Journal of Peace Research* 1, no. 1 (1964): 55–64.

Snyder, Jack. *Myths of Empire: Domestic Politics and International Ambition*. Ithaca: Cornell University Press, 1991.

Snyder, Scott A. *South Korea at the Crossroads: Autonomy and Alliance in an Era of Rival Powers*. New York: Columbia University Press, 2018.

Snyder, Scott. "South Korean Identity Under Park Geun-hye: Crosscurrents & Choppy Waters." *Joint U.S.– Korea Academic Studies*, Korea Economic Institute of America, October 6, 2016. http://www.keia.org /publication/south-korean-identity-under-park-geun-hye-crosscurrents-choppy-waters, accessed July 18, 2022.

Soeya, Yoshihide. "The Evolution of Japan's Public Diplomacy: Haunted by Its Past History." In *Understanding Public Diplomacy in East Asia: Middle Powers in a Troubled Region*, edited by Jan Melissen and Yul Sohn, 79–105. New York: Palgrave Macmillan, 2015.

Soeya, Yoshihide. "Japan's Relations with China." In *The Golden Age of the U.S.–China–Japan Triangle, 1972– 1989*, edited by Ezra F. Vogel, Ming Yuan, and Akihiko Tanaka, 210–226. Cambridge, MA: Harvard University Press, 2002.

Soeya, Yoshihide, David A. Welch, and Masayuki Tadokoro, eds. *Japan as a "Normal Country"? A Nation in Search of Its Place in the World*. Toronto: University of Toronto Press, 2011.

Song, Qiang, Zhang Zangzang, Qiao Bian, Tang Zhengyu, and Gu Qingsheng. *Zhongguo Keyi Shuo Bu— Lengzhanhou Shidai de Zhengzhi yu Qinggan Jueze* [China Can Say No—Political and Emotional Choices in the Post-Cold War Era]. Beijing: Zhonghua, 1996.

Soompi. "K-Pop Artists Claim 34 Out of 100 Spots on Oricon's 2021 Year-End Album Chart." *Soompi*, December 22, 2021. http://www.soompi.com/article/1505165wpp/k-pop-artists-claim-34-out-of -100-spots-on-oricons-2021-year-end-album-chart.

Solomon, Michael R. "The Role of Products as Social Stimuli: A Symbolic Interactionism Perspective." *Journal of Consumer Research* 10, no. 3 (1983): 319–29.

Solomon, Robert C. *The Passions: Emotions and the Meaning of Life*. Garden City, NY: Anchor, 1976.

South China Morning Post. "Chinese Humiliation." *South China Morning Post*, October 2, 2003.

Stanovich, Keith E., and Richard F. West. "Individual Differences in Reasoning: Implications for the Rationality Debate?" *Behavioral and Brain Sciences* 23, no. 5 (2000): 645–65.

Steele, Brent J. *Ontological Security in International Relations: Self-identity and the IR State*. London: Routledge, 2008.

Storry, Richard. *Japan and the Decline of the West in Asia: 1894–1943*. New York: Macmillan, 1979.

Stroud, Barry. *The Significance of Philosophical Skepticism*. Oxford: Oxford University Press, 1984.

Sugimoto, Yoshio, and Ross E. Mouer. "Reappraising Images of Japanese Society." *Social Analysis: The International Journal of Anthropology* 5–6 (December 1980): 5–19.

Sun, Jing. *Japan and China as Charm Rivals: Soft Power in Regional Diplomacy*. Ann Arbor: University of Michigan Press, 2012.

Suzuki, Daisetz T. *Zen and Japanese Culture*. Princeton: Princeton University Press, 2019; originally published 1959.

Suzuki, Shogo. "The Importance of 'Othering' in China's National Identity: Sino-Japanese Relations as a Stage of Identity Conflicts." *Pacific Review* 20, no. 1 (2007): 23–47.

Suzuki, Shogo. "Japanese Revisionists and the 'Korea Threat': Insights from Ontological Security." *Cambridge Review of International Affairs* 32, no. 3 (2019): 303–21.

Sydney Morning Herald. "Furious Chinese Claim Japanese Tourists Had More than Sex on Their Minds." *Sydney Morning Herald*, September 30, 2003.

Takayoshi, Matsuo. "The Development of Democracy in Japan—Taishō Democracy: Its Flowering and Breakdown." *Developing Economies* 4, no. 4 (1966): 612–32.

Takenaka, Kiyoshi. "Abe Sees World War One Echoes in Japan–China Tensions." *Reuters*, January 23, 2014. http://www.reuters.com/article/uk-japan-china/abe-sees-world-war-one-echoes-in-japan-china -tensions-idUKBREA0M08K20140123, accessed July 2, 2022.

Takenaka, Kiyoshi, and Sui-Lee Wee. "Japan Infuriates China by Agreeing to Buy Disputed Isles." *Reuters*, September 10, 2012. http://www.reuters.com/article/us-china-japan/japan-infuriates-china -by-agreeing-to-buy-disputed-isles-idUSBRE8890AU20120910, accessed July 5, 2022.

Tam, Yue-him. "Who Engineered the Anti-Japanese Protests in 2005?" *Macalester International* 18, no. 25 (Spring 2007): 281–99. http://digitalcommons.macalester.edu/macintl/vol18/iss1/25.

Tamaki, Taku. *Deconstructing Japan's Image of South Korea: Identity in Foreign Policy*. New York: Palgrave Macmillan, 2010.

Tamamoto, Masaru. "Ambiguous Japan: Japanese National Identity at Century's End." In *International Relations Theory and the Asia-Pacific*, edited by G. John Ikenberry and Michael Mastanduno, 191–212. New York: Columbia University Press, 2003.

Tanaka, Yuki, and John W. Dower. *Hidden Horrors: Japanese War Crimes in World War II*. New York: Routledge, 1996.

Tankha, Brij, ed. *Okakura Tenshin and Pan-Asianism: Shadows of the Past*. Leiden, the Netherlands: Global Oriental, 2008.

Tanter, Raymond. *Rogue Regimes: Terrorism and Proliferation*. New York: Palgrave Macmillan, 1999.

Terracciano, Antonio et al. "National Character Does Not Reflect Mean Personality Trait Levels in 49 Cultures." *Science* 310 (October 7, 2005): 96–100.

Thaden, Edward C. "The Beginnings of Romantic Nationalism in Russia." *American Slavic and East European Review* 13, no. 4 (December 1954): 500–21.

Thomas, Ronan. "The Capitol, Seoul." *History Today* 47, no. 1 (1997): 62–63.

Thompson, William R. "Democracy and Peace: Putting the Cart before the Horse?" *International Organization* 50, no. 1 (Winter 1996): 141–74.

Thorsten, Marie. *Superhuman Japan: Knowledge, Nation and Culture in US–Japan Relations*. London: Routledge, 2012.

Thanh, Hélène Vu. "The Role of the Franciscans in the Establishment of Diplomatic Relations between the Philippines and Japan in the 16th–17th Centuries: Transpacific Geopolitics?" *Itinerario* 40, no. 2 (2016): 239–56.

Thies, Cameron G. "The Construction of a Latin American Interstate Culture of Rivalry." *International Interactions* 34, no. 3 (2008): 231–57.

Thies, Cameron G. "Role Theory and Foreign Policy." In *The International Studies Encyclopedia*, vol. X, edited by Robert A. Denemark, 6335–56. Oxford: Wiley-Blackwell, 2010.

Thies, Cameron G. "A Social Psychological Approach to Enduring Rivalries." *Political Psychology* 22, no. 4 (2001): 693–725.

Thies, Cameron G. *The United States, Israel, and the Search for International Order: Socializing States*. New York: Routledge, 2013.

Thies, Cameron G., and Mark David Nieman. *Rising Powers and Foreign Policy Revisionism: Understanding BRICS Identity and Behavior through Time*. Ann Arbor: University of Michigan Press, 2017.

Thrall, Trevor, and Jane K. Cramer, eds. *American Foreign Policy and the Politics of Fear: Threat Inflation since 9/11*. London: Routledge, 2009.

Thucydides. *The History of the Peloponnesian War*. Translated by Richard Crawley. Project Gutenberg, 2003. http://www.gutenberg.org/files/7142/7142-h/7142-h.htm.

Tiezzi, Shannon. "China Decries New US-Japan Defense Guidelines." *Diplomat*, May 1, 2015. http:// thediplomat.com/2015/05/china-decries-new-us-japan-defense-guidelines, accessed July 6, 2022.

Titchener, Edward Bradford. *A Text-book of Psychology*. New York: Macmillan, 1910.

Tikhonov, V. M. *Modern Korea and Its Others: Perceptions of the Neighbouring Countries and Korean Modernity*. London: Routledge, 2016.

TNS Singapore. "Opinion Poll on Japan in Six ASEAN Countries." February–March 2008. Japan Ministry of Foreign Affairs. http://www.mofa.go.jp/region/asia-paci/asean/survey/qa0803.pdf, accessed December 8, 2021.

Tomkins, Silvan S. "Affect as Amplification: Some Modifications in Theory." In *Emotion: Theory, Research and Experience*, edited by Robert Plutchik and Henry Kellerman, 141–87. New York: Academic Press, 1980.

Tomkins, Silvan S. *Affect Imagery Consciousness: The Complete Edition*. New York: Springer, 2008; originally published in 1962 and 1963.

Tomlinson, Alan, and Christopher Young, eds. *National Identity and Global Sports Events: Culture, Politics, and Spectacle in the Olympics and the Football World Cup*. Albany: State University of New York Press, 2006.

Towle, Philip. *From Ally to Enemy: Anglo-Japanese Military Relations, 1900–45*. Folkestone, England: Global Oriental, 2006.

Trezise, Philip H. "Japan, the Enemy?" *Brookings Review* 8, no. 1 (Winter 1989/1990): 3–13.

Tsui, Lokman. "The Panopticon as the Antithesis of a Space of Freedom: Control and Regulation of the Internet in China." *China Information* 17, no. 2 (2003): 65–82.

Tsuzuki, Keiroku. "Social Intercourse between Japanese and Westerners." In *An Episode from the Life of Count Inouye etc.*, edited by Tsuzuki Keiroku, 157–89. Tokyo: Sanshusha, 1912.

Turner, Frederick Jackson. *The Frontier in American History*. New York: Holt, 1920.

UPI. "S. Korea Discloses Sensitive Documents." *United Press International*, January 17, 2005. http://www.upi.com/Top_News/2005/01/17/SKorea-discloses-sensitive-documents/UPI-38131105952315/, accessed July 13, 2022.

Valaskivi, Katja. "A Brand New Future? Cool Japan and the Social Imaginary of the Branded Nation." *Japan Forum* 25, no. 4 (2013): 485–504.

Van Dyke, Jon M. "Legal Issues Related to Sovereignty over Dokdo and Its Maritime Boundary." *Ocean Development & International Law* 38, no. 1–2 (2007): 157–224.

Van Evera, Stephen. "Causes of War." PhD diss., University of California, Berkeley, 1984.

Van Ree, Erik. "Heroes and Merchants: Stalin's Understanding of National Character." *Kritika: Explorations in Russian and Eurasian History* 8, no. 1 (2007): 41–65.

Varadarajan, Latha. "Constructivism, Identity and Neoliberal (In)security." *Review of International Studies* 30, no. 3 (2004): 319–41.

Vekasi, Kristin, and Jiwon Nam. "Boycotting Japan: Explaining Divergence in Chinese and South Korean Economic Backlash." *Journal of Asian Security and International Affairs* 6, no. 3 (2019): 299–326.

Vickers, Edward. "Smothering Diversity: Patriotism in China's School Curriculum under Xi Jinping." *Journal of Genocide Research* 24, no. 2 (2022): 158–70.

Villacorta, Wilfrido V. "Japan's Asian Identity: Concerns for ASEAN–Japan Relations." *ASEAN Economic Bulletin* 11, no. 1 (July1994): 79–92.

Vogel, Ezra F., Ming Yuan, and Akihiko Tanaka, eds. *The Golden Age of the U.S.–China–Japan Triangle, 1972–1989*. Cambridge, United Kingdom: Cambridge University Press, 2002.

Vyas, Utpal. *Soft Power in Japan–China Relations: State, Sub-State and Non-state Relations*. London: Routledge, 2010.

Wagenaar, Wester. "Wacky Japan: A New Face of Orientalism." *Asia in Focus* 3 (Summer 2016): 46–54.

Wakker, Peter P. *Prospect Theory: For Risk and Ambiguity*. Cambridge, United Kingdom: Cambridge University Press, 2010.

Waldron, Arthur. *The Great Wall of China: From History to Myth*. Cambridge, United Kingdom: Cambridge University Press, 1990.

Walker, R. B. J. *Inside/Outside: International Relations as Political Theory*. Cambridge, United Kingdom: Cambridge University Press, 1993.

Walker, Stephen G. "National Role Conceptions and Systemic Outcomes." In *Psychological Models in International Politics*, edited by Lawrence S. Falkowski, 169–210. Boulder, CO: Westview, 1979.

Walker, Stephen G. *Role Theory and the Cognitive Architecture of British Appeasement Decisions: Symbolic and Strategic Interaction in World Politics.* New York: Routledge, 2013.

Walker, Stephen G. *Role Theory and Foreign Policy Analysis.* Durham, NC: Duke University Press, 1987.

Walker, Stephen G., Akan Malici, and Mark Schafer. *Rethinking Foreign Policy Analysis: States, Leaders, and the Microfoundations of Behavioral International Relations.* New York: Routledge, 2010.

Wallace, Jeremy L., and Jessica Chen Weiss. "The Political Geography of Nationalist Protest in China: Cities and the 2012 Anti-Japanese Protests." *China Quarterly* 222 (2015): 403–29.

Walt, Stephen M. "Alliance Formation and the Balance of World Power." *International Security* 9, no. 4 (1985): 3–43.

Walt, Stephen M. *The Origins of Alliances.* Ithaca: Cornell University Press, 1987.

Waltz, Kenneth N. *Foreign Policy and Democratic Politics: The American and British Experience.* Boston: Little, Brown and Company, 1967.

Waltz, Kenneth N. *Man, the State, and War: A Theoretical Analysis.* New York: Columbia University Press, 1959.

Waltz, Kenneth N. *Theory of International Relations.* New York: Random House, 1979.

Wang, Jian. "The Power and Limits of Branding in National Image Communication in Global Society." *Journal of International Communication* 14, no. 2 (2008): 9–24.

Wang, Min. *Hontō wa Nihon ni Akogareru Chūgoku-Jin: "Han-Nichi" Kanjō no Shinsō Bunseki* [The Chinese Who Actually Yearn for Japan: A Deep Analysis of Anti-Japanese Sentiment]. Tokyo: PHP Kenkyūjo, 2005.

Wang, Mingming. *Empire and Local Worlds: A Chinese Model of Long-Term Historical Anthropology.* Walnut Creek, CA: Left Coast Press, 2009.

Wang, Yaqiu. "The Business of Censorship: Documents Show How Weibo Filters Sensitive News in China." *CPJ Blog,* Committee to Protect Journalists, March 3, 2016. http://cpj.org/blog/2016/03/the -business-of-censorship-documents-show-how-weib.php, accessed July 18, 2022.

Wang, Zheng. "National Humiliation, History Education, and the Politics of Historical Memory: Patriotic Education Campaign in China." *International Studies Quarterly* 52, no. 4 (2008): 783–806.

Wang, Zheng. *Never Forget National Humiliation: Historical Memory in Chinese Politics and Foreign Relations.* New York: Columbia University Press, 2014.

Wang, Zhenping. *Ambassadors from the Islands of Immortals: China–Japan Relations in the Han-Tang Period.* Honolulu: University of Hawaii Press, 2005.

Watanabe, Akio. "Japan between East and West." *Asia-Pacific Review* 17, no. 1 (2010): 21–28.

Watanabe, Yasushi, and David L. McConnell, eds. *Soft Power Superpowers: Cultural and National Assets of Japan and the United States.* Armonk, NY: M. E. Sharpe, 2008.

Watson, David, and Auke Tellegen. "Toward a Consensual Structure of Mood." *Psychological Bulletin* 98, no. 2 (1985): 219–35.

Watson, John Broadus. *Psychology: From the Standpoint of a Behaviorist.* Philadelphia: J. B. Lippincott, 1919.

Wehner, Leslie E. "The Narration of Roles in Foreign Policy Analysis." *Journal of International Relations and Development* 23, no. 2 (2020): 359–84.

Wehner, Leslie E., and Cameron G. Thies. "Role Theory, Narratives, and Interpretation: The Domestic Contestation of Roles." *International Studies Review* 16, no. 3 (2014): 411–36.

Weidner, Jason. "Nation Branding, Technologies of the Self, and the Political Subject of the Nation-State." Paper presented at the Annual Meeting of the International Studies Association, Montreal, March 16–19, 2011.

Weinstein, Michael. "South Korea–Japan Dokdo/Takeshima Dispute: Toward Confrontation." *Asia-Pacific Journal: Japan Focus* 4, no. 5 (May 6, 2006): 1–7.

Weisman, Steven R. "Japanese Express Remorse to Korea." *New York Times,* May 25, 1990.

Weiss, Jessica Chen. "How Hawkish Is the Chinese Public? Another Look at 'Rising Nationalism' and Chinese Foreign Policy." *Journal of Contemporary China* 28, no. 119 (2019): 679–95.

Weiss, Jessica Chen. *Powerful Patriots: Nationalist Protest in China's Foreign Relations.* New York: Oxford University Press, 2014.

Wen, Jiabao, and Kan Naoto. "Premier Wen Jiabao Holds Talks with His Japanese Counterpart Naoto Kan." *Chinese Ministry of Foreign Affairs Website*, May 22, 2011. http://www.mfa.gov.cn/ce/ceus//eng/zgyw/t825172.htm, accessed August 7, 2022.

Wendt, Alexander. "Anarchy Is What States Make of It: The Social Construction of Power Politics." *International Organization* 46, no. 2 (1992): 391–425.

Wendt, Alexander. "Collective Identity Formation and the International State." *American Political Science Review* 88, no. 2 (1994): 384–96.

Wendt, Alexander. *Social Theory of International Politics*. Cambridge, United Kingdom: Cambridge University Press, 1999.

Wendt, Alexander. "The State as Person in International Theory." *Review of International Studies* 30, no. 2 (2004): 289–316.

Wenger, Marion A. "Emotion as Visceral Action: An Extension of Lange's Theory." In *The Second International Symposium on Feelings and Emotions*, edited by Martin L. Reymert, 3–10. New York: McGraw-Hill, 1950.

Werther, Charlotte. "Rebranding Britain: Cool Britannia, the Millennium Dome and the 2012 Olympics." *Moderna Språk* 105, no. 1 (2011): 1–14.

White, Ralph K. *Fearful Warriors: A Psychological Profile of U.S.–Soviet Relations*. New York: Free Press, 1984.

Whiting, Allen S. *China Eyes Japan*. Berkeley: University of California Press, 1989.

Whitmer, Jennifer M. "You Are Your Brand: Self-Branding and the Marketization of Self." *Sociology Compass* 13, no. 3 (2019): e12662. https://doi.org/10.1111/soc4.12662.

Whitney, Christopher B., and David Shambaugh. *Soft Power in Asia: Results of a 2008 Multinational Survey of Public Opinion*. Chicago: The Chicago Council on Global Affairs, 2009. http://www.brookings.edu/wp-content/uploads/2012/04/0617_east_asia_report.pdf.

Wick, Shelley D. "Capabilities, Cooperation, and Culture: Mapping American Ambivalence toward China." *Foreign Policy Analysis* 10, no. 3 (2014): 289–309.

Wiegand, Krista E., and Ajin Choi. "Nationalism, Public Opinion, and Dispute Resolution: The Dokdo/Takeshima Dispute." *Journal of Asian Pacific Communication* 27, no. 2 (2017): 232–45.

Wilkinson, Endymion. *Gokai, Yōroppa vs. Nihon* [Misunderstanding: Europe versus Japan]. Tokyo: Chuokoron-sha, 1982.

Wilkinson, Endymion. *Japan versus the West: Image and Reality*. London: Penguin, 1990.

Winthrop, Robert. *Dictionary of Concepts in Cultural Anthropology*. New York: Greenwood Press, 1991.

Wish, Naomi. "Foreign Policy Makers and Their National Role Conceptions." *International Studies Quarterly* 24, no. 4 (1980): 532–54.

Wong, Seanon S. "Mapping the Repertoire of Emotions and Their Communicative Functions in Face-to-Face Diplomacy." *International Studies Review* 22, no. 1 (2020): 77–97.

Wong, Seanon S. "Stoics and Hotheads: Leaders' Temperament, Anger, and the Expression of Resolve in Face-to-Face Diplomacy." *Journal of Global Security Studies* 4, no. 2 (2019): 190–208.

Worringer, Renée. *Ottomans Imagining Japan: East, Middle East, and Non-Western Modernity at the Turn of the Twentieth Century*. New York: Palgrave Macmillan, 2014.

Wundt, Wilhelm Max. *An Introduction to Psychology*. Translated by Rudolf Pintner. London: Allen & Unwin, 1912.

Wuthnow, Joel, and Phillip C. Saunders. *Chinese Military Reform in the Age of Xi Jinping: Drivers, Challenges, and Implications*. Washington, DC: National Defense University Press, 2017.

Xi, Jinping. "Guanyu 'Zhonggong Zhongyang Guanyu Quanmian Tuijin yi Fazhi Guo Ruogan Zhongda Wenti de Jueding' de Shuoming" [Elaboration Concerning the Chinese Communist Party Central Committee's Decision on Major Questions Concerning All-Around Development of a Nation Ruled by Law]. *Xinhuanet*, October 28, 2014. http://cpc.people.com.cn/n/2014/1028/c64094-25926150.html, accessed July 18, 2022.

Xinhua. "China Scathes Abe's Yasukuni Visit." *People's Daily*, December 27, 2013. http://en.people.cn/90883/8496810.html, accessed June 23, 2022.

Xinhua. "China Strongly Dissatisfied with Japan's New Defense White Paper." *China Daily*, July 22, 2015. http://www.chinadaily.com.cn/world/2015-07/22/content_21375442.htm, accessed July 6, 2022.

Yahuda, Michael. "China's New Assertiveness in the South China Sea." *Journal of Contemporary China* 22, no. 81 (2013): 446–59.

Yamaguchi, Mari. "Review Confirms Basis of Japan's Sex Slave Apology." *AP News*, June 21, 2014. http://apnews.com/article/73d0fa8f6f7e446e9e05d0b1d68b8f36, accessed July 13, 2022.

Yang, Jiechi. "Yang Jiechi Voices Solemn Stance of China to Japan over Forcing Through the New Security Bills by the House of Representatives of the National Diet of Japan." *Chinese Ministry of Foreign Affairs Website*, July 16, 2015. http://www.mfa.gov.cn/ce/cegv/eng/wjyw/t1282552.htm, accessed July 6, 2022.

Yee, Herbert, and Ian Storey. *China Threat: Perceptions, Myths, and Reality*. London: Routledge, 2002.

Yokoyama, Toshio. *Japan in the Victorian Mind: A Study of Stereotyped Images of a Nation 1850–80*. London: Macmillan, 1987.

Yoon, Hong-Key. *The Culture of Fengshui in Korea: An Exploration of East Asian Geomancy*. Lanham, MD: Lexington Books, 2006.

Yoshihara, Mari. *Embracing the East: White Women and American Orientalism*. Oxford: Oxford University Press, 2002.

Yoshimatsu, Hidetaka. "Japan's Role Conception in Multilateral Initiatives: The Evolution from Hatoyama to Abe." *Australian Journal of International Affairs* 72, no. 2 (2018): 129–44.

Yoshino, Kosaku. *Cultural Nationalism in Contemporary Japan: A Sociological Enquiry*. London: Routledge, 1992.

Yue, Jianyong. "The Limits to China's Peaceful Rise—Deep Integration and a New Cold War." *Global Policy* 13, no. 1 (2022): 91–106.

Yuge, Toshihiro. *Chūgoku Taiwan ni Okeru Nihonzō: Eiga, Kyōkasho, Honyaku ga Tsutaeru Nihon* [Images of Japan in China and Taiwan: Japan Conveyed in Movies, Textbooks, and Translations]. Tokyo: Tōhō Shoten, 2011.

Yun, Seong-Hun. "An Overdue Critical Look at Soft Power Measurement: The Construct Validity of the Soft Power 30 in Focus." *Journal of International and Area Studies* 25, no. 2 (2018): 1–19.

Zaborowski, Robert. "Plato's 'Phaedrus' 253e5–255a1 Revisited. A Reappraisal of Plato's View on the Soul." *Organon* 50 (2018): 165–207.

Zajonc, Robert B. "Feeling and Thinking: Preferences Need No Inferences." *American Psychologist* 35, no. 2 (1980): 151–75.

Zehfuss, Maja. "Constructivism and Identity: A Dangerous Liaison." *European Journal of International Relations* 7, no. 3 (2001): 315–48.

Zeki, Semir, and John Paul Romaya. "Neural Correlates of Hate." *PloS One* 3, no. 10 (2008): e3556.

Zevelev, Igor. "Russian National Identity and Foreign Policy." *CSIS Russia and Eurasia Program Report*. Washington: Center for Strategic and International Studies, 2016.

Zhang, Lifen. "Transcript of Interview with Wang Yi." *Financial Times*, January 29, 2014.

Zhang, Tuosheng. "China's Relations with Japan." In *The Golden Age of the U.S.–China–Japan Triangle, 1972–1989*, edited by Ezra F. Vogel, Ming Yuan, and Akihiko Tanaka, 191–209. Cambridge, MA: Harvard University Press, 2002.

Zhang, Xiaoming. "China's Perceptions of and Responses to Abe's Foreign Policy." *Asian Perspective* 39, no. 3 (July–September 2015): 423–439.

Zhang, Yongjin. *China in International Society since 1949: Alienation and Beyond*. London: Palgrave, 1998.

Zhao, Suisheng. "China's Pragmatic Nationalism: Is It Manageable?" *Washington Quarterly* 29, no. 1 (2005/06): 131–44.

Zhao, Suisheng. "A State-Led Nationalism: The Patriotic Education Campaign in Post-Tiananmen China." *Communist and Post-Communist Studies* 31, no. 3 (1998): 287–302.

Zhao, Yuezhi. *Communication in China: Political Economy, Power, and Conflict*. Lanham, MD: Rowman & Littlefield, 2008.

Zhao, Yuezhi. *Media, Market, and Democracy in China: Between the Party Line and the Bottom Line*. Urbana: University of Illinois Press, 1998.

Zheng, Bijian. "China's Peaceful Rise to Great-Power Status." *Foreign Affairs* 84, no. 5 (2005): 18–24.

Zheng, Yongnian. *Discovering Chinese Nationalism in China: Modernization, Identity, and International Relations*. Cambridge, United Kingdom: Cambridge University Press, 1999.

Zhou, Min, and Hanning Wang. "Participation in Anti-Japanese Demonstrations in China: Evidence from a Survey on Three Elite Universities in Beijing." *Journal of East Asian Studies* 16, no. 3 (2016): 391–413.

INDEX

ABOUT THE AUTHOR

Paul A. Kowert is associate professor and chair of the Department of Political Science at the University of Massachusetts Boston. He is a specialist in East Asian foreign policy and the politics of national identity in international relations. His previous work—including books on *Groupthink or Deadlock, Cultures of Order,* and *Psychology and Constructivism in International Relations*—explore the way leaders differ in their use of information and advice, the way people form perceptions of other countries, and the role of emotion and normative frameworks in foreign policy.